WHERE'S WALDO?

THE TOTALLY ESSENTIAL

TRAVEL

COLLECTION

MARTIN HANDFORD

CANDLEWICK PRESS

HI, WALDO-WATCHER!

ARE YOU READY TO JOIN ME ON MY SEVEN
FANTASTIC ADVENTURES?

WHERE'S WALDO?
WHERE'S WALDO NOW?
WHERE'S WALDO? THE FANTASTIC JOURNEY
WHERE'S WALDO? IN HOLLYWOOD
WHERE'S WALDO? THE WONDER BOOK
WHERE'S WALDO? THE GREAT PICTURE HUNT!
WHERE'S WALDO? THE INCREDIBLE PAPER CHASE

CAN YOU FIND THE FIVE INTREPID TRAVELERS
AND THEIR PRECIOUS ITEMS IN EVERY SCENE?

ODLAW   WIZARD   WENDA   WOOF   WALDO
         WHITEBEARD

 WALDO'S KEY   WOOF'S BONE   WENDA'S CAMERA

 WIZARD WHITEBEARD'S   ODLAW'S BINOCULARS
SCROLL

WAIT, THERE'S MORE! AT THE BEGINNING AND
END OF EACH ADVENTURE, FIND A FOLD-OUT
CHECKLIST WITH HUNDREDS MORE THINGS
TO LOOK FOR.

WOW! WHAT A SEARCH!

BON VOYAGE!

WHERE'S WALDO?

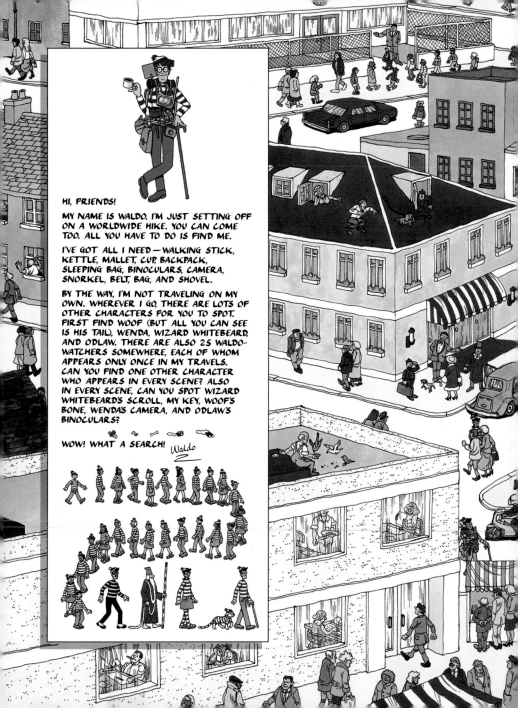

HI, FRIENDS!

MY NAME IS WALDO. I'M JUST SETTING OFF ON A WORLDWIDE HIKE. YOU CAN COME TOO. ALL YOU HAVE TO DO IS FIND ME.

I'VE GOT ALL I NEED — WALKING STICK, KETTLE, MALLET, CUP, BACKPACK, SLEEPING BAG, BINOCULARS, CAMERA, SNORKEL, BELT, BAG, AND SHOVEL.

BY THE WAY, I'M NOT TRAVELING ON MY OWN. WHEREVER I GO, THERE ARE LOTS OF OTHER CHARACTERS FOR YOU TO SPOT. FIRST FIND WOOF (BUT ALL YOU CAN SEE IS HIS TAIL), WENDA, WIZARD WHITEBEARD, AND ODLAW. THERE ARE ALSO 25 WALDO-WATCHERS SOMEWHERE, EACH OF WHOM APPEARS ONLY ONCE IN MY TRAVELS. CAN YOU FIND ONE OTHER CHARACTER WHO APPEARS IN EVERY SCENE? ALSO IN EVERY SCENE, CAN YOU SPOT WIZARD WHITEBEARD'S SCROLL, MY KEY, WOOF'S BONE, WENDA'S CAMERA, AND ODLAW'S BINOCULARS?

WOW! WHAT A SEARCH! Waldo

THE GREAT WHERE'S WALDO? CHECKLIST: PART ONE
Hundreds of things for Waldo-Watchers to watch out for! Don't forget PART TWO at the end of this adventure!

IN TOWN

- [ ] A dog on a roof
- [ ] A man on a fountain
- [ ] A man about to trip over a dog's leash
- [ ] A car crash
- [ ] A happy barber
- [ ] People on a street, watching TV
- [ ] A puncture caused by a Roman arrow
- [ ] A tearful tune
- [ ] A boy attacked by a plant
- [ ] A waiter who isn't concentrating
- [ ] A robber who's been clobbered
- [ ] A face on a wall
- [ ] A man coming out of a manhole
- [ ] A man feeding pigeons
- [ ] A bicycle crash

ON THE BEACH

- [ ] A dog biting a boy's bottom
- [ ] A man who is overdressed
- [ ] A muscular man with a medal
- [ ] A popular girl
- [ ] A water-skier on water
- [ ] A striped photo
- [ ] A punctured air mattress
- [ ] A donkey who likes ice cream
- [ ] A man being squashed
- [ ] A punctured beach ball
- [ ] A human pyramid
- [ ] A human stepping-stone
- [ ] Two odd friends
- [ ] A cowboy
- [ ] A human donkey
- [ ] Age and beauty
- [ ] A boy who follows in his father's footsteps
- [ ] Two men with vests, one without
- [ ] A boy being tortured by a spider
- [ ] A show-off with sand castles
- [ ] A gang of hat robbers
- [ ] An Arab making pyramids
- [ ] Three protruding tongues
- [ ] Two oddly fitting hats
- [ ] An odd couple
- [ ] Five spiders
- [ ] A towel with a hole in it
- [ ] A punctured pontoon boat
- [ ] A boy who's not allowed any ice cream

SKI SLOPES

- [ ] A man reading on a roof
- [ ] A flying skier
- [ ] A runaway skier
- [ ] A backward skier
- [ ] A portrait in snow
- [ ] An illegal fisherman
- [ ] A snowball in the neck
- [ ] Two unconscious skiers
- [ ] Two skiers hitting trees
- [ ] An Alpine horn
- [ ] A snow skier
- [ ] A flag collector
- [ ] Two very scruffy skiers
- [ ] A skier up a tree
- [ ] A water-skier on snow
- [ ] An abominable snowman
- [ ] A skiing reindeer
- [ ] A roof jumper
- [ ] A heap of skaters

CAMPSITE

- [ ] A bull in a hedge
- [ ] Bull horns
- [ ] A shark in a canal
- [ ] A bull seeing red
- [ ] A careless kick
- [ ] Tea in a lap
- [ ] A low bridge
- [ ] People knocked over by a mallet
- [ ] A man surprised undressing
- [ ] A bicycle tire about to be punctured
- [ ] Camper's camels
- [ ] A scarecrow that doesn't work
- [ ] A wigwam
- [ ] Large biceps
- [ ] A collapsed tent
- [ ] A smoking barbecue
- [ ] A fisherman catching old boots
- [ ] An old-fashioned bicycle
- [ ] Boy Scouts making fire
- [ ] A roller-skating hiker
- [ ] A man blowing up a boat
- [ ] A camper's butler
- [ ] Runners on a road
- [ ] A bull chasing children
- [ ] Scruffy campers
- [ ] Thirsty walkers

THE TRAIN STATION

- [ ] A boy falling from a train
- [ ] A breakdown on tracks
- [ ] Naughty children on a train roof
- [ ] People being knocked over by a door
- [ ] A man about to step on a ball
- [ ] Three different times at the same time
- [ ] A wheelbarrow baby carriage
- [ ] A face on a train
- [ ] Five people reading one newspaper
- [ ] A struggling bag carrier
- [ ] A show-off with suitcases
- [ ] A man losing everything from his cases
- [ ] A smoking train
- [ ] A squeeze on a bench
- [ ] A dog tearing a man's trousers
- [ ] Fare dodgers
- [ ] A hand caught between doors
- [ ] A cattle stampede
- [ ] A man breaking a weighing machine

AIRPORT

- [ ] A flying saucer
- [ ] A boy who's been hiding in a suitcase
- [ ] A child firing a catapult
- [ ] A leaking fuel pipe
- [ ] Flight controllers playing badminton
- [ ] A rocket
- [ ] A turret
- [ ] Three watch smugglers
- [ ] Naughty children on a plane
- [ ] A forklift truck
- [ ] A wind sock
- [ ] A chopper
- [ ] A plane that doesn't fly
- [ ] A flying Ace
- [ ] Dracula
- [ ] Five men blowing up a balloon
- [ ] Runners on a runway
- [ ] Four smoking people
- [ ] Four people falling from a plane
- [ ] A cargo of cattle
- [ ] A fire engine
- [ ] Three childish pilots
- [ ] A blimp being punctured

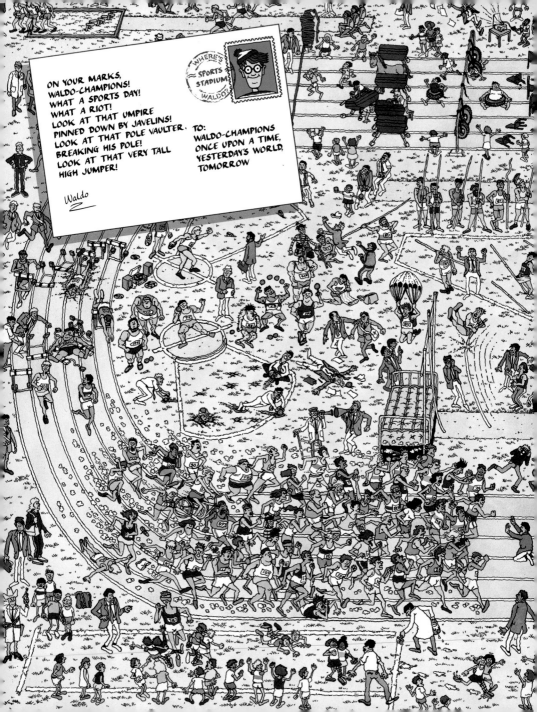

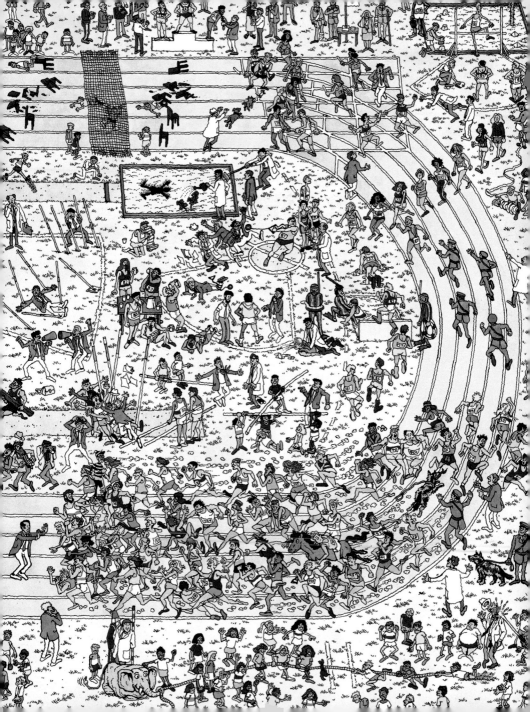

HEY, WALDO-WATCHERS!
SAW SOME TRULY TERRIFIC
SIGHTS TODAY — SOMEONE
BURNING TROUSERS WITH
AN IRON; A LONG THIN MAN
WITH A LONG THIN TIE;
A GLOVE ATTACKING A MAN.
PHEW! INCREDIBLE!

Waldo

TO:
WALDO-WATCHERS
OVER THE MOON,
THE WILD WEST,
NOW

WHERE'S
DEPARTMENT
STORE
WALDO?

THE GREAT WHERE'S WALDO?
CHECKLIST: PART TWO

SPORTS STADIUM

- [ ] Three pairs of feet, sticking out of sand
- [ ] A cowboy starting races
- [ ] Hopeless hurdlers
- [ ] Ten children with fifteen legs
- [ ] A record thrower
- [ ] A shot put juggler
- [ ] An ear trumpet
- [ ] A vaulting horse
- [ ] A runner with two wheels
- [ ] A parachuting vaulter
- [ ] A Scotsman with a pole
- [ ] An elephant pulling a rope
- [ ] People being knocked over by a hammer
- [ ] A gardener
- [ ] Three frogmen
- [ ] A nude runner
- [ ] A bed
- [ ] A bandaged boy
- [ ] A runner with four legs
- [ ] A sunken jumper
- [ ] A man with an odd pair of legs
- [ ] A man chasing a dog chasing a cat
- [ ] A boy squirting water

MUSEUM

- [ ] A very big skeleton
- [ ] A clown squirting water
- [ ] A catapult firing a child
- [ ] A bird's nest in a woman's hair
- [ ] A highwayman
- [ ] A popping bicep
- [ ] An arrow in the neck
- [ ] A knight watching TV
- [ ] Picture robbers
- [ ] A smoking picture
- [ ] A leaking watercolor
- [ ] Fighting pictures
- [ ] A king and queen
- [ ] A fat picture and a thin one
- [ ] Three cavemen
- [ ] A game of catch with a bomb
- [ ] Charioteers
- [ ] A collapsing pillar

AT SEA

- [ ] A windsurfer
- [ ] A boat punctured by an arrow
- [ ] A sword fight with a swordfish
- [ ] A school of whales
- [ ] Seasick sailors
- [ ] A leaking diver
- [ ] A boat crash
- [ ] A bathtub
- [ ] A seabed
- [ ] A game of tic-tac-toe
- [ ] A lucky fisherman
- [ ] Three lumberjacks
- [ ] Unlucky fishermen
- [ ] Two water-skiers in a tangle
- [ ] Fish robbers
- [ ] A sea cowboy
- [ ] A fishy photo
- [ ] A man being strangled by an octopus
- [ ] Stowaways
- [ ] A Chinese junk
- [ ] A wave at sea

SAFARI PARK

- [ ] Noah's ark
- [ ] A message in a bottle
- [ ] A hippo having its teeth cleaned
- [ ] A bird's nest in an antler
- [ ] A hungry giraffe
- [ ] An ice cream robber
- [ ] A zebra crossing
- [ ] Santa Claus
- [ ] Three owls
- [ ] A unicorn
- [ ] Caged people
- [ ] A lion driving a car
- [ ] Bears
- [ ] Tarzan
- [ ] Lion cubs
- [ ] An Indian tiger
- [ ] Two lines for the restrooms
- [ ] Animals' beauty parlor
- [ ] An elephant squirting water

DEPARTMENT STORE

- [ ] An ironing demonstration
- [ ] A woman surprised undressing
- [ ] A man whose boots face the wrong way
- [ ] A man with heavy packages
- [ ] A misbehaving vacuum cleaner
- [ ] Ties that match their wearers
- [ ] A man washing his clothes
- [ ] A man trying on a jacket that's too big
- [ ] A woman tripping over toys
- [ ] A boy pulling a girl's hair
- [ ] A boy riding in a shopping cart
- [ ] A glove that's alive

FAIRGROUND

- [ ] A cannon at a rifle range
- [ ] A bumper car run wild
- [ ] A sword swallower
- [ ] A one-armed bandit
- [ ] A helium-balloon seller
- [ ] A runaway rocket
- [ ] A runaway merry-go-round horse
- [ ] A haunted house
- [ ] Seven lost children and a lost dog
- [ ] A tank crash
- [ ] A weight lifter dropping his weights
- [ ] Three clowns
- [ ] Three men dressed as bears

WOW! WHAT A SEARCH!

Did you find Waldo, all his friends, and all the things they lost? Did you find the one scene where Waldo and Odlaw both lost their binoculars? Odlaw's binoculars are the ones nearest to him. Did you find the extra character who appears in every scene? If not, keep looking! Wow! Fantastic!

THE
ABSOLUTELY
HUGE AND
ENORMOUSLY
INTERESTING
BOOK OF
CAVEMEN,

CAVE WOMEN,
CAVE DOGS,
AND ALL SORTS
OF EXTREMELY
SAVAGE
STONE AGE
BEASTS.

HI THERE, BOOKWORMS!

SOME PARTS OF HISTORY ARE AMAZING!
I SIT HERE READING ALL THESE BOOKS
ABOUT THE WORLD LONG AGO, AND IT'S
LIKE RIDING A TIME MACHINE. WHY NOT
TRY IT FOR YOURSELVES? JUST SEARCH
EACH PICTURE AND FIND ME, WOOF
(REMEMBER, ALL YOU CAN SEE IS HIS
TAIL), WENDA, WIZARD WHITEBEARD, AND
ODLAW. THEN LOOK FOR MY KEY, WOOF'S
BONE (IN THIS SCENE IT'S THE BONE
THAT'S NEAREST TO HIS TAIL), WENDA'S
CAMERA, WIZARD WHITEBEARD'S SCROLL,
AND ODLAW'S BINOCULARS.

THERE ARE ALSO 25 WALDO-WATCHERS,
EACH OF WHOM APPEARS ONLY ONCE
SOMEWHERE ON MY TRAVELS. AND ONE
MORE THING! CAN YOU FIND ANOTHER
CHARACTER, NOT SHOWN BELOW, WHO
APPEARS ONCE IN EVERY PICTURE?

Waldo

THE
ABSOLUTELY
HUGE AND
ENORMOUSLY
INTERESTING
BOOK OF
CAVEMEN,

CAVE WOMEN,
CAVE DOGS,
AND ALL SORTS
OF EXTREMELY
SAVAGE
STONE AGE
BEASTS.

HI THERE, BOOKWORMS!

SOME PARTS OF HISTORY ARE AMAZING!
I SIT HERE READING ALL THESE BOOKS
ABOUT THE WORLD LONG AGO, AND IT'S
LIKE RIDING A TIME MACHINE. WHY NOT
TRY IT FOR YOURSELVES? JUST SEARCH
EACH PICTURE AND FIND ME, WOOF
(REMEMBER, ALL YOU CAN SEE IS HIS
TAIL), WENDA, WIZARD WHITEBEARD, AND
ODLAW. THEN LOOK FOR MY KEY, WOOF'S
BONE (IN THIS SCENE IT'S THE BONE
THAT'S NEAREST TO HIS TAIL), WENDA'S
CAMERA, WIZARD WHITEBEARD'S SCROLL,
AND ODLAW'S BINOCULARS.

THERE ARE ALSO 25 WALDO-WATCHERS,
EACH OF WHOM APPEARS ONLY ONCE
SOMEWHERE ON MY TRAVELS. AND ONE
MORE THING! CAN YOU FIND ANOTHER
CHARACTER, NOT SHOWN BELOW, WHO
APPEARS ONCE IN EVERY PICTURE?

Waldo

THE GREAT WHERE'S WALDO NOW? CHECKLIST: PART ONE

Hundreds more things for time travelers to look for! Don't forget PART TWO at the end of this adventure!

THE STONE AGE

- [ ] Four cavemen swinging into trouble
- [ ] An accident with an ax
- [ ] A great invention
- [ ] A Stone Age rodeo
- [ ] Boars chasing a man
- [ ] Men chasing a boar
- [ ] A romantic caveman
- [ ] A mammoth squirt
- [ ] A man who has overeaten
- [ ] A bear trap
- [ ] A mammoth in the river
- [ ] A fruit stall
- [ ] Charging woolly rhinos
- [ ] A big cover-up
- [ ] A trunk holding a trunk
- [ ] A knockout game of baseball
- [ ] A rocky picture show
- [ ] An upside-down boar
- [ ] A spoiled dog
- [ ] A lesson on dinosaurs
- [ ] A very scruffy family
- [ ] Some dangerous spear fishermen

THE RIDDLE OF THE PYRAMIDS

- [ ] An upside-down pyramid
- [ ] An upside-down sarcophagus
- [ ] A group of posing gods
- [ ] Two protruding hands
- [ ] Two protruding feet
- [ ] A fat man and his picture
- [ ] Seventeen protruding tongues
- [ ] Stones defying gravity
- [ ] Egyptian vandals
- [ ] Egyptian graffiti
- [ ] A man sweeping dirt under a pyramid
- [ ] A thirsty sphinx
- [ ] A runaway block of stone
- [ ] A loud blast
- [ ] A happy leopard
- [ ] A picture firing an arrow
- [ ] A careless water carrier
- [ ] Sunbathers in peril
- [ ] A messy milking session
- [ ] A mummy and a baby
- [ ] Pyramids of sand

FUN AND GAMES IN ANCIENT ROME

- [ ] A charioteer who has lost his chariot
- [ ] Coliseum cleaners
- [ ] An unequal contest with spears
- [ ] A winner who is about to lose
- [ ] A lion with good table manners
- [ ] A deadly set of wheels
- [ ] Lion cubs being teased
- [ ] Four shields that match their owners
- [ ] A pyramid of lions
- [ ] Lions giving the paws down
- [ ] A leopard chasing a leopard skin
- [ ] A piggyback puncher
- [ ] An awful musician
- [ ] A painful fork-lift
- [ ] A horse holding the reins
- [ ] A leopard in love
- [ ] A Roman keeping count
- [ ] A gladiator losing his sandals

ON TOUR WITH THE VIKINGS

- [ ] A happy figurehead
- [ ] Figureheads in love
- [ ] A man being used as a club
- [ ] A tearful sheep
- [ ] Two hopeless hiding places
- [ ] Childish Vikings
- [ ] A beard with a foot on it
- [ ] An eagle posing as a helmet
- [ ] A sailor tearing a sail
- [ ] A heavily armed Viking
- [ ] A ride on a braid
- [ ] Three spears being beheaded
- [ ] A burning behind
- [ ] A bent boat
- [ ] A frightened figurehead
- [ ] Locked horns
- [ ] A helmet of spiders
- [ ] A helmet of smoke
- [ ] A bullfight

THE END OF THE CRUSADES

- [ ] A cat about to be catapulted
- [ ] A man about to be catapulted
- [ ] A human bridge
- [ ] A key that is out of reach
- [ ] A message for the milkman
- [ ] A cauldron of boiling oil
- [ ] A battering ram
- [ ] Crusaders caught by their necks
- [ ] A load of washing
- [ ] Two catapult catastrophes
- [ ] A catapult aiming the wrong way
- [ ] Three snakes
- [ ] A crusader fast asleep
- [ ] Crusaders soaking up the sun
- [ ] Flattened crusaders
- [ ] Rock faces
- [ ] A crusader who broke a ladder
- [ ] A ticklish situation

ONCE UPON A SATURDAY MORNING

- [ ] A dirty downpour
- [ ] Archers missing the target
- [ ] A jouster sitting back to front
- [ ] A dog stalking a cat stalking some birds
- [ ] A long line of pickpockets
- [ ] A jouster who needs lots of practice
- [ ] A man making a bear dance
- [ ] A bear making a man dance
- [ ] Hats that are tied together
- [ ] Fruit and vegetable thieves
- [ ] An unexpected puddle
- [ ] A juggling jester
- [ ] A very long drink
- [ ] A heavily burdened beast
- [ ] Drunken friars
- [ ] A man scything hats
- [ ] An angry fish
- [ ] A ticklish torture
- [ ] Minstrels making an awful noise

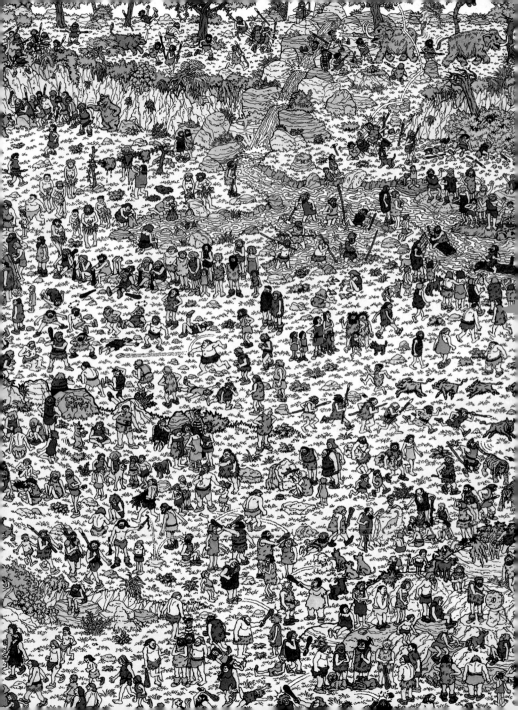

2,000 YEARS AGO

FVN AND GAMES IN ANCIENT ROME

THE ROMANS SPENT MOST OF THEIR TIME FIGHTING, CONQVERING, LEARNING LATIN AND MAKING ROADS. THEY ALWAYS HAD GAMES AT THE COLISEVM. THEIR FAVORITE GAMES WERE FIGHTING, CHARIOT RACING, FIGHTING, AND FEEDING CHRISTIANS TO THE LIONS. WHEN THE CROWD GAVE A GLADIATOR THE THVMBS DOWN, IT MEANT KILL YOVR OPPONENT. THVMBS VP MEANT LET HIM GO. THVMBS VP FOR YOV IF YOV CAN FIND ME AT THE GAMES.

1,003 YEARS AGO

ON TOUR
WITH THE
VIKINGS

At home, the Vikings were quiet people who liked knitting, cheese tasting and boring things like that. But on tour, they went wild. They put on their best horned hats and sailed across the sea, singing and shouting like mad. If you heard them coming, it was best to run away. But don't you run away before you find me.

800 YEARS AGO

The End of the Crusades

After 200 years of fierce argument with the Saladins and Paladins, who would not tell them the way to Jerusalem, the Crusaders finally ran out of clean T-shirts, so they came home. For years afterward they dined out on stories of the castles they had battered and besieged and the fascinating people they had thrown rocks at. Go on your own crusade to find me.

600 YEARS AGO

ONCE UPON A SATURDAY MORNING

The Middle Ages were a very merry time to be alive, especially on Saturdays. Short skirts and striped tights were in fashion for men; everybody knew lots of jokes; there was widespread juggling, jousting, archery, jesting and fun. But if you got into trouble, the Middle Ages could be miserable. For the man in the stocks or the pillory or about to lose his head, Saturday morning was no laughing matter. Don't joke around, look for me here.

171,185 DAYS AGO

THE LAST DAYS OF THE AZTECS

The Aztecs lived in sunny Mexico and were rich and strong and liked swinging from poles pretending to be eagles. They also liked making human sacrifices to their gods, so it was best to agree with everything they said. The Spanish were also rich and strong and some of them, called conquistadores, came to Mexico to find gold. They thought the Aztecs a complete nuisance. Get swinging and find me in Mexico.

400 YEARS AGO

Is red better than blue? What do you mean your poem about cherry blossoms is better than mine? Shall we have another cup of tea? Over difficult questions such as these, the Japanese fought fiercely for hundreds of years. The fiercest fighters of all were the samurai, who wore flags on their backs so that their mommies could find them. The fighters without flags were called ashigaru. I don't have a flag either, but find me anyway.

TROUBLE IN OLD JAPAN

250 YEARS AGO

BEING A PIRATE

(Shiver-me-timbers!)

It really was a lot of fun being a pirate, especially if you were very hairy and didn't have much in the way of brains. It also helped if you had only one leg, or one eye, or two noses, and had a pirate's hat with your name tag sewn inside and a treasure map and a rusty cutlass. Once there were lots of pirates, but they died out in the end because too many of them were men. Shiver me timbers and find me here.

MORE THAN 100 YEARS AGO

HAVING A BALL   IN GAYE PAREE

The history of France has some very bad parts, like getting your head chopped off by Madame Guillotine in the French Revolution; and some very good parts, like the invention of smelly cheese. In 1870 Napoleon (the third one) threw a ball in Paris to celebrate. All the beautiful people came and danced the night away to a band called the Third Republic. Waltz right in and find me.

100 YEARS AGO

THE GOLD RUSH

At the end of the nineteenth century large numbers of **AMERICANS** were frequently seen to be **RUSHING** toward **HOLES** in the ground, hoping to find **GOLD**. Most of them never even found the holes in the ground. But at least they all got **EXERCISE** and **FRESH AIR**, which kept them **HEALTHY**. And health is more important than **GOLD** . . . isn't it? You get the **GOLD** if you can spot me.

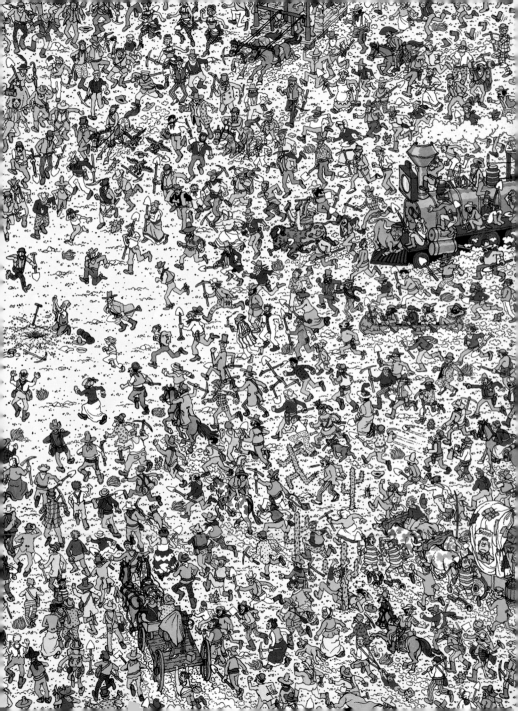

THE GREAT WHERE'S WALDO NOW?
CHECKLIST: PART TWO

THE LAST DAYS OF THE AZTECS

- A tall headdress
- Aztecs in a spin
- A conquistador with his fingers in his ears
- Three archers causing one man pain
- A picture looking sideways
- A tussle for a flag
- A human missile
- A drummer perched on high
- A kissing conquistador
- A frightened horse
- Yellow teeth
- A scabbard in the eye
- An eagle bombing raid
- A boy robbing a robber
- An Aztec ball game
- Five knockouts with one slingshot

TROUBLE IN OLD JAPAN

- Three warriors trapped on a bridge
- Warriors with daggers in their mouths
- A warrior caught by his pony-tail
- A sword being cut in two
- A warrior bending over backward
- A wrestler out for the count
- An easily scared horse
- Warriors making a splash
- Warriors running under a bridge
- A heavy passenger
- A downtrodden warrior
- Two gangs of arrow thieves
- A shot under a hat
- A flag full of arrows
- A spear thrown backward

BEING A PIRATE

- An unpopular woman
- A big pushover
- A pirate pinched by a crab
- A sniper in a palm tree
- A backfiring blunderbuss
- A pirate with four pistols and a sword
- Sharks ready to eat
- A skull with an eye patch
- A feeble cannon shot
- Feet sticking out of a cannon
- A modest figurehead
- A three-way clubbing
- A winking skull
- A creature with eight arms
- A crow's nest
- A cannonball puncher
- A deadly handshake
- A boat in a bathtub
- An empty treasure chest
- A cargo of heavyweights
- A human surfboard

HAVING A BALL IN GAYE PAREE

- Cancan dancers
- Two musicians fighting with their bows
- A scruffy man
- A waiter spilling a drink
- A man in a dress
- A tall, thin man with a short, fat woman
- A man caught by a statue
- Guests swinging from the chandeliers
- An eye-catching violinist
- A heavy pair of trousers
- A man about to get a crashing headache
- A man weighed down by his medals
- A curious assortment of weapons
- A man wearing a pile of hats
- An insolent statue
- A dangerous dancer
- A harpist firing an arrow
- A woman losing her dress

THE GOLD RUSH

- An overloaded donkey
- A running cactus
- A man being dragged by his horse
- Running boots
- Running tools
- A man falling over a barrel
- A dog taking his pick
- A man on a buffalo
- A canoe out of water
- A clown on a unicycle
- Men who have come off the rails
- Prospecting vultures
- Three escaped convicts
- A man running into a cactus
- A moving house
- A man on an old-fashioned bicycle
- Men in their night clothes
- A man being dragged by his dog
- Prospecting snakes
- A man taking a photograph
- A horse wearing a hat

THE FUTURE

- A smiling satellite
- Mercury
- Hitchhikers in the Galaxy
- Spaceships on a collision course
- A robot and his dog
- A creature holding six drinks
- Humans laughing at aliens
- A biplane
- Saturn being sat on
- Identical twin aliens
- Space traffic lights
- An alien with two noses on his face
- Aliens laughing at humans
- A crash landing
- The Great Bear
- Costumes from every page of this book
- Flying saucers
- Neptune
- The Milky Way
- A blue alien with hand in pocket

WHAT A MYSTERY!

Wow, Waldo-Watchers! As well as finding Waldo and his friends, did you find all the things they lost? Did you find the mystery character in every picture? It may be difficult, but keep searching and eventually you'll find her (now, that's a clue!). And one last thing: Somewhere one of the Waldo watchers lost the bobble from his hat. Can you spot which one and find the bobble?

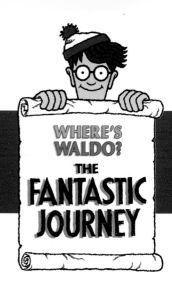

THE GOBBLING GLUTTONS

ONCE UPON A TIME, WALDO
EMBARKED UPON A FANTASTIC
JOURNEY. FIRST, AMONG A
THRONG OF GOBBLING GLUTTONS,
HE MET WIZARD WHITEBEARD, WHO
COMMANDED HIM TO FIND A SCROLL AND
THEN TO FIND ANOTHER AT EVERY STAGE OF
HIS JOURNEY. FOR WHEN HE HAD FOUND
12 SCROLLS, HE WOULD UNDERSTAND THE
TRUTH ABOUT HIMSELF.

IN EVERY PICTURE FIND WALDO, WOOF (BUT
ALL YOU CAN SEE IS HIS TAIL), WENDA, WIZARD
WHITEBEARD, ODLAW, AND THE SCROLL. THEN
FIND WALDO'S KEY, WOOF'S BONE (IN THIS SCENE
IT'S THE BONE THAT'S NEAREST TO HIS TAIL),
WENDA'S CAMERA, AND ODLAW'S BINOCULARS.

THERE ARE ALSO 25 WALDO-WATCHERS, EACH OF
WHOM APPEARS ONLY ONCE SOMEWHERE IN
THE FOLLOWING 12 PICTURES. AND ONE MORE
THING! CAN YOU FIND ANOTHER CHARACTER,
NOT SHOWN BELOW, WHO APPEARS ONCE IN
EVERY PICTURE EXCEPT THE LAST?

THE GREAT WHERE'S WALDO? THE FANTASTIC JOURNEY CHECKLIST: PART ONE

Hundreds more things for Waldo followers to look for! Don't forget PART TWO at the end of this adventure!

THE GOBBLING GLUTTONS

- [ ] A strong waiter and a weak one
- [ ] Long-distance smells
- [ ] Unequal portions of pie
- [ ] A man who has had too much to drink
- [ ] People who are going the wrong way
- [ ] Very tough dishes
- [ ] An upside-down dish
- [ ] A very hot dinner
- [ ] Knights drinking through straws
- [ ] A clever drink pourer
- [ ] Giant sausages
- [ ] A custard fight
- [ ] An overloaded seat
- [ ] Beard-flavored soup
- [ ] Men pulling legs
- [ ] A painful spillage
- [ ] A poke in the eye
- [ ] A man tied up in spaghetti
- [ ] A knockout dish
- [ ] A man who has eaten too much
- [ ] A tall diner eating a tall dish
- [ ] An exploding pie
- [ ] A giant sausage breaking in half
- [ ] A smell traveling through two people

THE BATTLING MONKS

- [ ] Two fire engines
- [ ] Hotfooted monks
- [ ] A bridge made of monks
- [ ] A smart-alecky monk
- [ ] A diving monk
- [ ] A scared statue
- [ ] Fire meeting water
- [ ] A snaking jet of water
- [ ] Chasers being chased
- [ ] A smug statue
- [ ] A snaking jet of flame
- [ ] A five-way washout
- [ ] A burning bridge
- [ ] Seven burning backsides
- [ ] Monks worshipping the Flowing Bucket of Water
- [ ] Monks shielding themselves from lava
- [ ] Thirteen trapped and extremely worried monks
- [ ] A monk seeing an oncoming jet of flame
- [ ] Monks worshipping the Mighty Erupting Volcano
- [ ] A very worried monk confronted by two opponents
- [ ] A burning hose
- [ ] Monks and lava pouring out of a volcano
- [ ] A chain of water
- [ ] Two monks accidentally attacking their brothers

THE CARPET FLYERS

- [ ] Two carpets on a collison course
- [ ] An overweight flyer
- [ ] A pedestrian crossing
- [ ] A carpet pinup
- [ ] Three hangers-on
- [ ] Flying hitchhikers
- [ ] An unsatisfied customer
- [ ] A used-carpet salesman
- [ ] A topsy-turvy tower
- [ ] A spiky crash
- [ ] Carpet cops and robbers
- [ ] A passing fruit thief
- [ ] Upside-down flyers
- [ ] A carpet repair shop
- [ ] Popular male and female flyers
- [ ] A flying tower
- [ ] A stair carpet
- [ ] Flying highwaymen
- [ ] Rich and poor flyers
- [ ] A carpet-breakdown rescue service
- [ ] Carpets flying on carpet flyers
- [ ] A carpet traffic policeman
- [ ] A flying carpet without a flyer

THE GREAT BALLGAME PLAYERS

- [ ] A three-way drink
- [ ] A row of handheld banners
- [ ] A chase that goes around in circles
- [ ] A spectator surrounded by three rival supporters
- [ ] Players who can't see where they are going
- [ ] Two tall players versus short ones
- [ ] Seven awful singers
- [ ] A face made of balls
- [ ] Players who are digging for victory
- [ ] A face about to hit a fist
- [ ] A shot that breaks the woodwork
- [ ] A mob chasing a player backward
- [ ] A player chasing a mob
- [ ] Players pulling one another's hoods
- [ ] A flag with a hole in it
- [ ] A mob of players all holding balls
- [ ] A player heading a ball
- [ ] A player tripping over a rock
- [ ] A player punching a ball
- [ ] A spectator accidentally hitting two others
- [ ] A player sticking his tongue out at a mob
- [ ] A mouth pulled open by a beard
- [ ] A backside shot

THE FEROCIOUS RED DWARFS

- [ ] A spear-breaking slingshot
- [ ] Two punches causing chain reactions
- [ ] Fat and thin spears and spearmen
- [ ] A spearman being knocked through a flag
- [ ] A collar made out of a shield
- [ ] A prison made of spears
- [ ] Tangled spears
- [ ] A devious disarmer
- [ ] Dwarfs disguised as spearmen
- [ ] A stickup machine
- [ ] A spearman trapped by his battle dress
- [ ] A sneaky spear bender
- [ ] An ax head causing headaches
- [ ] A dwarf who is on the wrong side
- [ ] Prankish target practice
- [ ] Opponents charging through each other
- [ ] A spearman running away from a spear
- [ ] A slingshot causing a chain reaction
- [ ] A sword cutting through a shield
- [ ] A dwarf hiding up a spear
- [ ] Spearmen who have jumped out of their clothes
- [ ] A spear knocking off a dwarf's helmet

THE NASTY NASTIES

- [ ] A vampire who is scared of ghosts
- [ ] Two vampire bears
- [ ] Vampires drinking through straws
- [ ] Gargoyle lovers
- [ ] An upside-down torture
- [ ] A baseball bat
- [ ] Three wolfmen
- [ ] A mummy who is coming undone
- [ ] A vampire mirror test
- [ ] A frightened skeleton
- [ ] Dog, cat, and mouse doorways
- [ ] Courting cats
- [ ] A ghoulish bowling game
- [ ] A gargoyle being poked in the eye
- [ ] An upside-down gargoyle
- [ ] Ghoulish flight controllers
- [ ] Three witches flying backward
- [ ] A witch losing her broomstick
- [ ] A broomstick flying a witch
- [ ] A ticklish torture
- [ ] A vampire about to get the chop
- [ ] A ghost train
- [ ] A vampire who doesn't fit his coffin
- [ ] A three-eyed, hooded torturer

THE GOBBLING GLUTTONS

ONCE UPON A TIME, WALDO
EMBARKED UPON A FANTASTIC
JOURNEY. FIRST, AMONG A
THRONG OF GOBBLING GLUTTONS,
HE MET WIZARD WHITEBEARD, WHO
COMMANDED HIM TO FIND A SCROLL AND
THEN TO FIND ANOTHER AT EVERY STAGE OF
HIS JOURNEY. FOR WHEN HE HAD FOUND
12 SCROLLS, HE WOULD UNDERSTAND THE
TRUTH ABOUT HIMSELF.

IN EVERY PICTURE FIND WALDO, WOOF (BUT
ALL YOU CAN SEE IS HIS TAIL), WENDA, WIZARD
WHITEBEARD, ODLAW, AND THE SCROLL. THEN
FIND WALDO'S KEY, WOOF'S BONE (IN THIS SCENE
IT'S THE BONE THAT'S NEAREST TO HIS TAIL),
WENDA'S CAMERA, AND ODLAW'S BINOCULARS.

THERE ARE ALSO 25 WALDO-WATCHERS, EACH OF
WHOM APPEARS ONLY ONCE SOMEWHERE IN
THE FOLLOWING 12 PICTURES. AND ONE MORE
THING! CAN YOU FIND ANOTHER CHARACTER,
NOT SHOWN BELOW, WHO APPEARS ONCE IN
EVERY PICTURE EXCEPT THE LAST?

THE BATTLING MONKS

THEN WALDO AND WIZARD WHITEBEARD CAME
TO THE PLACE WHERE THE INVISIBLE MONKS
OF FIRE FOUGHT THE MONKS OF WATER. AND
AS WALDO SEARCHED FOR THE SECOND
SCROLL, HE SAW THAT MANY WALDOS HAD BEEN THIS WAY
BEFORE. AND WHEN HE FOUND THE SCROLL, IT WAS TIME TO
CONTINUE WITH HIS JOURNEY.

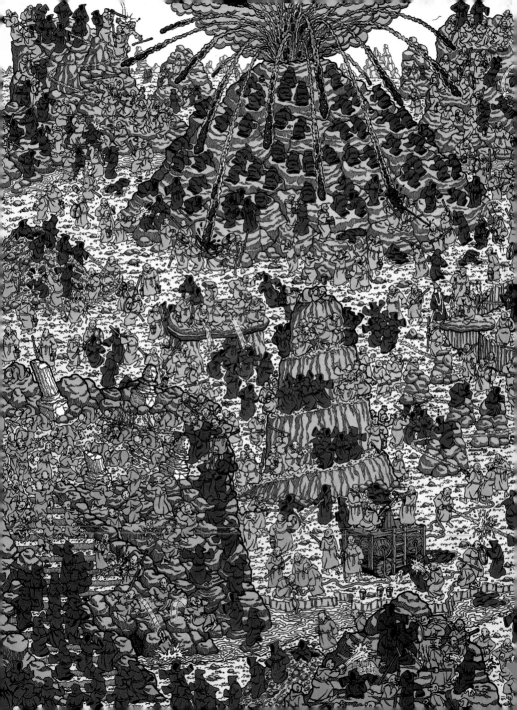

THE CARPET FLYERS

THEN WALDO AND WIZARD WHITEBEARD
CAME TO THE LAND OF THE CARPET FLYERS,
WHERE MANY WALDOS HAD BEEN BEFORE.
AND WALDO SAW THAT THERE WERE MANY
CARPETS IN THE SKY AND MANY RED BIRDS
(HOW MANY, O BRAINY BIRD AND CARPET WATCHERS?).
AND WHEN WALDO FOUND THE THIRD SCROLL, IT WAS
TIME TO CONTINUE WITH HIS JOURNEY.

THE GREAT BALLGAME PLAYERS

THEN WALDO AND WIZARD WHITEBEARD CAME TO
THE PLAYING FIELD OF THE GREAT BALLGAME
PLAYERS, WHERE MANY WALDOS HAD BEEN
BEFORE. AND WALDO SAW THAT FOUR TEAMS WERE
PLAYING AGAINST ONE ANOTHER (BUT WAS ANYONE WINNING?
WHAT WAS THE SCORE? CAN YOU FIGURE OUT THE RULES?).
THEN WALDO FOUND THE FOURTH SCROLL AND CONTINUED
WITH HIS JOURNEY.

THE FEROCIOUS RED DWARFS

THEN WALDO AND WIZARD WHITEBEARD CAME AMONG THE FEROCIOUS RED DWARFS, WHERE MANY WALDOS HAD BEEN BEFORE. AND THE DWARFS WERE ATTACKING THE MANY-COLORED SPEARMEN, CAUSING MIGHTY MAYHEM AND HORRID HAVOC. AND WALDO FOUND THE FIFTH SCROLL AND CONTINUED WITH HIS JOURNEY.

THE NASTY NASTIES

THEN WALDO AND WIZARD WHITEBEARD CAME TO
THE CASTLE OF THE NASTY NASTIES, WHERE
MANY WALDOS HAD BEEN BEFORE. AND
WHEREVER WALDO WALKED, THERE WAS A FEARFUL CLATTERING
OF BONES (WOOF'S BONE IN THIS SCENE IS THE ONE NEAREST TO
HIS TAIL) AND A FOUL SLURPING OF FILTHY FOOD. AND WALDO
FOUND THE SIXTH SCROLL AND CONTINUED WITH HIS JOURNEY.

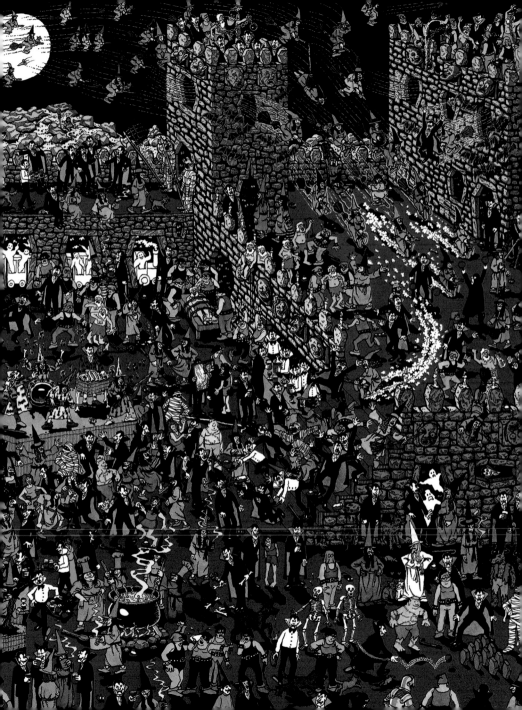

THE FIGHTING FORESTERS

THEN WALDO AND WIZARD WHITEBEARD CAME
AMONG THE FIGHTING FORESTERS, WHERE
MANY WALDOS HAD BEEN BEFORE. AND IN
THEIR BATTLE WITH THE EVIL BLACK KNIGHTS,
THE FOREST WOMEN WERE AIDED BY THE ANIMALS, BY
THE LIVING MUD, EVEN BY THE TREES THEMSELVES. AND
WALDO FOUND THE SEVENTH SCROLL AND CONTINUED
WITH HIS JOURNEY.

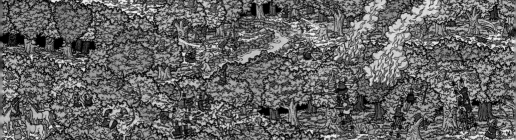

THE DEEP-SEA DIVERS

THEN WALDO AND WIZARD WHITEBEARD CAME
TO THE WATERY WORLD OF THE DEEP-SEA
DIVERS, WHERE MANY WALDOS HAD BEEN
BEFORE. AND WALDO SEARCHED FOR THE EIGHTH
SCROLL AMONG THE MONSTERS OF THE DEEP, AMONG THE
MERMAIDS, FISHERMEN, AND FISH. AND WHEN HE FOUND IT,
IT WAS TIME TO CONTINUE WITH HIS JOURNEY.

THE KNIGHTS OF THE MAGIC FLAG

THEN WALDO AND WIZARD WHITEBEARD CAME
TO A PLACE MORE CROWDED THAN ANY WALDO
HAD SEEN BEFORE, WHERE TWO ARMIES WITH
MANY MAGIC FLAGS WERE LOCKED IN COMBAT.
AND WALDO SAW THAT MANY WALDOS HAD BEEN THIS WAY
BEFORE. AND WHEN HE FOUND THE NINTH SCROLL, IT WAS
TIME TO CONTINUE WITH HIS JOURNEY.

THE UNFRIENDLY GIANTS

THEN WALDO AND WIZARD WHITEBEARD CAME
TO THE LAND OF THE UNFRIENDLY GIANTS,
WHERE MANY WALDOS HAD BEEN BEFORE.
AND WALDO SAW THAT THE GIANTS WERE
HORRIDLY HARASSING THE LITTLE PEOPLE. AND WHEN HE
FOUND THE TENTH SCROLL, IT WAS TIME TO CONTINUE WITH
HIS JOURNEY.

THE UNDERGROUND HUNTERS

THEN WALDO AND WIZARD WHITEBEARD CAME
AMONG THE UNDERGROUND HUNTERS, WHERE
MANY WALDOS HAD BEEN BEFORE. THERE WAS
MUCH MENACE IN THIS PLACE, AND A
MULTITUDE OF MALEVOLENT MONSTERS. WALDO
FOUND THE ELEVENTH SCROLL AND CONTINUED WITH
HIS JOURNEY.

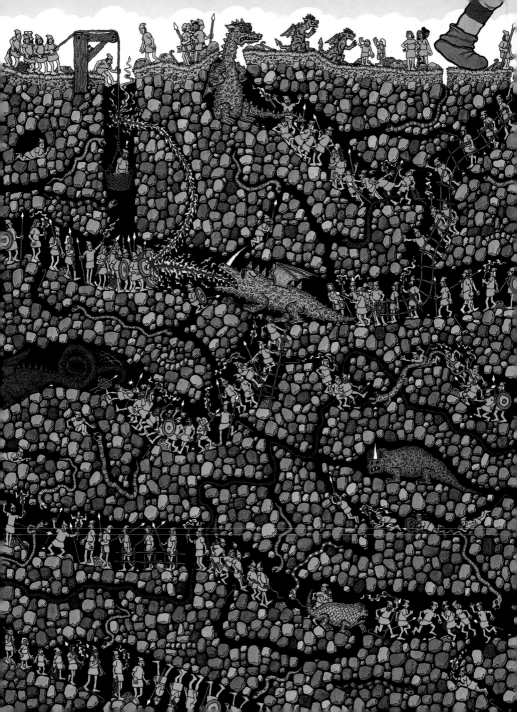

THE LAND OF WALDOS

THEN WALDO FOUND THE TWELFTH SCROLL AND SAW THE TRUTH ABOUT HIMSELF, THAT HE WAS JUST ONE WALDO AMONG MANY. HE SAW, TOO, THAT WALDOS OFTEN LOSE THINGS, FOR HE HIMSELF HAD LOST ONE SHOE. AND AS HE LOOKED FOR HIS SHOE, HE DISCOVERED THAT WIZARD WHITEBEARD WAS NOT HIS ONLY FELLOW TRAVELER. THERE WERE NOW ELEVEN OTHERS—ONE FROM EVERY PLACE HE HAD BEEN TO— WHO HAD JOINED HIM ONE BY ONE ALONG THE WAY. SO NOW (O LOYAL FOLLOWERS OF WALDO!) FIND THE REAL WALDO AND HELP HIM FIND HIS MISSING SHOE. AND THERE, IN THE LAND OF WALDOS, MAY WALDO LIVE HAPPILY EVER AFTER.

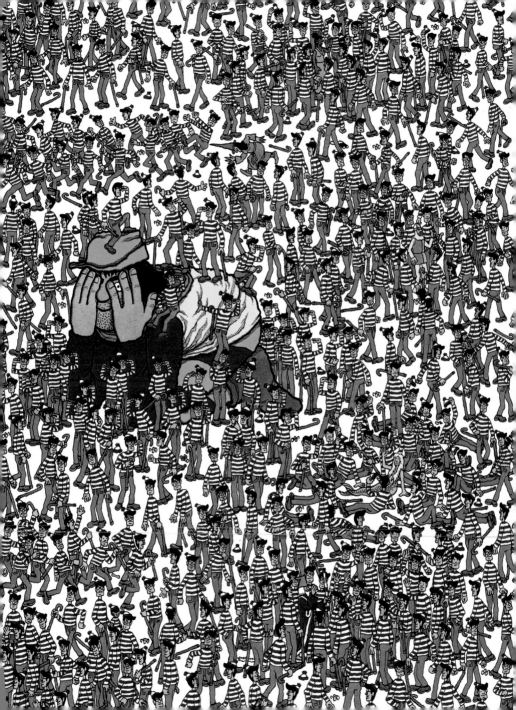

THE GREAT WHERE'S WALDO?
THE FANTASTIC JOURNEY CHECKLIST: PART TWO

THE FIGHTING FORESTERS

- [ ] Three long legs
- [ ] A three-legged knight
- [ ] Knights being chopped down by a tree
- [ ] Two multiple knockouts
- [ ] A lazy lady
- [ ] A tree with a lot of puff
- [ ] Hardheaded women
- [ ] Attackers about to be attacked
- [ ] A strong woman and a weak one
- [ ] An easily frightened horse
- [ ] Eight pairs of upside-down feet
- [ ] Knights shooting arrows at knights
- [ ] An upside-down ladder
- [ ] Loving trees
- [ ] An upside-down trunk
- [ ] A two-headed unicorn
- [ ] A unicorn in a tree
- [ ] Trees with two faces
- [ ] Muddy mudslingers
- [ ] A tearful small tree
- [ ] Spears getting sharpened tips
- [ ] Trees branching out violently
- [ ] Stilts being chewed up

THE DEEP-SEA DIVERS

- [ ] A two-headed fish
- [ ] A sword fight with a swordfish
- [ ] A sea lion
- [ ] A seabed
- [ ] A fish face
- [ ] A catfish and a dogfish
- [ ] A jellyfish
- [ ] A fish with two tails
- [ ] A skate
- [ ] Two fish-shaped formations
- [ ] Treacherous treasure
- [ ] Oyster beds
- [ ] Canned fish, flying fish, and fish fingers
- [ ] Electric eels
- [ ] A deck of cards
- [ ] A bottle in a message
- [ ] A fake fin
- [ ] A backward mermaid
- [ ] A sea horse–drawn carriage
- [ ] A boat's compass
- [ ] A fish catching men
- [ ] An underwater beach scene
- [ ] Divers drawing on an angry sea monster

THE KNIGHTS OF THE MAGIC FLAG

- [ ] Unfaithful royals
- [ ] A flag full of fists
- [ ] A game of tic-tac-toe
- [ ] A sword-fighting reindeer
- [ ] A man behind bars
- [ ] A mouse among lions
- [ ] Flags within a flag
- [ ] A tangle of tongues
- [ ] A zebra crossing
- [ ] An eagle dropping an eyeful
- [ ] A puffing spoilsport
- [ ] A battering-ram door key
- [ ] Snakes and ladders
- [ ] A flame-throwing dragon
- [ ] Diminishing desserts
- [ ] A crown thief
- [ ] A thirsty lion
- [ ] A weapon's imbalance
- [ ] A foot being tickled by a feather
- [ ] Some rude soldiers
- [ ] A surrendering reindeer
- [ ] A dog straining to get a bone
- [ ] A helmet with three eyes

THE UNFRIENDLY GIANTS

- [ ] Trappers about to be trapped
- [ ] A catapulted missile hitting people
- [ ] A hairy bird's nest
- [ ] Ducks out of water
- [ ] A mocking giant about to come unstuck
- [ ] Two broom trees
- [ ] Two giants who are out for the count
- [ ] Two windmill knockouts
- [ ] A polite giant about to get a headache
- [ ] A giant with a roof over his head
- [ ] Three people in a giant hood
- [ ] A battering-ram fist
- [ ] A house shaker
- [ ] A thumbtack trap
- [ ] A landslide of boulders
- [ ] Six people strapped inside giant belts
- [ ] People being swept off their feet
- [ ] People taking part in a board game
- [ ] Rope pullers being pulled
- [ ] Birds being disturbed by a giant
- [ ] Two game watchers slapping people
- [ ] Four shy ladies being flattered
- [ ] A powerful burst of pond water

THE UNDERGROUND HUNTERS

- [ ] A hunter about to put his foot in it
- [ ] Four frightened flames
- [ ] A snaky hat thief
- [ ] An underground traffic policeman
- [ ] Three surrendering flames
- [ ] A two-headed snake
- [ ] A snaky tickle
- [ ] A ridiculously long snake
- [ ] Three dragons wearing sunglasses
- [ ] A dragon that attacks with both ends
- [ ] Angry snake parents
- [ ] Five broken spears
- [ ] A monstrous bridge
- [ ] Five rock faces
- [ ] Upside-down hunters
- [ ] A snake that is trapped
- [ ] A very long ladder
- [ ] A torch setting fire to spears
- [ ] Hunters tripped by a tongue
- [ ] A hunter with an extra-long spear
- [ ] Hunters about to collide
- [ ] Hunters going around in a circle
- [ ] A shocked tail puller

THE LAND OF WALDOS

- [ ] Waldos waving
- [ ] Waldos walking
- [ ] Waldos running
- [ ] Waldos sitting
- [ ] Waldos lying down
- [ ] Waldos sliding
- [ ] Waldos standing still
- [ ] Waldos smiling
- [ ] Waldos searching
- [ ] Waldos being chased
- [ ] Waldos giving the thumbs up
- [ ] Waldos looking frightened
- [ ] Waldos with bobble hats
- [ ] Waldos without bobble hats
- [ ] Waldos raising their bobble hats
- [ ] Waldos with walking sticks
- [ ] Waldos without walking sticks
- [ ] Waldos with glasses
- [ ] Waldos without glasses
- [ ] A Waldo on a hat
- [ ] A Waldo holding a wing
- [ ] Waldo

THE FANTASTIC JOURNEY

Did you find Waldo, his friends, and all the things that they had lost? Did you find the mystery character who appeared in every scene except the Land of Waldos? It may be difficult, but keep searching and eventually you'll find him—now that's a clue! And one last thing: Somewhere one of the Waldo-Watchers lost the bobble from his hat. Can you find which one, and find the bobble?

A DREAM COME TRUE

WOW, WALDO-WATCHERS, THIS IS FANTASTIC, I'M REALLY IN HOLLYWOOD! LOOK AT THE FILM PEOPLE EVERYWHERE – I WONDER WHAT MOVIES THEY'RE MAKING. THIS IS MY DREAM COME TRUE . . . TO MEET THE DIRECTORS AND ACTORS, TO WALK THROUGH THE CROWDS OF EXTRAS, TO SEE BEHIND THE SCENES! PHEW, I WONDER IF I'LL APPEAR IN A MOVIE MYSELF!

★ ★ ★ WHAT TO LOOK FOR IN HOLLYWOOD! ★ ★ ★

WELCOME TO TINSELTOWN, WALDO-WATCHERS! THESE ARE THE PEOPLE AND THINGS TO LOOK FOR AS YOU WALK THROUGH THE FILM SETS WITH WALDO.

★ FIRST (OF COURSE!) WHERE'S WALDO?

★ NEXT FIND WALDO'S CANINE COMPANION, WOOF – REMEMBER, ALL YOU CAN SEE IS HIS TAIL!

★ THEN FIND WALDO'S FRIEND WENDA!

★ ABRACADABRA! NOW FOCUS IN ON WIZARD WHITEBEARD!

★ BOO! HISS! HERE COMES THE BAD GUY, ODLAW!

★ NOW SPOT THESE 25 WALDO-WATCHERS, EACH OF WHOM APPEARS ONLY ONCE BEFORE THE FINAL FANTASTIC SCENE!

★ WOW! INCREDIBLE! SPOT ONE OTHER CHARACTER WHO APPEARS IN EVERY SCENE EXCEPT THE LAST!

★ ★ KEEP ON SEARCHING! THERE'S MORE TO FIND! ★ ★

ON EVERY SET FIND WALDO'S LOST KEY

WOOF'S LOST BONE! WENDA'S LOST CAMERA! WIZARD WHITEBEARD'S SCROLL! ODLAW'S LOST BINOCULARS! AND A MISSING CAN OF FILM!

★ ★ ★ ★ ★ ★ AND MORE AND MORE! ★ ★ ★ ★ ★ ★ ★

EACH OF THE FOUR POSTERS ON THE WALL OVER THERE IS PART OF ONE OF THE FILM SETS WALDO IS ABOUT TO VISIT. ★ FIND OUT WHERE THE POSTERS CAME FROM. ★ THEN SPOT ANY DIFFERENCES BETWEEN THE POSTERS AND THE SETS.

THE GREAT WHERE'S WALDO? IN HOLLYWOOD CHECKLIST: PART ONE

Lots more things for Waldo-Watchers to look for! Don't forget PART TWO at the end of this adventure!

★ ★ ★ A DREAM COME TRUE ★ ★ ★

- [ ] A soldier capturing some food
- [ ] A double agent in a spy film
- [ ] Someone walking tall
- [ ] A swing band
- [ ] A green star on a yellow ball
- [ ] A wind machine blowing out of control
- [ ] A romantic scene
- [ ] A girl in a swimsuit with a yellow hat
- [ ] Eight pieces of heart-shaped film equipment
- [ ] Ten studio security guards
- [ ] Twenty-one pirates in striped clothing
- [ ] Three shields
- [ ] Someone who has put their foot in it
- [ ] Three people with skis
- [ ] A scenic painter
- [ ] A man with a red-and-white-spotted tie
- [ ] A friendly pirate

★ ★ SHHH! THIS IS A SILENT MOVIE ★ ★

- [ ] A watchtower
- [ ] Two mobile cameras
- [ ] A director with a giant megaphone
- [ ] A searchlight
- [ ] A runaway wheel
- [ ] Two butterfly catchers
- [ ] Thirteen balloons
- [ ] A man in plus fours trousers
- [ ] Seven megaphones
- [ ] A trail of leaking buckets
- [ ] Nine four-legged animals
- [ ] Fifteen cameras
- [ ] Some flowers being watered
- [ ] Three men slipping on some fruit
- [ ] A hose cut by an ax
- [ ] Four fire chiefs wearing pointed hats
- [ ] A railway-track ladder
- [ ] Three men wearing red shirts and suspenders
- [ ] Two umbrellas

★ ★ ★ HORSEPLAY IN TROY ★ ★ ★

- [ ] Five blue soldiers with red-crested helmets
- [ ] One soldier wearing sandals
- [ ] Thirteen real four-legged animals
- [ ] Some ancient traffic police
- [ ] Five red soldiers with blue-crested helmets
- [ ] Two soldiers with slings
- [ ] Four first-aid soldiers
- [ ] Five yellow soldiers with blue-crested helmets
- [ ] Five soldiers with brooms
- [ ] One soldier with a square shield
- [ ] Three film crew members wearing sunglasses
- [ ] Three soldiers with extra-long cloaks
- [ ] Two statues waving at each other
- [ ] Three Trojans drinking coffee
- [ ] Ten arrows that are stuck in shields
- [ ] A trash can
- [ ] Soldiers arguing about the time

★ ★ FUN IN THE FOREIGN LEGION ★ ★

- [ ] Some date trees
- [ ] Twelve camels
- [ ] A modern airplane ruining a camera shot
- [ ] Four trees surrendering
- [ ] A rock hitting sixteen people
- [ ] Two men being shaken out of a tree
- [ ] The right costumes in the wrong colors
- [ ] A horseman riding in the wrong direction
- [ ] A French flag with colors in the wrong order
- [ ] Five men wearing undershirts and boxers
- [ ] Some enemies fighting back-to-back
- [ ] An unpopular musician
- [ ] A man reading a newspaper
- [ ] Three men hiding underneath animals
- [ ] An animal stepping on a man's foot
- [ ] A man surrendering to a shovel

★ A TREMENDOUS SONG AND DANCE ★

- [ ] One dancer wearing a blue carnation
- [ ] Some tap dancers
- [ ] A grand piano
- [ ] A musician playing a double bass
- [ ] Dancers wearing top hats and tails
- [ ] Sailors saluting the ship's "N" sign
- [ ] The captain's log
- [ ] Sailors with bell-bottom pants
- [ ] A vice admiral
- [ ] A piano keyboard
- [ ] Four orange feathers
- [ ] A soldier on the wrong set
- [ ] Five real anchors
- [ ] Three watery creatures
- [ ] Nine mops
- [ ] Four sailors with tattoos

★ ALI BABA AND THE FORTY THIEVES ★

- [ ] A man asleep in bed
- [ ] Another man awake in bed
- [ ] Five animals
- [ ] A man wearing yellow shoes
- [ ] A man wearing green shoes
- [ ] A man wearing a red shoe and a white shoe
- [ ] A man wearing a red shoe and a pink shoe
- [ ] A chest of drawers
- [ ] A man with jewels in his beard
- [ ] Two careless carpet carriers
- [ ] A man wearing a green turban
- [ ] A man wearing a yellow turban
- [ ] Four real genies
- [ ] A man carrying a gray treasure chest
- [ ] A man with a red star on his turban
- [ ] A man with a yellow tassel on his fez
- [ ] A man with a green tassel on his fez

★ ★ ★ THE WILD, WILD WEST ★ ★ ★

- [ ] Two cowboys about to draw against each other
- [ ] Drinkers raising their glasses to a lady
- [ ] Outlaws holding up a stagecoach
- [ ] Some boisterous cowboys painting the town red
- [ ] Doc holiday
- [ ] The film wardrobe department
- [ ] Buffalo Bill
- [ ] The loan ranger
- [ ] Gamblers playing cards
- [ ] A couple of gunslingers
- [ ] Calamity Jane
- [ ] A buffalo **stampede**
- [ ] A spaghetti western
- [ ] A horse-drawn wagon
- [ ] Billy the kid
- [ ] Townspeople saluting General Store
- [ ] A band of outlaws
- [ ] Two cowboys shouting, "This town ain't big enough for the both of us."

A DREAM COME TRUE

WOW, WALDO-WATCHERS, THIS IS FANTASTIC, I'M REALLY IN HOLLYWOOD! LOOK AT THE FILM PEOPLE EVERYWHERE – I WONDER WHAT MOVIES THEY'RE MAKING. THIS IS MY DREAM COME TRUE . . . TO MEET THE DIRECTORS AND ACTORS, TO WALK THROUGH THE CROWDS OF EXTRAS, TO SEE BEHIND THE SCENES! PHEW, I WONDER IF I'LL APPEAR IN A MOVIE MYSELF!

★ ★ ★ WHAT TO LOOK FOR IN HOLLYWOOD! ★ ★ ★

WELCOME TO TINSELTOWN, WALDO-WATCHERS! THESE ARE THE PEOPLE AND THINGS TO LOOK FOR AS YOU WALK THROUGH THE FILM SETS WITH WALDO.

★ FIRST (OF COURSE!) WHERE'S WALDO?

★ NEXT FIND WALDO'S CANINE COMPANION, WOOF – REMEMBER, ALL YOU CAN SEE IS HIS TAIL!

★ THEN FIND WALDO'S FRIEND WENDA!

★ ABRACADABRA! NOW FOCUS IN ON WIZARD WHITEBEARD!

★ BOO! HISS! HERE COMES THE BAD GUY, ODLAW!

★ NOW SPOT THESE 25 WALDO-WATCHERS, EACH OF WHOM APPEARS ONLY ONCE BEFORE THE FINAL FANTASTIC SCENE!

★ WOW! INCREDIBLE! SPOT ONE OTHER CHARACTER WHO APPEARS IN EVERY SCENE EXCEPT THE LAST!

★ ★ KEEP ON SEARCHING! THERE'S MORE TO FIND! ★ ★

ON EVERY SET FIND WALDO'S LOST KEY!

WOOF'S LOST BONE! WENDA'S LOST CAMERA! WIZARD WHITEBEARD'S SCROLL! ODLAW'S LOST BINOCULARS! AND A MISSING CAN OF FILM!

★ ★ ★ ★ ★ ★ AND MORE AND MORE! ★ ★ ★ ★ ★ ★ ★

EACH OF THE FOUR POSTERS ON THE WALL OVER THERE IS PART OF ONE OF THE FILM SETS WALDO IS ABOUT TO VISIT. ★ FIND OUT WHERE THE POSTERS CAME FROM. ★ THEN SPOT ANY DIFFERENCES BETWEEN THE POSTERS AND THE SETS.

SHHH! THIS IS A SILENT MOVIE

SO THIS IS HOW THE HOLLYWOOD DREAM BEGAN – WITH SILENT MOVIES MADE IN BLACK AND WHITE. IT LOOKS CRAZY AND IT MAKES YOU LAUGH. ACTING IN SLAPSTICK COMEDIES MUST BE REALLY HARD – LOOK HOW MANY ACCIDENTS ARE HAPPENING. BUT THE GREAT THING IS THAT NONE OF THE ACTORS EVER GET HURT, HOWEVER OFTEN THEY FALL FLAT ON THEIR FACES!

$10,000

FUN IN THE FOREIGN LEGION

PHEW, MOVIE FANS. DON'T GET OVERHEATED. THIS IS THE MOST SIZZLING LOCATION SO FAR! EVERYONE'S SWELTERING, FROM STARS TO SAND-SHIFTERS. SOME OF THOSE EXTRAS LOOK LIKE THEY'RE LOSING THEIR COOL – HAVE THEY FORGOTTEN THIS IS ONLY A FILM? PERHAPS IT'S TIME A FEW MORE OF THEM DESERTED THE DESERT AND JOINED THE RUSH FOR ICE CREAM!

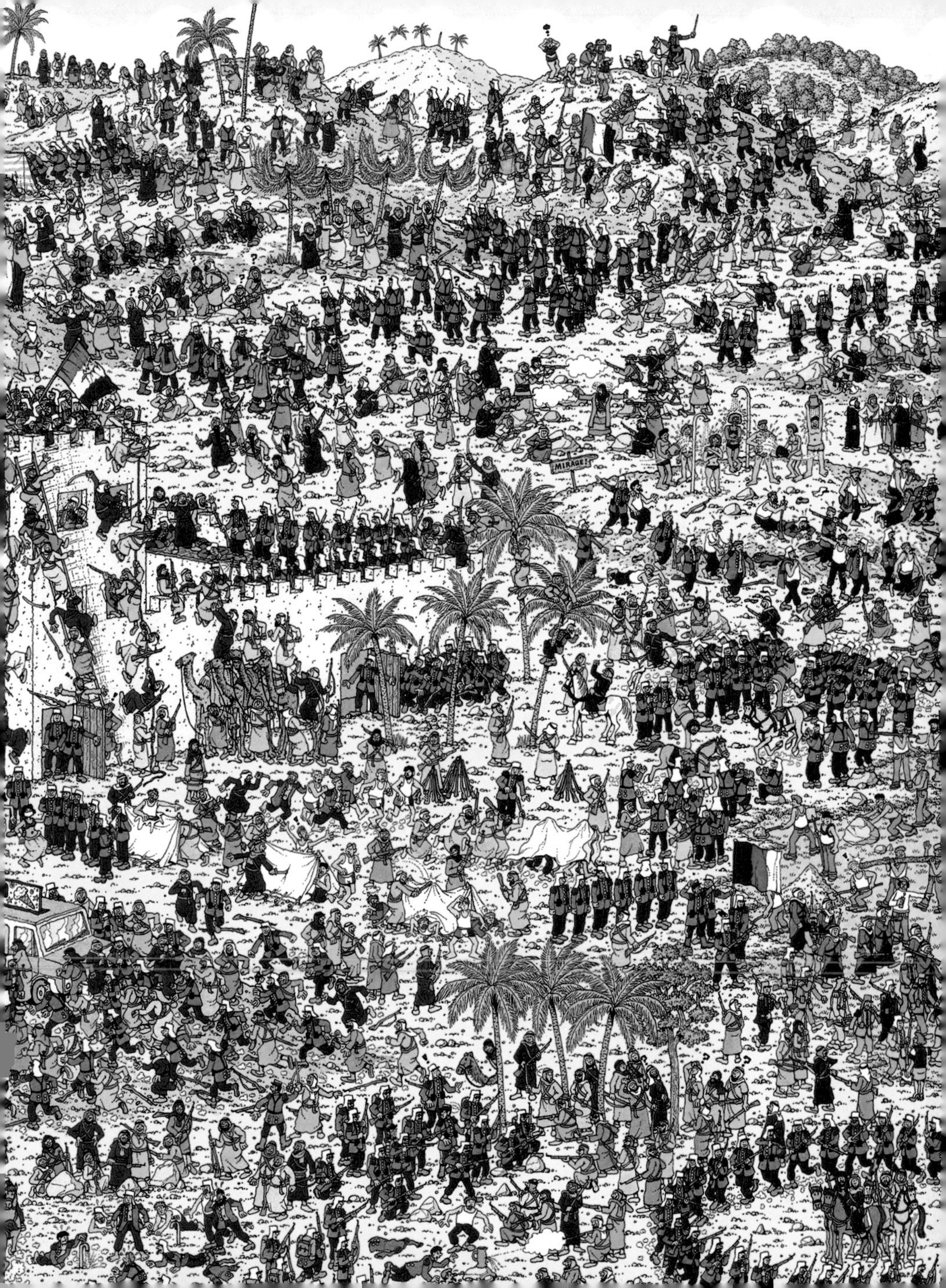
MIRAGE!

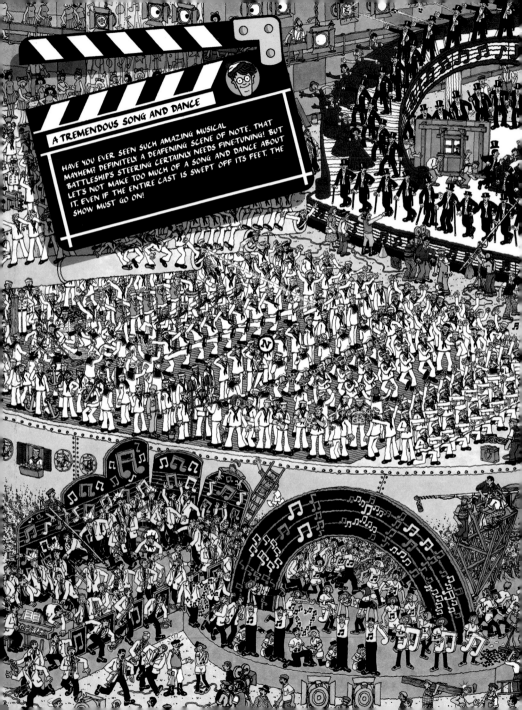

A TREMENDOUS SONG AND DANCE

HAVE YOU EVER SEEN SUCH AMAZING MUSICAL MAYHEM? DEFINITELY A DEAFENING SCENE OF NOTE. THAT BATTLESHIP'S STEERING CERTAINLY NEEDS FINE-TUNING! BUT LET'S NOT MAKE TOO MUCH OF A SONG AND DANCE ABOUT IT. EVEN IF THE ENTIRE CAST IS SWEPT OFF ITS FEET, THE SHOW MUST GO ON!

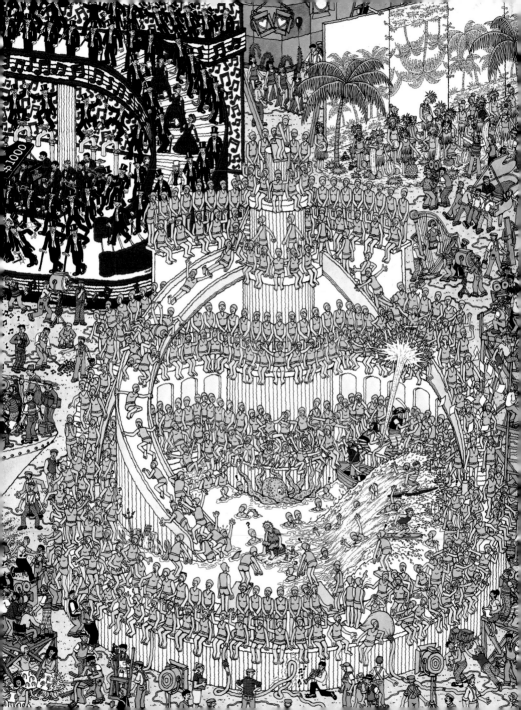

ALI BABA AND THE FORTY THIEVES

WHAT A CRUSH IN THE CAVE, WALDO-FOLLOWERS, BUT PAN IN ON THOSE POTS OF TREASURE! HOW MANY THIEVES WERE IN THE STORY? I BELIEVE THIS DIRECTOR THINKS FORTY THOUSAND! HAVE YOU SPOTTED ALI BABA? HE'S IN THE ALLEY, CUTTING HAIR – THE SCRIPTWRITER THINKS HIS NAME'S ALLEY BARBER! JANGLING GENIES – WHAT A FEARFULLY FUNNY FLICK THIS IS!

THE WILD, WILD WEST

YEEE-HA, WALDO-WATCHERS. HAVE YOU EVER SEEN SUCH A WILD, WILD WESTERN? HERE COMES THE WAGON TRAIN, STEAMING INTO TOWN; THE GOLD RUSH IS ON AND A COWBOY IS RIDING OFF INTO THE SUNSET! THERE'S SO MUCH ACTION, SO MUCH EXCITEMENT! I WONDER IF THE REAL WILD WEST WAS AS BRIGHT AND COLORFUL AS THIS!

THE SWASHBUCKLING MUSKETEERS

ALL FOR ONE, ONE FOR ALL! – WASN'T THAT THE MOTTO OF THE THREE MUSKETEERS? NOW LOOK AT THIS FREE-FOR-ALL! CAN YOU SPOT OUR THREE GALLANT HEROES BATTLING WITH THE RED-COATED CARDINAL'S GUARDS? WITH ALL THIS SWASHBUCKLING ACTION GOING ON, I WONDER HOW THE CAMERAMEN CAN CAPTURE IT ALL ON FILM!

DINOSAURS, SPACEMEN, AND GHOULS

PHEW, INCREDIBLE! TIME, SPACE, AND HORROR ARE IN A MIGHTY MUDDLE HERE! WHAT COSMIC COSTUMES AND WHAT GREAT SPECIAL EFFECTS! ONE OF THOSE FLYING SAUCERS LOOKS LIKE IT'S REALLY FLYING! ARE THOSE REAL ALIENS INSIDE, NOT ACTORS AT ALL? SO WHAT'S REAL AND WHAT'S MADE UP IN FILMS LIKE THESE?

ROBIN HOOD'S MERRY MESS-UP

LOOK HOW MANY MERRY MEN HAVE LEFT SHERWOOD
FOREST FOR A DAY OUT IN NOTTINGHAM CASTLE!
AND WHAT A MERRY TIME THEY'RE HAVING, MESSING
UP THE SHERIFF'S PARADE. WHICH ONE IS ROBIN HOOD? THE
ONE WEARING A ROBIN HOOD, OF COURSE! WHEN
YOU GO TO SEE THIS MOVIE, YOU'LL THINK IT'S ALL REAL,
BUT THE CASTLE'S STONE WALLS ARE MADE OF WOOD!

WHEN THE STARS COME OUT

WOW, WALDO-WATCHERS, THIS IS WHAT I CALL GLAMOUR! I'M AT A MAJOR MOVIE PREMIERE. THE STARS HAVE COME TO SEE THE FILM: THE CROWDS HAVE COME TO SEE THE STARS. LOOK AT THAT PINK STRETCH LIMO – NOW THAT'S A PERFECT CAR FOR A STAR. AND WHO'S IN THE BONE-MOBILE BEHIND? AND DOESN'T KING KONG LOOK NICER IN LIFE THAN WHEN HE'S ON THE SCREEN?

WHERE'S WALDO? THE MUSICAL

WOW, WHAT AN EXTRAVAGANZA, WALDO-WATCHERS – THIS ALL-SINGING, ALL-DANCING MOVIE IS ALL ABOUT ME AND MY FRIENDS! LOOK HOW MANY ACTORS ARE DRESSED UP AS ME! AND LOOK AT ALL THE WOOFS, WENDAS, WIZARD WHITEBEARDS, AND ODLAWS. HAVE YOU NOTICED THAT THE WARDROBE DEPARTMENT HAS MADE MISTAKES WITH SOME OF THE ACTORS' COSTUMES? BUT THAT WON'T HELP YOU FIND THE REAL ME AND MY FOUR FRIENDS IN THIS FILM! I'LL GIVE YOU SOME CLUES. I'M THE WALDO WITH SOMETHING EXTRA FOR WOOF. ALL YOU CAN SEE OF THE REAL WOOF IS HIS TAIL. THE REAL WENDA HAS A CAMERA. THE REAL WIZARD WHITEBEARD IS WEARING A HAT BENT TO THE LEFT. AND THE REAL ODLAW IS HOLDING A WALKING STICK.

THERE'S JUST ONE MORE THING. I'VE BEEN FOLLOWED HERE BY ONE CHARACTER FROM EVERY SET I'VE VISITED. SO CAN YOU SPOT ALL ELEVEN OF THEM IN THIS SCENE? AND CAN YOU FIND OUT WHEN EACH CHARACTER FIRST JOINED ME, AND CATCH ALL THEIR APPEARANCES THROUGHOUT MY TRAVELS?

THE GREAT WHERE'S WALDO? IN HOLLYWOOD CHECKLIST: PART TWO

Even more things for
Waldo-Watchers
to look for.

★ THE SWASHBUCKLING MUSKETEERS ★

- Eleven gentlemen bowing
- Two wheelbarrows
- Twelve spouts of water
- A tear-jerking emotional scene
- A gentleman with only one glove
- Three musket tears
- One lost glove
- A man wearing different colored gloves
- A hat with a striped plume
- Badly dressed men turned away from the dance
- A bouncer
- Two swordfighting ladies
- Two dueling film directors
- Three angry gardeners
- Two swordsmen fencing
- Three mixed-up statues
- A man having his foot tickled
- Four ladies being presented with flowers
- Four real animals

★ DINOSAURS, SPACEMEN, AND GHOULS ★

- "Hand" luggage
- A fly in saucer
- A ticklish dinosaur
- A greedy green alien
- A dozing dinosaur
- A spaceship
- A smart-alecky dinosaur
- Stars in a star's dressing room
- A wolfman having a howling good time
- Eight characters in craters
- A planet picnic
- A game of ringtoss
- A space castle
- Two people reading books
- Four cavemen going up in the world
- An astronaut without helmet, gloves, or boots
- Three other astronauts without helmets
- Two bottles of ketchup

★ ROBIN HOOD'S MERRY MESS-UP ★

- Eight ladies in medieval costume
- "Little" John leading some men
- Sixteen flags
- Two archers with long bows
- "Maid" Marian cleaning up
- A medieval extra with a radio
- A sheriff's soldier with rolled-up sleeves
- "Fryer" Tuck
- A night in armor
- A knight with a pink plume in his helmet
- The Sheriff of Nottingham
- A man with a bow and arrow
- A soldier with a large shield
- Medieval soldiers wearing the wrong pants
- A prisoner with a giant ball and chain
- Five real four-legged animals
- Twenty-one ladders
- Seven helmets with animal crests

★ ★ WHEN THE STARS COME OUT ★ ★

- Twenty-nine lights
- Two rival news reporters
- Someone who has it all wrapped up
- A policeman wanting an autograph
- Three cowboys
- Ten hearts
- Seven large palms
- Someone with a bird's-eye view
- A handful of spectators
- A celebrity wearing a new dress
- Someone making their mark
- Two astronauts
- A sleepy spectator with an alarm clock
- A twisting telescope
- An extra-long straw
- Four celebrities wearing sunglasses

★ ★ WHERE'S WALDO? THE MUSICAL ★ ★

- A Waldo sweater with stripes in reverse order
- A Waldo with blond hair
- A Waldo with a beard
- A Wenda without any shoes
- A Waldo wearing shades
- An Odlaw without a mustache
- A Waldo sweater with extra stripes
- A haredresser
- A Waldo wearing a hat without a bobble
- A Waldo without pockets on his jeans
- A Wizard Whitebeard wearing glasses
- A Waldo script reading
- A sound mixer
- A Wenda with a blue-and-white-striped umbrella
- A walking stick
- Two Wizard Whitebeards without beards
- A Waldo without glasses
- An Odlaw wearing a hat without a bobble
- A Wenda with blonde hair
- A Waldo wearing a bobble hat in reverse colors
- A Wenda without glasses
- A Wizard Whitebeard wearing a red hat
- A Woof wearing a bobble hat in reverse colors
- A Wenda wearing round Waldo glasses
- A Waldo tickling another Waldo
- A Woof without a bobble hat
- A Wenda with no pockets on her skirt
- A Waldo holding a walking stick the wrong way up
- A Woof wearing a hat without a bobble
- A Woof wearing shades
- A back view of a Wenda
- A Waldo in blue-and-white stripes
- A Wenda who is not wearing a bobble hat
- An Odlaw without shades
- A Wizard Whitebeard dancing
- A back view of a Waldo
- A Wizard Whitebeard wearing a bobble hat
- A Woof wearing a blue-and-white bobble hat
- Two Wizard Whitebeards without white beards
- A Wenda wearing a hat without a bobble
- A Waldo with two bobble hats

★ ★ ★ BACK TO THE BEGINNING ★ ★ ★

Did you find Waldo, all his friends, and all
the things they lost? Did you find the mystery
character who appears in every scene except the
last? And one more thing: Somewhere one of the
Waldo-Watchers lost the bobble from his hat.
Can you spot which one and find the bobble?

★ ★ ★ THE FINAL FILM TEST ★ ★ ★

Nearly all the faces in the sprocket holes on
this and on part one of the checklist appear in
color somewhere else in the book. Can you
find where? But . . . ten of them do not appear
anywhere else! Can you tell which ten? Lastly
. . . some faces appear more than once in the
sprocket holes. Can you see which ones and
how many times each one appears?

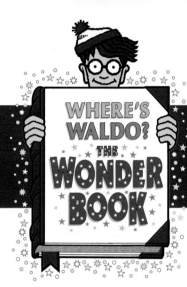

THE GREAT WHERE'S WALDO? THE WONDER BOOK CHECKLIST: PART ONE

More wonderful things for Waldo fans to check out! Don't forget PART TWO at the end of this adventure!

ONCE UPON A PAGE . . .

- [ ] Helen of Troy and Paris
- [ ] Rudyard Kipling and the jungle book
- [ ] Sir Francis and his drake
- [ ] Wild Bill hiccup
- [ ] A shopping centaur
- [ ] Handel's water music
- [ ] George washing ton
- [ ] Samuel peeps at his diary
- [ ] Guy forks
- [ ] Tchaikovsky and the nut cracker sweet
- [ ] A Roundhead with a round head
- [ ] Pythagoras and the square of the hippopotamus
- [ ] William shakes spear
- [ ] Madame two swords
- [ ] Garibaldi and his biscuits
- [ ] Florence and her nightingale
- [ ] The pilgrim fathers
- [ ] Captain cook
- [ ] Hamlet making an omelet
- [ ] Jason and the juggernauts
- [ ] Whistling Whistler painting his mother
- [ ] Ali barber
- [ ] Lincoln and the Gettysburg address
- [ ] Billy the kid
- [ ] Two knights fighting the war of the roses
- [ ] The Duke of Wellington's wellington

THE MIGHTY FRUIT FIGHT

- [ ] A box of dates next to a box of dates
- [ ] A pair of date palms
- [ ] "An apple a day keeps the doctor away!"
- [ ] Six crab apples
- [ ] Four naval oranges
- [ ] Blueberries wearing blue berets
- [ ] A kiwi fruit
- [ ] A banana doing the splits
- [ ] A pine apple
- [ ] Three fruit fools
- [ ] A bowl of fruit and a can of fruit
- [ ] Cranberry saws
- [ ] An orange upsetting the apple cart
- [ ] A banana tree
- [ ] Cooking apples
- [ ] Elder berry wine
- [ ] Seven wild cherries
- [ ] Goose berries
- [ ] A pound of apples
- [ ] A partridge in a pear tree
- [ ] A fruit cock tail
- [ ] Two peach halves
- [ ] "The Big Apple"
- [ ] One sour apple without a beard
- [ ] Paw paw fruit
- [ ] Another apple cart being upset

THE GAME OF GAMES

- [ ] Some stair cases
- [ ] Maize inside a maze
- [ ] A cross word
- [ ] A flight of stairs
- [ ] A map reading
- [ ] A player rolling the dice
- [ ] A tightrope walking
- [ ] A player with a map and a pair of compasses
- [ ] A player throwing a six
- [ ] One player not wearing gloves
- [ ] One lost glove
- [ ] The other lost glove
- [ ] A missing puzzle piece
- [ ] A bad mathematician
- [ ] Eight shovels
- [ ] Twenty-nine hoops
- [ ] Two cans of paint
- [ ] An upside-down question mark on a player's tunic
- [ ] A blue player holding a green block
- [ ] A player with a magnet
- [ ] Five referees with their arms folded
- [ ] Five crying players with handkerchiefs
- [ ] Two players reading newspapers
- [ ] A smoke signal
- [ ] Three ticklish players
- [ ] Eight messages in bottles

TOYS! TOYS! TOYS!

- [ ] Two spinning tops and a top spinning
- [ ] Jack in the box
- [ ] A jack in a box
- [ ] A toy soldier being decorated
- [ ] A toy soldier in full dress uniform
- [ ] A toy drill sergeant
- [ ] A fish tank
- [ ] Two anchors
- [ ] A toy figure on skis
- [ ] A chalkboard
- [ ] A toy figure pushing a wheelbarrow
- [ ] A crow's nest
- [ ] An apple-tree bookend
- [ ] A goal
- [ ] Five big red books
- [ ] A bear on a rocking horse
- [ ] A toy bandsman holding cymbals
- [ ] A toy performer balancing two chairs in the air
- [ ] Five wooden ladders
- [ ] A giraffe with a red-and-white-striped scarf
- [ ] A pirate carrying a barrel
- [ ] Toy figures climbing up a long scarf
- [ ] A teddy bear wearing a green scarf
- [ ] Two giraffes in the ark
- [ ] A robot holding a red tray

BRIGHT LIGHTS AND NIGHT FRIGHTS

- [ ] Street lights
- [ ] Lime light
- [ ] A rowboat
- [ ] An octo-puss
- [ ] Moon light
- [ ] Light entertainers
- [ ] A very light house
- [ ] Day light
- [ ] A fishing boat
- [ ] A standard lamp
- [ ] Christmas tree lights
- [ ] A light weight boxer
- [ ] Star light
- [ ] A light at the end of the tunnel
- [ ] Stage lights
- [ ] A motorboat
- [ ] A sailor walking the plank
- [ ] A diving board
- [ ] Candle light
- [ ] A bedside light
- [ ] The deep blue C
- [ ] A Chinese lantern
- [ ] A search light
- [ ] A sleeping monster
- [ ] A mirror
- [ ] Four sailors looking through telescopes

THE CAKE FACTORY

- [ ] A loading bay
- [ ] Conveyor belts
- [ ] Two Danish pastries
- [ ] A gingerbread man
- [ ] Two workers blowing cream horns
- [ ] Maple syrup
- [ ] Hot cross buns
- [ ] A Viennese whirl
- [ ] A Swiss roll
- [ ] A pan cake
- [ ] A chocolate moose
- [ ] A custard-pie fight
- [ ] Apple pie
- [ ] Black forest gateau
- [ ] A fish cake
- [ ] Rock cakes
- [ ] Dough nuts
- [ ] A doe nut
- [ ] Baked Alaska
- [ ] A fairy cake
- [ ] Mississippi mud pie
- [ ] Upside-down cake
- [ ] Carrot cake
- [ ] A cup cake
- [ ] Sponge cakes
- [ ] A cake carrying a worker

ONCE UPON A PAGE...

HEY, WALDO FANS! LOOK AT ALL THESE BRILLIANT BOOKS! LOOK AT ALL THE CHARACTERS WHO HAVE STEPPED OUT FROM THEIR PAGES! WOW! WHAT A MAGIC SCENE! THESE BOOKS HAVE REALLY COME ALIVE! FANTASTIC — THAT BOOK OVER THERE IS ABOUT MY TRAVELS! AND WOOF, WENDA, WIZARD WHITEBEARD, AND ODLAW ALL HAVE SPECIAL BOOKS OF THEIR OWN. NOW YOU CAN JOIN US TOO, IF YOU CAN FIND US, AND WE'LL TRAVEL TOGETHER THROUGH ALL THE OTHER WONDERFUL SCENES IN THIS WONDER BOOK. ONE SCENE IS MY SPECIAL FAVORITE — YOU'LL NEVER GUESS WHAT MAKES IT SO GREAT. THE BOOKMARK MARKS IT, SO WHEN WE GET THERE, YOU WILL KNOW. NOW GET SEARCHING, WALDO-FOLLOWERS, AND OFF WE GO! AND BE PREPARED FOR LOTS OF SURPRISES ALONG THE WAY!

Waldo

THE SEARCH IS ON! FIND THESE FIVE INTREPID TRAVELERS IN EVERY SCENE IN THE WONDER BOOK!

- FIND WALDO . . . WHO LEADS THE WAY!
- FIND WOOF . . . WHO WAGS HIS TAIL! (WHICH IS USUALLY ALL YOU CAN SEE!)
- FIND WENDA . . . WHO TAKES THE PICTURES!
- FIND WIZARD WHITEBEARD . . . WHO CASTS THE SPELLS!
- FIND ODLAW . . . WHOSE GOOD DEEDS ARE FEW INDEED!

THE SEARCH CONTINUES! NEXT FIND THESE IMPORTANT THINGS THE TRAVELERS HAVE LOST!

- FIND WALDO'S LOST KEY!
- FIND WOOF'S LOST BONE!
- FIND WENDA'S LOST CAMERA!
- FIND WIZARD WHITEBEARD'S MAGIC SCROLL!
- FIND ODLAW'S LOST BINOCULARS!

THE GREAT BOOK OF ODLAW'S GOOD DEEDS

CLASSIC STORIES FROM LITERATURE

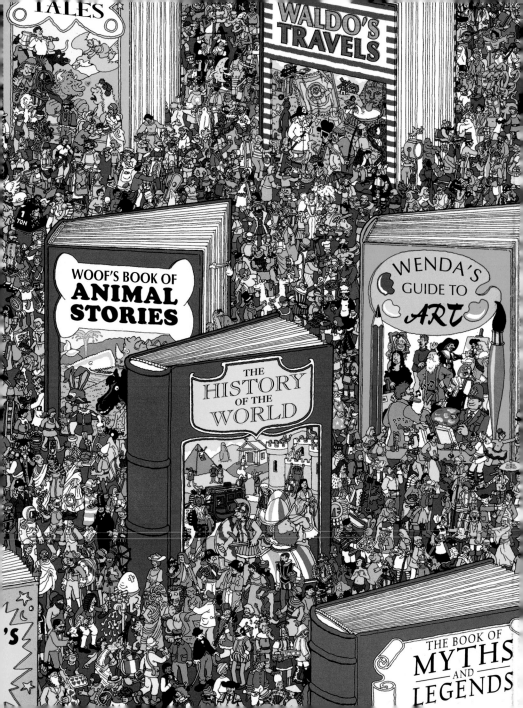

THE MIGHTY FRUIT FIGHT

WOW! AMAZING! HAVE YOU EVER IN YOUR LIVES SEEN A PLACE SO FULL OF FRUIT? HOW SWEET IT IS TO SAIL LEMON BOATS DOWN ORANGE JUICE RIVERS! BUT WATCH OUT, WALDO FANS! THE APPLES HAVE TURNED SOUR AND THEY'RE ATTACKING ALL THE OTHER FRUIT. WHOOSH! SQUIRT! SPLOOOOOSH! THERE'S A FRUIT JAM IN THE RIVER, SCUFFLES ON THE BANANA BRIDGES, AND SUGAR BEING POURED ALL OVER THE STRAWBERRIES! PHEW! WHAT A MIGHTY FRUIT FIGHT!

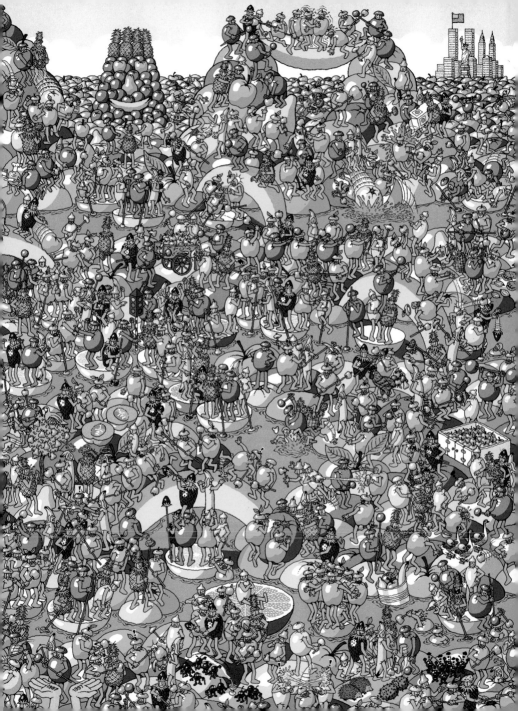

THE GAME OF GAMES

STARTED! CAN YOU SPOT THE ONLY ORANGE TEAM PLAYER WHO HAS FINISHED? AND THE ONLY GREEN TEAM PLAYER WHO HAS NOT YET BEGUN?

FOUR HUGE TEAMS ARE PLAYING THIS GREAT GAME OF GAMES. THE REFEREES ARE TRYING TO SEE THAT NO ONE BREAKS THE RULES. BETWEEN THE STARTING LINE AT THE TOP AND THE FINISH LINE AT THE BOTTOM, THERE ARE LOTS OF PUZZLES, BOOBY TRAPS, AND TESTS. THE GREEN TEAMS NEARLY WON, AND THE ORANGE TEAMS HARDLY

THE CAKE FACTORY

Mmmm! Feast your eyes, Waldo-watchers! Sniff the delicious smells of baking cakes! Drool at the tasty toppings! Can you see a cake like a teapot, a cake like a house, a cake so tall a worker on the floor above is licking it? Cakes, cakes, everywhere! How scrumptious! How yum-yum-yumptious! Look

at the oozing sugar icing and the shiny red cherries on the roof up there! That room is where the factory controllers work, but have they lost control?

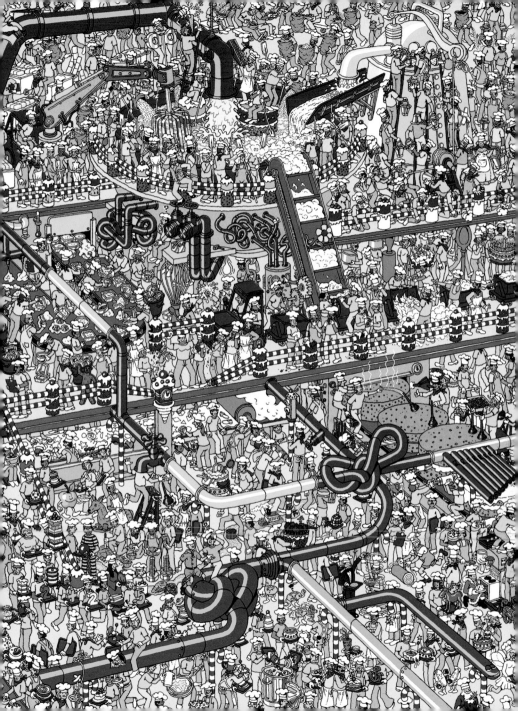

THE BATTLE OF THE BANDS

BOOM, BOOM, RAT-A-TAT-TAT! HAVE YOU EVER HEARD SUCH A BEATING OF DRUMS? ROOT-A-TOOT, TAN-TARA! OR SUCH AN EAR-SPLITTING BLAST OF TRUMPETS? A HOSTILE ARMY OF BANDSMEN IS MASSING BENEATH THE RAMPARTS OF THE GRAND CASTLE OF MUSIC. SOME ARE BEING PUSHED ALONG IN BANDSTANDS! OTHERS ARE CLIMBING MUSIC-NOTE LADDERS! BUT WHAT A STRANGE THING! THEY ARE ALL DRESSED AS ANIMALS! SEE THE ELEPHANTS, THE BEARS, THE CROCS, AND THE DUCKS! AND JUST LIKE THEIR MUSIC, THEY ARE WILD AND WACKY!

THE ODLAW SWAMP

THE BRAVE ARMY OF MANY HATS IS TRYING TO GET THROUGH THIS FEARFUL SWAMP. HUNDREDS OF ODLAWS AND BLACK-AND-YELLOW SWAMP CREATURES ARE CAUSING TROUBLE IN THE UNDERGROWTH. THE REAL ODLAW IS THE ONE CLOSEST TO HIS LOST PAIR OF BINOCULARS. CAN YOU FIND HIM, X-RAY-EYED ONES? HOW MANY

DIFFERENT KINDS OF HATS CAN YOU SEE ON THE SOLDIERS' HEADS? SQUELCH! SQUELCH! I'M GLAD I'M NOT IN THEIR SHOES! ESPECIALLY AS THEIR FEET ARE IN THE MURKY MUD!

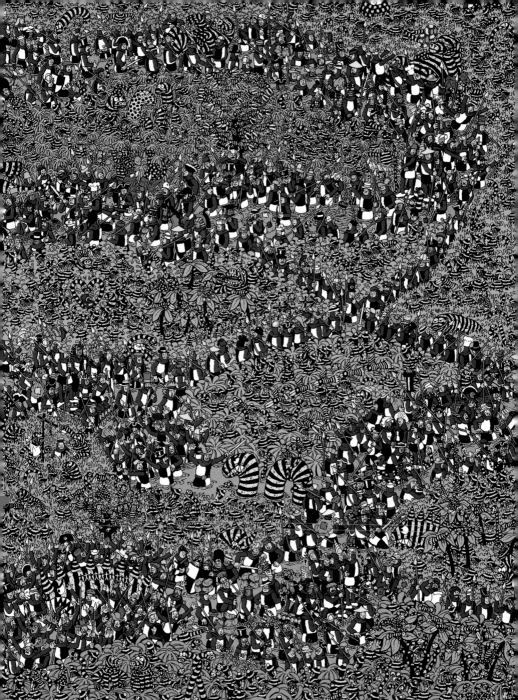

CLOWN TOWN

CLAP YOUR FEET, WALDO-JOKERS! STAMP YOUR HANDS! YOU'LL GO OOGLY-BOOGLY-WOOGLY-EYED WITH WONDER! HERE ARE HUNDREDS OF CLOWNS PLAYING PRANKS AND MAKING MISCHIEF! LOOK AT THEIR COLORFUL COSTUMES — WITH FLUFFY POM-POMS GALORE! AND THEIR BRIGHT AND SHINY NOSES! TOOT, TOOT! CAN YOU SEE A CAR WITH ITS TONGUE STICKING OUT?

TING-A-LING! AND A BIKE WITH SQUARE WHEELS? TEE-HEE! HA-HA! WHAT HAPPINESS IT IS TO BE IN CLOWN TOWN! SPLASH! SPLAT! EXCEPT FOR ALL THOSE SQUIRTY FLOWERS AND CUSTARD PIES!

THE CORRIDORS OF TIME

TICK-TOCK, TICK-TOCK! THE HANDS OF ALL THE CLOCKS EXCEPT ONE SAY A QUARTER TO TWELVE. WHAT A DING-DONG THERE WILL BE WHEN THEY STRIKE! CAN YOU FIND THE ONLY CLOCK THAT TELLS A DIFFERENT TIME? IN THIS SCENE ARE THIRTY-SEVEN DOORS. ABOVE EACH DOOR APPEARS THE SHAPE OF THE KEY THAT WILL UNLOCK IT. CAN YOU FIND THE KEYS IN THE CROWD, BRAINY ONES, AND MATCH THEM TO THE SHAPES? OH, NO! ONE DOOR HAS NO SHAPE ABOVE IT! EVEN SO, YOU MUST FIND ITS KEY!

THE LAND OF WOOFS

HEY! LOOK AT ALL THESE DOGS THAT ARE DRESSED LIKE WOOF! BOW WOW WOW! IN THIS LAND A DOG'S LIFE IS THE HIGHLIFE! THERE'S A LUXURY WOOF HOTEL WITH A BONE-SHAPED SWIMMING POOL, AND AT THE WOOF RACETRACK, LOTS OF WOOFS ARE CHASING ATTENDANTS DRESSED AS CATS, SAUSAGES, AND POSTMEN! THE BOOKMARK IS ON THIS PAGE, WALDO-FOLLOWERS, SO NOW YOU KNOW, THIS IS MY FAVORITE SCENE! THIS IS THE ONLY SCENE IN THE BOOK WHERE YOU CAN SEE MORE OF THE REAL WOOF THAN JUST HIS TAIL! BUT CAN YOU FIND HIM? HE'S THE ONLY ONE WITH FIVE RED STRIPES ON HIS TAIL! HERE'S ANOTHER CHALLENGE! ELEVEN

TRAVELERS HAVE FOLLOWED ME HERE — ONE FROM EVERY SCENE. CAN YOU SEE THEM? AND CAN YOU FIND WHERE EACH ONE JOINED ME ON MY ADVENTURES, AND SPOT ALL THEIR APPEARANCES AFTERWARD? KEEP ON SEARCHING, WALDO FANS! HAVE A WONDERFUL, WONDERFUL TIME!

THE GREAT WHERE'S WALDO?
THE WONDER BOOK CHECKLIST: PART TWO

THE BATTLE OF THE BANDS

- A rubber band
- A piano forty
- A pipe band
- Bandsmen "playing" their instruments
- A fan fair
- Bandsmen with saxophones and sacks of phones
- A steel band
- A swing band
- Sheet music
- Racing bandsmen "beating" their drums
- A rock band
- Kettle drums
- A mouth organ
- A baby sitar
- A 1-man band
- A French horn
- A barrel organ
- Some violin bows
- A rock and roll band
- Bandsmen playing cornets
- A drummer with drumsticks
- A big elephant trunk
- Bandsmen making a drum kit
- The orchestra pit
- A bag piper
- Some cheetah bandsmen cheating

THE ODLAW SWAMP

- Two soldiers disguised as Odlaws
- A soldier wearing a bowler hat
- A soldier wearing a stovepipe hat
- A soldier wearing a riding helmet
- A soldier wearing a straw hat
- Three soldiers wearing peaked caps
- A lady wearing an Easter bonnet
- Two soldiers wearing football helmets
- Two soldiers wearing baseball caps
- A big shield next to a little shield
- A lady wearing a sun hat
- A soldier with two big feathers in his hat
- Some rattle snakes
- Five romantic snakes
- Seven wooden rafts
- Three small wooden boats
- Four birds' nests
- One Odlaw in disguise
- A swamp creature without stripes
- A monster cleaning its teeth
- A monster asleep, but not for long
- A soldier floating on a package
- A very big monster with a very small head
- One charmed snake
- Five charmed spears
- A snake reading

CLOWN TOWN

- A clown reading a newspaper
- A starry umbrella
- A clown with a blue teapot
- Two hoses leaking
- A clown with two hoops on each arm
- A clown looking through a telescope
- Two clowns holding big hammers
- A clown with a bag of party favors
- Two clowns holding flowerpots
- A clown swinging a pillow
- A clown combing the roof of a Clown Town house
- A clown bursting a balloon
- Six flowers squirting the same clown
- A clown wearing a jack-in-the-box hat
- Three cars
- Three watering cans
- A clown with a fishing rod
- One hat joining two clowns
- A clown about to catapult a custard pie
- Clowns wearing tea shirts
- Three clowns with buckets of water
- A clown with a yo-yo
- A clown stepping into a custard pie
- Seventeen clouds
- A clown having his foot tickled
- One clown with a green nose

THE FANTASTIC FLOWER GARDEN

- The yellow rose of Texas
- Flower pots and flower beds
- Butter flies
- Gardeners sowing seeds and planting bulbs
- A garden nursery
- A bird bath and a bird table
- House plants, wall flowers, and blue bells
- Dandy lions, tiger lilies, and fox gloves
- Cabbage patches, letters leaves, and a collie flower
- A hedgehog next to a hedge hog
- A flower border and a flower show
- A bull frog
- Earth worms
- A wheelbarrow full of wheels
- A cricket match
- Parsley, sage, Rosemary, and time
- A queen bee near a honey comb
- A landscape gardener
- A sun dial next to a sundial
- Gardeners dancing to the beetles
- A green house and a tree house
- A spring onion and a leek with a leak
- Door mice
- An apple tree
- Weeping willows and climbing roses
- Rock pool

THE CORRIDORS OF TIME

- The clock striking twelve
- Wall clocks, clock faces, and a clock tower
- An egg timer
- A very loud alarm clock
- A traveling clock
- A runner racing against time
- Roman numerals
- Time flies
- An hour glass
- Old Father Time and Big Ben
- Grandfather clocks
- A walking stick
- Thirty-six pairs of almost identical twins
- One pair of identical twins
- A man's suspenders being pulled in opposite directions
- A swinging pendulum
- Coattails tied in a knot
- A door and thirteen clocks on their sides
- A very tall top hat
- A sundial
- A pair of hooked umbrellas
- A clock cuckoo
- A pair of tangled walking sticks

THE LAND OF WOOFS

- Dog biscuits
- A mountain dog
- A hot dog getting cool
- A gray hound bus
- Dog baskets
- A pair of swimming trunks
- A sheep dog
- A watch dog
- A bull dog
- A great Dane
- A guard dog
- A dog in a wet suit
- Some swimming costumes
- A dog with a red collar
- A dog wearing a yellow collar with a blue disk
- A dog with a blue bobble on his hat
- A top dog
- A sausage dog with sausages
- A dog wearing a blue collar with a green disk
- A cat dressed like a Woof dog
- The puppies' pool
- A dog doing a paw stand
- A Scottie dog
- Two dogs having a massage
- A sniffer dog
- Twenty-two red-and-white striped towels

★ CLOWNING AROUND! ★

Ha, ha! What a joker! The clown who follows Waldo and his friends to the end of the book changes the color of his hatband in one scene! Can you find which scene it is? What color does his hatband change to?

EXHIBIT 1 – ODLAW'S PICTURE PANDEMONIUM

- A green-skinned pirate
- Two ghost imposters
- Five mummies
- A bandaged finger
- Two spiders
- A head and crossbones
- A drooping flower
- Two teddy tattoos
- A black cat
- The sun
- Eight striped witches' hats
- Fourteen ladders
- Twelve vultures
- An upside-down skull and crossbones
- Four flying witches
- A pair of heart-shaped sunglasses
- Three spike-topped helmets
- A puzzled, fangless vampire
- A drinking straw
- A squashed Viking

EXHIBIT 2 – A SPORTING LIFE

- Hitting a hole in one
- A centaur circle
- A volleyball court
- Serving an ace
- A boxer saved by the belle
- Four under Pa
- The baseball batter's swing
- A pool table
- A Jim instructor
- Dancers at a soccer ball
- Team subs
- A marshal arts class
- Weight lifters pumping iron
- Shadowboxers
- A football quarterback
- Snow-peaked caps
- A pair of swimming trunks
- An archer with a long bow
- A steeplechase
- A pear skating

EXHIBIT 4 – BROWN SAILORS AND GREEN SCALERS AGAIN
ANSWERS
SPOT-THE-DIFFERENCES

- A missing tail-end
- An absent cloud
- A brown balloon
- A balloon number missing
- A missing tooth
- A missing lasso
- Some smoke missing
- A missing flag
- A monster without spots
- A backward number
- A flag number missing
- A missing monster
- An absent sailor
- A missing telescope
- A man with a yellow beard
- Some missing green slime
- An extra sailor
- A slime gun without a nozzle
- A brown sea creature
- A sailor in a white top

EXHIBIT 5 – THE PINK PARADISE PARTY

- Two skate on skates
- A broken heel
- A heavy-metal guitarist
- Two banana skins
- A pencil skirt
- Ball room dancers
- Two bugs jitterbugging
- A sole singer
- Dancers tripping on beads
- A Miniskirt
- A tea-shirt
- Two foxtrotters
- Platform shoes
- Some disc jockeys
- Oliver Twisting
- A Duke box and jukebox
- Dancing the knight away
- Beehive hairdos
- Squares square-dancing
- Two doormen

EXHIBIT 6 – OLD FRIENDS

- A lady in a blue ball gown
- A snowman
- A monster in a man-suit
- A red astronaut
- A woman with a green bag
- A pirate surfing
- A thirsty boy
- A cook with a dough nut
- A crab clipping a toenail
- A hippo with a jumbo-size toothbrush
- A pole vaulter taking a break
- A rude statue
- A bullfrog
- A man holding a flower
- A man in a manhole
- A horse-drawn wagon
- A woman with a clipboard
- A swimmer in shades
- A dog in the shade
- A woman holding a hairbrush

EXHIBIT 1 — ODLAW'S PICTURE PANDEMONIUM

WOW, WALDO FANS, WHAT PORTRAIT PANDEMONIUM! HAVE YOU EVER SEEN SO MANY YELLOW AND BLACK STRIPES IN ONE PLACE? STRIPE-TASTIC! WE'RE HERE IN ODLAW'S PICTURE GALLERY, AND JUST LOOK AT WHAT HIS ARTFUL ASSOCIATES HAVE CARRIED IN — 30 PECULIAR PORTRAITS IN AN ODDITY OF FRAMES. AMAZING! THERE'S QUITE A CAST OF CHARACTERS IN THESE PAINTINGS, AND THEY ALL APPEAR AGAIN ELSEWHERE IN THE BOOK. AND PICTURE THIS: ONE OF THEM EVEN APPEARS SOMEWHERE IN THIS CRAZY CROWD! GOOD LUCK ON YOUR HUNT FOR THE PLACES WITH THE FACES. WHAT A PICTURE!

EXHIBIT 1 — ODLAW'S PICTURE PANDEMONIUM

WOW, WALDO FANS, WHAT PORTRAIT PANDEMONIUM! HAVE YOU EVER SEEN SO MANY YELLOW AND BLACK STRIPES IN ONE PLACE? STRIPE-TASTIC! WE'RE HERE IN ODLAW'S PICTURE GALLERY, AND JUST LOOK AT WHAT HIS ARTFUL ASSOCIATES HAVE CARRIED IN — 30 PECULIAR PORTRAITS IN AN ODDITY OF FRAMES. AMAZING! THERE'S QUITE A CAST OF CHARACTERS IN THESE PAINTINGS, AND THEY ALL APPEAR AGAIN ELSEWHERE IN THE BOOK. AND PICTURE THIS: ONE OF THEM EVEN APPEARS SOMEWHERE IN THIS CRAZY CROWD! GOOD LUCK ON YOUR HUNT FOR THE PLACES WITH THE FACES. WHAT A PICTURE!

THE GREAT PICTURE HUNT!

HEY, WALDO FANS, WELCOME TO THE GREAT PICTURE HUNT!

THE FUN STARTS IN EXHIBIT 1, ODLAW'S PICTURE PANDEMONIUM, WHERE YOU'LL FIND 30 ENORMOUS PORTRAITS. WOW! EXAMINE THEM CAREFULLY, BECAUSE EVERY ONE OF THE PORTRAIT SUBJECTS CAN BE FOUND SOMEWHERE ELSE IN THIS BOOK . . . BUT ONLY ONCE. YOUR CHALLENGE IS TO FIND THESE SLIPPERY SUBJECTS WHEREVER THEY MIGHT BE HIDING.

ARE YOU READY FOR AN ART ADVENTURE, GALLERY GAZERS? HAVE FUN!

Waldo

EXHIBIT 2 —
A SPORTING LIFE

WELCOME, PICTURE HUNT PALS,
TO MY SPECIAL REPORT FROM THE
LAND OF SPORTS. FANTASTIC! IT'S LIKE
THE OLYMPICS EVERY DAY HERE, BUT WITH
SO MANY ATHLETIC EVENTS ON THE MENU,
THERE'S NO TIME LEFT FOR ANY REST AND
RELAXATION. BUT THERE'S NOTHING TOO
STRENUOUS ABOUT OUR MAIN EVENT, THE
GREAT PICTURE HUNT, SO KEEP YOUR
EYES ON THE BALL AND YOUR POINTER
FINGER READY. ON YOUR MARK,
GET SET, GO!

EXHIBIT 3 —
BROWN SAILORS AND
GREEN SCALERS

WHAT WINGED WONDERS ARE THESE,
WALDO-WATCHERS? DRAGONS AND GOO, BOATS
IN THE BLUE, AND AS FOR THOSE BALLOONS,
WHAT A NUMBERING NIGHTMARE!
ANCHORS AWEIGH!

EXHIBIT 5 — THE PINK PARADISE PARTY

IT'S SATURDAY NIGHT, THE TEMPERATURE IS RISING, AND IT LOOKS AS IF A RASH OF MUSICAL MAYHEM AND DISCO FEVER HAS BROKEN OUT IN THIS DIZZY DANCE HALL. WHEW! IT'S HOT! HIP HIP-HOPPERS, ROCK-AND-ROLLERS, AND BODY-AND-SOULERS — IT'S A PACKED-OUT, PARTYGOERS' PINK PARADISE. SO GET ON DOWN, CUT YOUR GROOVE, AND MAKE YOUR MOVES — IT'S TIME TO SHUFFLE YOUR FEET TO THE PICTURE HUNT BEAT!

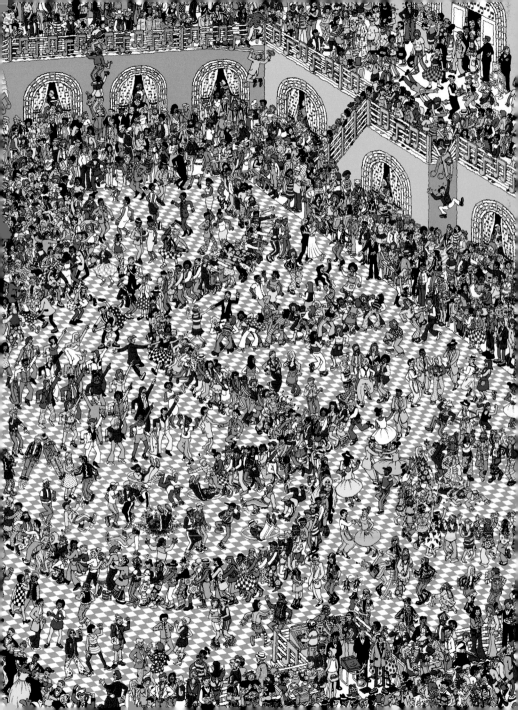

EXHIBIT 6 — OLD FRIENDS

AH, PICTURE HUNT PALS, HOW I LOVE TO LOOK THROUGH MY
SCRAPBOOKS OF MEMORIES AND SOUVENIRS. THIS PAGE IS
ONE OF MY FAVORITES: A COLLAGE CRAMMED WITH FAMILIAR
FACES FROM MY EARLIER ADVENTURES. FANTASTIC! EVEN
THE MOST DEDICATED OF WALDO-WATCHERS AMONG YOU
MAY HAVE TROUBLE RECOGNIZING ALL THE OLD FRIENDS
HERE — IT'S QUITE A CHALLENGE. BUT HERE'S AN EASIER
TEASER THAT ANYONE CAN DO: JUST LOOK AT THE CIRCLED
FACES IN THE BORDER OF THIS FRAME, THEN SEE IF YOU CAN
SPOT THEM IN THE SURROUNDING PICTURE.

EXHIBIT 7 — OLD FRIENDS AGAIN

IT'S ALWAYS NICE WHEN FRIENDS CAN STAY A LITTLE LONGER.... HERE'S A COLLECTION OF PORTRAITS OF SOME OF THE OLD FRIENDS FROM NEXT DOOR — BUT IN SILHOUETTE FORM. CAN YOU MATCH UP THE BLAST-FROM-THE-PAST CHARACTERS ON THE PREVIOUS PAGE WITH THEIR SILHOUETTES HERE? JUST TO MAKE IT INTERESTING, SOME OF THEM ARE UPSIDE DOWN OR SIDEWAYS. SO, ONWARD AND UPWARD (AND DOWNWARD AND SIDEWAYS!), PICTURE HUNTERS!

EXHIBIT 8 — THE MONSTER MASTERPIECE

YIKES, SPIKES, AND SCALY SEGMENTS, I'M LOST IN THE LAND OF THE MONSTERS. WHAT A CREATURE FEATURE! WHO'S IN CHARGE HERE, ANYWAY? THE HELMETED HUNTERS OR THEIR QUARRELSOME QUARRY? YOU'D BETTER WATCH OUT FOR BOTH AS YOU DIVE INTO THIS MONSTER MAYHEM, ART FANS — THERE ARE STILL SOME PORTRAIT SUBJECTS TO FIND. WHAT A MONSTROSITY!

EXHIBIT 9 — WALDOWORLD
WHAT A WEIRD AND WACKY WORLD WE'RE IN,
GALLERY GAZERS — NOT JUST A WORLD OF WALDOS
BUT A WORLD OF WHITEBEARDS, WENDAS, WOOFS,
AND AN ODDITY OF ODLAWS AS WELL. AMAZING!
BUT LOOK AGAIN. . . . THERE'S ONLY ONE REAL WALDO
HERE, AND THE SAME GOES FOR MY FRIENDS, TOO.
DON'T FORGET THAT YOU CAN TELL IF WE'RE THE
GENUINE ARTICLES BY OUR CORRECT ARRANGEMENT
OF STRIPES. SO CAST YOUR EYES ACROSS THIS
COLLECTION OF IMPOSTERS AND IMPERSONATORS
AND SEE IF YOU CAN FIND THE REAL US!

EXHIBIT 10 — WALDOWORLD AGAIN

DON'T BE DAUNTED BY HAVING TO DALLY OVER THIS DIZZY DIORAMA OF DOPPELGANGERS, DEAR READERS. EVERYTHING IS NOT AS IT APPEARS. WE'RE ALL STILL HERE, BUT THIS TIME THERE ARE 20 VARIATIONS FROM THE SCENE ON THE LEFT. CAN YOU SPOT ALL THE DIFFERENCES? AND HAVE YOU FOUND THE REAL WHITEBEARD, WENDA, WOOF, AND ODLAW YET? IF YOU'RE STILL HAVING TROUBLE FINDING THE REAL US, WHY NOT CHECK OUT HOW WE LOOK IN THE KEY AT THE BEGINNING OF THE BOOK?

EXHIBIT 12 — THE GREAT PORTRAIT EXHIBITION
OUR JOURNEY IS NOW OVER, WALDO FANS, BUT WHAT A
FITTING FINALE — A FANTASTIC EXHIBITION IN A PROPER ART
GALLERY! THE CROWD HERE SEEMS MUCH MORE WELCOMING
THAN ODLAW'S ODD ENSEMBLE FROM THE FIRST SCENE. I'M
ALSO REALLY PLEASED THAT ALL 30 OF THE CHARACTERS WE'VE
BEEN SEARCHING FOR IN THE EARLIER SCENES APPEAR AGAIN
HERE AMONG THE GALLERY GAZERS. SEE IF YOU CAN SPOT THEM
AS THEY TRY TO BLEND INTO THE CROWD AND ENJOY THE
SHOW. I HOPE YOU FOUND THEM IN THE PREVIOUS PAGES, TOO.
IF NOT, THERE'S STILL PLENTY OF TIME TO DO SO — THE
EXHIBITION NEVER CLOSES!

THE SUPER WHERE'S WALDO?
THE GREAT PICTURE HUNT CHECKLIST: PART TWO

EXHIBIT 10 – WALDOWORLD AGAIN
ANSWERS
SPOT-THE-DIFFERENCES

☐ A missing wizard
☐ A Waldo no longer smiling
☐ A Woof missing a tail
☐ An Odlaw missing a hat
☐ An Odlaw wearing different glasses
☐ A Wenda in blue-and-white tights
☐ A walking stick missing a tip
☐ An Odlaw in yellow pants
☐ A Wenda with vertical stripes
☐ A wizard beard that has changed color
☐ A Wenda wearing a red skirt
☐ A Whitebeard wearing a red hat
☐ A Waldo whose stripes have shifted
☐ A Whitebeard whose staff is missing
☐ A hat that has lost its pompom
☐ A Waldo in striped pants
☐ A Wenda who has lost her glasses
☐ A Woof with a longer tail
☐ A missing walking stick
☐ A spotted Odlaw

EXHIBIT 8 – THE MONSTER MASTERPIECE

☐ Salt and pepper shakers
☐ A ropey snakebite
☐ A monster wearing a napkin
☐ A tail lassoing a foot
☐ Two hunters using hankies
☐ A raft made from snakes
☐ A ticklish monster
☐ A snake tripping up hunters
☐ A pointed helmet prodding a hunter
☐ A monster munching timber
☐ One round shield
☐ Six arrows rebounding off monsters
☐ A swimming race
☐ A bunch of flowers
☐ A log stuck on a horn
☐ A monster wielding three swords
☐ A hunter held upside down
☐ A long tongue lassoing a leg
☐ A monster chewing spears
☐ Two hunter-boys sliding

EXHIBIT 11 – PIRATE PANORAMA

☐ Seven bottles
☐ Diving boards
☐ A massage in a bottle
☐ A giant wave
☐ A school of whales
☐ A pirate riding the serf
☐ Five birds
☐ A deck of cards
☐ Seven flags
☐ A pirate walking the plank
☐ A dessert island
☐ Eleven cannons
☐ The deep blue C
☐ Eight fins
☐ A pirate with an ax and a cutlass
☐ A tap
☐ Lobster beds
☐ Four cannonballs
☐ A two-foot gun barrel
☐ Two colored patches

EXHIBIT 12 – THE GREAT PICTURE EXHIBITION

☐ Nineteen flowers
☐ A woman guitarist
☐ A leaking watercolor
☐ Two dueling artists
☐ Eleven horses
☐ Four brooms
☐ An empty red frame
☐ Two cavewomen
☐ A very long white beard
☐ Nine fish
☐ An artist with seven brushes
☐ A gray donkey
☐ A rude shield
☐ Two brushes in a hatband
☐ A hungry wolf
☐ A red bow tie
☐ An artist with a big brush
☐ Five stools
☐ Red-and-yellow striped sleeves
☐ A cracked vase

AND JUST ONE MORE THING . . .

Why not brush up on your math with this arithmetic problem?

Add the number of frames containing pictures of men in Exhibit 1 to the number of blue picture frames in Exhibit 7.

Then subtract the number of triangular frames in Exhibit 12.

THE GREAT WHERE'S WALDO? THE INCREDIBLE PAPER CHASE CHECKLIST: PART ONE

Hundreds more spectacular things to search for! Don't forget PART TWO at the end of this adventure!

THE CASTLE SIEGE

- [ ] Five blue-coated soldiers wearing blue plumes
- [ ] Five red-coated soldiers wearing red plumes
- [ ] A blue-coated soldier wearing a red plume
- [ ] A red-coated soldier wearing a blue plume
- [ ] Four blue-coated archers
- [ ] Five characters holding white feathers
- [ ] Some pike men holding pikes
- [ ] Minors digging a tunnel
- [ ] Twenty-two ladders
- [ ] Some longbowmen wearing long bows
- [ ] Eight catapults
- [ ] Twenty-seven ladies dressed in blue
- [ ] Twelve men with white beards
- [ ] A wishing well
- [ ] Two tidy witches
- [ ] Nine blue shields
- [ ] Four horses
- [ ] Three round red shields
- [ ] A prisoner in a puzzling position
- [ ] Eight men snoozing
- [ ] Someone with by far the longest hair
- [ ] A soldier with one bare foot
- [ ] Eighteen characters with their tongues out
- [ ] Five tents

THE JURASSIC GAMES

- [ ] A dinosaur volleyball game
- [ ] A dinosaur rowing race
- [ ] Dinosaurs playing cricket
- [ ] A dinosaur soccer match
- [ ] A dinosaur windsurfer race
- [ ] Dinosaurs playing baseball
- [ ] A dinosaur football game
- [ ] Dinosaurs playing basketball
- [ ] Dinosaurs playing golf
- [ ] A dinosaur steeplechase race
- [ ] A dinosaur polo match
- [ ] Four sets of dinosaur cheerleaders
- [ ] Dinosaurs keeping score with their tails
- [ ] Some show-jumping dinosaurs

PICTURE THIS

- [ ] A bird escaped from its frame
- [ ] An angry dragon
- [ ] An airplane with real wings
- [ ] An alarm clock
- [ ] A running cactus
- [ ] A rude tree trunk
- [ ] Some fish fingers
- [ ] A mermaid in reverse
- [ ] Three skiers
- [ ] A messy eater
- [ ] An upside-down picture
- [ ] A giant foot
- [ ] Three romantic animals
- [ ] A foot being tickled
- [ ] A picture within a picture
- [ ] Two men sharing the same hat
- [ ] Two helmets worn back-to-front
- [ ] Someone drinking through a straw
- [ ] Three flags
- [ ] Nine tongues hanging out
- [ ] A caveman escaped from his frame
- [ ] Seven dogs and a dogfish
- [ ] A bandaged finger
- [ ] A braided mustache
- [ ] Four bears
- [ ] Three helmets with red plumes
- [ ] Four cats
- [ ] Four ducks
- [ ] Yellow, blue, and red picture frames

THE GREAT RETREAT

- [ ] A shield suddenly vacated
- [ ] A heart on a soldier's tunic
- [ ] One curved sword
- [ ] A soldier carrying a hammer
- [ ] One striped spear
- [ ] A soldier not wearing a top
- [ ] Two runaway boots
- [ ] A horseless rider
- [ ] A soldier with a sword and an ax
- [ ] Three bare feet
- [ ] Four pink tails
- [ ] A spear with tips at both ends
- [ ] A helmet with a blue plume
- [ ] A soldier with a red boot and a blue boot
- [ ] A helmet with a red plume

WHAT A DOG FIGHT

- [ ] A gundog soldier
- [ ] A guard-dog soldier
- [ ] A boxer-dog soldier
- [ ] A bloodhound soldier
- [ ] A prize poodle soldier
- [ ] Two soldiers begging for bones
- [ ] Two soldiers running to fetch a ball
- [ ] Four stars on one tunic
- [ ] A dog basket
- [ ] A dog wearing a man mask
- [ ] Four ticklish feet
- [ ] A soldier with two tails
- [ ] A white star on a cream tunic
- [ ] Cream eyes on a white dog mask
- [ ] A soldier with a black leg and a brown leg
- [ ] A cream glove on a blue striped arm
- [ ] A cream glove on a black striped arm
- [ ] A brown dog mask on a blue tunic
- [ ] A blue nose on a brown dog mask

THE BEAT OF THE DRUMS

- [ ] A rude back row
- [ ] Courtesy causing a pile-up
- [ ] Some very short spears
- [ ] A group facing in all directions
- [ ] A domino effect
- [ ] A never-ending spear
- [ ] Two hats joined together
- [ ] Some very scruffy soldiers
- [ ] A soldier wearing only one shoe
- [ ] A soldier wearing red shoes
- [ ] Thirty-five horses
- [ ] A pink hatband and a blue hatband
- [ ] One blue spear
- [ ] One lost shoe
- [ ] One hat with a yellow feather
- [ ] One hat with a red hatband

THE GREAT ESCAPE

- [ ] Ten men wearing green hoods
- [ ] Ten men wearing only one glove
- [ ] Ten men wearing hoods not matching gloves
- [ ] Ten men wearing two different colored gloves
- [ ] Ten men wearing short and long gloves
- [ ] Ten lost gloves
- [ ] Ten men wearing one fingerless glove
- [ ] Six ladders
- [ ] Nineteen shovels
- [ ] Five question mark shapes formed by the hedge

THE JURASSIC GAMES

GOODNESS CRETACEOUS! WHO WILL YOU SUPPORT FROM THE SIDELINES: THE BLUE STRIPY-SAURUS TEAM OR THE PINK SPOTTY-DOCUS TEAM? WILL YOU CHEER FOR CRICKET, ROWING, OR BASKETBALL? DON'T FORGET TO WAVE IF YOU SEE A T. REX—THEY'RE NOT ON ANY TEAM, BUT YOU WOULDN'T WANT TO GET ON THEIR BAD SIDE!

PICTURE THIS

PHEW! LOOK AT ALL THESE FRAMED PORTRAITS. ALTHOUGH THEY MAY BE COLORED DIFFERENTLY, SOME OF THESE ARE CHARACTERS I HAVE MET ON MY OTHER TRAVELS. THERE ARE ALSO SOME WHO APPEAR ELSEWHERE IN THIS BOOK. CAN YOU SPOT FOUR CHARACTERS THAT APPEAR TWICE IN THIS SPECTACULAR DISPLAY?

THE GREAT RETREAT

YIKES! A FEROCIOUS MAN-EATING
MONSTER IS WANDERING FREE,
AND HE'S HUNGRY — HE'S GOBBLED
14 SOLDIERS FOR LUNCH ALREADY!
I'VE DRAWN THE SHAPES OF EIGHT
SOLDIERS ON THE RUN — CAN YOU
MATCH THEM WITH EIGHT SOLDIERS
IN THE CROWD BEFORE THE MONSTER
EATS THEM FOR HIS DESSERT?

WHAT A DOG FIGHT!

BOW WOW WOW! TWO ARMIES ARE LOCKED IN BATTLE, ALL WITH DOG MASKS ON. ONE ARMY IS DRESSED IN BLUE, BLACK, AND WHITE, AND THE OTHER IN RED, BROWN, AND CREAM. CAN YOU FIND EIGHT SOLDIERS, FOUR FROM EACH SIDE, WITH SOMETHING IN ONE OF THE OTHER SIDE'S COLORS? OH, AND WHERE IS WOOF IN THIS DOG PACK?

THE ENORMOUS PARTY

WOW! HOW EXCITING! ARE YOU IN THE MOOD FOR A PARTY, WALDO-WATCHERS? LOOK AT THE BALLOONS, THE STREAMERS, AND ALL THE SMILING FACES! THE FLAGS OF 18 COUNTRIES ARE FLYING HERE—CAN YOU SPOT SIX FLAGS THAT HAVE SOMETHING WRONG WITH THEM? *

* THE ANSWERS ARE UNDER THE FLAP. NO CHEATING!

THE ENORMOUS PARTY — ANSWERS

THE ENORMOUS PARTY

WOW! HOW EXCITING! ARE YOU IN THE MOOD FOR A PARTY, WALDO-WATCHERS? LOOK AT ALL THE BALLOONS, THE STREAMERS, AND ALL THE SMILING FACES! THE FLAGS OF 18 COUNTRIES ARE FLYING HERE — CAN YOU SPOT SIX FLAGS THAT HAVE SOMETHING WRONG WITH THEM? *+

* THE ANSWERS ARE AT THE BACK OF THIS BOOK. HO GREAT!HA!

1 France	10 Switzerland		
2 The Netherlands	11 U.S.A.		
3 United Kingdom	12 Canada		
4 Sweden	13 Belgium		
5 Australia	14 New Zealand		
6 Norway	15 Finland		
7 Spain	16 Austria		
8 Japan	17 Germany		
9 Denmark	18 Brazil		

FLAGS WITH FAULTS

3	Diagonal red stripes missing
4	Flying backward
5	One star missing
11	Red and white stripes reversed
12	Maple leaf upside-down
14	Diagonal red stripes missing

THE ENORMOUS PARTY

- [ ] Five back views of Waldo's head
- [ ] A servant bending over backward
- [ ] Two muscle-men being ignored
- [ ] An eight-man band
- [ ] A helmet worn backward
- [ ] Eight front wheels
- [ ] Two upside-down faces of Waldo
- [ ] A man wrapped in a streamer
- [ ] Someone wearing a blue beret
- [ ] A reluctant arm-rest

PENCIL AND PAPER

Did you find the eight tiny pieces of paper that Waldo dropped from his notepad — one in every scene? Waldo has also left his pencil somewhere on the journey — can you go back and find it, super-seekers?

AND TWO MORE THINGS!

Dozens of Waldo-Watchers appear in this book (there is at least one in every scene, but some scenes have many more!).

There's another character — apart from Waldo, Woof, Wenda, Wizard Whitebeard, and Odlaw — in every scene. Can you find her?

First U.S. edition in this format 2013

ISBN 978-0-7636-6178-6 (collection)

13 14 15 16 17 WKT 10 9 8 7 6 5 4 3

Printed in Shenzhen, Guangdong, China

This book was typeset in Optima and Wallyfont.
The illustrations were done in watercolor and water-based ink.

Candlewick Press, 99 Dover Street, Somerville, Massachusetts 02144
visit us at www.candlewick.com

COMPLETE POETRY AND PROSE

THE
OTHER VOICE
IN
EARLY MODERN
EUROPE

A Series Edited by Margaret L. King and Albert Rabil Jr.

RECENT BOOKS IN THE SERIES

Louise Labé

COMPLETE POETRY
AND PROSE
A Bilingual Edition

ॐ

*Edited with Critical Introductions and
Prose Translations by Deborah Lesko Baker and
Poetry Translations by Annie Finch*

THE UNIVERSITY OF CHICAGO PRESS
Chicago & London

Louise Labé, 1522–1566

Deborah Lesko Baker is professor and chair of French at
Georgetown University. She is the author of *The Subject of Desire:
Petrarchan Poetics and the Female Voice in Louise Labé.*

Annie Finch is director of the Stonecoast Low-Residency MFA in
Creative Writing Program at the University of Southern Maine.
Her most recent book of poems is *Calendars.*

The University of Chicago Press, Chicago 60637
The University of Chicago Press, Ltd., London
© 2006 by The University of Chicago
All rights reserved. Published 2006
Printed in the United States of America

15 14 13 12 11 10 09 08 07 06 1 2 3 4 5

ISBN: 0-226-46714-7 (cloth)
ISBN: 0-226-46715-5 (paper)

The University of Chicago gratefully acknowledges the generous support of
James E. Rabil, in memory of Scottie W. Rabil, toward the publication of this book.

Library of Congress Cataloging-in-Publication Data

Labé, Louise, 1526?–1566.
[Works. English & French. 2006]
Complete poetry and prose : a bilingual edition / Louise Labé ;
edited with critical introductions and prose translation by
Deborah Lesko Baker ; poetry translation by Annie Finch.— 1st ed.
p. cm. — (The other voice in early modern Europe)
Includes bibliographical references and index.
ISBN 0-226-46714-7 (cloth : alk. paper) — ISBN 0-226-46715-5 (pbk : alk. paper)
1. Labé, Louise, 1526?–1566—Translations into English.   I. Baker, Deborah Lesko.
II. Finch, Annie, 1956–   III. Title.   IV. Series.
PQ1628.L2A23 2006
841'.3—dc22
2005029665

For Glen
(A. F.)

In memory of my mother, Stefania Barna Lesko (1921–2003)
(D. L. B.)

CONTENTS

ACKNOWLEDGMENTS

The appearance of this first bilingual critical edition of Louise Labé's complete works has been made possible by a number of fruitful collaborations. We are grateful, first of all, to Albert Rabil, co-editor of the University of Chicago Press Other Voice series, who supported from the outset an edition containing the entirety of Labé's literary production, who encouraged its fully bilingual presentation and who worked astutely and patiently with the volume editor and translators through challenging times. Our thanks go as well to the University of Chicago Press poetry editor, Randy Petilos, for his ongoing counsel and indispensible help in locating Labé's portrait and manuscript illustrations, to copy editor Susan Tarcov for her meticulous corrections, to Maia Rigas for her attentive assistance in the final stages of preparation, and to the anonymous reader who prepared a remarkably detailed and helpful report on the original manuscript. Georgetown University provided generous support through competitive research grants to several phases of our work.

We are pleased to have on facing pages for the translations throughout this volume the definitive French text established and annotated by François Rigolot in his newly updated 2004 edition of Labé's *Oeuvres complètes,* and we express to him and to Hélène Fiamma, literary director of Flammarion Press in Paris, our sincere appreciation. Anne-Marie Bourbon kindly shared with us the electronic files of Labé's prose texts from Rigolot's French edition used in her own recent translation of the dedicatory letter and the *Debate of Folly and Love.* Mitchell Brown graciously reviewed early versions of the poetry translations. Alissa Webel reviewed a preliminary draft of the prose translations and helped to decipher a number of difficult constructions and obscure locutions. Peter Baker read and commented on the three criti-

cal introductions, and gave precious and unwavering support to the entire project.

Annie Finch's translations of many of Labé's sonnets have been published or produced in other venues, whose permission to reprint we gratefully acknowledge here:

Sonnets 1, 9, and 16 appeared in *Kestrel* (spring 2002).

Sonnets 2, 4, and 18 and Elegy 3 appeared in *Iambs and Trochees* (spring 2002).

Sonnets 9 and 12 appeared in *Marlboro Review* (winter 1998).

Sonnets 10, 13, 14, and 16 appeared on Ablemuse.com.

Sonnets 5, 11, and 15 appeared in *S, P, M & H.*

Sonnet 22 appeared in *Iron Horse* (summer 2005).

Sonnets 7 and 16 appeared in *Ars Interpres* [Stockholm] (winter 2004).

Sonnet 3 appeared in *World Poetry: An Anthology of Verse from Antiquity to Our Time,* edited by John Major and Katherine Washburn (New York: Norton, 1998).

Sonnet 8 was reprinted in Philip Soergel, *The Renaissance,* Arts and Humanities through the Ages (Farmington Hills, MI: Gale Publishing, 2004).

Sonnet 18 was set to music by Deborah Drattell as "Kiss Me Again" and premiered by Lauren Flanagan at the Metropolitan Museum of Art, New York, February 14, 2003.

Sonnet 20 was set to music by Kevin Warren for the Lyric Recovery Festival in Carnegie Hall, New York, March 22, 2004.

Deborah Lesko Baker and Annie Finch

THE OTHER VOICE IN
EARLY MODERN EUROPE:
INTRODUCTION TO THE SERIES
Margaret L. King and Albert Rabil Jr.

THE OLD VOICE AND THE OTHER VOICE

In western Europe and the United States, women are nearing equality in the professions, in business, and in politics. Most enjoy access to education, reproductive rights, and autonomy in financial affairs. Issues vital to women are on the public agenda: equal pay, child care, domestic abuse, breast cancer research, and curricular revision with an eye to the inclusion of women.

These recent achievements have their origins in things women (and some male supporters) said for the first time about six hundred years ago. Theirs is the "other voice," in contradistinction to the "first voice," the voice of the educated men who created Western culture. Coincident with a general reshaping of European culture in the period 1300–1700 (called the Renaissance or early modern period), questions of female equality and opportunity were raised that still resound and are still unresolved.

The other voice emerged against the backdrop of a three-thousand-year history of the derogation of women rooted in the civilizations related to Western culture: Hebrew, Greek, Roman, and Christian. Negative attitudes toward women inherited from these traditions pervaded the intellectual, medical, legal, religious, and social systems that developed during the European Middle Ages.

The following pages describe the traditional, overwhelmingly male views of women's nature inherited by early modern Europeans and the new tradition that the "other voice" called into being to begin to challenge reigning assumptions. This review should serve as a framework for understanding the texts published in the series. The Other Voice in Early Modern Europe. Introductions specific to each text and author follow this essay in all the volumes of the series.

TRADITIONAL VIEWS OF WOMEN, 500 B.C.E.–1500 C.E.

Embedded in the philosophical and medical theories of the ancient Greeks were perceptions of the female as inferior to the male in both mind and body. Similarly, the structure of civil legislation inherited from the ancient Romans was biased against women, and the views on women developed by Christian thinkers out of the Hebrew Bible and the Christian New Testament were negative and disabling. Literary works composed in the vernacular of ordinary people, and widely recited or read, conveyed these negative assumptions. The social networks within which most women lived—those of the family and the institutions of the Roman Catholic Church—were shaped by this negative tradition and sharply limited the areas in which women might act in and upon the world.

GREEK PHILOSOPHY AND FEMALE NATURE. Greek biology assumed that women were inferior to men and defined them as merely childbearers and housekeepers. This view was authoritatively expressed in the works of the philosopher Aristotle.

Aristotle thought in dualities. He considered action superior to inaction, form (the inner design or structure of any object) superior to matter, completion to incompletion, possession to deprivation. In each of these dualities, he associated the male principle with the superior quality and the female with the inferior. "The male principle in nature," he argued, "is associated with active, formative and perfected characteristics, while the female is passive, material and deprived, desiring the male in order to become complete." [1] Men are always identified with virile qualities, such as judgment, courage, and stamina, and women with their opposites—irrationality, cowardice, and weakness.

The masculine principle was considered superior even in the womb. The man's semen, Aristotle believed, created the form of a new human creature, while the female body contributed only matter. (The existence of the ovum, and with it the other facts of human embryology, was not established until the seventeenth century.) Although the later Greek physician Galen believed there was a female component in generation, contributed by "female semen," the followers of both Aristotle and Galen saw the male role in human generation as more active and more important.

In the Aristotelian view, the male principle sought always to reproduce itself. The creation of a female was always a mistake, therefore, resulting from

---

1. Aristotle, *Physics* 1.9.192a20–24, in *The Complete Works of Aristotle,* ed. Jonathan Barnes, rev. Oxford trans., 2 vols. (Princeton, 1984), 1:328.

an imperfect act of generation. Every female born was considered a "defective" or "mutilated" male (as Aristotle's terminology has variously been translated), a "monstrosity" of nature.[2]

For Greek theorists, the biology of males and females was the key to their psychology. The female was softer and more docile, more apt to be despondent, querulous, and deceitful. Being incomplete, moreover, she craved sexual fulfillment in intercourse with a male. The male was intellectual, active, and in control of his passions.

These psychological polarities derived from the theory that the universe consisted of four elements (earth, fire, air, and water), expressed in human bodies as four "humors" (black bile, yellow bile, blood, and phlegm) considered, respectively, dry, hot, damp, and cold and corresponding to mental states ("melancholic," "choleric," "sanguine," "phlegmatic"). In this scheme the male, sharing the principles of earth and fire, was dry and hot; the female, sharing the principles of air and water, was cold and damp.

Female psychology was further affected by her dominant organ, the uterus (womb), *hystera* in Greek. The passions generated by the womb made women lustful, deceitful, talkative, irrational, indeed—when these affects were in excess—"hysterical."

Aristotle's biology also had social and political consequences. If the male principle was superior and the female inferior, then in the household, as in the state, men should rule and women must be subordinate. That hierarchy did not rule out the companionship of husband and wife, whose cooperation was necessary for the welfare of children and the preservation of property. Such mutuality supported male preeminence.

Aristotle's teacher Plato suggested a different possibility: that men and women might possess the same virtues. The setting for this proposal is the imaginary and ideal Republic that Plato sketches in a dialogue of that name. Here, for a privileged elite capable of leading wisely, all distinctions of class and wealth dissolve, as, consequently, do those of gender. Without households or property, as Plato constructs his ideal society, there is no need for the subordination of women. Women may therefore be educated to the same level as men to assume leadership. Plato's Republic remained imaginary, however. In real societies, the subordination of women remained the norm and the prescription.

The views of women inherited from the Greek philosophical tradition became the basis for medieval thought. In the thirteenth century, the supreme Scholastic philosopher Thomas Aquinas, among others, still echoed

2. Aristotle, *Generation of Animals* 2.3.737a27–28, in ibid., 1:1144.

Aristotle's views of human reproduction, of male and female personalities, and of the preeminent male role in the social hierarchy.

ROMAN LAW AND THE FEMALE CONDITION. Roman law, like Greek philosophy, underlay medieval thought and shaped medieval society. The ancient belief that adult property-owning men should administer households and make decisions affecting the community at large is the very fulcrum of Roman law.

About 450 B.C.E., during Rome's republican era, the community's customary law was recorded (legendarily) on twelve tablets erected in the city's central forum. It was later elaborated by professional jurists whose activity increased in the imperial era, when much new legislation was passed, especially on issues affecting family and inheritance. This growing, changing body of laws was eventually codified in the *Corpus of Civil Law* under the direction of the emperor Justinian, generations after the empire ceased to be ruled from Rome. That *Corpus*, read and commented on by medieval scholars from the eleventh century on, inspired the legal systems of most of the cities and kingdoms of Europe.

Laws regarding dowries, divorce, and inheritance pertain primarily to women. Since those laws aimed to maintain and preserve property, the women concerned were those from the property-owning minority. Their subordination to male family members points to the even greater subordination of lower-class and slave women, about whom the laws speak little.

In the early republic, the *paterfamilias*, or "father of the family," possessed *patria potestas*, "paternal power." The term *pater*, "father," in both these cases does not necessarily mean biological father but denotes the head of a household. The father was the person who owned the household's property and, indeed, its human members. The *paterfamilias* had absolute power—including the power, rarely exercised, of life or death—over his wife, his children, and his slaves, as much as his cattle.

Male children could be "emancipated," an act that granted legal autonomy and the right to own property. Those over fourteen could be emancipated by a special grant from the father or automatically by their father's death. But females could never be emancipated; instead, they passed from the authority of their father to that of a husband or, if widowed or orphaned while still unmarried, to a guardian or tutor.

Marriage in its traditional form placed the woman under her husband's authority, or *manus*. He could divorce her on grounds of adultery, drinking wine, or stealing from the household, but she could not divorce him. She could neither possess property in her own right nor bequeath any to her

children upon her death. When her husband died, the household property passed not to her but to his male heirs. And when her father died, she had no claim to any family inheritance, which was directed to her brothers or more remote male relatives. The effect of these laws was to exclude women from civil society, itself based on property ownership.

In the later republican and imperial periods, these rules were significantly modified. Women rarely married according to the traditional form. The practice of "free" marriage allowed a woman to remain under her father's authority, to possess property given her by her father (most frequently the "dowry," recoverable from the husband's household on his death), and to inherit from her father. She could also bequeath property to her own children and divorce her husband, just as he could divorce her.

Despite this greater freedom, women still suffered enormous disability under Roman law. Heirs could belong only to the father's side, never the mother's. Moreover, although she could bequeath her property to her children, she could not establish a line of succession in doing so. A woman was "the beginning and end of her own family," said the jurist Ulpian. Moreover, women could play no public role. They could not hold public office, represent anyone in a legal case, or even witness a will. Women had only a private existence and no public personality.

The dowry system, the guardian, women's limited ability to transmit wealth, and total political disability are all features of Roman law adopted by the medieval communities of western Europe, although modified according to local customary laws.

CHRISTIAN DOCTRINE AND WOMEN'S PLACE. The Hebrew Bible and the Christian New Testament authorized later writers to limit women to the realm of the family and to burden them with the guilt of original sin. The passages most fruitful for this purpose were the creation narratives in Genesis and sentences from the Epistles defining women's role within the Christian family and community.

Each of the first two chapters of Genesis contains a creation narrative. In the first "God created man in his own image, in the image of God he created him; male and female he created them" (Gn 1:27). In the second, God created Eve from Adam's rib (2:21–23). Christian theologians relied principally on Genesis 2 for their understanding of the relation between man and woman, interpreting the creation of Eve from Adam as proof of her subordination to him.

The creation story in Genesis 2 leads to that of the temptations in Genesis 3: of Eve by the wily serpent and of Adam by Eve. As read by Christian

theologians from Tertullian to Thomas Aquinas, the narrative made Eve responsible for the Fall and its consequences. She instigated the act; she deceived her husband; she suffered the greater punishment. Her disobedience made it necessary for Jesus to be incarnated and to die on the cross. From the pulpit, moralists and preachers for centuries conveyed to women the guilt that they bore for original sin.

The Epistles offered advice to early Christians on building communities of the faithful. Among the matters to be regulated was the place of women. Paul offered views favorable to women in Galatians 3:28: "There is neither Jew nor Greek, there is neither slave nor free, there is neither male nor female; for you are all one in Christ Jesus." Paul also referred to women as his coworkers and placed them on a par with himself and his male coworkers (Phlm 4:2–3; Rom 16:1–3; 1 Cor 16:19). Elsewhere, Paul limited women's possibilities: "But I want you to understand that the head of every man is Christ, the head of a woman is her husband, and the head of Christ is God" (1 Cor 11:3).

Biblical passages by later writers (although attributed to Paul) enjoined women to forgo jewels, expensive clothes, and elaborate coiffures; and they forbade women to "teach or have authority over men," telling them to "learn in silence with all submissiveness" as is proper for one responsible for sin, consoling them, however, with the thought that they will be saved through childbearing (1 Tm 2:9–15). Other texts among the later Epistles defined women as the weaker sex and emphasized their subordination to their husbands (1 Pt 3:7; Col 3:18; Eph 5:22–23).

These passages from the New Testament became the arsenal employed by theologians of the early church to transmit negative attitudes toward women to medieval Christian culture—above all, Tertullian (*On the Apparel of Women*), Jerome (*Against Jovinian*), and Augustine (*The Literal Meaning of Genesis*).

THE IMAGE OF WOMEN IN MEDIEVAL LITERATURE. The philosophical, legal, and religious traditions born in antiquity formed the basis of the medieval intellectual synthesis wrought by trained thinkers, mostly clerics, writing in Latin and based largely in universities. The vernacular literary tradition that developed alongside the learned tradition also spoke about female nature and women's roles. Medieval stories, poems, and epics also portrayed women negatively—as lustful and deceitful—while praising good housekeepers and loyal wives as replicas of the Virgin Mary or the female saints and martyrs.

There is an exception in the movement of "courtly love" that evolved in southern France from the twelfth century. Courtly love was the erotic love between a nobleman and noblewoman, the latter usually superior in social

rank. It was always adulterous. From the conventions of courtly love derive modern Western notions of romantic love. The tradition has had an impact disproportionate to its size, for it affected only a tiny elite, and very few women. The exaltation of the female lover probably does not reflect a higher evaluation of women or a step toward their sexual liberation. More likely it gives expression to the social and sexual tensions besetting the knightly class at a specific historical juncture.

The literary fashion of courtly love was on the wane by the thirteenth century, when the widely read *Romance of the Rose* was composed in French by two authors of significantly different dispositions. Guillaume de Lorris composed the initial four thousand verses about 1235, and Jean de Meun added about seventeen thousand verses—more than four times the original— about 1265.

The fragment composed by Guillaume de Lorris stands squarely in the tradition of courtly love. Here the poet, in a dream, is admitted into a walled garden where he finds a magic fountain in which a rosebush is reflected. He longs to pick one rose, but the thorns prevent his doing so, even as he is wounded by arrows from the god of love, whose commands he agrees to obey. The rest of this part of the poem recounts the poet's unsuccessful efforts to pluck the rose.

The longer part of the *Romance* by Jean de Meun also describes a dream. But here allegorical characters give long didactic speeches, providing a social satire on a variety of themes, some pertaining to women. Love is an anxious and tormented state, the poem explains: women are greedy and manipulative, marriage is miserable, beautiful women are lustful, ugly ones cease to please, and a chaste woman is as rare as a black swan.

Shortly after Jean de Meun completed *The Romance of the Rose*, Mathéolus penned his *Lamentations*, a long Latin diatribe against marriage translated into French about a century later. The *Lamentations* sum up medieval attitudes toward women and provoked the important response by Christine de Pizan in her *Book of the City of Ladies*.

In 1355, Giovanni Boccaccio wrote *Il Corbaccio*, another antifeminist manifesto, although ironically by an author whose other works pioneered new directions in Renaissance thought. The former husband of his lover appears to Boccaccio, condemning his unmoderated lust and detailing the defects of women. Boccaccio concedes at the end "how much men naturally surpass women in nobility" and is cured of his desires.[3]

---

3. Giovanni Boccaccio, *The Corbaccio, or The Labyrinth of Love*, trans. and ed. Anthony K. Cassell, rev. ed. (Binghamton, NY, 1993), 71.

WOMEN'S ROLES: THE FAMILY. The negative perceptions of women expressed in the intellectual tradition are also implicit in the actual roles that women played in European society. Assigned to subordinate positions in the household and the church, they were barred from significant participation in public life.

Medieval European households, like those in antiquity and in non-Western civilizations, were headed by males. It was the male serf (or peasant), feudal lord, town merchant, or citizen who was polled or taxed or succeeded to an inheritance or had any acknowledged public role, although his wife or widow could stand as a temporary surrogate. From about 1100, the position of property-holding males was further enhanced: inheritance was confined to the male, or agnate, line—with depressing consequences for women.

A wife never fully belonged to her husband's family, nor was she a daughter to her father's family. She left her father's house young to marry whomever her parents chose. Her dowry was managed by her husband, and at her death it normally passed to her children by him.

A married woman's life was occupied nearly constantly with cycles of pregnancy, childbearing, and lactation. Women bore children through all the years of their fertility, and many died in childbirth. They were also responsible for raising young children up to six or seven. In the propertied classes that responsibility was shared, since it was common for a wet nurse to take over breast-feeding and for servants to perform other chores.

Women trained their daughters in the household duties appropriate to their status, nearly always tasks associated with textiles: spinning, weaving, sewing, embroidering. Their sons were sent out of the house as apprentices or students, or their training was assumed by fathers in later childhood and adolescence. On the death of her husband, a woman's children became the responsibility of his family. She generally did not take "his" children with her to a new marriage or back to her father's house, except sometimes in the artisan classes.

Women also worked. Rural peasants performed farm chores, merchant wives often practiced their husbands' trades, the unmarried daughters of the urban poor worked as servants or prostitutes. All wives produced or embellished textiles and did the housekeeping, while wealthy ones managed servants. These labors were unpaid or poorly paid but often contributed substantially to family wealth.

WOMEN'S ROLES: THE CHURCH. Membership in a household, whether a father's or a husband's, meant for women a lifelong subordination to others. In western Europe, the Roman Catholic Church offered an

alternative to the career of wife and mother. A woman could enter a convent, parallel in function to the monasteries for men that evolved in the early Christian centuries.

In the convent, a woman pledged herself to a celibate life, lived according to strict community rules, and worshiped daily. Often the convent offered training in Latin, allowing some women to become considerable scholars and authors as well as scribes, artists, and musicians. For women who chose the conventual life, the benefits could be enormous, but for numerous others placed in convents by paternal choice, the life could be restrictive and burdensome.

The conventual life declined as an alternative for women as the modern age approached. Reformed monastic institutions resisted responsibility for related female orders. The church increasingly restricted female institutional life by insisting on closer male supervision.

Women often sought other options. Some joined the communities of laywomen that sprang up spontaneously in the thirteenth century in the urban zones of western Europe, especially in Flanders and Italy. Some joined the heretical movements that flourished in late medieval Christendom, whose anticlerical and often antifamily positions particularly appealed to women. In these communities, some women were acclaimed as "holy women" or "saints," whereas others often were condemned as frauds or heretics.

In all, although the options offered to women by the church were sometimes less than satisfactory, they were sometimes richly rewarding. After 1520, the convent remained an option only in Roman Catholic territories. Protestantism engendered an ideal of marriage as a heroic endeavor and appeared to place husband and wife on a more equal footing. Sermons and treatises, however, still called for female subordination and obedience.

THE OTHER VOICE, 1300–1700

When the modern era opened, European culture was so firmly structured by a framework of negative attitudes toward women that to dismantle it was a monumental labor. The process began as part of a larger cultural movement that entailed the critical reexamination of ideas inherited from the ancient and medieval past. The humanists launched that critical reexamination.

THE HUMANIST FOUNDATION. Originating in Italy in the fourteenth century, humanism quickly became the dominant intellectual movement in Europe. Spreading in the sixteenth century from Italy to the rest of Europe,

The effect of Humanism on women.

it fueled the literary, scientific, and philosophical movements of the era and laid the basis for the eighteenth-century Enlightenment.

Humanists regarded the Scholastic philosophy of medieval universities as out of touch with the realities of urban life. They found in the rhetorical discourse of classical Rome a language adapted to civic life and public speech. They learned to read, speak, and write classical Latin and, eventually, classical Greek. They founded schools to teach others to do so, establishing the pattern for elementary and secondary education for the next three hundred years.

In the service of complex government bureaucracies, humanists employed their skills to write eloquent letters, deliver public orations, and formulate public policy. They developed new scripts for copying manuscripts and used the new printing press to disseminate texts, for which they created methods of critical editing.

Humanism was a movement led by males who accepted the evaluation of women in ancient texts and generally shared the misogynist perceptions of their culture. (Female humanists, as we will see, did not.) Yet humanism also opened the door to a reevaluation of the nature and capacity of women. By calling authors, texts, and ideas into question, it made possible the fundamental rereading of the whole intellectual tradition that was required in order to free women from cultural prejudice and social subordination.

A DIFFERENT CITY. The other voice first appeared when, after so many centuries, the accumulation of misogynist concepts evoked a response from a capable female defender: Christine de Pizan (1365–1431). Introducing her *Book of the City of Ladies* (1405), she described how she was affected by reading Mathéolus's *Lamentations*: "Just the sight of this book . . . made me wonder how it happened that so many different men . . . are so inclined to express both in speaking and in their treatises and writings so many wicked insults about women and their behavior."[4] These statements impelled her to detest herself "and the entire feminine sex, as though we were monstrosities in nature."[5]

The rest of *The Book of the City of Ladies* presents a justification of the female sex and a vision of an ideal community of women. A pioneer, she has received the message of female inferiority and rejected it. From the fourteenth to the seventeenth century, a huge body of literature accumulated that responded to the dominant tradition.

4. Christine de Pizan, *The Book of the City of Ladies*, trans. Earl Jeffrey Richards, foreword by Marina Warner (New York, 1982), 1.1.1, pp. 3–4.

5. Ibid., 1.1.1–2, p. 5.

The result was a literary explosion consisting of works by both men and women, in Latin and in the vernaculars: works enumerating the achievements of notable women; works rebutting the main accusations made against women; works arguing for the equal education of men and women; works defining and redefining women's proper role in the family, at court, in public; works describing women's lives and experiences. Recent monographs and articles have begun to hint at the great range of this movement, involving probably several thousand titles. The protofeminism of these "other voices" constitutes a significant fraction of the literary product of the early modern era.

THE CATALOGS. About 1365, the same Boccaccio whose *Corbaccio* rehearses the usual charges against female nature wrote another work, *Concerning Famous Women*. A humanist treatise drawing on classical texts, it praised 106 notable women: ninety-eight of them from pagan Greek and Roman antiquity, one (Eve) from the Bible, and seven from the medieval religious and cultural tradition; his book helped make all readers aware of a sex normally condemned or forgotten. Boccaccio's outlook nevertheless was unfriendly to women, for it singled out for praise those women who possessed the traditional virtues of chastity, silence, and obedience. Women who were active in the public realm—for example, rulers and warriors—were depicted as usually being lascivious and as suffering terrible punishments for entering the masculine sphere. Women were his subject, but Boccaccio's standard remained male.

Christine de Pizan's *Book of the City of Ladies* contains a second catalog, one responding specifically to Boccaccio's. Whereas Boccaccio portrays female virtue as exceptional, she depicts it as universal. Many women in history were leaders, or remained chaste despite the lascivious approaches of men, or were visionaries and brave martyrs.

The work of Boccaccio inspired a series of catalogs of illustrious women of the biblical, classical, Christian, and local pasts, among them Filippo da Bergamo's *Of Illustrious Women*, Pierre de Brantôme's *Lives of Illustrious Women*, Pierre Le Moyne's *Gallerie of Heroic Women*, and Pietro Paolo de Ribera's *Immortal Triumphs and Heroic Enterprises of 845 Women*. Whatever their embedded prejudices, these works drove home to the public the possibility of female excellence.

THE DEBATE. At the same time, many questions remained: Could a woman be virtuous? Could she perform noteworthy deeds? Was she even, strictly speaking, of the same human species as men? These questions

were debated over four centuries, in French, German, Italian, Spanish, and English, by authors male and female, among Catholics, Protestants, and Jews, in ponderous volumes and breezy pamphlets. The whole literary genre has been called the *querelle des femmes*, the "woman question."

The opening volley of this battle occurred in the first years of the fifteenth century, in a literary debate sparked by Christine de Pizan. She exchanged letters critical of Jean de Meun's contribution to *The Romance of the Rose* with two French royal secretaries, Jean de Montreuil and Gontier Col. When the matter became public, Jean Gerson, one of Europe's leading theologians, supported de Pizan's arguments against de Meun, for the moment silencing the opposition.

The debate resurfaced repeatedly over the next two hundred years. *The Triumph of Women* (1438) by Juan Rodríguez de la Camara (or Juan Rodríguez del Padron) struck a new note by presenting arguments for the superiority of women to men. *The Champion of Women* (1440–42) by Martin Le Franc addresses once again the negative views of women presented in *The Romance of the Rose* and offers counterevidence of female virtue and achievement.

A cameo of the debate on women is included in *The Courtier,* one of the most widely read books of the era, published by the Italian Baldassare Castiglione in 1528 and immediately translated into other European vernaculars. *The Courtier* depicts a series of evenings at the court of the duke of Urbino in which many men and some women of the highest social stratum amuse themselves by discussing a range of literary and social issues. The "woman question" is a pervasive theme throughout, and the third of its four books is devoted entirely to that issue.

In a verbal duel, Gasparo Pallavicino and Giuliano de' Medici present the main claims of the two traditions. Gasparo argues the innate inferiority of women and their inclination to vice. Only in bearing children do they profit the world. Giuliano counters that women share the same spiritual and mental capacities as men and may excel in wisdom and action. Men and women are of the same essence: just as no stone can be more perfectly a stone than another, so no human being can be more perfectly human than others, whether male or female. It was an astonishing assertion, boldly made to an audience as large as all Europe.

THE TREATISES. Humanism provided the materials for a positive counterconcept to the misogyny embedded in Scholastic philosophy and law and inherited from the Greek, Roman, and Christian pasts. A series of humanist treatises on marriage and family, on education and deportment, and on the nature of women helped construct these new perspectives.

The works by Francesco Barbaro and Leon Battista Alberti—*On Marriage* (1415) and *On the Family* (1434–37)—far from defending female equality, reasserted women's responsibility for rearing children and managing the housekeeping while being obedient, chaste, and silent. Nevertheless, they served the cause of reexamining the issue of women's nature by placing domestic issues at the center of scholarly concern and reopening the pertinent classical texts. In addition, Barbaro emphasized the companionate nature of marriage and the importance of a wife's spiritual and mental qualities for the well-being of the family.

These themes reappear in later humanist works on marriage and the education of women by Juan Luis Vives and Erasmus. Both were moderately sympathetic to the condition of women without reaching beyond the usual masculine prescriptions for female behavior.

An outlook more favorable to women characterizes the nearly unknown work *In Praise of Women* (ca. 1487) by the Italian humanist Bartolommeo Goggio. In addition to providing a catalog of illustrious women, Goggio argued that male and female are the same in essence, but that women (reworking the Adam and Eve narrative from quite a new angle) are actually superior. In the same vein, the Italian humanist Mario Equicola asserted the spiritual equality of men and women in *On Women* (1501). In 1525, Galeazzo Flavio Capra (or Capella) published his work *On the Excellence and Dignity of Women*. This humanist tradition of treatises defending the worthiness of women culminates in the work of Henricus Cornelius Agrippa *On the Nobility and Preeminence of the Female Sex*. No work by a male humanist more succinctly or explicitly presents the case for female dignity.

THE WITCH BOOKS. While humanists grappled with the issues pertaining to women and family, other learned men turned their attention to what they perceived as a very great problem: witches. Witch-hunting manuals, explorations of the witch phenomenon, and even defenses of witches are not at first glance pertinent to the tradition of the other voice. But they do relate in this way: most accused witches were women. The hostility aroused by supposed witch activity is comparable to the hostility aroused by women. The evil deeds the victims of the hunt were charged with were exaggerations of the vices to which, many believed, all women were prone.

The connection between the witch accusation and the hatred of women is explicit in the notorious witch-hunting manual *The Hammer of Witches* (1486) by two Dominican inquisitors, Heinrich Krämer and Jacob Sprenger. Here the inconstancy, deceitfulness, and lustfulness traditionally associated with women are depicted in exaggerated form as the core features of witch

behavior. These traits inclined women to make a bargain with the devil—sealed by sexual intercourse—by which they acquired unholy powers. Such bizarre claims, far from being rejected by rational men, were broadcast by intellectuals. The German Ulrich Molitur, the Frenchman Nicolas Rémy, and the Italian Stefano Guazzo all coolly informed the public of sinister orgies and midnight pacts with the devil. The celebrated French jurist, historian, and political philosopher Jean Bodin argued that because women were especially prone to diabolism, regular legal procedures could properly be suspended in order to try those accused of this "exceptional crime."

A few experts such as the physician Johann Weyer, a student of Agrippa's, raised their voices in protest. In 1563, he explained the witch phenomenon thus, without discarding belief in diabolism: the devil deluded foolish old women afflicted by melancholia, causing them to believe they had magical powers. Weyer's rational skepticism, which had good credibility in the community of the learned, worked to revise the conventional views of women and witchcraft.

WOMEN'S WORKS. To the many categories of works produced on the question of women's worth must be added nearly all works written by women. A woman writing was in herself a statement of women's claim to dignity.

Only a few women wrote anything before the dawn of the modern era, for three reasons. First, they rarely received the education that would enable them to write. Second, they were not admitted to the public roles—as administrator, bureaucrat, lawyer or notary, or university professor—in which they might gain knowledge of the kinds of things the literate public thought worth writing about. Third, the culture imposed silence on women, considering speaking out a form of unchastity. Given these conditions, it is remarkable that any women wrote. Those who did before the fourteenth century were almost always nuns or religious women whose isolation made their pronouncements more acceptable.

From the fourteenth century on, the volume of women's writings rose. Women continued to write devotional literature, although not always as cloistered nuns. They also wrote diaries, often intended as keepsakes for their children; books of advice to their sons and daughters; letters to family members and friends; and family memoirs, in a few cases elaborate enough to be considered histories.

A few women wrote works directly concerning the "woman question," and some of these, such as the humanists Isotta Nogarola, Cassandra Fedele, Laura Cereta, and Olympia Morata, were highly trained. A few were

professional writers, living by the income of their pens; the very first among them was Christine de Pizan, noteworthy in this context as in so many others. In addition to *The Book of the City of Ladies* and her critiques of *The Romance of the Rose*, she wrote *The Treasure of the City of Ladies* (a guide to social decorum for women), an advice book for her son, much courtly verse, and a full-scale history of the reign of King Charles V of France.

WOMEN PATRONS. Women who did not themselves write but encouraged others to do so boosted the development of an alternative tradition. Highly placed women patrons supported authors, artists, musicians, poets, and learned men. Such patrons, drawn mostly from the Italian elites and the courts of northern Europe, figure disproportionately as the dedicatees of the important works of early feminism.

For a start, it might be noted that the catalogs of Boccaccio and Alvaro de Luna were dedicated to the Florentine noblewoman Andrea Acciaiuoli and to Doña María, first wife of King Juan II of Castile, while the French translation of Boccaccio's work was commissioned by Anne of Brittany, wife of King Charles VIII of France. The humanist treatises of Goggio, Equicola, Vives, and Agrippa were dedicated, respectively, to Eleanora of Aragon, wife of Ercole I d'Este, Duke of Ferrara; to Margherita Cantelma of Mantua; to Catherine of Aragon, wife of King Henry VIII of England; and to Margaret, Duchess of Austria and regent of the Netherlands. As late as 1696, Mary Astell's *Serious Proposal to the Ladies, for the Advancement of Their True and Greatest Interest* was dedicated to Princess Anne of Denmark.

These authors presumed that their efforts would be welcome to female patrons, or they may have written at the bidding of those patrons. Silent themselves, perhaps even unresponsive, these loftily placed women helped shape the tradition of the other voice.

THE ISSUES. The literary forms and patterns in which the tradition of the other voice presented itself have now been sketched. It remains to highlight the major issues around which this tradition crystallizes. In brief, there are four problems to which our authors return again and again, in plays and catalogs, in verse and letters, in treatises and dialogues, in every language: the problem of chastity, the problem of power, the problem of speech, and the problem of knowledge. Of these the greatest, preconditioning the others, is the problem of chastity.

THE PROBLEM OF CHASTITY. In traditional European culture, as in those of antiquity and others around the globe, chastity was perceived as woman's

quintessential virtue—in contrast to courage, or generosity, or leadership, or rationality, seen as virtues characteristic of men. Opponents of women charged them with insatiable lust. Women themselves and their defenders—without disputing the validity of the standard—responded that women were capable of chastity.

The requirement of chastity kept women at home, silenced them, isolated them, left them in ignorance. It was the source of all other impediments. Why was it so important to the society of men, of whom chastity was not required, and who more often than not considered it their right to violate the chastity of any woman they encountered?

Female chastity ensured the continuity of the male-headed household. If a man's wife was not chaste, he could not be sure of the legitimacy of his offspring. If they were not his and they acquired his property, it was not his household, but some other man's, that had endured. If his daughter was not chaste, she could not be transferred to another man's household as his wife, and he was dishonored.

The whole system of the integrity of the household and the transmission of property was bound up in female chastity. Such a requirement pertained only to property-owning classes, of course. Poor women could not expect to maintain their chastity, least of all if they were in contact with high-status men to whom all women but those of their own household were prey.

In Catholic Europe, the requirement of chastity was further buttressed by moral and religious imperatives. Original sin was inextricably linked with the sexual act. Virginity was seen as heroic virtue, far more impressive than, say, the avoidance of idleness or greed. Monasticism, the cultural institution that dominated medieval Europe for centuries, was grounded in the renunciation of the flesh. The Catholic reform of the eleventh century imposed a similar standard on all the clergy and a heightened awareness of sexual requirements on all the laity. Although men were asked to be chaste, female unchastity was much worse: it led to the devil, as Eve had led mankind to sin.

To such requirements, women and their defenders protested their innocence. Furthermore, following the example of holy women who had escaped the requirements of family and sought the religious life, some women began to conceive of female communities as alternatives both to family and to the cloister. Christine de Pizan's city of ladies was such a community. Moderata Fonte and Mary Astell envisioned others. The luxurious salons of the French *précieuses* of the seventeenth century, or the comfortable English drawing rooms of the next, may have been born of the same impulse. Here women

not only might escape, if briefly, the subordinate position that life in the family entailed but might also make claims to power, exercise their capacity for speech, and display their knowledge.

THE PROBLEM OF POWER. Women were excluded from power: the whole cultural tradition insisted on it. Only men were citizens, only men bore arms, only men could be chiefs or lords or kings. There were exceptions that did not disprove the rule, when wives or widows or mothers took the place of men, awaiting their return or the maturation of a male heir. A woman who attempted to rule in her own right was perceived as an anomaly, a monster, at once a deformed woman and an insufficient male, sexually confused and consequently unsafe.

The association of such images with women who held or sought power explains some otherwise odd features of early modern culture. Queen Elizabeth I of England, one of the few women to hold full regal authority in European history, played with such male/female images—positive ones, of course—in representing herself to her subjects. She was a prince, and manly, even though she was female. She was also (she claimed) virginal, a condition absolutely essential if she was to avoid the attacks of her opponents. Catherine de' Medici, who ruled France as widow and regent for her sons, also adopted such imagery in defining her position. She chose as one symbol the figure of Artemisia, an androgynous ancient warrior-heroine who combined a female persona with masculine powers.

Power in a woman, without such sexual imagery, seems to have been indigestible by the culture. A rare note was struck by the Englishman Sir Thomas Elyot in his *Defence of Good Women* (1540), justifying both women's participation in civic life and their prowess in arms. The old tune was sung by the Scots reformer John Knox in his *First Blast of the Trumpet against the Monstrous Regiment of Women* (1558); for him rule by women, defects in nature, was a hideous contradiction in terms.

The confused sexuality of the imagery of female potency was not reserved for rulers. Any woman who excelled was likely to be called an Amazon, recalling the self-mutilated warrior women of antiquity who repudiated all men, gave up their sons, and raised only their daughters. She was often said to have "exceeded her sex" or to have possessed "masculine virtue"—as the very fact of conspicuous excellence conferred masculinity even on the female subject. The catalogs of notable women often showed those female heroes dressed in armor, armed to the teeth, like men. Amazonian heroines romp through the epics of the age—Ariosto's *Orlando Furioso* (1532) and Spenser's *Faerie Queene* (1590–1609). Excellence in a woman was perceived as a claim for power, and power was reserved for the masculine

realm. A woman who possessed either one was masculinized and lost title to her own female identity.

THE PROBLEM OF SPEECH. Just as power had a sexual dimension when it was claimed by women, so did speech. A good woman spoke little. Excessive speech was an indication of unchastity. By speech, women seduced men. Eve had lured Adam into sin by her speech. Accused witches were commonly accused of having spoken abusively, or irrationally, or simply too much. As enlightened a figure as Francesco Barbaro insisted on silence in a woman, which he linked to her perfect unanimity with her husband's will and her unblemished virtue (her chastity). Another Italian humanist, Leonardo Bruni, in advising a noblewoman on her studies, barred her not from speech but from public speaking. That was reserved for men.

Related to the problem of speech was that of costume—another, if silent, form of self-expression. Assigned the task of pleasing men as their primary occupation, elite women often tended toward elaborate costume, hairdressing, and the use of cosmetics. Clergy and secular moralists alike condemned these practices. The appropriate function of costume and adornment was to announce the status of a woman's husband or father. Any further indulgence in adornment was akin to unchastity.

THE PROBLEM OF KNOWLEDGE. When the Italian noblewoman Isotta Nogarola had begun to attain a reputation as a humanist, she was accused of incest—a telling instance of the association of learning in women with unchastity. That chilling association inclined any woman who was educated to deny that she was or to make exaggerated claims of heroic chastity.

If educated women were pursued with suspicions of sexual misconduct, women seeking an education faced an even more daunting obstacle: the assumption that women were by nature incapable of learning, that reasoning was a particularly masculine ability. Just as they proclaimed their chastity, women and their defenders insisted on their capacity for learning. The major work by a male writer on female education—that by Juan Luis Vives, *On the Education of a Christian Woman* (1523)—granted female capacity for intellection but still argued that a woman's whole education was to be shaped around the requirement of chastity and a future within the household. Female writers of the following generations—Marie de Gournay in France, Anna Maria van Schurman in Holland, and Mary Astell in England—began to envision other possibilities.

The pioneers of female education were the Italian women humanists who managed to attain a literacy in Latin and a knowledge of classical and Christian literature equivalent to that of prominent men. Their works implicitly and explicitly raise questions about women's social roles, defining

problems that beset women attempting to break out of the cultural limits that had bound them. Like Christine de Pizan, who achieved an advanced education through her father's tutoring and her own devices, their bold questioning makes clear the importance of training. Only when women were educated to the same standard as male leaders would they be able to raise that other voice and insist on their dignity as human beings morally, intellectually, and legally equal to men.

THE OTHER VOICE. The other voice, a voice of protest, was mostly female, but it was also male. It spoke in the vernaculars and in Latin, in treatises and dialogues, in plays and poetry, in letters and diaries, and in pamphlets. It battered at the wall of prejudice that encircled women and raised a banner announcing its claims. The female was equal (or even superior) to the male in essential nature—moral, spiritual, and intellectual. Women were capable of higher education, of holding positions of power and influence in the public realm, and of speaking and writing persuasively. The last bastion of masculine supremacy, centered on the notions of a woman's primary domestic responsibility and the requirement of female chastity, was not as yet assaulted—although visions of productive female communities as alternatives to the family indicated an awareness of the problem.

During the period 1300–1700, the other voice remained only a voice, and one only dimly heard. It did not result—yet—in an alteration of social patterns. Indeed, to this day they have not entirely been altered. Yet the call for justice issued as long as six centuries ago by those writing in the tradition of the other voice must be recognized as the source and origin of the mature feminist tradition and of the realignment of social institutions accomplished in the modern age.

We thank the volume editors in this series, who responded with many suggestions to an earlier draft of this introduction, making it a collaborative enterprise. Many of their suggestions and criticisms have resulted in revisions of this introduction, although we remain responsible for the final product.

PROJECTED TITLES IN THE SERIES

Francesco Barbaro et al., *On Marriage and the Family*, edited and translated by Margaret L. King

Francesco Buoninsegni and Arcangela Tarabotti, *Menippean Satire: "Against Feminine Extravagance" and "Antisatire,"* edited and translated by Elissa Weaver

Rosalba Carriera, *Letters, Diaries, and Art*, edited and translated by Catherine M. Sama

Madame du Chatelet, *Selected Works*, edited by Judith Zinsser

Vittoria Colonna, Chiara Matraini, and Lucrezia Marinella, *Marian Writings*, edited and translated by Susan Haskins

Princess Elizabeth of Bohemia, *Correspondence with Descartes*, edited and translated by Lisa Shapiro

Isabella d'Este, *Selected Letters*, edited and translated by Deanna Shemek

Fairy Tales by Seventeenth-Century French Women Writers, edited and translated by Lewis Seifert and Domna C. Stanton

Moderata Fonte, *Floridoro*, edited and translated by Valeria Finucci

Moderata Fonte and Lucrezia Marinella, *Religious Narratives*, edited and translated by Virginia Cox

Catharina Regina von Greiffenberg, *Meditations on the Life of Christ*, edited and translated by Lynne Tatlock

In Praise of Women: Italian Fifteenth-Century Defenses of Women, edited and translated by Daniel Bornstein

Lucrezia Marinella, *L'Enrico, or Byzantium Conquered*, edited and translated by Virginia Cox

Lucrezia Marinella, *Happy Arcadia*, edited and translated by Susan Haskins and Letizia Panizza

Chiara Matraini, *Selected Poetry and Prose*, edited and translated by Elaine MacLachlan

Alessandro Piccolomini, *Rethinking Marriage in Sixteenth-Century Italy*, edited and translated by Letizia Panizza

Christine de Pizan, *Debate over the "Romance of the Rose,"* edited and translated by David F. Hult

Christine de Pizan, *Life of Charles V*, edited and translated by Nadia Margolis

Christine de Pizan, *The Long Road of Learning*, edited and translated by Andrea Tarnowski

Madeleine and Catherine des Roches, *From Mother and Daughter: Poems, Dialogues, and Letters*, edited and translated by Anne Larsen

Oliva Sabuco, *The New Philosophy: True Medicine*, edited and translated by Gianna Pomata

Margherita Sarrocchi, *La Scanderbeide*, edited and translated by Rinaldina Russell

Gabrielle Suchon, *"On Philosophy" and "On Morality,"* edited and translated by Domna Stanton with Rebecca Wilkin

Sara Copio Sullam, *Sara Copio Sullam: Jewish Poet and Intellectual in Early Seventeenth-Century Venice*, edited and translated by Don Harrán

Arcangela Tarabotti, *Convent Life as Inferno: A Report*, introduction and notes by Francesca Medioli, translated by Letizia Panizza

Laura Terracina, *Works*, edited and translated by Michael Sherberg

Katharina Schütz Zell, *Selected Writings*, edited and translated by Elsie McKee

Figure 1. Engraved portrait of Louise Labé by Pierre Woeriot in Lyon in 1555, the only known portrait drawn during her lifetime. Courtesy Printing Museum of Lyon.

VOLUME EDITOR'S
INTRODUCTION

THE OTHER VOICE

The notion of the "other voice" takes on multiple dimensions when it comes to the literary legacy of Louise Labé, one of the most gifted and controversial women writers of early modern Europe. At once revered and maligned, acclaimed and brushed aside — in her own and subsequent times — Louise Labé has left for the contemporary reader both the seductive cultural mythology and the meticulous artistic labor of a Renaissance woman's coming to writing (*la venue à l'écriture*, as Hélène Cixous would have it), coming to selfhood, and coming to understanding of the individual's timeless struggle to connect with others in the world. But unlike the voices of many other female authors and the male authors who supported them, Labé's "other voice" has rarely lacked either writerly or biographical notoriety, and her poetic works — in particular her love sonnets — have attracted numerous translators and commentators and have long earned her at least a cameo appearance in the canon of French and European literature. Yet beyond the achingly erotic verses in which so many readers have been impelled to hear the thinly veiled confession of a strikingly unconventional life, the poet's voice has been shown in recent years to be infinitely complex in its interweaving and rewriting of the rich traditions of classical elegy and Petrarchan lyric from the vantage point of a female speaking subject.

Furthermore, this deeper and more subtle understanding of Labé's lyric voice has stimulated more fervent interest in the entirety of her production and in the varied narrative voices she fashions in her less-known prose works. Whether adopting the authorial first person as a champion of women's rights to education and public self-expression, or appropriating the mouthpieces of mythological characters involved in dialogue and debate on gender, art, and love, Labé trumpets at once the plight and the potential of women seeking to navigate the cultural expectations and social norms inherent in their times. *1*

And still, from this multiplicity of speaking postures — public and private, narrative and poetic — there ultimately emerges the unified voice of an authentic female subject that reveals, that defines, and that endlessly tests who she is both as a gendered being and as a common partner in the human experience. In the new translations to follow we hope to recapture the many remarkable facets of this integrated voice.

LIFE AND WRITINGS

The small amount of verifiable biographical documentation available on Louise Labé has given rise to a number of colorful elaborations in which it is difficult to distinguish fact from fiction. We know that she was born in Lyon, probably sometime between 1520 and 1522, and lived her entire life in or around the city, which reigned as the cultural capital of France throughout the first half of the sixteenth century.[1] Lyon enjoyed this privileged status thanks to a confluence of powerful factors: its commercial vitality in banking, trade, and the silk and printing industries, its role as a center of humanism frequented by writers, scholars, and the royal courts of Kings Francis I and Henri II, and its geographical proximity to the thriving economic and cultural theaters of the Italian Renaissance.

Labé was the daughter of a well-to-do Lyonnais rope maker, Pierre Charly, and his second wife, Etiennette Roybet, who died around 1523. Curiously, as Ann Rosalind Jones, Madeleine Lazard, and François Rigolot note, the name Labé came to the family via Pierre's first wife, Guillemette Humbert,

---

1. The most comprehensive biographical and sociohistorical study of Labé to date can be found in Madeleine Lazard's magisterial 2004 volume, *Louise Labé* (Paris: Fayard). For a selection of other recent discussions on elements of Labé's biography and/or the significance of her positioning as a woman living and writing in sixteenth-century Lyon, see Karine Berriot, *Louise Labé: La Belle Rebelle et le François nouveau, suivi des Œuvres complètes* (Paris: Seuil, 1985); Evelyne Berriot-Salvadore, *Les femmes dans la société française de la Renaissance* (Geneva: Droz, 1991); Keith Cameron, *Louise Labé: Feminist and Poet of the Renaissance* (New York: Berg Women's Series, 1990), 17–26; Natalie Zemon Davis, "City Women and Religious Change," in *Society and Culture in Early Modern France* (Stanford: Stanford University Press, 1975), 65–95; Enzo Giudici, *Louise Labé: Essai* (Paris: Nizet, 1981); Ann Rosalind Jones, "Eros Equalized: Literary Cross-Dressing and the Defense of Women in Louise Labé and Veronica Franco," in *The Currency of Eros: Women's Love Lyric in Europe, 1540–1620* (Bloomington: Indiana University Press, 1990), esp. 155–60; Constance Jordan, *Renaissance Feminism: Literary Texts and Political Models* (Ithaca, NY: Cornell University Press, 1990), esp. 174–77; Madeleine Lazard, *Images littéraires de la femme à la Renaissance* (Paris: Presses Universitaires de France, 1985); Jeanne Prine, "Louise Labé, Poet of Lyon," in *Women Writers of the Renaissance and Reformation*, ed. Katharina M. Wilson (Athens, GA: University of Georgia Press, 1987), 132–34; François Rigolot, *Louise Labé Lyonnaise ou la Renaissance au féminin* (Paris: Honoré Champion, 1997), esp. 9–30; and François Rigolot, ed., Chronologie, in *Louise Labé: Œuvres complètes*, 2nd ed. (Paris: Flammarion, 2004), 269–77.

whose own previous husband — a rope maker in his own right — had owned a property called Labé (also spelled L'Abbé) and who, like Montaigne famously after him, followed the contemporary custom of adopting its name.[2] Upon his marriage to Guillemette, Pierre came into ownership of this property and likewise assumed the name Labé, which his daughter would retain throughout her life, eschewing her original paternal and her subsequent marital appellation.

Raised by her father and stepmother, Antoinette Taillard (whom Pierre married after his second wife's death), Louise benefited from an apparently progressive attitude toward female education on the part of her father, who, although illiterate himself, followed the pattern of certain successful and upwardly mobile bourgeois citizens of Lyon and allowed her to be schooled, like her brothers, in the typically male domains of ancient and modern languages, fencing, and equestrian sports, as well as the traditionally "feminine" arts of music and needlework. Although this example of paternal enlightenment did not prevent Pierre Labé from negotiating sometime between 1542 and 1544 a conventional arranged marriage for his daughter with Ennemond Perrin, a fellow rope maker well advanced in age, the poetess also benefited from the apparently progressive attitude in cosmopolitan Lyon toward certain kinds of traditional class and gender hierarchies, a phenomenon attributable both to the city's independence from the Paris court and from Sorbonniste authority, and to the strong participation in its civic governance by flourishing craftsmen and merchants. It was this blurring of class distinctions, exemplified by the practice wherein daughters of certain prosperous bourgeois citizens came to be educated in skills and disciplines normally reserved for the aristocracy, that enabled a talented woman who was noble neither by birth nor by marriage to write and publish works and participate in intellectual conversations with the male-dominated literary world.[3]

Possessing little in common with her financially secure but uneducated husband, Louise Labé thus rejected a conventional domestic role and exploited the social flexibility and cultural dynamism that Lyonnais society provided her. Frequenting and at times probably hosting members of the city's established literary circles, she cultivated exchanges and friendships

2. See Jones, *Currency of Eros,* 156; Lazard, *Louise Labé,* 30–31; and Rigolot, *Louise Labé Lyonnaise,* 230–31. Since Pierre Charly assumed the artisanal business and venue of his wife's first husband, the adoption of his predecessor's "professional" name was commercially expedient.

3. Berriot (*La Belle Rebelle,* 167) and Jones (*Currency of Eros,* 156) have both stressed the political and economic factors that contributed to this occasional flexibility in Lyonnais class hierarchies. For a discussion and assessment of the various theories advanced over the years regarding the enigma of Labé's education, see Lazard (*Louise Labé,* 41–52).

with well-known resident poets of the time, including the celebrated Petrar-
chan imitator Maurice Scève and his female protégé, Pernette du Guillet, and
came into contact with many others, including Clément Marot, Joachim du
Bellay, Pierre de Ronsard, and less well remembered figures such as Pontus
de Tyard, Jean-Antoine de Baïf, Jacques Peletier du Mans, and Olivier de
Magny, with whom she was rumored to have had a love affair.[4] She published
her own volume of complete works in 1555 through the prestigious printing
establishment of Jean de Tournes. This volume, accompanied by two dozen
poems paying homage to Labé by her male literary contemporaries, was re-
published a year later in three different editions (two in Lyon and one in
Rouen) and enjoyed a success attesting to the author's sparkling public noto-
riety. However, Labé's star that burned so brightly was short-lived; she re-
tired to a country property outside of Lyon around 1557, and following her
husband's death sometime in the early 1560s, she continued to live in relative
obscurity until her own death in 1566, when she was barely forty-five.

AFTERLIFE OF LABÉ AND HER WRITINGS

For several centuries after her death, Labé suffered the fate common to
female love poets from Sappho to Edna St. Vincent Millay, attracting more
attention from legends concerning her personal life than from her artis-
tic production: supposed liaisons with Magny and other poets, with army
officers, and even with the dauphin and future king Henri II, as well as her
purported taste for cross-dressing and military exercises, as illustrated in
a widely circulated story of her appearance in battle against the Spanish
at the 1542 siege of Perpignan. In contrast to the lavish praise for her
beauty, courageous spirit, intelligence, and artistic talent documented in her
volume's concluding *Hommage*, as well as in other contemporary writings, slan-
der and innuendo centering on her sexual mores and taste for male activities
flew thick and fast from the pens of her detractors in the years after her
death.[5] Some portrayed her suggestively as a courtesan, in the style of the

---

4. To read the texts of what Rigolot calls the poetic dialogue between Labé's second sonnet and
a sonnet published one year later in *Les Souspirs* of Magny, as well as an excerpt of one of his 1559
Odes, see Rigolot's edition of Labé's *Œuvres poétiques*, 223–29. Jones also mentions another
1559 ode in which Magny derisively addresses Labé's husband Ennemond as "Sire Aymon" and
contrasts her beauty and musical gifts to the rope maker's soiled working attire (*Currency of
Eros*, 160).

5. The range of both laudatory and negative reactions to Labé's works and to her perceived per-
son by her contemporaries, as well as by writers and scholars up through the early 1980s, can be
gauged from the twenty-four poems in homage to Louise Labé from the 1555 edition and the
quotations entitled "Regards sur Louise Labé" in Rigolot's edition of her *Œuvres complètes* (137–200

famed Italian *cortegiana honesta,* typified by Venetian poet Veronica Franco: a well-educated and cultivated woman who through the support she received from wealthy men attended and hosted literary salons and became known and respected for her talent in conversing and writing. Others adopted more coarse invective, among whom perhaps the most vituperative was John Calvin, who in a famous 1561 letter from Geneva made reference to Labé as a *"plebeia meretrix"*(common prostitute).[6]

Yet despite the persistence of such insinuations and of such ambivalent epithets as "La Belle Cordière" (the Beautiful Wife of the Rope Maker), also used by Calvin, "Capitaine Louise," and "La Belle Amazone," and despite the fact that no new editions of her collected works appeared between 1566 and 1762 (and no scholarly edition until that of Charles Boy in 1887), Louise Labé *as writer* never completely dropped off the radar screen. Her prose dialogue appears to have inspired Jean de la Fontaine's fable "Love and Folly," and her various works are evoked by writers including Voltaire, nineteenth-century female poet Marceline Desbordes-Valmore, Sainte-Beuve, Louis Aragon, Léon-Paul Fargue, Léopold Senghor, and Rainer Maria Rilke, who also translated her sonnets into German. Scholarly interest in her writings grew modestly in the first two-thirds of the twentieth century, generally still with a strong overlay of biographical speculation and debate, and during this period five editions of her love sonnets translated into English appeared.[7] Yet only relatively recently, from the 1960s on, and especially in the context of the energetic recovery of early modern women authors in the 1980s and 1990s, have critics begun to devote thorough and sophisticated attention to Labé's unified body of work.[8] Even a brief overview of this body

---

and 231–62). Included among these are remarks by several of her early biographers, Jean Pernetti, in his 1757 *Recherches pour servir à l'histoire de Lyon;* Breghot du Lut in the *Notice* to his 1824 edition of her works; Charles Boy in the critical commentary of his 1887 scholarly edition (*Œuvres de Louise Labé,* reprinted in Geneva by Slatkine, 1968); and Dorothy O'Conner in her 1926 monograph *Louise Labé, Sa vie et son œuvre* (Paris: Les Presses Françaises). Boy's 1887 edition of Labé's *Œuvres* also includes comments made about Louise Labé by her contemporaries (2:89–114).

6. Lazard (*Louise Labé,* 75–77) documents the fascinating historical anecdote that explains the background of Calvin's notorious remark.

7. These English translations of the sonnets include those by Frederic Prokosch (New York: New Directions, 1947); Frances Lobb (London: Euphorian Books, 1950); Alta Lind Cook (Toronto: University of Toronto Press, 1950); Bettina Knapp (Paris: Minard, 1964); and Graham Dunstan Martin (Austin: University of Texas Press, 1972).

8. One key index of the ongoing revalidation of Labé's works into the twenty-first century is their first-time selection for inclusion among the texts featured in the 2005 French university *agrégation* competition for *lettres modernes.* In conjunction with this event, a new volume compiling important articles on Labé was published in December 2004: Béatrice Alonso and Eliane

of work reveals just why her writing attracted such visceral reactions — both positive and negative — particularly from her male contemporaries, and why for so long it proved less problematic for posterity to focus on moral judgment and romanticization of her biographical profile rather than on what amounted to a subversive, original, and enlightening authorial voice.

After all, despite the relative freedom and flexibility that Lyonnais society offered her, Labé nevertheless moved clearly against the grain of what was generally considered appropriate conduct and discourse for a woman of her era, and her literary production as a whole speaks to the powerful and emancipated role that she envisioned for women in both public and private life.

LABÉ'S FEMINISM

Labé's 1555 volume begins with a short (ninety-line) *epistre,* or dedicatory letter, to a young Lyonnais noblewoman, Clémence de Bourges, that serves as a now classic statement of what can appropriately be called the "feminist" issues and concerns of women in early modern Europe.[9] In this manifesto, Labé begins by emphasizing the importance of broader access to education for women, thereby championing the right of other women to the unusual

---

Viennot, eds., *Louise Labé 2005* (Saint-Etienne: Publications Universitaires de Saint-Etienne, 2004). Moreover, in addition to the key works cited in note 1 above, which combine textual interpretation with biographical and cultural contextualization, other recent book-length studies analyzing Labé's *Complete Works* include Deborah Lesko Baker, *The Subject of Desire: Petrarchan Poetics and the Female Voice in Louise Labé* (West Lafayette, IN: Purdue University Press, 1996); Guy Demerson, ed., *Louise Labé: Les voix du lyrisme* (Paris: Éditions du CNRS, 1990); Daniel Martin, *Signe(s) d'Amante: L'agencement des Evvres de Louize Labé Lionnoize* (Paris: Honoré Champion, 1999); and Chiara Sibona, *Le Sens qui résonne: Une étude sur le sonnet français à travers l'œuvre de Louise Labé* (Ravenna: Longo, 1984).

Beside the contributions compiled in Béatrice Alonso's and Guy Demerson's volumes, among other important post-1980 articles and book chapters devoted to Labé's works, see especially the essays by Deborah Lesko Baker, Wilson Baldridge, Edith Benkov, Françoise Charpentier, Lance Donaldson-Evans, Tom Conley, Robert Cottrell, Michel Dassonville, Carla Freccero, Floyd Gray, Ann Rosalind Jones, Peggy Kamuf, William J. Kennedy, Anne Larsen, Deborah N. Losse, Daniel Martin, Mary B. Moore, Jerry Nash, Sharlene May Poliner, Kirk Read, François Rigolot, Paula Sommers, Marcel Tetel, Karen Wiley, Colette Winn, and Cathy Yandell listed in the bibliography.

9. The origins of the connection between Labé and Clémence de Bourges, the daughter of a Lyonnais magistrate, have sparked much interest, as they attest to the flexibility of urban class boundaries to which I alluded earlier. As Rigolot states in his edition of the complete works, the two most likely met at a convent where Labé was probably sent to be schooled after her mother's death (Chronologie, 278). In her brief overview of Clémence's life, Lazard nevertheless maintains that there is no documented proof of a friendship between Louise and her dedicatee, who was ten to fifteen years younger (*Louise Labé,* 121–22).

advantage that was offered to her as a member of the nonaristocratic class. In this defense of education, in which she calls upon women to move beyond their traditional and subservient domestic roles, Labé advances one of her essential beliefs: the importance of reciprocity and equality between men and women, both as working partners in society and in their own mutual relationships. She then turns in the final section of this dedicatory letter to a second core belief: that women should also be encouraged to write, since writing puts into motion a process through which any individual — whether male or female — can forge a sense of selfhood that leads to a fuller, more conscious life. In implicit contrast to the deceptions and disappointments of erotic attachments, she stresses the pleasure derived from a woman's "relationship" with her own text — her alternation between the actual act of writing and her study of the written word on the page — and how this pleasure in itself becomes an enriching experience, based as it is on the recording of individual memories and their subsequent contemplation at different points in time.

Labé's dedicatory letter, setting forth so cogently her advocacy of women's entrance onto the public and literary stage, as well as her assertion of female identity as complex and separate from the lens of the male gaze, is followed in the volume by a much longer prose work of over two thousand lines, entitled *Debate of Folly and Love*. The *Debate* is a mythological play in prose, organized in five discourses, or acts, that exploits the popular models of medieval-Renaissance dialogue, allegories embodying human problems in divine characters, and satiric critique as typified in Erasmus's *Praise of Folly* in order to address in a different context Labé's vision of male-female partnership in the arenas of both social interaction and erotic love.[10] What Labé ingeniously achieves in the *Debate* is a concrete enactment of the *Dedicatory Letter*'s precepts in theatrical form — a drama pitting the god of Love (Amour, or Cupid) and the goddess of Folly (Folie) against one another in a dispute over their respective social standing and roles. This allegorical drama allows the reader a sense of playful fantasy and an attendant sense of distance from which to consider in a more detached way some of the controversial points Labé makes about traditional male authority. In other words, her critique of male-female relations and power dynamics is less threatening to a conventional male and female reading public when presented in the guise of often comic argumentative exchanges between the two mythological protagonists, as well as in the philosophical oratory of each character's public

---

10. The Erasmian intertext is fundamental, for several editions of *Praise of Folly* had been published in Lyon beginning in 1511, as well as a French translation in 1520.

defender (the gods Apollo and Mercury, respectively) when the couple's dispute is referred to Jupiter's court of law. The celestial king's tersely enigmatic final verdict compels the reader to reflect on the ambiguities and vulnerabilities that challenge any conventional simplification of gendered relations. In its elaborate combination of dramatic convention and prose oration, the *Debate* revisits and extends certain key concerns thematized at the heart of the dedicatory letter: the power of oral and written language, the importance of self-knowledge and knowledge of others in the world, the assertion of equal partnership between men and women in public and private spheres, and the very possibility of change, whether in the way the social order conceives of gender roles or in the way the literary culture configures romantic or erotic love. These are among the most prominent concerns that the author goes on to privilege throughout the lyric verse culminating her complete works.

Louise Labé composed and published her own poetry — three hundred-line elegies and twenty-four sonnets — against the backdrop of a fertile intersection of classical, native French, and Italian influences, including the great trio of Latin elegists Propertius, Tibullus, and Ovid; the early sixteenth-century court poet who first introduced the elegy in France, Clément Marot; the fifteenth- and sixteenth-century Florentine Neoplatonists, chief among them Marsilio Ficino; and, most prominently of all, the lyric giant of the Italian Renaissance, Francesco Petrarca (1304–74) and his great French male imitators, Maurice Scève, Joachim du Bellay, and Pierre de Ronsard.[11] Indeed, Labé wrote at the highest moment of the Petrarchan tradition in France, a tradition that captivated all of early modern Europe through its fashioning of male-female love experience according to the perspective of the male speaker in Petrarch's *Canzoniere*.[12] The modality at the heart of

11. For useful summaries of these contributing influences, see Cameron, *Louise Labé*, chap. 3, and Lazard, *Louise Labé*, chap. 5; for specific background on Labé's appropriation of the classical and Marotic elegy form, see Michel Dassonville, "Louise Labé et le genre élégiaque," in *Pre-Pléiade Poetry*, ed. Jerry Nash (Lexington, KY: French Forum, 1985), 77–83; Gertrude S. Hanisch, *Love Elegies of the Renaissance: Marot, Louise Labé, and Ronsard*, Stanford French and Italian Studies (Saratoga, CA: Anma Libri, 1979); Daniel Martin, *Signe(s) d'Amante*, 167–78; and Rigolot, Préface, in his edition of Labé's works. The major volumes by French male poets imitating Petrarch's *Canzoniere* are Scève's *Délie* (1544), Du Bellay's *Olive* (1550), and Ronsard's *Amours* (1552). The major Neoplatonic texts having an impact on these poets, as well as on Labé, include Marsilio Ficino's Latin translation and commentary on Plato's *Symposium* (translated into French in 1546); Baldassare Castiglione's *Book of the Courtier* (translated into French in 1537); Pietro Bembo's *Asolani* (translated into French in 1545); Leone Ebreo's *Love Dialogues* (translated into French in 1551); and Speroni's *Dialogues* (1542).

12. Recent fundamental book-length studies devoted either entirely or substantially to Petrarch and his tradition include Howard Bloom, ed., *Petrarch: Modern Critical Views* (New York: Chelsea House, 1989); Gordon Braden, *Petrarchan Love and the Continental Renaissance* (New Haven: Yale University Press, 1999); JoAnn DellaNeva, *Song and Counter-song: Scève's "Délie" and Petrarch's "Rime"*

the Petrarchan lyric is a male speaker's lament over the love of an unattainable woman and the struggles he encounters in his spiritual journey through this crisis. What is most innovative and crucial in this tradition from a literary, historical, and psychological point of view is the poet's complex construction of an individual self and subjectivity. In developing this subjectivity the male speaker descends in his anguish to ever-deepening areas of self-absorption, such that the female love object, more than an actual concrete other, becomes an abstract catalyst through which he accesses and perpetuates his own psychic struggle. The reader thus perceives throughout the Petrarchan tradition, and especially as adapted in early- to mid-sixteenth- century France, a tendency to privilege the ontological conflict and fragmentation of the male subject, and actually to celebrate them as the constitutive elements of a paradoxically heroic posture. Given that Louise Labé, like all her contemporaries working in the milieu of Renaissance humanism, sought to imitate classical and Italian models as a preliminary validation of her own literary endeavors, a fundamental and fascinating question arises. What new dimensions come into play when a female voice begins to manipulate this tradition, and when the woman is no longer an

---

(Lexington, KY: French Forum, 1983); Heather Dubrow, *Echoes of Desire: English Petrarchism and Its Counterdiscourses* (Ithaca, NY: Cornell University Press, 1995); Robert Durling, ed. and trans., Introduction, *Petrarch's Lyric Poems* (Cambridge: Harvard University Press, 1976); Roland Greene, *Post-Petrarchism: Origins and Innovations of the Western Lyric Sequence* (Princeton: Princeton University Press, 1991); Thomas M. Greene, *The Light in Troy: Imitation and Discovery in Renaissance Poetry* (New Haven: Yale University Press, 1982); Olivia Holmes, *Assembling the Lyric Self: Authorship from Troubadour Song to Italian Poetry Book* (Minneapolis: University of Minnesota Press, 2000); William J. Kennedy, *The Site of Petrarchism: Early Modern National Sentiment in Italy, France, and England* (Baltimore: Johns Hopkins University Press, 2003), and *Authorizing Petrarch* (Ithaca, NY: Cornell University Press, 1994); Giuseppe Mazzotta, ed., *The Worlds of Petrarch* (Durham, NC: Duke University Press, 1993); Mark Musa, ed. and trans., Introduction, *The "Canzoniere," or Rerum vulgarium fragmenta* (Bloomington: Indiana University Press, 1996); Timothy Reiss, *Mirages of the Selfe: Patterns of Personhood in Ancient and Early Modern Europe* (Stanford: Stanford University Press, 2003); Sara Sturm-Maddox, *Ronsard, Petrarch, and the "Amours"* (Gainesville: University Press of Florida, 1999), *Petrarch's Laurels* (University Park, PA: Pennsylvania State University Press, 1992), and *Petrarch's Metamorphoses: Text and Subtext in the "Rime Sparse"* (Columbia: University of Missouri Press, 1985); and Marguerite Waller, *Petrarch's Poetics and Literary History* (Amherst: University of Massachusetts Press, 1980).

To honor the seven-hundredth anniversary of Petrarch's birth, the fall 2004 volume (22) of the international journal *Annali d'italianistica* (ed. Dino Cervigni) is devoted specifically to new articles on Petrarch and Petrarchism. In addition to these articles and the contributions compiled in the above-listed volumes of Howard Bloom and Giuseppe Mazzotta, which include the classic articles of John Freccero ("The Fig Tree and the Laurel: Petrarch's Poetics,") and of Mazzotta himself ("The *Canzoniere* and the Language of the Self"), among other important post-1980 articles and book chapters devoted to Petrarch, see the essays by Gordon Braden, Lynn Enterline, Thomas Greene, and Nancy Vickers listed in the volume editor's bibliography.

abstract object of male desire but rather becomes the subject of desire in her own right, one who narrates her own journey through the vicissitudes of love?[13]

Although throughout the itinerary detailed in her love elegies and sonnets Labé incorporates many of the conventions, settings, and metaphors standard in Petrarchan practice, she displaces the priority placed on psychic conflict, narcissistic self-reflection, and eternal futility in the fashioning of the traditional male speaker. She is moreover not content to settle for the only foreseeable solution projected by the male speaker in face of his dilemma: the anticipation of a spiritual release and metaphorical union with the beloved after death. Labé rejects this idea of heavenly escape in favor of concrete scenarios and possibilities — even if they do not become reality — whereby earthly union and reciprocity between a male and a female lover can take place. Thanks to these imaginative scenarios, she transforms the fundamental desire activating her female speaker's experience — a desire seen in the male Petrarchan ethos as a sinful drive to be eradicated — into a positive, life-giving force that can bring not only intense suffering but a fulfilling connection to the beloved and a more acute understanding of self. Through her lyric speaker, then, she proposes an ontological model of a unified human being who continues to validate the possibility of joyful partnership with another loved human being on this earth. Labé's investigation of self and its relation to a "privileged" other in her poetry also leads her, as it does in her more public writings, to embrace the wider community of women and men who likewise undergo the challenges and sufferings of love, to seek a compassionate and reciprocal dialogue with them, and therefore to affirm an openness to otherness in the world that situates the ultimate equality of all human spirits in the common crucible of their existential struggles.

Deborah Lesko Baker

13. Juliana Schiesari has addressed this question brilliantly with respect to Italian women poets Gaspara Stampa and Isabella di Morra in chapter 3 of her book *The Gendering of Melancholia: Feminism, Psychoanalysis, and the Symbolics of Loss in Renaissance Literature* (Ithaca, NY: Cornell University Press, 1992).

VOLUME EDITOR'S
BIBLIOGRAPHY

PRINCIPAL EDITIONS OF LOUISE LABÉ'S WORKS

Evvres de Lovize Labé Lionnoize. A Lyon par Jean de Tournes, avec Privilege du Roy. 1555.

Evvres de Lovïze Labé Lionnoize. Ed. N. F. Cochard and Breghot du Lut. Lyon: Durand et Perrin, 1824.

Œuvres de Louise Labé. Ed. Prosper Blanchemain. Paris: Librairie des Bibliophiles, 1875.

Œuvres de Louise Labé. Ed. Charles Boy. 2 vols. Paris: Alphonse Lemerre, 1887. Reprint, Geneva: Slatkine, 1968.

Œuvres complètes. Ed. Enzo Giudici. TLF no. 292. Geneva: Droz, 1981.

Œuvres poétiques précédées des 'Rymes' de Pernette de Guillet avec un choix de Blasons du corps féminin. Ed. Françoise Charpentier. Paris: Gallimard, 1983.

Œuvres complètes. Ed. Karine Berriot. In *Louise Labé: La Belle Rebelle et le François nouveau.* Paris: Seuil, 1985.

Œuvres complètes: Sonnets, élégies, "Débat de Folie et d'Amour," poésies. Ed. François Rigolot. 2nd ed. Paris: Flammarion, 2004. Orig. pub. 1986.

PRINCIPAL PREVIOUS TRANSLATIONS
OF LOUISE LABÉ'S WORKS INTO ENGLISH

The Debate Betweene Follie and Love. Trans. Robert Greene, Maister of Artes. 4th ed. London: H. Lownes, 1608.

The Debate between Folly and Cupid. Trans. Edwin Marion Cox. London: Williams & Norgate, 1925.

Louise Labé: Love Sonnets. Trans. Frederic Prokosch. New York: New Directions, 1947.

Louise Labé: The Twenty-four Love Sonnets. Trans. Frances Lobb. London: Euphorion Books, 1950.

Louise Labé, "La Belle Cordière": Sonnets. Trans. Alta Lind Cook. Toronto: University of Toronto Press, 1950.

Louise Labé: Les Sonnets. Trans. Bettina L. Knapp. Paris: Minard, 1964.

Louise Labé: Sonnets. Trans. Graham Dunstan Martin. Ed. and with a preface by Peter Sharratt. Edinburgh Bilingual Library. Austin: University of Texas Press, 1972.

Louise Labé's Complete Works. Ed. and trans. Edith R. Farrell. Troy, NY: Whitson, 1986.

Debate of Folly and Love. Trans. Anne-Marie Bourbon. New York: Peter Lang Publishers, 2000. Includes a translation of the *Dedicatory Letter.*

DICTIONARIES OF SIXTEENTH-CENTURY FRENCH LANGUAGE

Cotgrave, Randle. *A Dictionarie of the French and English Tongues,* reproduced from the first edition [London, 1611]. Introd. William S. Woods. Columbia: University of South Carolina Press, 1950, 1968.
Huguet, Edmond. *Dictionnaire de la langue française du seizième siècle.* 7 vols. Paris: Didier, 1950.

SELECTED CRITICAL STUDIES IN ENGLISH

Benkov, Edith Joyce. "The Pantheon Revisited: Myth and Metaphor in Louise Labé." *Classical and Modern Literature* 5, no. 1 (1984): 23–31.
———. "The Re-making of Love: Louise Labé's *Débat de Folie et d'Amour.*" *Symposium* 46, no. 2 (1992): 94–104.
Bloom, Harold, ed. *Petrarch: Modern Critical Views.* New York: Chelsea House, 1989.
Braden, Gordon. "Love and Fame: The Petrarchan Career." In *Pragmatism's Freud: The Moral Disposition of Psychoanalysis,* ed. Joseph H. Smith and William Kerrigan, 126–58. Baltimore: Johns Hopkins University Press, 1986.
———. *Petrarchan Love and the Continental Renaissance.* New Haven: Yale University Press, 1999.
Cameron, Keith. *A Concordance to Louise Labé: Œuvres poétiques.* Exeter, UK: Dept. of French and Italian, University of Exeter, 1986.
———. *Louise Labé: Feminist and Poet of the Renaissance.* New York: Berg Women's Series, 1990.
Cervigni, Dino, ed. *Petrarch and the European Literary Tradition.* A special volume of *Annali d'Italianistica* 22 (2004).
Clark-Evans, Christine. "The Feminine Exemplum in Writing: Humanist Instruction in Louise Labé's Letter Preface to Clémence de Bourge." *Exemplaria* 6, no. 1 (1994): 205–21. Rpt. in Alonso and Viennot, *Louise Labé 2005,* 91–106.
Conley, Tom. "Engendering Letters: Louise Labé's Polygraph." In Larsen and Winn, *Renaissance Women Writers: French Texts/American Contexts,* 160–71.
———. "A Space of One's Own." Foreword to Lesko Baker, *Subject of Desire,* xi–xiii.
Cottrell, Robert D. "The Problematics of Opposition in Louise Labé's *Débat de Folie et d'Amour.*" *French Forum* 12, no. 1 (1987): 27–42.
Cox, Virginia. *The Renaissance Dialogue: Literary Dialogue in Its Social and Political Contexts, Castiglione to Galileo.* Cambridge, UK: Cambridge University Press, 1992.
Davis, Natalie Zemon. *Society and Culture in Early Modern France.* Stanford: Stanford University Press, 1975.
DeJean, Joan. *Fictions of Sappho: 1546–1937.* Chicago: University of Chicago Press, 1989.
DellaNeva, Joann. *Song and Counter-song: Scève's "Délie" and Petrarch's "Rime."* Lexington, KY: French Forum, 1983.

Donaldson-Evans, Lance K. *Love's Fatal Glance: A Study of Eye Imagery in the Poets of the "Ecole lyonnaise."* University, MS: Romance Monographs, Inc., 1980.

Dubrow, Heather. *Echoes of Desire: English Petrarchism and Its Counterdiscourses.* Ithaca, NY: Cornell University Press, 1995.

Durling, Robert, ed. and trans. Introduction. *Petrarch's Lyric Poems.* Cambridge: Harvard University Press, 1976.

Enterline, Lynn. *The Rhetoric of the Body from Ovid to Shakespeare.* Cambridge: Cambridge University Press, 2000.

Freccero, Carla. "Louise Labé's Feminist Poetics." In *Distant Voices Still Heard: Contemporary Readings of French Renaissance Literature,* ed. J. O'Brien and M. Quainton. Liverpool: Liverpool University Press, 2000.

Freccero, John. "The Fig Tree and the Laurel: Petrarch's Poetics." *Diacritics* (spring 1975): 34–40; reprinted in Bloom, *Petrarch,* 43–55.

Gray, Floyd. *Gender, Rhetoric and Print Culture in French Renaissance Writing.* Cambridge: Cambridge University Press, 2000.

Greene, Roland. *Post-Petrarchism: Origins and Innovations of the Western Lyric Sequence.* Princeton: Princeton University Press, 1991.

Greene, Thomas M. *The Light in Troy: Imitation and Discovery in Renaissance Poetry.* New Haven: Yale University Press, 1982.

———. "Petrarch Viator." In *The Vulnerable Text: Essays on Renaissance Literature,* 18–45. New York: Columbia University Press, 1986.

Hanisch, Gertrude S. *Love Elegies of the Renaissance: Marot, Louise Labé, and Ronsard.* Stanford French and Italian Studies. Saratoga, CA: Anma Libri, 1979.

Holmes, Olivia. *Assembling the Lyric Self: Authorship from Troubadour Song to Italian Poetry Book.* Minneapolis: University of Minnesota Press, 2000.

Jones, Ann Rosalind. "Assimilation with a Difference: Renaissance Women Poets and Literary Influence." *Yale French Studies* 62 (1981): 135–53.

———, with Nancy J. Vickers. "Canon Rule and the Restoration Renaissance." *Yale French Studies* 75 (1988): 9–25.

———. "City Women and Their Audiences: Louise Labé and Veronica Franco." In *Rewriting the Renaissance: The Discourses of Sexual Difference in Early Modern Europe,* ed. Margaret W. Ferguson, Maureen Quilligan, and Nancy J. Vickers, 299–316. Chicago: University of Chicago Press, 1986.

———. *The Currency of Eros: Women's Love Lyric in Europe, 1540–1620.* Bloomington: Indiana University Press, 1990.

Jordan, Constance. *Renaissance Feminism: Literary Texts and Political Models.* Ithaca: Cornell University Press, 1990.

Kamuf, Peggy. "A Double Life (Femmeninism II)." In *Men in Feminism,* ed. Alice Jardine and Paul Smith, 93–97. New York: Methuen, 1987.

Kennedy, William J. *Authorizing Petrarch.* Ithaca: Cornell University Press, 1994.

———. *The Site of Petrarchism: Early Modern National Sentiment in Italy, France, and England.* Baltimore: Johns Hopkins University Press, 2003.

Larsen, Anne R. "Louise Labé's *Débat de Folie et d'Amour*: Feminism and the Defense of Learning." *Tulsa Studies in Women's Literature* 2 (1983): 43–55.

———. "'Un honneste passetems': Strategies of Legitimation in French Renaissance Women's Prefaces." *L'Esprit Créateur* 30, no. 4 (1990): 11–22.

Larsen, Anne R., and Colette H. Winn, eds. *Renaissance Women Writers: French Texts/American Contexts.* Detroit: Wayne State University Press, 1994.

Lesko Baker, Deborah. "Louise Labé's Conditional Imperatives: Subversion and Transcendence of the Petrarchan Tradition." *Sixteenth Century Journal* 21 no. 4 (1990): 523–41. Rpt. in Alonso and Viennot, *Louise Labé 2005*, 133–50.

———. "Re-reading the 'folie': Louise Labé's Sonnet XVIII and the Renaissance Love Heritage." *Renaissance and Reformation/Renaissance et Réforme* 17, no. 1 (1993): 5–14.

———. *The Subject of Desire: Petrarchan Poetics and the Female Voice in Louise Labé.* West Lafayette, IN: Purdue University Press, 1996.

Losse, Deborah N. *Sampling the Book: Renaissance Prologues and the French Conteurs.* Lewisburg, PA: Bucknell University Press, 1994.

———. "Women Addressing Women: The Differentiated Text." In Larsen and Winn, *Renaissance Women Writers*, 23–37.

Mazzotta, Giuseppe. "The *Canzoniere* and the Language of the Self." *Studies in Philology* 75 (1978): 271–96. Rpt. in Mazzotta, *Worlds of Petrarch*, 58–79, and in Bloom, *Petrarch*, 57–78.

———, ed. *The Worlds of Petrarch.* Durham: Duke University Press, 1993.

Moore, Mary B. *Desiring Voices: Women Sonneteers and Petrachism.* Carbondale: Southern Illinois University Press, 2000.

Musa, Mark, ed. and trans. Introduction. *The 'Canzoniere,' or Rerum vulgarium fragmenta.* Bloomington: Indiana University Press, 1996.

Nash, Jerry. "Louise Labé and Learned Levity." *Romance Notes* 21, no. 2 (1980): 227–33.

———. "'Ne veuillez point condamner ma simplesse': Louise Labé and Literary Simplicity." *Res Publica Litterarum* 3 (1980): 91–100.

———, ed. *Pre-Pléiade Poetry.* Lexington, KY: French Forum, 1985.

Poliner, Sharlene May. "'Signes d'Amante' and the Dispossessed Lover: Louise Labé's Poetics of Inheritance." *Bibliothèque d'Humanisme et Renaissance* 46, no. 2 (1984): 323–42.

Prine, Jeanne. "Louise Labé, Poet of Lyon." In *Women Writers of the Renaissance and Reformation*, ed. Katharina M. Wilson, 132–57. Athens: University of Georgia Press, 1987.

Read, Kirk. "Louise Labé in Search of Time Past: Prefatory Strategies and Rhetorical Transformations." *Critical Matrix: Princeton Working Papers in Women's Studies* (spring–summer 1990): 63–88.

Reiss, Timothy. *Mirages of the Selfe: Patterns of Personhood in Ancient and Early Modern Europe.* Stanford: Stanford University Press, 2003.

Rigolot, François. "Gender vs. Sex Difference in Louise Labé's Grammar of Love." In *Rewriting the Renaissance: The Discourses of Sexual Difference in Early Modern Europe*, ed. Margaret W. Ferguson, Maureen Quilligan, and Nancy J. Vickers, 287–98. Chicago: University of Chicago Press, 1986.

———. "Louise Labé." In *French Women Writers: A Bio-bibliographical Source Book*, ed. Eva Martin Sartori and Dorothy Wynne Zimmerman, 262–71. New York: Greenwood Press, 1991.

———, ed. and introd. "Writing in the Feminine in the Renaissance." Special issue of *L'Esprit Créateur* 30 (winter 1990).

Schiesari, Juliana. *The Gendering of Melancholia: Feminism, Psychoanalysis, and the Symbolics of Loss in Renaissance Literature.* Ithaca: Cornell University Press, 1992.

Sommers, Paula. "Louise Labé: The Mysterious Case of the Body in the Text." In Larsen and Winn, *Renaissance Women Writers*, 85–98.

Sturm-Maddox, Sara. *Petrarch's Laurels.* University Park: Pennsylvania State University Press, 1992.

———. *Petrarch's Metamorphoses: Text and Subtext in the "Rime Sparse."* Columbia: University of Missouri Press, 1985.

———. *Ronsard, Petrarch, and the "Amours."* Gainesville: University Press of Florida, 1999.

Vickers, Nancy. "Diana Described: Scattered Woman and Scattered Rhyme." *Critical Inquiry* 8 (1981): 265–79.

Wiley, Karen F. "Louise Labé's Deceptive Petrarchism." *Modern Language Studies* 9 (1981): 51–60.

Winn, Colette H., ed. *The Dialogue in Early Modern France, 1547–1630: Art and Argument.* Washington, DC: Catholic University of America Press, 1993.

Yandell, Cathy. *Carpe Corpus: Time and Gender in Early Modern France.* Newark: University of Delaware Press, 2000.

———. "Carpe Diem, Poetic Immortality, and the Gendered Ideology of Time." In Larsen and Winn, *Renaissance Women Writers*, 115–29.

SELECTED CRITICAL STUDIES IN FRENCH

Alonso, Béatrice. "En guise de Préambule: Ecriture 'féminine,' écriture féministe." In Alonso and Viennot, *Louise Labé 2005*, 7–16.

——— and Eliane Viennot, eds. *Louise Labé 2005.* Collection "L'École du genre," special publication no. 1. Saint-Etienne, France: Publications Universitaires de Saint-Etienne, 2004.

Baldridge, Wilson. "Le langage de la séparation chez Louise Labé." *Etudes littéraires* 20, no. 2 (1987): 61–76.

———. "La présence de la folie dans les *Œuvres* de Louise Labé." *Renaissance et Réforme* 25, no. 4 (1989): 371–79. Rpt. in Alonso and Viennot, *Louise Labé 2005*, 71–78.

Berriot, Karine. *Louise Labé: La Belle Rebelle et le François nouveau, suivi des Œuvres complètes.* Paris: Seuil, 1985.

Berriot-Salvadore, Evelyne. *Les femmes dans la société française de la Renaissance.* Geneva: Droz, 1991.

———. "Les héritières de Louise Labé." In Alonso and Viennot, *Louise Labé 2005*, 119–29.

Budini, Paolo. "Un verso ambiguo di Louise Labé." *Francofonia* 18 (1989): 83–92. Rpt. in Alonso and Viennot, *Louise Labé 2005*, 161–68.

———. "Le sonnet italien de Louise Labé." *Francofonia* 20 (1991): 47–59. Rpt. in Alonso and Viennot, *Louise Labé 2005*, 151–60.

Charpentier, Françoise. "Le débat de Louise et d'amour: une poétique?" In Demerson, *Louise Labé*, 147–59. Rpt. in Alonso and Viennot, *Louise Labé 2005*, 209–18.

———. "Les voix du désir: Le *Débat de Folie et d'Amour* de Louise Labé." In *Le signe et le texte: Études sur l'écriture au XVIe siècle en France*, ed. Lawrence D. Kritzman. Lexington, KY: French Forum, 1990. 27–38. Rpt. in Alonso and Viennot, *Louise Labé 2005*, 197–208.

—, ed. Préface. *Louise Labé: Œuvres poétiques*, 7–30. Paris: Gallimard, 1983.

Dassonville, Michel. "Louise Labé et le genre élégiaque." In Nash, *Pre-Pléiade Poetry*, 77–83.

Demerson, Guy, ed. *Louise Labé: Les voix du lyrisme*. Paris: Éditions du CNRS, 1990.

Fontaine, Marie-Madeleine. "Politique de Louise Labé." In Demerson, *Louise Labé*, 223–41. Rpt. in Alonso and Viennot, *Louise Labé 2005*, 219–32.

Jones-Davies, M. T., ed. *Le dialogue au temps de la Renaissance*. Paris: Jean Touzot, 1984.

Lauvergnat-Gagnière, Christiane. "La rhétorique dans le *Débat de Folie et d'Amour* de Louise Labé." In Demerson, *Louise Labé*, 53–67. Rpt. in Alonso and Viennot, *Louise Labé 2005*, 233–44.

Lazard, Madeleine. *Images littéraires de la femme à la Renaissance*. Paris: Presses Universitaires de France, 1985.

—. "Protestations et revendications féminines dans la littérature française du XVIe siècle." *Revue d'histoire littéraire de la France* 91, no. 6 (1991): 859–77.

—. *Louise Labé*. Paris: Fayard, 2004.

Lecercle, François. "L'erreur d'Ulysse: Quelques hypothèses sur l'organisation du *Canzoniere* de Louise Labé." In Demerson, *Louise Labé*, 207–21. Rpt. in Alonso and Viennot, *Louise Labé 2005*, 169–80.

Logan, Marie-Rose. "La portée théorique du *Debat de Folie et d'Amour* de Louise Labé." *Saggi e ricerche di letteratura francese* 16 (1977): 9–25. Rpt. in Alonso and Viennot, *Louise Labé 2005*, 245–54.

Martin, Daniel. "Les *Elégies* de Louise Labé: Le faix d'Amour et le faix de l'Ecriture." *Etudes littéraires* 27, no. 2 (1994): 39–52.

—. *Signe(s) d'Amante: L'agencement des Evvres de Louize Labé Lionnoize*. Paris: Honoré Champion, 1999.

—. "Bibliographie générale" (Pour la Société Française d'Études du Seizième Siècle). In Alonso and Viennot, *Louise Labé 2005*, 255–69.

Mathieu-Castellani, Gisèle. "Les marques du féminin dans la parole amoureuse de Louise Labé." In Demerson, *Louise Labé*, 189–205. Rpt. in Alonso and Viennot, *Louise Labé 2005*, 197–218.

O'Connor, Dorothy. *Louise Labé: Sa vie et son œuvre*. Paris: Les Presses françaises, 1926. Rpt. Geneva: Slatkine, 1972.

Pérouse, Gabriel-André. "Louise Labé, Claude de Taillemont et le monde poétique de Jeanne Flore." In Demerson, *Louise Labé*, 35–52. Rpt. in Alonso and Viennot, *Louise Labé 2005*, 79–90.

Read, Kirk, and François Rigolot. "Discours liminaire et identité littéraire: Remarques sur la préface féminine au XVIe siècle." *Versants* 15 (1989): 75–98.

Rigolot, François. "Louise Labé et la redécouverte de Sappho." *Nouvelle revue du seizième siècle* 1 (1983): 19–31.

—. "Quel genre d'amour pour Louise Labé?" *Poétique* 55 (1983): 303–17.

—. "Signature et signification: Les Baisers de Louise Labé." *Romanic Review* 75, no. 1 (1984): 10–24. Rpt. in Alonso and Viennot, *Louise Labé 2005*, 57–70.

—. Préface. *Œuvres complètes*, 7–27.

—. "Le 'Subtils ouvrages' de Louise Labé, ou: quand Pallas devient Arachné." *Etudes littéraires* 20, no. 2 (1987): 43–60.

—. "La préface à la Renaissance: un discours sexué?" *Cahiers de l'association internationale des études françaises* 42 (1990): 121–35.

———, and Julianne Jones Wright. "Les irruptions de Folie: Fonction idéologique du porte-parole dans les *Œuvres* de Louise Labé." *L'Esprit Créateur* 30, no. 4 (1990): 72–84.

———. "Louise Labé et les 'Dames lionnoises': les ambiguités de la censure." In *Le signe et le texte: Etudes sur l'écriture au XVIe siècle en France*, ed. Lawrence D. Kritzman, 13–25. Lexington, KY: French Forum, 1990.

———. "Orphée aux mains des femmes: L'exemple de Louise Labé à la Renaissance." *Versants* 24 (1993): 17–33.

———. *Louise Labé Lyonnaise ou la Renaissance au féminin*. Paris: Honoré Champion, 1997.

Sibona, Chiara. *Le sens qui résonne: une étude sur le sonnet français à travers l'œuvre de Louise Labé.* Ravenna: Longo, 1984.

Tetel, Marcel. "Le luth et la lyre de l'Ecole Lyonnaise." In *Il Rinascimento a Lione*, 951–62. Acts of the 1995 International Congress at Macerata. Rome: Edizioni dell'Ateneo, 1988.

Viennot, Eliane. "La Diffusion du féminisme au temps de Louise Labé." In Alonso and Viennot, *Louise Labé 2005*, 19–36.

Wilson, Dudley B. "La poésie amoureuse de Louise Labé." In Demerson, *Louise Labé*, 17–34. Rpt. in Alonso and Viennot, *Louise Labé 2005*, 181–95.

Winn, Colette H. "La femme écrivain au XVIe siècle: Ecriture et transgression." *Poétique* 84 (1990): 435–52.

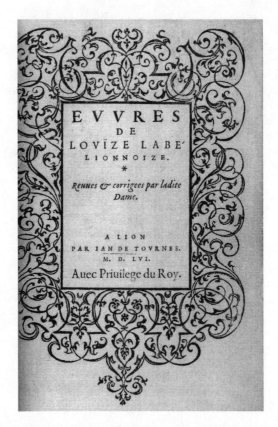

EVVRES

DE

LOVÏZE LABE'

LIONNOIZE.

*

Reuues & corrigees par ladite
Dame.

A LION

PAR IAN DE TOVRNES.

M. D. LVI.

Auec Priuilege du Roy.

Figure 2. Title page from the second edition of Labé's works, "Evvres de Louïze Labé Lionnoize. Reuues & corrigees par ladite Dame" (Gordon 1556.L25). Gordon Collections, Special Collections, University of Virginia Library.

I

PROSE

INTRODUCTION

When first introduced to Louise Labé's volume of complete works, readers may be taken by surprise that the female writer to whom they have likely been drawn by her celebrity as an unapologetic love poet in a man's lyric world actually composed more than three times as many lines of prose as of poetry. The reasons for this gap in familiarity go beyond the plausible arguments that an early modern woman's personal erotic verse may be of more immediate access and appeal than her narrative social and literary commentary — and even that the poetry has sustained its extraordinary afterlife because it ultimately constitutes the pearl of Labé's creative genius. An important point to make at the outset is that Labé's prose is dense, structurally elaborate, and consequently often difficult. Like her literary peers, she strives toward a rhetorical richness frequently reflected in lengthy, convoluted sentences brimming over with enumerations, images, and broadranging allusions — in short, a prose style in keeping with her times, but one that can sometimes intimidate the modern reader.

A related and equally important factor in the relative obscurity of Labé's prose works as compared with her poetry over time is the connection between this rhetorical exuberance—alternately serious and humorous in tone—and the posture and goals of the authorial speaker (in the case of the dedicatory letter) or the characters who take on her voice (in the case of the *Debate*). Even as they come to inscribe the revisionary poetics embodied in her verse, Labé's two prose texts are clearly and openly polemical, passionately addressing the status of women (and men) in the culture and society of her times, and advocating change in social rules, expectations, and prejudices that perpetuate conventional gender roles. Labé's participation via these texts in the thriving public debate known as the *Querelle des femmes* paradoxically did not, for understandable reasons, enhance the public visibility of her

prose during most of the time since her death, inasmuch as the "other voice" adopted in her overtly polemical work (as in that of other women authors) continued to be largely overshadowed by the hegemony of traditional hierarchies. That we are now filling in that gap between knowledge and appreciation of the two (public and private) faces of Louise Labé's work newly empowers the contemporary reader to discover, in the challenging prose writings of a brave yet compassionate social critic, the genesis of a great poet.

DEDICATORY LETTER (EPISTRE DEDICATOIRE)

Since the time has now come, Mademoiselle, when men's harsh laws no longer prevent women from applying themselves to study and learning, it seems to me that those who have the means should take advantage of this well-deserved freedom — so fervently desired by our sex in the past — to pursue them.

[Estant le tems venu, Madamoiselle, que les severes loix des hommes n'empeschent plus les femmes de s'apliquer aus sciences et disciplines: il me semble que celles qui ont la commodité, doivent employer cette honneste liberté, que notre sexe ha autre fois tant desiree, à icelles aprendre. (Pp. 42–43 below)][1]

Thus begins the first part of the dedicatory letter's elaborate opening pronouncement.[2] Declaring in a direct address to her young dedicatee the need for a break with past limitations placed on women's pursuit of learning, Labé simultaneously inaugurates two levels of dialogue: one with her designated sister compatriot from the city of Lyon, and one with the flourishing social debate of the *Querelle* concerning the worth and appropriate role of women.[3] After she proceeds in the rest of her lengthy opening sentence to confront the "wrong" (tort [p. 42 below]) long perpetuated by men in their prohibition of female education, she immediately moves on to broaden the parameters of her challenge so as to encourage women not only to study, but to *write*, thereby offering them the promise of a more durable and organic gift than the "chains, rings, and lavish clothing" (chaines, anneaus, et somptueus habits [p. 42 below]) offered to them as external markers of male attainment. At the same time, she extends the scope of her dialogue to women as a whole with the repeated use of the collective first-person-plural pronoun, to which she will return insistently at subsequent points of her letter: "But the honor that education brings *us* will be entirely *our own*, and cannot be taken away *from us* — neither by a thief's trickery, nor by an enemy's force, nor by the passage of time" (Mais l'honneur que la science *nous* procurera,

sera entierement *notre:* et ne *nous* pourra estre oté, ne par finesse de larron, ne force d'ennemis, ne longueur du tems [p. 42 below; emphasis added]).

Ever conscious of the judgment of her readers, both male and female (as we shall see again in portions of her poetry), Labé then introduces a dual rhetorical strategy that she will exploit to shrewd advantage throughout her prefatory text. In order to moderate the assertiveness of her confrontational opening gesture, she draws back into a humble stance in which she denies any intention of presenting herself as a model to embody this emancipatory cause: "If the heavens had blessed me with a mind intelligent enough to understand whatever it wanted to, I would hold myself up here as an *example,* instead of simply giving advice" (Si j'eusse esté tant favorisee des Cieus, que d'avoir l'esprit grand assez pour comprendre ce dont il ha ù envie, je servirois en cet endroit plus d'*exemple* que d'amonicion [p. 42 below; emphasis added]). If Labé's disavowal here of the "exemplary" status embraced openly in her autobiographical verse functions on one hand as a potential buffer against negative criticism, it also reveals the originality of her place in the feminist polemic, since the dedicatory letter represents the first sixteenth-century French prose document authored *by a woman* in defense or praise of women based primarily *not* on *exempla* (individual examples) of laudable female characters in classical and biblical mythology, or on depictions of idealized Petrarchan stereotypes, but rather on sustained argumentation grounded in current social practice.[4]

Following a brief reinforcement of this deferential posture through passing remarks on the conventionally "acceptable" strand of her youthful education ("being trained in music" [l'exercice de la Musique (p. 42 below)]) and her own intellectual limits ("la rudesse de mon entendement" [p. 42 below]), Labé reassumes a more assertive voice to conclude the first half of her letter, calling upon women at large to push beyond the limits of their traditional homebound roles to assume their rightful place *alongside* men in both public and private matters:

> I can do no more than urge virtuous ladies to raise their minds a bit above their distaffs and spindles, and to dedicate themselves to making the world understand that if we are not made to be in command, we nevertheless should not be scorned as partners, in domestic as in public affairs, by those who rule and demand obedience.
>
> [Je ne puis faire autre chose que prier les vertueuses Dames d'eslever un peu leurs esprits par-dessus leurs quenoilles et fuseaus, et s'employer à faire entendre au monde que si nous ne sommes faites pour commander, si ne devons nous estre desdaignees pour compagnes tant

es afaires domestiques que publiques, de ceus qui gouvernent et se font obeïr. (Pp. 42–43 below)]

Probably the most famous sentence of the entire preface (thanks to its appropriation of the ancient Greek "distaff and spindle" emblem), Labé's complex formulation balances both deferential and confrontational diction in presenting an initial assertion of the principle of male-female reciprocity that informs all of her works.[5] Reciprocity for the author does not imply sameness, and the recommended female uprising from the domestic hearth (already softened by the qualification "a bit" ["un peu"]) pointedly cedes to men the continuing prerogative to lead and to rule, provided that women's active participation in educational, literary, and social affairs is validated rather than dismissed. Such dedicated involvement represents a challenge requiring, as the speaker urges a few lines later, the ongoing mutual solidarity of women themselves: "For this reason, we have to spur one another on to such a worthy undertaking" (Pource, nous faut il animer l'une l'autre à si louable entreprise [p. 42 below]).

This imperative for mutual encouragement invites the reader to contemplate what, precisely, defines the character of the *"virtuous* Ladies" (*vertueuses Dames*) to whom Labé refers — especially given that she employs some form of the term "virtue" three times in this section of the text. Indeed, as confirmed by dictionaries of sixteenth-century French language, *vertu* is a word of multiple resonances and in conventional practice is often attributed along gendered lines, such that "virtue" for women is typically associated with moral goodness, especially chastity, whereas for men it more often carries the connotations of strength, courage, and power, stemming etymologically from the Italian *virtù* and, by extension, from the Latin *virtus*.[6] One of Labé's *coups de force* here is that at the same time as she rhetorically underlines the requisite social acceptability anticipated in her call to "virtuous" women, she suggests by her very call to action that such women are courageous and possess the capacity to empower themselves. And since, as Cathy Yandell has recently argued, there is a crucial link between the early modern notion of female virtue and the ideology of time, Labé's emphasis on this term provides the transition to the second part of her letter, in which she presents her vision and justification for how her "Dames vertueuses" should consider spending their own time.[7]

The consideration of this question leads to a commentary in several stages on the benefits of study, and subsequently of writing, to the individual woman as a representative of the broader community of women:

Yet if there is something else beyond fame and honor to recommend in the study of letters, the *pleasure* it typically provides ought to be an

incentive to *every one of us.* This pleasure is different from other diversions, for when people have gotten as much enjoyment from them as they want, they can boast of nothing except having passed the time. Study, on the contrary, brings with it a *unique inner satisfaction* that stays with us far longer.

[S'il y ha quelque chose recommandable apres la gloire et l'honneur, *le plaisir* que l'estude des lettres ha acoutumé donner *nous* y doit *chacune* inciter: qui est autre que les autres recreations: desquelles quand on en ha pris tant que lon veut, on ne se peut vanter d'autre chose, que d'avoir passé le tems. Mais celle de l'estude laisse un *contentement de soy,* qui nous demeure plus longuement. (Pp. 42–45 below; emphasis added)]

In addition to the emphasis on each individual woman ("chacune") within the female collective ("nous"), another key shift in attention is apparent in this passage: the focus on private *pleasure* rather than on public acclaim. Thus the polemical solicitation (reflected previously in verbs such as *prier* and *animer*) to pursue study and education as vehicles to enact social change gives way to a more personal solicitation (reflected above in the parallel verb *inciter*) to seek through study the longer-lasting self-contentment not yielded by other pastimes (what Labé calls "recreations"— a term suggesting the potential link between enjoyable activity and self-renewal). Indeed, in this change of perspective Labé draws a crucial connection between a woman's intellectual inquiry and the affirmation of her very *selfhood.* She develops this notion of female selfhood and further details how it can be attained by analyzing the particularity and breadth of the pleasure derived from mental exercise.

This analysis involves first a juxtaposition of intellectual pleasure with another category of "recreations"— sensory or sensual pleasures — in terms of their relationship to time: "We take joy in the past, and it serves us better than the present, but the pleasures of the senses immediately slip away and never return, and the memory of them is sometimes as painful as the acts were sweet" (Car le passé nous resjouit, et sert plus que le present: mais les plaisirs des sentimens se perdent incontinent, et ne reviennent jamais, et en est quelquefois la memoire autant facheuse, comme les actes ont esté delectables [pp. 44–45 below]). The core phenomenological problem as Labé conceives it involves the unreliability of memory in recovering and preserving the original affective state associated with sensory experience. Such sensory pleasures, or "voluptez," as she also designates them, are catalysts of *illusory* mental "imprints" of the past and are therefore inadequate sources of genuine self-enrichment or growth: "and no matter how powerful the image *imprinted* in our minds, we still know perfectly well it is merely a *shadow* of the past that misleads and deceives us" (Et quelque imaginacion forte que nous

imprimions en la teste, si connoissons nous bien que ce n'est qu'une *ombre* du passé qui nous abuse et trompe [pp. 44–45; emphasis added]).

This shadowy character of memory leads Labé finally to contrast the mind's self-generated "imprints" of the past with the concrete "imprinting" of thoughts on paper in the act of writing. She argues for writing as the deepest source of intellectual pleasure not only because it builds an archive enabling the recovery of authentic past impressions undistorted by later recollection, but also because it stimulates active evaluation and reexamination of these past impressions through the maturer optic of the present — a fulfilling process by which selfhood is enhanced and achieved: "the judgment that our second impressions allow us to make of our earlier ones repays us with an unparalleled satisfaction" (le jugement que font nos secondes concepcions des premieres, nous rend un singulier contentement [pp. 44–45 below]).[8]

In the selected quotations above, as throughout this portion of the dedicatory letter, Louise Labé's repeated terminology evoking the satisfaction to be derived from study and writing suggests a new conception of pleasure available to women that transcends the spheres of coquetry, seduction, erotic adulation, and domestic contentment to which early modern male writers assigned them.[9] In hinting not so subtly at the transitory, troubling enjoyment of sensual attachments as compared to the enduring pleasure of mental application, the author in her preface figuratively eroticizes the intellectual and creative processes that foster a mutually fulfilling relationship between a woman and the texts she reads and writes — and the dialogue between her past and present ruminations experienced over time. Or as François Rigolot puts it: "This pleasure that the poet possesses in communicating him- or herself to a reader who is perhaps none other than him- or herself would coincide with the desire of a lover to give herself to her beloved" (Ce plaisir qu'a le poète à se communiquer à un lecteur [une lectrice] qui n'est peut-être que lui-même [elle-même] voudrait ne faire qu'un avec le désir qu'a l'amante de se donner à son amant).[10]

The rich theorization of the benefits of writing to private female growth implicitly reengages the hope for female literary production in the public sphere, and as such provides the transition to the concluding section of Labé's letter. Thus toward the end of the panegyric to writing, the predominance of the first-person-plural collective pronoun (*nous*) gives way to the reappearance of the second-person pronoun designating Clémence de Bourges, whom the author addressed specifically at the beginning of her text. The cyclic return to the invocation of her dedicatee in the closing is likewise accompanied by the author's self-referential return to her own writerly endeavor and by the reassumption of a modest, even self-deprecatory stance — a move

designed here in part to neutralize any potential defensive response to the new parameters of female pleasure she has just set forth:

> As for me, both when I first wrote these youthful works, and when I had occasion to look over them again more recently, I was seeking nothing more than a worthwhile pastime and a way to keep from being idle. I never meant for anyone else to see them. But since some of my friends managed to read them without my knowledge and since (how easily we believe those who praise us!) they persuaded me that I ought to make them public, I didn't dare say no to them — although I did threaten to make them drink down half the shame that might come out of it.

> [Quant à moy tant en escrivant premierement ces jeunesses que en les revoyant depuis, je n'y cherchois autre chose qu'un honneste passetems et moyen de fuir oisiveté: et n'avois point intencion que personne que moy les dust jamais voir. Mais depuis que quelcuns de mes amis ont trouvé moyen de les lire sans que j'en susse rien, et que (ainsi comme aisément nous croyons ceus qui nous louent) ils m'ont fait à croire que les devois mettre en lumiere: je ne les ay osé esconduire, les menassant ce pendant de leur faire boire la moitié de la honte qui en proviendroit. (Pp. 44–45 below)]

If Labé's recourse to a humble posture when discussing her own works is a common rhetorical strategy among both male and female early modern writers, it serves nonetheless proactively to forestall attacks by her reading public in a particularly clever way, in that it assigns responsibility for the appearance of her volume to the friends (male and female, given the masculine plural form of the word *amis*) who form a powerful cohort of that very public.[11] Not only does she imply agreement on the part of these readers that by writing she has used her time well, but she includes them as almost organic participants in the assimilation (or "drinking down") of any negative consequences following the publication of her work.[12] She refers to such criticism or scandal by the highly-charged term "honte" (literally, "shame"), which in early modern use frequently serves as a term of social reproach for women who breach conventional codes of propriety. By applying this term in equal measure to herself and to her (male) readers, Labé destabilizes its typical female gendering and in the notion of shared blame finds yet another way to affirm male-female reciprocity. Thus, even as she moves ostensibly to efface herself and her own writing in the dedicatory letter's final sentence by passing the torch of literary production on to her dedicatee, the author

urges us — through the multileveled dialogue begun here with her Lyonnais co-citizen, her female collectivity, her male audience, and even with the process of writing itself — to heed in the *œuvre* to follow the imperatives of her powerful voice.

DEBATE OF FOLLY AND LOVE
(DEBAT DE FOLIE ET D'AMOUR)

The dialogic voice assumes new dimensions in what is by far Labé's longest work and her most challenging in terms of structural and linguistic readability, the *Debate of Folly and Love*. As noted in the volume editor's introduction, the *Debate* features a striking heterogeneity of medieval and Renaissance genres, including allegorical debate, Neoplatonic dialogue and treatise, Erasmian satire, and mythological fable, and a diversity of diction and tone ranging from comedic conversation to high oratory — all incorporated in a five-act drama (five discourses [*discours*], as Labé calls them) in which Olympian characters flesh out and weigh in on the social and literary causes prized by their author.[13] In its key transitional position within Labé's volume, the *Debate* at once mobilizes the polemical concerns presented in the dedicatory letter and reinforces their inseparability from the values and ethos informing the love lyric. As I outline below the overall development of the *Debate*, I will selectively highlight key aspects of this double focus revealed in the action, dialogue, and language of the text.

The Opening Discourse

Discourse 1 stages an inflammatory scene of male-female confrontation between Love and Folly — a confrontation on which all subsequent "acts" of the drama are based, and which can be briefly summarized as follows. As the two title characters arrive quasi-simultaneously at the door of Jupiter's palace to attend a banquet for the gods, Folly pushes ahead of Love to gain entrance first, thereby incensing him and inciting an animated dispute over the worthiness, power, and standing that each of them exercises in the world. When Folly refuses to be intimidated by Love's menacing arguments, in frustration he fires one of his arrows at her, but is foiled again when she escapes his attack by making herself invisible. In retaliation for this attempted violation, Folly puts out Love's eyes and then seals his blindness by applying a bandage received from the Fates that can never be removed.[14]

This scene's dramatic reenactment of the central issues raised in the dedicatory letter is discernible on a number of levels. In a global sense, as Anne Larsen was one of the first to argue, Folly's refusal to back down — first

verbally, then physically — from Love's insults and threats reaffirms the letter's advancement of the female voice itself to address women's goals and capabilities in a man's world that has often done them "wrong." [15] But the reader need only return to the action depicted in the very first exchange between the protagonists to see an actualization of the challenging gestures that in the dedicatory letter alternate with the narrator's more conventionally self-deprecating posture:

> FOLLY: From what I can see, I'll be the last to arrive at Jupiter's banquet, where I believe everyone's expecting me. But I see, too, so it seems, Venus's son, who is just as late as I am. I must get past him, so that no one accuses me of being late and lazy.
> LOVE: Who is this madwoman pushing past me so rudely? [16] What's her big hurry? If I'd seen you, I would have stopped you from getting ahead of me.
> FOLLY: You wouldn't have been able to stop me, young and weak as you are . . .

> [FOLIE: A ce que je voy, je seray la derniere au festin de Jupiter, ou je croy que lon m'atent. Mais je voy, ce me semble, le fils de Venus, qui y va aussi tart que moy. Il faut que je le passe: à fin que lon ne m'apelle tardive et paresseuse.
> AMOUR: Qui est cette fole qui me pousse si rudement? quelle grande háte la presse? Si je t'usse aperçue, je t'usse bien gardé de passer.
> FOLIE: Tu ne m'usses pù empescher, estant si jeune et foible . . .
> (Pp. 46–49 below)]

Folly demonstrates from the outset a perceptive understanding both of her position in the gods' social hierarchy and of what she must do to change it. Indeed, although she knows that she and Cupid are in fact on *equal* footing in this instance, since he is "just as late" as she is, she realizes that it is she, as a woman, who will be negatively stereotyped as late and lazy, and that to change this she must assertively *get past* him. Labé repeats here the same verb (*passer*) that she employs in the dedicatory letter when exhorting her female counterparts to move beyond their distaffs and spindles, so that her own sex might "*surpass* or equal men not only in physical beauty, but in knowledge and virtue" (non en beauté seulement, mais en science et vertu *passer* ou egaler les hommes; emphasis added). Love, on the other hand, already showing his figurative blindness, denies any knowledge whatsoever of Folly's identity, maligning her as "this madwoman" and vowing that he would have blocked her passage if he had seen her — a vow that Folly immediately

refutes, casting her own aspersion on the "young and weak" deity. The crumbling of male-imposed barriers to female advancement is of course the change Labé trumpets at the beginning of her dedicatory letter, and once again the same verb affirming that men's laws no longer "prevent" women's pursuit of study (les severes loix des hommes *n'empeschent plus* les femmes de s'apliquer aus sciences et disciplines; emphasis added) finds its way into Folly's retort at the palace door: "You wouldn't have been able to stop me" (Tu ne m'usses pù *empescher*).

The issues and dynamics introduced in microcosm in this exchange are elaborated throughout the rest of the opening *discours*.[17] Both characters engage in extended verbal sparring to assert their power and authority, Love via shameless self-aggrandizement and repeated misogynist slurs against the goddess, and Folly via the systematic deflation of his puffed-up self-image and by her own appropriation of aggressive male bravado — as when she expounds that she would not be afraid of Cupid "even if [she] had one arm tied behind [her] back" (quand j'aurois un bras lié, si ne te creindrois je gueres [pp. 48–49 below]). A key feature of Love's own misogynist discourse is his ongoing insistence on referring to Folly as "a woman he doesn't even know" (femme *inconnue*; emphasis added) and a conflation of her gender with ignorance, an association suggesting that traditionally dismissive attitude toward female learning that Labé's dedicatory letter seeks to eradicate: "Your youth, your sex, and the way you act already prove you wrong, but even more than that your *ignorance*, which keeps you from recognizing the high rank I hold" (ta jeunesse, ton sexe, ta façon de faire te dementent assez; mais plus ton *ignorance*, qui ne te permet connoitre le grand degré que je tiens [pp. 48–49 below; emphasis added]).[18] Folly, however, turns the tables on Love in respect to the issue of knowledge and ignorance, proposing that his inability to recognize her and his misplaced view of his own grandeur reveal his failure to recognize his own immaturity, that is, to know himself: "you simply don't know yourself for who you are" (te mesconnois bien toymesme [pp. 48–49 below]).

Love's flawed self-knowledge derives in large part from his perceived possession of an autonomy and self-sufficiency unique among gods and men: "But I have no weapons, council, ammunition, or support other than myself" (Mais je n'ay autres armes, conseil, municion, ayde, que moymesme [pp. 50–51 below]). When Folly's refutation of this view incites Love to fire his arrow at her, she counters with an assertion of their *equal* status as celestial deities (I am a goddess, just as you are a god ["Je suis Deesse, comme tu es Dieu" (pp. 52–53 below)])— an equality she verifies by showing that she, like Love, has the power to make herself invisible. Moreover, she exploits this act of disappearance as an illustration of the very *interdependency* they share.

Striving to dismantle Love's narcissistic sense of self-sufficiency, the goddess points out that each of them has a different but indispensable role in causing people to fall in love, Cupid as the shooter of passion's arrows and herself as their director to her desired targets: "You raise your bow and let the arrows fly into the air; but I make them lodge in whatever hearts I want" (Tu lasches l'arc, et gettes les flesches en l'air; mais je les assois aus coeurs que je veus [pp. 52–53 below]). This dramatic depiction of interdependency — a notion that for Labé is a defining factor in any equal relationship — also dramatizes the dedicatory letter's argument that male-female equality does not mean sameness, that men and women may exercise distinct and complementary roles as partners ("compagnes") in society and in life.

Driven by Love's continuing insults and stubborn self-centeredness to put out his eyes — that is, to literalize his metaphoric blindness — Folly declares war on the love god's narcissism in a way that relates back suggestively to issues of perception and recognition raised in Labé's letter. The restrictive portrayal of women as keepers of the hearth and as beneficiaries of male wealth ("chains, rings, and lavish clothing") constitutes a solipsistic gesture in that it paints them as mere reflections of a male privilege that ignores their very otherness.[19] If women are to be known for who they truly are, they must first learn to know themselves, through the labor of study, writing, and self-evaluation that Labé proposes — fundamentally antinarcissistic activities because they aim toward an authentic self-understanding (as against Love's misguided self-absorption) that will promote their capacity to live and work more fruitfully alongside men and women alike.

Folly's concluding act in this crucial first discourse — her application onto Love's now lost eyes of the unremovable bandage made by the Fates — constitutes a powerful example of how solidarity among women can move to realign the patriarchal order, given that not even Jupiter can undo this deed. In moving to dispel Love's illusion of self-sufficiency, Folly in effect joins forces with the Fates (figured mythologically as three women who together weave the threads of human destiny), who themselves have here transformed their "spindles" from an emblem of domestic confinement to an instrument of social resistance and change. Thus, Folly's complicity with the Fates refigures and hyperbolizes in collective form her transgressive opening push past Love at the palace door.

The Intermediary Discourses

Discourses 2, 3, and 4 introduce the remaining cast of characters and function as a transition between the central opening confrontation of the *Debate* and its lengthy final act, in which Love's complaint against Folly is taken up in the celestial court. To review the action briefly, in discourse 2 Cupid

deplores his misadventure to his mother, the goddess of love, Venus, whose predictable maternal outrage adds a new and contrasting female voice to the drama. She, in turn, beseeches Jupiter for revenge in discourse 3, after which the reigning king calls upon Folly to appear alongside Venus so that he can decide in their joint presence how to handle the quarrel. Having determined to bring the matter to trial, he summons Apollo and Mercury to appoint them as the defenders of Love and Folly, respectively, in the legal hearing to begin the following day. Then, as the parties disperse to prepare their arguments, Cupid himself seeks out Jupiter in discourse 4 for a rich and in some ways surprising pretrial discussion.

The presence of Venus in both discourses 2 and 3 adds important new dimensions to the scope of the dispute. First of all, in her exchanges both with her son and with Jupiter, she herself takes on the exclamations of misogynist invective brandished by Love throughout the opening scene, stripping Folly of both divine and human qualities and relegating her to the basest regions of the underworld: "O hateful enemy of all wisdom! O you depraved woman! Goddess unworthy of the name . . . the most wretched thing of them all. . . . She is Folly, the most despicable Fury that hell has ever known!" (O maudite ennemie de toute sapience, ô femme abandonnee, ô à tort nommée Deesse . . . la plus miserable chose au monde. . . . C'est Folie, la plus outrageuse Furie qui onques fut es Enfers [pp. 60–63 below]). Venus's appropriation of this rhetoric intimates in part the displacement of the quarrel into a fight between two women — a displacement dramatizing the specter of female divisiveness that Labé strives to avert not only in the dedicatory letter but in her love poetry as well. In submitting this conflict to Jupiter's patriarchal authority, as Rigolot and Wright's analysis has shown, Venus assumes another rhetorical posture, that of the stereotypically helpless woman whose emotions compromise her very ability to speak: "Since I am the most aggrieved mother in the world, *I can only speak as those who grieve*" (Estant la plus afligee mere du monde, *je ne puis parler, que comme les afligees* [pp. 62–63 below; emphasis added]).[20] As the reader might expect, Folly's rhetoric when called before Jupiter exhibits no such pity-provoking ploy, as she announces herself "ready to respond" (preste à respondre [pp. 62–63 below]) to Cupid's charges; however, she demonstrates a realistic awareness of the more powerful influence of male language, and therefore requests that her defense be handled by Mercury.

Whereas even Folly's submission to male linguistic authority defines her as attuned to the dynamics of the external world, both Love and his mother Venus in their own dialogue fall into the net of narcissistic interiority that in all her works Labé assiduously strives to escape. Declaring himself "fed up

with all of this" (las de toute chose [pp. 58–59 below]) and ready to shoot his remaining arrows at random and give up his bow, Love falls into the same self-absorbed languor that often besieges his own male victims in the Petrarchan lyric tradition. Nor is Venus immune from the solipsistic features of Petrarchan love, as she focuses her lament not on her son's loss but on the deprivation his blindness entails for her: "And thus Folly . . . has the power to rob Venus of the greatest pleasure she had in life — which was to have her son, Love, be able to *look at* her. This was her delight, her desire, her joy. . . . My only source of wealth is my beauty — and what does that matter to a blind man?" (Et donques Folie . . . ha le pouvoir d'oter à Venus le plus grand plaisir qu'elle ust en ce monde: qui estoit quand son fils Amour la *voyoit.* En ce estoit son contentement, son desir, sa felicité. . . . Mon tresor n'est que beauté, de laquelle que chaut il à un aveugle? [pp. 60–61 below; emphasis added]). By designating the authentication of her physical beauty through her son's *visual* admiration as the sole source of her own happiness, the goddess implicitly raises yet again Labé's critique of the objectifying power of the male gaze in the cultural formation and in the literary establishment. This critique will continue to surface in her lyric poetry, both in her occasional satiric refocusing of the female gaze on male physical attributes, and in her overall transformation of the mute female object into a multifaceted speaking subject.[21]

A final element in the mother-son interchange that anticipates discourse 4's conversation between Love and Jupiter is the thorny issue of equality — this time specifically in respect to the realm of love. One result of Cupid's blindness is that he can no longer target the recipients of his arrows so as to perpetuate his ideology of highborn love, an ideology that promotes passion strictly between those of *equal* beauty and breeding — as Venus calls it, "the passion appropriate only to higher souls" (la passion propre aus bons esprits [pp. 58–59 below]).[22] Based paradoxically on a fundamental adherence to class differences or *in*equalities, this popular courtly and Petrarchan notion is thwarted in the *Debate* by Folly's retaliatory attack and will be challenged throughout Labé's poetry, where love is seen not as a restrictive privilege among social equals but as a force to which all humans are susceptible, and thus the great *equalizer* of all individuals.

The approach to the core notions of equality and inequality in love changes pointedly and significantly as Love and Jupiter enter into dialogue in discourse 4. The catalyst of this change is an interesting shift in the postures of the two characters. Jupiter lets down the armor of his mighty image by marveling at Cupid's ongoing popularity among gods and men, as he confesses his own failure to make himself loved despite his many amorous exploits. Cupid, in response, shakes off his lethargy and childish belligerence

by assuming the higher stance of a teacher-philosopher, as he advises the celestial king on two sets of curiously contradictory relational dynamics that determine the development and quality of love among men and women. First, he addresses Jupiter's surprise over why he himself is loved even by the unhappy victims of his arrows: "The true greatness of Love lies in this: when we love someone who treats us badly" (En ce se montre la grandeur d'Amour, quand on ayme celui dont on est mal traité [pp. 66–67 below]). With this statement he evinces the reality of how *unequal* treatment — unyielding adoration by one person despite indifference or rejection by another — can feed love's very intensity and power. Yet almost immediately afterward, Cupid at least ostensibly abandons this dictum in order to instruct Jupiter on a more effective means to win love than the celestial king's typical metamorphoses and forced seductions: "love thrives best when things are equal. It's no more than a yoke that needs to be carried by two well-paired oxen; otherwise the harness will not stay on straight" (Amour se plait de choses egales. Ce n'est qu'un joug, lequel faut qu'il soit porté par deus Taureaus semblables: autrement le harnois n'ira pas droit [pp. 68–69 below]). Having already used the unlikely rustic image of the two oxen, he goes on to recommend that Jupiter descend to earth anonymously without his royal trappings, and assures him that in simply giving love openly and honestly, he will enjoy the fruits of being loved in return: "And then you will feel a kind of satisfaction unlike anything you have known in the past, and you will experience twice the pleasure. For there's every bit as much pleasure to be had in being kissed and loved, as in kissing and loving" (Lors tu sentiras bien un autre contentement, que ceus que tu as uz par le passé: et au lieu d'un simple plaisir, en recevras un double. Car autant y ha il de plaisir à estre baisé et aymé, que de baiser et aymer [pp. 68–69 below]).

What is the reader to make of the troubling dissonance between Cupid's affirmations of both *unequal* treatment and *equal* partnerships as insurers of love? In communicating these mixed messages through the voice of the love god himself, Labé actually engages him in an interrogation of his own mythology that anticipates the revisionary values to be worked out in her poetics. Clearly, Cupid's notion of unequal treatment when applied to lover and beloved defines the classic power dynamics of the Petrarchan tradition, in which the male speaker becomes ever more fixated on the taciturn female object who remains inaccessible to him. In contrast, Cupid's instructive scenario envisioning love as a shared earthly "yoke" through which mutual pleasure proliferates intimates the very subversion of the traditional model that Labé's lyric undertakes — and this on several levels.[23] In its promise to afford the discovery of a different kind of satisfaction and twice as much pleasure,

Cupid's commentary repeats the same charged language used in the dedicatory letter to describe the joys available through the active *mutual* relationship between a woman and her own text. But even more strikingly, in contradiction with his seeming earlier alignment with the Neoplatonic and Petrarchan sublimation of sensuality ("Lust and fire in the loins have nothing, or very little, to do with love" [La lubricité et ardeur de reins n'a rien de commun, ou bien peu, avec Amour"], pp. 68–69 below), Love here illustrates his newfound praise of mutuality by invoking the reciprocal actions of *physical* love: kissing and being kissed. And in a final equivocation on the Petrarchan mythology of the lover's powerlessness (over which Cupid himself reigns), the love god advances the possibility — and desirability — of self-change, if necessary, to gain the love of another person. Love's unlikely advocacy of mutuality, physical passion, and self-empowerment in love thus not only mirrors Labean principles of change but imagines their possible acceptance by the gatekeepers of tradition.

The Closing Discourse

When Jupiter hurriedly ends his conversation with Love by stating that the trial is about to begin, the dialogue moves immediately to discourse 5 and the judicial orations of Apollo and Mercury, whose combined defenses of the two protagonists are more than twice the length of the previous four discourses put together. Although this move marks the rather abrupt end of the shorter theatrical dialogues that facilitate the reader's engagement with the text, the love god's reflections in discourse 4 in fact prepare the transition to the final act in two important ways. First, they signal the move to the more didactic expository style and to the thematic postulations on love that prevail in the speeches of both Apollo and Mercury. But, even more, the surprisingly mixed character of Cupid's lessons on love anticipates the equally surprising linkages between the supposedly opposing arguments and positions of the two defenders. Therefore, just as Folly and Love have both served as mouthpieces for certain of Labé's views, Apollo and Mercury will also share the presentation of her ethos, demonstrating that the author's goal is to reveal the phenomena of gendered relations and human love in their totality and in their numerous ambiguities situated beyond the realm of pure reason. I will review here several of the most salient issues that surface or resurface in the dense and protracted arguments of the closing discourse.

Given the polemical setting, as well as Apollo's and Mercury's identities as the gods of poetry and eloquence, respectively, the thematization of language both as an instrument of power and as a vehicle of self-expression

remains an ongoing motor of the text. Predictably, Apollo reactivates a misogynist perspective concerning Love's confrontation with Folly at the palace gate, focusing, however, not so much on her transgressive actions as on her verbal aggression: "She responds with further *insults not befitting a respectable lady.* Then she starts to *boast,* glorifying herself, and demeaning Love" (Elle lui dit plus *d'injures, qu'il n'apartient à une femme de bien à dire.* De là elle commence *se hausser en paroles,* se magnifier, fait Amour petit [pp. 70–71 below; emphasis added]). Even when evoking her eventual blinding and bandaging of Love, Apollo seems most outraged by her unabashed *telling* of her deed ("She who did the deed says so, proclaims it publicly, and tells her story far and wide" [Celle qui ha fait le coup, le dit, le presche, en fait ses contes par tout (pp. 72–73 below)])— thus figuring her female language as not only inappropriate but dangerous, and, as he says later, apt to the spreading of "nasty gossip" (mauvaises langues [pp. 92–93 below]) about innocent and honorable relationships. The poetry god's allusion to the impact of slanderous language is an excellent example of Labé's own double-edged position in this final discourse. On one hand, of course, through Apollo's negative comments she critiques, as in the dedicatory letter, the silencing of female voices as well as the traditional attribution of gossip to women. This critique will in fact be reenacted in Mercury's oration, where on four separate occasions the switch from third-person to first-person pronouns suggests Folly's will to reassert her own voice, even at the risk of interrupting the male defender whom she herself has chosen.[24] Yet when it comes to Apollo's specific plea that people be free in their comings and goings, unconstrained by fear of false censure and scandal, the author's own social experience and her poetic admonitions against the judgments of her female co-citizens imply her support for his broader position, if not for how he frames it.

In contrast to his deprecation of Folly's female language, Apollo's ongoing defense and praise of Love link his client with all the worthy powers of language in both social interaction and literary creation, since, as the poetry god affirms, "the greatest pleasure there is, after love, is talking about it" (le plus grand plaisir qui soit apres amour, c'est d'en *parler* [pp. 88–89 below; emphasis added]). This aphorism leads to his presentation of the fundamental symbiotic connection between Love (the god *and* the emotional phenomenon) and poetry: "from the very minute men fall in love, they start writing verses " (incontinent que les hommes commencent d'aymer, ils escrivent vers [pp. 88–89 below]). This is another instance in which Labé would align herself with the spirit, if not the letter, of Apollo's dictum. Her very first elegy confirms that falling in love is indeed the catalyst of her verse, but she revises the notion that both the source and the transmitters of poetic power

are inevitably male and that the dynamics of the transmission are fixed. It is no surprise that Apollo goes on to codify the male dominance of love lyric by listing famous poets, of which he selects several for particular notice:

> Cupid has surely won this point: that everyone must sing either of his own passions or those of others, or else embellish his speeches with love, knowing there's nothing else that can make him more popular. Ovid always said that he loved. *In his own language, Petrarch* raised his one great love close to the height of glory given to the poet who portrayed all the passions, customs, behaviors, and natures of all men — that is, Homer himself. When did Virgil ever sing better than when he told of Dido's love?

> [C'est Cupidon qui ha gaigné ce point, qu'il faut que chacun chante ou ses passions, ou celles d'autrui, ou couvre ses discours d'Amour, sachant qu'il n'y ha rien, qui le puisse faire mieus este reçu. Ovide ha tousjours dit qu'il aymoit. *Petrarque en son langage* ha fait sa seule afeccion aprocher à la gloire de celui, qui ha representé toutes les passions, coutumes, façons, et natures de tous les hommes, qui est Homere. Qu'a jamais mieus chanté Virgile, que les amours de la Dame de Carthage? (Pp. 88–89 below; emphasis added)]

After first connecting the ability of poets to recount love with their legitimation and standing in a long lyric tradition, he specifies those who in his view have done this most successfully, and to whom belong the highest reputations: Ovid, Petrarch, Homer, and Virgil. In so doing, as Robert Cottrell has argued, Apollo therefore aligns his client with the most authoritative figures in this tradition, and by extension presents Love as an emblem of conventional male lyric discourse.[25] This male discourse embodied by Love, moreover, is consistently viewed by Apollo as an enduring foundation of stability and harmony in the world: "If you take away Love, everything else is ruined" (Otant l'amour, tout est ruïné [pp. 72–73 below]). What the reader senses at the heart of this exposition is Labé's full awareness of the weight of male literary authority that bears on her own poetic pursuits. Moreover, the highlighting of Petrarch as the sole postclassical poet in Apollo's circle of greatest acclaim — and the artist who eschewed classical Latin to tell his love story in the vernacular — prefigures Labé's overarching goal, especially in the sonnets, to voice the trials and joys of love in her own language, dialoguing with her predecessor as she crafts innovations in his very tradition.

Given Apollo's attribution of poetic creation to Love, and his explicit linking of Love to the Petrarchan heritage, Mercury takes as his task in part

to dismantle the sacred and orderly veneer of this heritage by revealing and analyzing its underlying "follies." This strategy serves to validate the inseparable connection between his client and her accuser at the same time as it formulates the appropriation and revision of Petrarchan lyric enacted in Labé's poetics. Seeking moreover to entertain, rather than to alienate Apollo and the rest of his audience, Mercury presents a series of comical vignettes that satirize the portrayal of unattainable Petrarchan love.

In an opening scenario in which the conventional gender roles remain intact, the figures of the suffering male lover and the hardhearted Petrarchan lady are exaggerated to the point of absurdity:

> There are some men who come across cruel ladies who never show them any mercy. Other women are so tricky that after leading them on to the brink of their goal, they leave them high and dry. What do these men do? After they have sighed, cried, and complained endlessly over a long period of time, some become monks, others flee the country, and still others just give up and die.

> [Il y en ha qui rencontrent Dames cruelles, desquelles jamais on n'obtient merci. Autres sont si rusees, qu'apres les avoir menez jusques aupres du but, les laissent là. Que font ils? Apres avoir longuement soupiré, ploré, et crié, les uns se rendent Moynes: les autres abandonnent le païs: les autres se laissent mourir. (Pp. 118–119 below)]

Here, far from producing the kind of self-knowledge that Apollo posits as the fruit of love, the typically revered melancholy of the Petrarchan male speaker leads only to desperate escape from the world and to self-destruction.

But Mercury is also determined to show that women are equally vulnerable to the crises of unrequited or inaccessible love defining the Petrarchan lyric model:

> Might you think that women are more sensible when they fall in love?. . . But the sad thing is, more often than not, women have such bad luck that the more they love, the less they are loved in return.

> [Et penseriez vous, que les amours des femmes soient de beaucoup plus sages? . . . Mais le mal est, que le plus souvent elles rencontrent si mal: que plus ayment, et moins sont aymees. (Pp. 118–121 below)]

And as he goes on to illustrate in another set of amusing scenarios, women in love can well be subject to the same conflicting emotions and behaviors as their unhappily smitten male counterparts — a disordered state that Mercury seizes the opportunity to satirize by listing the whole gamut of hyperbolic vacillations and contradictions through which the Petrarchan male lover of-

ten describes his situation.²⁶ The god's move to universalize love's madness through a comic critique of the excesses of Petrarchan oxymoronic rhetoric cleverly allows him at the same time to legitimize a woman's right to assume the subject position of the conventional male speaker and to suggest that she might wish to define that position differently.

Indeed, in the closing pages of his oration Mercury raises in broad terms further elements of change that Labé will enact in her love lyric. Premier among them is an interrogation of the very notion of desire, which the god describes as coextensive with love itself:

> *Since Love is desire,* or since whatever it might be, it can't exist without desire, we must acknowledge that once this passion takes hold of a man, it *alters* and *changes* him. For desire ceaselessly *struggles* within the soul, always *stabbing* and arousing it. . . . [T]his *disturbance* of spirit . . . *unsettles* him to the point that *he turns into a totally different person from who he was.*

> [*Estant Amour desir,* ou, quoy que ce soit, ne pouvant estre sans desir: il faut confesser qu'incontinent que cette passion vient saisir l'homme, elle l'*altere* et *immue.* Car le desir incessamment *se demeine* dedens l'ame, la *poingnant* tousjours et resveillant. Cette *agitacion* d'esprit . . . le *malmeine,* en sorte *qu'il se fait tout autre qu'il n'estoit.* (Pp. 122–125 below; emphasis added)]

Through a vocabulary conceiving amatory desire as an involuntary, destabilizing, traumatic force, Mercury continues to challenge Apollo's idealization of Love as the catalyst of order and harmony in the world, insisting once again on the madly disruptive underpinnings from which the Petrarchan model cannot escape. Likewise, while not refuting Love's earlier advocacy of conscious self-change to win the beloved's affection (a principle also advanced by Apollo), Folly's defender presents desire itself as the primal, involuntary, and irrevocable catalyst of change in the soul of the person who loves. The key to whatever self-empowerment might follow, as Mercury goes on to argue, lies in how the lover views and responds to that desire:

> Once he's gotten started, the lover must do two things: he must let it be known he's in love, and *he must make himself loved in return.* For the first, he must have the ability to speak well, but that alone won't suffice. . . . For the most potent charm there is to make yourself loved, is simply to love. Conjure up as many sweet-smelling potions, magical spells, prayers, powders, and stones as you want: *but if you know how to help your own cause by how you reveal and declare your love,* there'll be no need for these extraordinary remedies.

[Estant une fois acheminé, il faut que le poursuivant en amours face deus choses: qu'il donne à connoitre qu'il ayme: et *qu'il se face aymer*. Pour le premier, le bien parler y est bien requis: mais seul ne suffira il. . . . Car le plus grand enchantement , qui soit pour estre aymé, c'est aymer. Ayez tant de sufumigacions, tant de characteres, adjuacions, poudres, et pierres, que voudrez: *mais si savez bien vous ayder, montrant et declarant votre amour:* il n'y aura besoin de ces estranges receptes. (Pp. 124–125 below; emphasis added)]

Mercury's directives in this passage on the "desirable" response to desire point the way to a key divergence that Labé will articulate in respect to the conventional Petrarchan ethos. In contrast to the male lyric speaker who remains trapped by the disruptive desire he tries to expunge as a pervasive moral flaw, Labé will assimilate and celebrate her desire as a defining feature of her very selfhood, transforming herself into the active "pursuer" (le poursuivant) of a relationship based on nurturing interactions between the self and the other. In embracing the idea that desire can indeed serve as a stimulus to enable one better to demonstrate and declare one's love — and this with the hope, if not the certainty, of making oneself loved in return — Labé will transcend the paralysis and self-absorption of the traditional male speaker and will define her journey as an active struggle to valorize and seek the joys of mutual love.

As shown in the intricately interwoven arguments of Apollo and Mercury, in Love's mixed verbal messages and Folly's paradoxical verbal wisdom, and in the physical aftermath of their dispute, the *Debate* as a whole seems to hinge, finally, on representations of the values of equality, reciprocity, and interdependency that motivate Labé's entire literary oeuvre. It is most fitting, then, that Jupiter's climactic pronouncement in the trial, in lieu of a definitive verdict, elects to perpetuate for an indefinite period of time the inevitable interdependency that Love and Folly share: "we order you to live together in peace, without hurting one another. Since Love is blind, Folly will be his guide, and will lead him wherever he wishes" (vous commandons vivre amiablement ensemble, sans vous outrager l'un l'autre. Et guidera Folie l'aveugle Amour, et le conduira par tout ou bon lui semblera [pp. 130–131 below]). But still, this imposed inseparability is not only provisional but ambiguous, for if Love and Folly are now ordered to share the very "yoke" that Love himself advocated as a means to enhance Jupiter's love relationships, the dynamics of this sharing are not entirely clear, and thus defy definitive rendering in English. Folly clearly will be the guide, but while as translator I have opted to choose Love as the navigator, it is nonetheless the case that

the original French indirect pronoun (*lui*) could apply to either character, and so it ultimately remains uncertain who will direct the path of the journey.[27] As such this final image of Love and Folly inextricably joined, commanded to face an indeterminate future with the balance of power not totally resolved, purposely defies any simplistic understanding of male-female equality and interdependency whether in society or in life, and shows that Labé's own journey into the future is informed and enriched by the ongoing challenges and ambiguities of human connections.

PROSE TRANSLATOR'S NOTE

The journey culminating in this new translation of Louise Labé's prose works has been a long and challenging one. Like most readers, I was first attracted to Labé's writings through her poetry, and given my focus on the early modern French lyric, I began to include her work, in the original French language, in the very first courses I taught on Renaissance poetry — although in my own university studies, I had been exposed only to the traditional male-authored canon. As I went on to develop my teaching and my own critical writing, my initial focus was on Labé's remarkable dialogue with the Petrarchan and Neoplatonic traditions in her sonnets. Then, as the idea took shape to extend the parameters of my work on Labé, I realized that the most enlightening approach to her 1555 volume would be to address in equal depth both her prose and her poetic production, this in order to explore both the variety and the internal coherence of her project and ethos.

In pursuing my own study, I found that I faced a substantial learning curve to reach a comfortable command of Labé's original French prose texts, and most especially of her *Debate of Folly and Love*. As with many other early modern French prose works, the length, density, and allusiveness of many of Labé's sentences, and the grammatical, syntactical, and lexical problems they pose in the evolving French of the sixteenth century, made multiple rereadings crucial — simply to understand the crux of what was being said, not to speak of analyzing its rhetorical, thematic, or social implications. Moreover, although I had some success with the shorter, more focused text of the dedicatory letter, my experiences of trying to teach portions of the *Debate* in the original French confirmed that it was very difficult for students to engage with the text. My students' problem in fact echoed my own in the earlier stages of my study: how can the reader — especially the more general reader — best extract and appreciate the richness of this work when the obstacles to readability are sometimes significant?

Not surprisingly, I came to the conclusion that for the Anglophone public, in addition to critical scholarship, translation is the other close to indispensable resource for the understanding of Labé's prose works — not only for those English speakers who do not read French, but also for the great majority of those who do. Indeed, without minimizing the privilege retained by the original text, for many native English readers with varying levels of training and competency in French, reading Labé's works in translation, side by side with the original French, will produce the most productive and satisfying learning experience.

By no means translated as widely as her sonnets, Labé's prose has nevertheless not been neglected by previous translators. The very first English translation of the *Debate*, by Robert Greene, appeared in England in 1584. Although it translates very loosely less than half of Labé's original text, it has historical importance, demonstrating that the *Debate* enjoyed considerable international interest and visibility in the years following its publication, despite the subsequent lack of attention it received as compared with the sonnets. Another, more literal, but minimally annotated translation of the entire *Debate* was published in England in 1925 by Edward Marion Cox. The most recent and far more accomplished translations of Labé's *Debate* and dedicatory letter are those by Edith Farrell, in the only previous edition of Labé's *Complete Works* in English (1986), and Anne-Marie Bourbon, in her dual language edition of the prose works only (2000). Jeanne Prine's translation of the dedicatory letter published along with a 1987 essay on Labé has also been circulated widely.

Vis-à-vis these most recent English versions, I undertook my own translation in two broad stages. I drafted a preliminary version without any concurrent consultation of the previous translations, this to insure a spontaneous, nonbiased response to the original texts. Working only with the Cotgrave and Huguet sixteenth-century French dictionaries and the standard Robert dictionary at this stage, I focused on locating and resolving points where diction and/or syntax seriously problematize basic comprehension, and on gaining a critical sense of the larger-scale rhetorical and structural issues posed for the translator, such as achieving the appropriate balance between oratorical and popular registers of diction and tone at play in the works. At this point, I made two basic decisions about the material presentation of the English text. First, given the lack of any paragraph breaks whatsoever in the expository portions of Labé's prose (the entire dedicatory letter, the entire fifth discourse of the *Debate*, and segments of the dialogues in the other four discourses), I decided to insert them, following Bourbon, Farrell, and Prine — although the positioning of my own paragraph breaks

does not always correspond to theirs. In order to facilitate a side-by-side reading of Labé's original text and my translation, bracketed paragraph symbols [¶] have been inserted in the French that can be matched up with corresponding paragraph indents in the English. Second, I decided, with Farrell, not to follow Labé's voluminous penchant for capitalizations and to use lower-case spellings except for proper names and in specific circumstances explained in the notes. Good arguments can certainly be made for one decision or the other, but as I moved on through my work on the *Debate*, I felt a certain ponderousness and artificiality in capitalizing multiple items in lists of such referents as animals, entertainments, and professions.

In preparing my second and final draft, I added all annotations, including both historical/mythological references and remarks on specific translation issues posed by the text such as ambiguous or missing grammatical referents, odd tense structures, and selected gender-specific or other polyvalent vocabulary. I also studied carefully the translations by Bourbon, Farrell, and Prine. Having by then confronted on my own the challenge of translating Labé's prose not only accurately but in readable fashion, I found that my respect for the work of these predecessors had grown deeper. I dialogue with them frequently in my notes, and my own final product owes debts of acknowledgment to all of them. With the model of their work before me, I have strived to determine, within textually justifiable bounds, how I could make the English version of these texts not only more accurate and idiomatic but simply more fun to read. I hope that the riches of Labé's lesser-known prose will come to resonate for the twenty-first-century reader in harmony with the riches of her very well-known verse, and that experiencing the whole will bring the "double pleasure" she prizes in both major facets of her work.

Deborah Lesko Baker

A M.C.D.B.L.

Estant le tems venu, Madamoiselle, que les severes loix des hommes n'empeschent plus les femmes de s'apliquer aus sciences et disciplines: il me semble que celles qui ont la commodité, doivent employer cette honneste liberté, que notre sexe ha autre fois tant desiree, à icelles aprendre: et montrer aus hommes le tort qu'ils nous faisoient en nous privant du bien et de l'honneur qui nous en pouvoit venir: Et si quelcune parvient en tel degré, que de pouvoir mettre ses concepcions par escrit, le faire songneusement et non dédaigner la gloire, et s'en parer plustot que de chaines, anneaus, et somptueus habits: lesquels ne pouvons vrayement estimer notres, que par usage. Mais l'honneur que la science nous procurera, sera entierement notre: et ne nous pourra estre oté, ne par finesse de larron, ne force d'ennemis, ne longueur du tems. [¶] Si j'eusse esté tant favorisee des Cieus, que d'avoir l'esprit grand assez pour comprendre ce dont il ha ù envie, je servirois en cet endroit plus d'exemple que d'amonicion. Mais ayant passé partie de ma jeunesse à l'exercice de la Musique, et ce qui m'a resté de tems l'ayant trouvé court pour la rudesse de mon entendement, et ne pouvant de moymesme satisfaire au bon vouloir que je porte à notre sexe, de le voir non en beauté seulement, mais en science et vertu passer ou egaler les hommes: je ne puis faire autre chose que prier les vertueuses Dames d'eslever un peu leurs esprits par-dessus leurs quenoilles et fuseaus, et s'employer à faire entendre au monde que si nous ne sommes faites pour commander, si ne devons nous estre desdaignees pour compagnes tant es afaires domestiques que publiques, de ceus qui gouvernent et se font obeïr. Et outre la reputacion que notre sexe en recevra, nous aurons valù au publiq, que les hommes mettront plus de peine et d'estude aus sciences vertueuses, de peur qu'ils n'ayent honte de voir preceder celles, desquelles ils ont pretendu estre tousjours superieurs quasi en tout. Pource, nous faut il animer l'une l'autre à si louable entreprise: De laquelle ne devez eslongner ny espargner votre esprit, jà de plusieurs et diverses graces acompagné: ny votre jeunesse, et autres faveurs de fortune, pour aquerir cet honneur que les lettres et sciences ont acoutumé porter aus personnes qui les suyvent. [¶] S'il y ha quelque chose recommandable apres la gloire et l'honneur, le plaisir que l'estude des lettres ha acoutumé donner nous y doit chacune inciter: qui est autre que les autres recreations: desquelles quand on en ha pris tant que lon veut, on ne se peut vanter d'autre chose, que d'avoir passé le tems. Mais celle de l'estude laisse un contentement de soy, qui nous demeure plus longuement. Car le passé nous resjouit, et sert plus que le pre-

DEDICATORY LETTER

TO M.C.D.B.L.[28]

Since the time has now come, Mademoiselle, when men's harsh laws no longer prevent women from applying themselves to study and learning, it seems to me that those who have the means should take advantage of this well-deserved freedom — so fervently desired by our sex in the past — to pursue them, and to show men how wrong they were to deprive us of the benefit and recognition these things might have given us.[29] And if any of us succeeds to the point where she can put her ideas down in writing, she should do it seriously and not disdain fame, but adorn herself with it, rather than with chains, rings, and lavish clothing, all of which we cannot truly consider our own except by social custom.[30] But the honor that education brings us will be entirely our own, and cannot be taken away from us — neither by a thief's trickery, nor by an enemy's force, nor by the passage of time.

If the heavens had blessed me with a mind intelligent enough to understand whatever it wanted to, I would hold myself up here as an example, instead of simply giving advice. But because I spent part of my youth being trained in music, and found the time left over to be too brief to apply my limited understanding, I cannot carry out on my own the sincere wish I have for our sex, to see it surpass or equal men not only in physical beauty, but in knowledge and virtue.[31] I can do no more than urge virtuous ladies to raise their minds a bit above their distaffs and spindles, and to dedicate themselves to making the world understand that if we are not made to be in command, we nevertheless should not be scorned as partners, in domestic as in public affairs, by those who rule and demand obedience.[32] Beyond the acclaim our sex will receive, we will benefit the public good, since men will put more effort and study into valuable domains of knowledge in order to avoid the shame of seeing themselves surpassed by women, over whom they have always claimed to be superior in almost everything. For this reason, we have to spur one another on to such a worthy undertaking. You must not abandon or be deterred from this goal, and you should thus devote your mind, already endowed with so many qualities, your youth, and whatever other gifts fortune has given you to obtaining the honor that letters and learning generally bring to people who pursue them.

Yet if there is something else beyond fame and honor to recommend in the study of letters, the pleasure it typically provides ought to be an incentive to every one of us. This pleasure is different from other diversions, for when people have gotten as much enjoyment from them as they want, they

sent: mais les plaisirs des sentimens se perdent incontinent, et ne reviennent jamais, et en est quelquefois la memoire autant facheuse, comme les actes ont esté delectables. Davantage les autres voluptez sont telles, que quelque souvenir qui en vienne, si ne nous peut il remettre en telle disposicion que nous estions: Et quelque imaginacion forte que nous imprimions en la teste, si connoissons nous bien que ce n'est qu'une ombre du passé qui nous abuse et trompe. [¶] Mais quand il avient que mettons par escrit nos concepcions, combien que puis apres notre cerveau coure par une infinité d'afaires et incessamment remue, si est ce que long tems apres, reprenans nos escrits, nous revenons au mesme point, et à la mesme disposicion ou nous estions. Lors nous redouble notre aise: car nous retrouvons le plaisir passé qu'avons ù ou en la matiere dont escrivions, ou en l'intelligence des sciences ou lors estions adonnez. Et outre ce, le jugement que font nos secondes concepcions des premieres, nous rend un singulier contentement. Ces deus biens qui proviennent d'escrire vous y doivent inciter, estant asseuree que le premier ne faudra d'acompagner vos escrits, comme il fait tous vos autres actes et façons de vivre. Le second sera en vous de le prendre, ou ne l'avoir point: ainsi que ce dont vous escrirez vous contentera. [¶] Quant à moy tant en escrivant premierement ces jeunesses que en les revoyant depuis, je n'y cherchois autre chose qu'un honneste passetems et moyen de fuir oisiveté: et n'avois point intencion que personne que moy les dust jamais voir. Mais depuis que quelcuns de mes amis ont trouvé moyen de les lire sans que j'en susse rien, et que (ainsi comme aisément nous croyons ceus qui nous louent) ils m'ont fait à croire que les devois mettre en lumiere: je ne les ay osé esconduire, les menassant ce pendant de leur faire boire la moitié de la honte qui en proviendroit. [¶] Et pource que les femmes ne se montrent volontiers en publiq seules, je vous ay choisie pour me servir de guide, vous dediant ce petit euvre, que ne vous envoye à autre fin que pour vous acertener du bon vouloir lequel de long tems je vous porte, et vous inciter et faire venir envie en voyant ce mien euvre rude et mal bati, d'en mettre en lumiere un autre qui soit mieus limé et de meilleure grace.

Dieu vous maintienne en santé. De Lion ce 24. Juillet 1555.
Votre humble amie Louïze Labé.

can boast of nothing except having passed the time. Study, on the contrary, brings with it a unique inner satisfaction that stays with us far longer.[33] We take joy in the past, and it serves us better than the present, but the pleasures of the senses immediately slip away and never return, and the memory of them is sometimes as painful as the acts were sweet. Besides this, other sensual pleasures are such that whatever memory we have of them cannot put us back in our previous state of mind; and no matter how powerful the image imprinted in our minds, we still know perfectly well it is merely a shadow of the past that misleads and deceives us.

But when we happen to put our thoughts down in writing — even though afterward our mind races through endless distractions and never stops moving — by going back much later to what we wrote, we can still recapture the moment and state of mind we were in before. Then we experience twice the enjoyment, for we rediscover the pleasure we had in the past, either in the subject we were writing about, or in our understanding of the fields of knowledge we were studying at the time. And beyond this, the judgment that our second impressions allow us to make of our earlier ones repays us with an unparalleled satisfaction. These two benefits attainable through writing should inspire you, for you can rest assured that the first one will not fail to go hand in hand with what you write, just as it does with all your other actions and your entire way of life. As for the second one, it will be up to you whether to take or leave it, depending on how happy you are with what you write.

As for me, both when I first wrote these youthful works, and when I had occasion to look over them again more recently, I was seeking nothing more than a worthwhile pastime and a way to keep from being idle. I never meant for anyone else to see them. But since some of my friends managed to read them without my knowledge and since (how easily we believe those who praise us!) they persuaded me that I ought to make them public, I didn't dare say no to them — although I did threaten to make them drink down half the shame that might come out of it.

And because women are reluctant to appear in public alone, I have chosen you as my guide and dedicate this little book to you. I send it with no other goal than to assure you of the good will that I have long had toward you, and to instill in you, after seeing this crude and badly constructed work of mine, the desire to produce another that may be more polished and more elegant.

May God keep you in good health. From Lyon, on this 24th day of July, 1555.
Your humble friend, Louise Labé

DEBAT DE FOLIE ET D'AMOUR

ARGUMENT

Jupiter faisoit un grand festin, où estoit commandé à tous les Dieus se trouver. Amour et Folie arrivent en mesme instant sur la porte du Palais: laquelle estant jà fermée, et n'ayant que le guichet ouvert, Folie voyant Amour jà prest à mettre un pied dedens, s'avance et passe la premiere. Amour se voyant poussé, entre en colere: Folie soutient lui apartenir de passer devant. Ils entrent en dispute sur leurs puissances, dinitez et préseances. Amour ne la pouvant veincre de paroles, met la main à son arc, et lui lasche une flesche, mais en vain: pource que Folie soudein se rend invisible: et se voulant venger, óte les yeus à Amour. Et pour couvrir le lieu où ils estoient, lui mit un bandeau, fait de tel artifice, qu'impossible est lui oter. Venus se pleint de Folie, Jupiter veut entendre leur diferent. Apolon et Mercure debatent le droit de l'une et l'autre partie. Jupiter les ayant longuement ouiz, en demande l'opinion aus Dieus: puis prononce sa sentence.

	FOLIE,	AMOUR,
Les personnes:	VENUS,	JUPITER,
	APOLON,	MERCURE.

DISCOURS I

FOLIE: A ce que je voy, je seray la derniere au festin de Jupiter, ou je croy que lon m'atent. Mais je voy, ce me semble, le fils de Venus, qui y va aussi tart que moy. Il faut que je le passe: à fin que lon ne m'apelle tardive et paresseuse.

THE DEBATE OF FOLLY AND LOVE

ARGUMENT

Jupiter[34] was hosting a grand banquet that all the gods were required to attend. Love[35] and Folly[36] arrive at the very same moment at the gates of the palace, where the main door is already closed, leaving open only a small side entrance.[37] Observing Love about to step inside, Folly moves past him and goes in first. Seeing himself pushed aside, Love gets angry: yet Folly continues to insist on her right to enter first. The two of them start arguing about their respective powers, rank, and authority. Unable to make her back down with words, Love takes up his bow and shoots an arrow at her, but to no avail, for Folly suddenly makes herself invisible and, seeking revenge, puts out Love's eyes. And further, to cover up the place where his eyes were, she applies a bandage devised so ingeniously that it is impossible for him to remove it. Venus[38] brings a complaint against Folly; Jupiter agrees to give their dispute a hearing. Apollo[39] and Mercury[40] debate the respective cases of the two sides. After listening to them both at length, Jupiter asks the opinion of the other gods and then pronounces his judgment.

	FOLLY,	LOVE,
The characters:	VENUS,	JUPITER,
	APOLLO,	MERCURY

DISCOURSE 1

FOLLY: From what I can see, I'll be the last to arrive at Jupiter's banquet, where I believe everyone's expecting me. But I see, too, so it seems, Venus's son, who is just as late as I am. I must get past him, so that no one accuses me of being late and lazy.

47

AMOUR: Qui est cette fole qui me pousse si rudement? quelle grande háte la presse? si je t'usse aperçue, je t'usse bien gardé de passer.

FOLIE: Tu ne m'usses pù empescher, estant si jeune et foible. Mais à Dieu te command', je vois devant dire que tu viens tout à loisir.

AMOUR: Il n'en ira pas ainsi: car avant que tu m'eschapes, je te donneray à connoitre que tu ne te dois atacher à moy.

FOLIE: Laisse moy aller, ne m'arreste point: car ce te sera honte de quereler avec une femme. Et si tu m'eschaufes une fois, tu n'auras du meilleur.

AMOUR: Quelles menasses sont ce cy? je n'ay trouvé encore personne qui m'ait menassé que cette fole.

FOLIE: Tu montres bien ton indiscrecion, de prendre en mal ce que je t'ay fait par jeu: et te mesconnois bien toymesme, trouvant mauvais que je pense avoir du meilleur si tu t'adresses à moy. Ne vois tu pas que tu n'es qu'un jeune garsonneau? de si foible taille que quand j'aurois un bras lié, si ne te creindrois je gueres.

AMOUR: Me connois tu bien?

FOLIE: Tu es Amour, fils de Venus.

AMOUR: Comment donques fais tu tant la brave aupres de moy, qui, quelque petit que tu me voyes, suis le plus creint et redouté entre les Dieus et les hommes? et toy femme inconnue, oses tu te faire plus grande que moy? ta jeunesse, ton sexe, ta façon de faire te dementent assez; mais plus ton ignorance, qui ne te permet connoitre le grand degré que je tiens.

FOLIE: Tu trionfes de dire. Ce n'est à moy à qui tu dois vendre tes coquilles. Mais di moy, quel est ce grand pouvoir dont tu te vantes?

AMOUR: Le ciel et la terre en rendent témoignage. Il n'y ha lieu ou n'aye laissé quelque trofee. Regarde au ciel tous les sieges des Dieus, et t'interrogue si quelcun d'entre eus s'est pù eschaper de mes mains. Commence au vieil Saturne, Jupiter, Mars, Apolon, et finiz aus Demidieus, Satires, Faunes et Silvains. Et n'auront honte les Deesses d'en confesser quelque chose. Et ne m'a Pallas espouventé de son bouclier: mais ne l'ay voulu interrompre de ses sutils ouvrages, ou jour et nuit elle s'employe. Baisse toy en terre, et di si tu trouveras gens de marque, qui ne soient ou ayent esté des miens. Voy en la furieuse mer, Neptune et ses Tritons, me prestans obeïssance. Penses tu que les infernaus s'en exemptent? ne les áy je fait sortir de leurs abimes, et venir espouven-

LOVE: Who is this madwoman[41] pushing past me so rudely? What's her big hurry? If I'd seen you, I would have stopped you from getting ahead of me.

FOLLY: You wouldn't have been able to stop me, young and weak as you are. So goodbye now, I'm going in to say that you're arriving at your own leisure.

LOVE: Oh no you won't, because before you get away from me, I'll show you that you mustn't meddle with me.

FOLLY: Let me go, and don't try to stop me, for it would be shameful of you to pick a fight with a woman. And if you wind up making me mad, you'll regret it.

LOVE: What kind of threats are these? I've never met anyone who has threatened me except this madwoman.

FOLLY: You're really showing how misguided you are to take so badly what I did to you in fun. You simply don't know yourself for who you are if you can't accept that I will have the upper hand if you get in my way. Don't you see that you're just a little boy — so puny in size that I would hardly be afraid of you even if I had one arm tied behind my back?

LOVE: Do you know who I am?

FOLLY: You are Love, the son of Venus.

LOVE: So how is it that you act so boldly in front of me, when — however small I may seem to you — I am the most feared and dreaded among gods and men? And you, a woman I don't even know, dare to consider yourself greater than me? Your youth, your sex, and the way you act already prove you wrong, but even more than that your ignorance, which keeps you from recognizing the high rank I hold.

*Il est homme.
ta femme
incomnu.*

FOLLY: You talk a good game. Don't try and strut your stuff with me.[42] But tell me then, what is this great power you're bragging about?

LOVE: Heaven and earth are my witnesses. There's not a single place where I haven't left my mark. Look at all the seats of the gods in heaven, and ask yourself if any one of them has been able to escape my grasp. Begin with old Saturn, Jupiter, Mars, Apollo and move right on down to the demigods, the satyrs, the fauns, and the sylvans.[43] The goddesses, too, won't be ashamed to admit it. Even Pallas didn't terrify me with her shield, but I decided not to interrupt the careful weaving to which she devotes herself day and night.[44] Go on down to earth, and tell me if you find any people of distinction who are not or have not been under my sway. Observe in the raging seas how Neptune and his Tritons obey me.[45] Do you think the gods of the underworld are

ter les humains, et ravir les filles à leurs meres, quelques juges qu'ils soient de telz forfaits et transgressions faites contre les loix? [¶] Et à fin que tu ne doutes avec quelles armes je fay tant de prouesses, voila mon Arc seul et mes flesches, qui m'ont fait toutes ces conquestes. Je n'ay besoin de Vulcan qui me forge de foudres, armet, escu, et glaive. Je ne suis acompagné de Furies, Harpies et tourmenteurs de monde, pour me faire creindre avant le combat. Je n'ay que faire de chariots, soudars, hommes darmes et grandes troupes de gens: sans lesquelles les hommes ne trionferoient la bas, estant d'eus si peu de chose, qu'un seul (quelque fort qu'il soit et puissant) est bien empesché alencontre de deus. Mais je n'ay autres armes, conseil, municion, ayde, que moy-mesme. Quand je voy les ennemis en campagne, je me presente avec mon Arc: et laschant une flesche les mets incontinent en route: et est aussi tot la victoire gaignee, que la bataille donnee.

FOLIE: J'excuse un peu ta jeunesse, autrement je te pourrois à bon droit nommer le plus presomptueus fol du monde. Il sembleroit à t'ouir que chacun tienne sa vie de ta merci: et que tu sois le vray Signeur et seul souverein tant en ciel qu'en terre. Tu t'es mal adressé pour me faire croire le contraire de ce que je say.

AMOUR: C'est une estrange façon de me nier tout ce que chacun confesse.

FOLIE: Je n'ay afaire du jugement des autres: mais quant à moy, je ne suis si aisee à tromper. Me penses tu de si peu d'entendement, que je ne connoisse à ton port, et à tes contenances, quel sens tu peus avoir? Et me feras tu passer devant les yeus, qu'un esprit leger comme le tien, et ton corps jeune et flouet, soit dine de telle signeurie, puissance et autorité, que tu t'atribues? Et si quelques aventures estranges, qui te sont avenues, te deçoivent, n'estime pas que je tombe en semblable erreur, sachant tresbien que ce n'est par ta force et vertu, que tant de miracles soient avenuz au monde: mais par mon industrie, par mon moyen et diligence: combien que tu ne me connoisses. Mais si tu veus un peu tenir moyen en ton courrous, je te feray connoitre en peu d'heure ton arc, et tes flesches, ou tant tu te glorifies, estre plus molz que paste, si je n'ay bandé l'arc, et trempé le fer de tes flesches.

any exception? Haven't I made them rise up from the depths to come terrify human beings, and snatch daughters away from their mothers, despite the fact that they themselves are the judges for such crimes and offenses committed against the law?[46]

And just so there's no doubt in your mind about the weapons I use to carry out such deeds, here are my bow and my arrows, all I ever needed to accomplish all these feats. I don't need Vulcan to forge me thunderbolts, breastplates, shields, and swords.[47] I don't surround myself with Furies, Harpies, or avengers to make myself feared even before battle.[48] I have no use for chariots, soldiers, men at arms, and impressive battle troops — without which mere men could never triumph, since each man alone (no matter how strong and powerful he might be) is unlikely to succeed when going up against two of his counterparts. But I have no weapons, council, ammunition, or support other than myself. When I see the enemy take the field, I come on with my bow, and by shooting just one arrow I set them all to flight, so my victory's won as soon as the battle begins.

FOLLY: I'm bearing with you because of your youth; otherwise I'd have every right to call you the most arrogant fool in the world. To hear you talk, it would appear that everyone's life is at your mercy, and that you are the true Lord and supreme ruler of heaven and earth. You're badly mistaken if you think you can make me believe the opposite of what I know is true.

LOVE: How strange to deny me what everyone else accepts.

FOLLY: I have nothing to do with the opinion of others, but, as for me, I'm not so easy to fool. Do you think I'm not smart enough to know from your appearance and attitude what kind of person you are? And that you could convince me, with a mind as silly as yours and with such a young, frail body, that you deserve all the control, power, and authority you take credit for? And if some bizarre adventures you've had delude you, don't imagine that I'll fall into the same trap. For I know full well it's not by your strength and power that so many miracles have happened in the world, but rather by my own ingenuity, skill, and diligence — despite the fact that you don't know me.[49] But if you'd like to keep testing me with your anger, I'll soon prove to you that the bow and arrows you show off to brag about yourself so much are softer than wet noodles, if I myself haven't tightened the bow and tempered the tips of your arrows.

AMOUR: Je croy que tu veus me faire perdre pacience. Je ne sache jamais que personne ait manié mon arc, que moy: et tu me veus faire à croire, que sans toy je n'en pourrois faire aucun effort. Mais puis qu'ainsi est que tu l'estimes si peu, tu en feras tout à cette heure la preuve.

Folie se fait invisible, tellement, qu'Amour ne la peut assener.

AMOUR: Mais qu'es tu devenue? comment m'es tu eschapee? Ou je n'ay sù t'ofenser, pour ne te voir, ou contre toy seule ha rebouché ma flesche: qui est bien le plus estrange cas qui jamais m'avint. Je pensoy estre seul d'entre les Dieus, qui me rendisse invisible à eus mesmes quand bon me sembloit: Et maintenant ay trouvé qui m'a esbloui les yeus. Aumoins di moy, quinconque sois, si à l'aventure ma flesche t'a frapee, et si elle t'a blessee.

FOLIE: Ne t'avoy je bien dit, que ton arc et tes flesches n'ont effort, que quand je suis de la partie. Et pourautant qu'il ne m'a plu d'estre navree, ton coup ha esté sans effort. Et ne t'esbahis si tu m'as perdue de vuë, car quand bon me semble, il n'y ha œil d'Aigle ou de serpent Épidaurien, qui me sache apercevoir. Et ne plus ne moins que le Cameleon, je pren quelquefois la semblance de ceus aupres desquelz je suis.

AMOUR: A ce que je voy, tu dois estre quelque sorciere ou enchanteresse. Es tu point quelque Circe, ou Medee, ou quelque Fée?

FOLIE: Tu m'outrages tousjours de paroles: et n'a tenu à toy que ne l'aye esté de fait. Je suis Deesse, comme tu es Dieu: mon nom est Folie. Je suis celle qui te fay grand, et abaisse à mon plaisir. Tu lasches l'arc, et gettes les flesches en l'air; mais je les assois aus cœurs que je veus. Quand tu te penses plus grand qu'il est possible d'estre, lors par quelque petit despit je te renge et remets avec le vulgaire. Tu t'adresses contre Jupiter: mais il est si puissant, et grand, que si je ne dressois ta main, si je n'avoy bien trempé ta flesche, tu n'aurois aucun pouvoir sur lui. [¶] Et quand toy seul ferois aymer, quelle seroit ta gloire si je ne faisois paroitre cet amour par mille invencions? Tu as fait aymer Jupiter: mais je l'ay fait transmuer en Cigne, en Taureau, en Or, en Aigle: en danger des plumassiers, des loups, des larrons, et chasseurs. Qui fit prendre Mars au piege avec ta mere, si non moy, qui l'avois

LOVE: I think you want me to lose my patience. I've never known anyone else to handle my bow but me, yet you want to make me believe that without you I couldn't do anything with it at all. And since you show so little respect for its power, I'll prove it to you right now.

Folly makes herself invisible, so that Love can't strike her.

LOVE: But where in the world have you disappeared to? How did you escape from me? Either I couldn't strike you because I couldn't see you, or else you're the only one ever to have blocked my arrow, which is the most incredible thing that's ever happened to me. I thought that I alone among the gods could make myself invisible to them at will, and now I've come across someone who's shocked my very eyes. Tell me, at least, whoever you are, if by any chance my arrow hit you, and if it wounded you.

FOLLY: Didn't I already tell you that your bow and arrows can't do anything unless I intervene? And since I didn't wish to be wounded, your attack had no effect at all. Don't be surprised you lost sight of me, for whenever I think it's an advantage to be invisible, neither the eye of an eagle nor the serpent of Epidaurus can catch a glimpse of me.[50] And just like the chameleon, at times I can assume the appearance of those around me.

[margin handwritten note: Elle est mystérieuse]

LOVE: From what I can tell, you must be some type of witch or enchantress. Are you perhaps someone like Circe or Medea, or some kind of fairy?[51]

FOLLY: You keep hurting me with your words, and if it had been up to you, you would have hurt me physically. I am a goddess, just as you are a god, and my name is Folly. I'm the one who makes you great or cuts you down to size, as I please. You raise your bow and let the arrows fly into the air; but I make them lodge in whatever hearts I want. When you fancy yourself greater than you could possibly be, then through some cunning tactic, I keep you in line and put you back in your place with the common herd. You take aim against Jupiter, but he is so mighty and great that if I didn't guide your hand, and if I hadn't properly tempered your arrow, you would have no power over him at all.

And even supposing that only you could make people fall in love, how famous would you be if I didn't reveal that love with a thousand imaginative strategies? You may have made Jupiter fall in love, but I was the one who turned him into a swan, a bull, a golden rain, and an eagle, making him a target for feather makers, wolves, thieves, and hunters.[52] Who do you think allowed Mars to fall into a trap with your

rendu si mal avisé, que venir faire un povre mari cocu dedens son lit mesme? [¶] Qu'ust ce esté, si Paris n'ust fait autre chose, qu'aymer He-leine? Il estoit à Troye, l'autre à Sparte: ils n'avoient garde d'eus as-sembler. Ne lui fis je dresser une armee de mer, aller chez Menelas, faire la court à sa femme, l'emmener parforce, et puis defendre sa querele injuste contre toute la Grece? Qui ust parlé des Amours de Dido, si elle n'ust fait semblant d'aller à la chasse pour avoir la com-modité de parler à Enee seule à seul, et lui montrer telle privauté, qu'il ne devoit avoir honte de prendre ce que volontiers elle ust donné, si à la fin n'ust couronné son amour d'une miserable mort? On n'ust non plus parlé d'elle, que de mile autres hotesses, qui font plaisir aus pas-sans. Je croy qu'aucune mencion ne seroit d'Artemise, si je ne lui usse fait boire les cendres de son mari. Car qui ust sù si son affeccion ust passé celle des autres femmes, qui ont aymé, et regretté leurs maris et leurs amis? [¶] Les effets et issues des choses les font louer ou mes-priser. Si tu fais aymer, j'en suis cause le plus souvent. Mais si quelque estrange aventure, ou grand effet en sort, en celà tu n'y as rien: mais en est à moy seule l'honneur. Tu n'as rien que le cœur: le demeurant est gouverné par moy. Tu ne scez quel moyen faut tenir. Et pour te de-clarer qu'il faut faire pour complaire, je te meine et condui: Et ne te ser-vent tes yeus non plus que la lumiere à un aveugle. Et à fin que tu me reconnoisses d'orenavant, et que me saches gré quand je te meneray ou conduiray: regarde si tu vois quelque chose de toymesme?

Folie tire les yeus à Amour.

AMOUR: O Jupiter! ô ma mere Venus! Jupiter, Jupiter, que m'a servi d'estre Dieu, fils de Venus tant bien voulu jusques ici, tant au ciel qu'en terre, si je suis suget à estre injurié et outragé, comme le plus vil esclave ou forsaire, qui soit au monde? Et qu'une femme inconnue m'ait pù crever les yeus? Qu'à la malheure fut ce banquet solennel institué pour moy. Me trouveray je en haut avecques les autres Dieus en tel or-dre? Ils se resjouiront, et ne feray que me pleindre. O femme cruelle! comment m'as tu ainsi acoutré.

FOLIE: Ainsi se chatient les jeunes et presomptueus, comme toy. Quelle temerité ha un enfant de s'adresser à une femme, et l'injurier et

mother, if not me, and to behave so recklessly that he turned her poor husband into a cuckold in his very own bed?[53]

What would it have been like if Paris had done no more than fall in love with Helen? He was in Troy, she was in Sparta, and they weren't planning to get together. But didn't I make him assemble a fleet of ships, sail to Menelaus's home, woo his wife, take her away by force, and then defend his unjust cause against all of Greece?[54] Who would ever have talked about Dido's love story, if she hadn't pretended to go hunting so she could speak to Aeneas alone and granted him such liberties that he didn't need to be ashamed to take what she would happily have given him — and if in the end she hadn't crowned her love with a pitiful death?[55] No one would have had anything more to say about her than about a thousand other hostesses who try to please passing travelers. I suspect no mention would be made of Artemisia, if I hadn't made her drink her husband's ashes.[56] For otherwise who would have known whether her passion went beyond that of other women who have loved and mourned the loss of their husbands and lovers?

The effects and outcomes of things are what determine whether they will be praised or blamed. Although you may be the one who makes people fall in love, I'm the one, most often, who is really behind it. But if it so happens that some bizarre event or extraordinary result comes out of it, you have absolutely nothing to do with it: the credit belongs to me. You only have control over the heart; the rest is up to me. Since you don't know how to get along by yourself, I lead you around and guide you to show what you need to do in order to succeed. Your eyes therefore do you no more good than light does for a blind man. And now, so you'll appreciate me from here on, and be grateful when I lead or guide you, check for yourself whether you can see anything on your own?

Folly puts out Love's eyes.

LOVE: Oh Jupiter, oh mother Venus! Jupiter, Jupiter, what good has it done me, Venus's son, to be a god until now so highly prized in heaven and on earth, if I'm to be subjected to abuse and humiliation like the lowliest slave or criminal in the world? And if a woman I don't even know has had the power to put out my eyes? What a disaster that this grand banquet was planned for me! Can I possibly show my face before the other gods in this condition? They'll all be having a good time, and I'll just be feeling sorry for myself. Oh you cruel woman, how could you have done this to me?

FOLLY: That's the price the young and the arrogant like you must pay. How foolhardy for a child to confront a woman, and to attack and

outrager de paroles: puis de voye de fait tacher à la tuer. Une autre fois estime ceus que tu ne connois estre, possible, plus grans que toy. Tu as ofensé la Royne des hommes, celle qui leur gouverne le cerveau, cœur, et esprit: à l'ombre de laquelle tous se retirent une fois en leur vie, et y demeurent les uns plus, les autres moins, selon leur merite. Tu as ofensé celle qui t'a fait avoir le bruit que tu as et ne s'est souciee de faire entendre au Monde, que la meilleure partie du loz qu'il te donnoit, lui estoit due. Si tu usses esté plus modeste, encore que je te fusse inconnue: cette faute ne te fust avenue.

AMOUR: Comment est il possible porter honneur à une personne, que lon n'a jamais vuë? Je ne t'ay point fait tant d'injure que tu dis, vù que ne te connoissois. Car si j'usse sù qui tu es, et combien tu as de pouvoir, je t'usse fait l'honneur que merite une grand' Dame. Mais est il possible, s'ainsi est que tant m'ayes aymé, et aydé en toutes mes entreprises, que m'ayant pardonné, me rendisses mes yeus?

FOLIE: Que tes yeux te soient renduz , ou non, il n'est en mon pouvoir. Mais je t'acoutreray bien le lieu ou ils estoient, en sorte que lon m'y verra point de diformité.

Folie bande Amour, et lui met des esles.

Et ce pendant que tu chercheras tes yeus, voici des esles que je te prestes, qui te conduiront aussi bien comme moy.

AMOUR: Mais ou avois tu pris ce bandeau si à propos pour me lier mes plaies?

FOLIE: En venant j'ay trouvé une des Parques, qui me l'a baillé, et m'a dit estre de telle nature, que jamais ne te pourra estre oté.

AMOUR: Comment oté! je suis donq aveugle à jamais? O meschante et traytresse! il ne te sufit pas de m'avoir crevé les yeus, mais tu as oté aus Dieus la puissance de me les pouvoir jamais rendre. O qu'il n'est pas dit sans cause, qu'il ne faut point recevoir present de la main de ses ennemis. La malheureuse m'a blessé, et me suis mis entre ses mains pour estre pensé. O cruelles Destinees! O noire journee! O moy trop credule! Ciel, Terre, Mer, n'aurez vous compassion de voir Amour aveugle? O infame et detestable, tu te vanteras que ne t'ay pù fraper, que tu m'as oté les yeus, et trompé en me fiant en toy. Mais que me sert

insult her with his words — and then while doing so to try and kill her. The next time, show some respect to those who just might be greater than you, whether you know it or not. You've offended the queen of men, her who rules their heads, hearts, and minds — and under whose shadow all people come at some point in their lives, and where some remain, for more or less time, according to their merit. You've offended the woman who made possible the very reputation you enjoy, and who didn't care at all about letting the world know that most of the glory it gave you should really have gone to her. If you'd been more modest, even though you didn't know who I was, this misfortune would never have befallen you.

LOVE: How can anyone pay homage to a person he's never seen? I didn't harm you nearly as much as you say, given that I didn't even know you. For if I'd realized who you were, and how much power you possess, I'd have shown you the esteem befitting a great lady. But if it's true that you've loved me so much and helped me in my every undertaking, do you think you could forgive me and give me back my eyes?

FOLLY: Whether or not you get your eyes back isn't up to me. But I'll carefully cover up the place where they were, so that no one will be able to tell you're disfigured.

Folly bandages up Love's eyes and gives him wings.

And while you're trying to figure out how to get your eyes back, I'm going to loan you these wings, which will take you around every bit as well as they do me.

LOVE: But where did you get this bandage you so conveniently had ready to bind up my wounds?

FOLLY: While I was on my way here, I ran into one of the Fates, who offered it to me and told me it's of a kind that can't ever be removed.[57]

LOVE: Can't be removed! So I'm going to be blind forever? Oh you wicked, treacherous woman! It's not enough that you've put out my eyes, but you've even taken away the power of the gods to give them back to me. Whoever said that no one should ever accept gifts from the hands of one's enemies knew what they were talking about. The wretched woman wounded me, and yet I surrendered myself to her to be bandaged. Oh cruel Fates! Oh dark day! How could I have been so naïve? Heaven, earth, and sea, won't you take pity when you see that Love is now blind? You vile, despicable woman, you're going to go around bragging that I couldn't strike you, that you put out my eyes, and that then you played a trick on me when I trusted you and let my guard down. But

de plorer ici? Il vaut mieus que me retire en quelque lieu apart, et laisse passer ce festin. Puis, s'il est ainsi que j'aye tant de faveur au Ciel ou en Terre: je trouveray moyen de me venger de la fausse Sorciere, qui tant m'a fait d'outrage.

DISCOURS 2

Amour sort du Palais de Jupiter, et va resvant à son infortune.

AMOUR: Ores suis je las de toute chose. Il vaut mieus par despit descharger mon carquois, et getter toutes mes flesches, puis rendre arc et trousse à Venus ma mere. Or aillent, ou elles pourront, ou en Ciel, ou en Terre, il ne m'en chaut: Aussi bien ne m'est plus loisible faire aymer qui bon me semblera. O que ces belles Destinees ont aujourdhui fait un beau trait, de m'avoir ordonné estre aveugle, à fin qu'indiferemment, et sans accepcion de personne, chacun soit au hazard de mes traits et de mes flesches. Je faisois aymer les jeunes pucelles, les jeunes hommes: j'acompagnois les plus jolies des plus beaus et plus adroits. Je pardon-nois aus laides, aus viles et basses personnes: je laissois la vieillesse en paix: Maintenant, pensant fraper un jeune, j'asseneray sus un vieil-lart: au lieu de quelque beau galand, quelque petit laideron à la bouche torse: Et aviendra qu'ils seront les plus amoureus, et qui plus voudront avoir de faveur en amours: et possible par importunité, presens, ou richesses, ou disgrace de quelques Dames, viendront au dessus de leur intencion: Et viendra mon regne en mespris entre les hommes, quand ils y verront tel desordre et mauvais gouvernement. Baste: en aille comme il pourra. Voila toutes mes flesches. Tel en soufrira, qui n'en pourra mais.

VENUS: Il estoit bien tems que je te trouvasse, mon cher fils, tant tu m'as donné de peine. A quoy tient il, que tu n'es venu au banquet de Jupiter? Tu as mis toute la compagnie en peine. Et en parlant de ton absence, Jupiter ha ouy dix mile pleintes de toy d'une infinité d'arti-sans, gens de labeur, esclaves, chambrieres, vieillars, vieilles edentees, crians tous à Jupiter qu'ils ayment: Et en sont les plus aparens fachez, trouvant mauvais, que tu les ayes en cet endroit egalez à ce vil popu-laire: et que la passion propre aus bons esprits soit aujourdhui familiere et commune aus plus lourds et grossiers.

AMOUR: Ne fust l'infortune, qui m'est avenue, j'usse assisté au banquet, comme les autres, et ne fussent les pleintes, qu'avez ouyes, esté faites.

what's the use of crying over it here? It's better if I go off and lie low somewhere, and just forget about this banquet. Then, if indeed I carry as much clout in heaven or on earth as I think I do, I'll find a way to get my revenge on this deceitful witch who has so unjustly wronged me.

DISCOURSE 2

Love leaves Jupiter's palace, and goes off contemplating his misfortune

LOVE: Now I'm fed up with all of this. I'm so upset I think it might be better for me just to empty my quiver and shoot off all my arrows, and then hand over my bow and weapon case to my mother, Venus. Let the arrows land where they will, in heaven or on earth: I just don't care anymore, now that I can no longer make whomever I want fall in love. Oh, those beauteous Fates pulled off quite a trick today — seeing to it that I should be blind, so that absolutely everyone runs the risk of being struck by my arrows. I used to make young maidens and young men fall in love; I paired the prettiest ones with the most handsome and clever partners. I spared the ugly, the worthless, and the lowborn. I left old people alone. Now, when I think I'm going to strike a youth, I may very well hit an old man — or instead of some handsome suitor, an ugly duckling with a crooked mouth. And it may very well be that they'll be the ones who fall most deeply in love, and who'll be the most anxious to win favor in their courtship. And perhaps by virtue of perseverance, presents, wealth, or even because of the unfortunate state of some women, they'll be even more successful than they dreamed. Then people will begin to scorn my rule, when they see such chaos and lack of control. Enough of this — whatever happens, happens. Here go all my arrows. Whoever gets hurt won't be able to do a thing about it.

VENUS: It's high time I found you, my dear son; I've been beside myself with worry. Why didn't you come to Jupiter's banquet? Everyone was concerned about where you were. And speaking of your absence, Jupiter has heard ten thousand complaints about you from a whole slew of craftsmen, laborers, slaves, chambermaids, old men, and toothless old women — all lamenting to him that they're in love. And the upper-class people are the most upset about this, taking offense that you've reduced them to the level of the lowly commoners, and that the passion appropriate only to higher souls has now become ordinary, and is experienced by the most dim-witted and vulgar people.

LOVE: If I hadn't fallen into such bad luck, I would have been at the banquet like everyone else, and these complaints you've heard would never have been made.

VENUS: Es tu blessé, mon fils? Qui t'a ainsi bandé les yeus?

AMOUR: Folie m'a tiré les yeus: et de peur qu'ils ne me fussent renduz, elle m'a mis ce bandeau qui jamais ne me peut estre oté.

VENUS: O quelle infortune! he moy miserable! Donq tu ne me verras plus, cher enfant? Au moins si te pouvois arroser la plaie de mes larmes.

Venus tache à desnouer la bande.

AMOUR: Tu pers ton tems: les neuz sont indissolubles.

VENUS: O maudite ennemie de toute sapience, ô femme abandonnee, ô à tort nommee Deesse, et à plus grand tort immortelle. Qui vid onq telle injure? Si Jupiter, et les Dieus me croient. A tout le moins que jamais cette meschante n'ait pouvoir sur toy, mon fils.

AMOUR: A tard se feront ces defenses, il les failloit faire avant que fusse aveugle: maintenant ne me serviront gueres!

VENUS: Et donques Folie, la plus miserable chose du monde, ha le pouvoir d'oter à Venus le plus grand plaisir qu'elle ust en ce monde: qui estoit quand son fils Amour la voyoit. En ce estoit son contentement, son desir, sa felicité. Helas, fils infortuné! O desastre d'Amour! O mere desolee! O Venus sans fruit belle! Tout ce que nous aquerons, nous le laissons à nos enfans: mon tresor n'est que beauté, de laquelle que chaut il à un aveugle? Amour tant cheri de tout le monde, comme as tu trouvé beste si furieuse, qui t'ait fait outrage! Qu'ainsi soit dit, que tous ceus qui aymeront (quelque faveur qu'ils ayent) ne soient sans mal, et infortune, à ce qu'ils ne se dient plus heureus, que le cher fils de Venus.

AMOUR: Cesse tes pleintes douce mere: et ne me redouble mon mal te voyant ennuiee. Laisse moy porter seul mon infortune: et ne desire point mal à ceus qui me suivront.

VENUS: Allons mon fils, vers Jupiter, et lui demandons vengeance de cette malheureuse.

DISCOURS 3

VENUS: Si onques tu uz pitié de moy, Jupiter, quand le fier Diomede me navra, lors que tu me voyois travailler pour sauver mon fils Enee de l'impetuosité des vents, vagues, et autres dangers,

VENUS: Are you injured, my son? Who bandaged your eyes like this?

LOVE: Folly put out my eyes, and for fear I might get them back, she wrapped this bandage around me, and it can never be removed.

VENUS: Oh what a terrible misfortune! How awful this makes me feel! So you'll never, ever be able to see me again, dear child? If at least I could wash your wound with my tears . . .

Venus tries to untie the bandage.

LOVE: You're wasting your time: these knots can't be undone.

VENUS: Oh hateful enemy of all wisdom! Oh you depraved woman! Goddess unworthy of the name, and more unworthy still of immortality! Who has ever witnessed such a crime? If only Jupiter and the gods will believe me! At least may this evil woman never have power over you, my son.

LOVE: It's too late to save me. You should have set up safe-guards like that before I was blind. They'll hardly be of any use to me now.

VENUS: And thus Folly, the most wretched thing of them all, has the power to rob Venus of the greatest pleasure she had in life — which was to have her son, Love, be able to look at her.[58] This was her delight, her desire, her joy. Alas, my luckless son! What a catastrophe for Love! What anguish for a mother! Oh Venus, her beauty now use-less! Everything we acquire, we leave to our children. My only source of wealth is my beauty — and what does that matter to a blind man? Love, so adored by everyone, what a mad beast you came up against, to have suffered such harm! Let it therefore be declared that from now on, no one who falls in love (however distinguished he might be) will escape pain and unhappiness, so that none of them will be able to con-sider himself more fortunate than Venus's dear son.

LOVE: Please, dear mother, calm your grief, and don't make me feel even worse by seeing you so distressed. Let me bear my troubles alone, and don't wish any ill on those who will follow in my footsteps.

VENUS: Then, my son, let's go before Jupiter, and ask him to punish this horrible woman.

DISCOURSE 3

VENUS: If ever you took pity on me, Jupiter, when fierce Diomedes wounded me as you watched me do everything in my power to save my son Aeneas from the raging winds, waves, and all the

esquels il fut tant au siege de Troye, que depuis: si mes pleurs pour la mort de mon Adonis te murent à compassion: la juste douleur, que j'ay pour l'injure faite à mon fils Amour, te devra faire avoir pitié de moy. Je dirois que c'est, si les larmes ne m'empeschoient. Mais regarde mon fils en quel estat il est, et tu connoitras pourquoy je me pleins.

JUPITER: Ma chere fille, que gaignes tu avec ces pleintes me provoquer à larmes? Ne scez tu l'amour que je t'ay portee de toute memoire? As tu defiance, ou que je ne te veuille secourir, ou que je ne puisse?

VENUS: Estant la plus afligee mere du monde, je ne puis parler, que comme les afligees. Encore que vous m'ayez tant montré de faveur et d'amitié, si est ce que je n'ose vous suplier, que de ce que facilement vous otroiriez au plus estrange de la terre. Je vous demande justice, et vengeance de la plus malheureuse femme qui fust jamais, qui m'a mis mon fils Cupidon en tel ordre que voyez. C'est Folie, la plus outrageuse Furie qui onques fut es Enfers.

JUPITER: Folie! ha elle esté si hardie d'atenter à ce, qui plus vous estoit cher? Croyez que si elle vous ha fait tort, que telle punicion en sera faite, qu'elle sera exemplaire. Je pensois qu'il n'y ust plus debats et noises qu'entre les hommes: mais si cette outrecuidee ha fait quelque desordre si pres de ma personne, il lui sera cher vendu. Toutefois il la faut ouir, à fin qu'elle ne se puisse pleindre. Car encore que je puisse savoir de moymesme la verité du fait, si ne veus je point mettre en avant cette coutume, qui pourroit tourner à consequence, de condamner une personne sans l'ouir. Pource, que Folie soit apelee.

FOLIE: Haut et souverein Jupiter, me voici preste à respondre à tout ce qu'Amour me voudra demander. Toutefois j'ay une requeste à te faire. Pource que je say que de premier bond la plus part de ces jeunes Dieux seront du coté d'Amour, et pourront faire trouver ma cause mauvaise en m'interrompant, et ayder celle d'Amour acompagnant son parler de douces acclamacions: je te suplie qu'il y ait quelcun des Dieux qui parle pour moy, et quelque autre pour Amour: à fin que la qualité des personnes ne soit plus tot consideree, que la verité du fait. Et pource que je crein ne trouver aucun, qui, de peur d'estre apelé fol, ou ami de Folie, veuille parler pour moy: je te suplie commander à quelcun de me prendre en sa garde et proteccion.

JUPITER: Demande qui tu voudras, et je le chargeray de parler pour toy.

other dangers he faced at the siege of Troy and afterward;[59] if the tears shed over my dear Adonis's death moved you to compassion;[60] then surely the rightful pain I now feel because of the injury done to my son, Love, should reawaken your pity for me. I would tell you all about it, if I weren't so choked up by my tears. But just take a look at my son and the sorry state he finds himself in, and you will know why I'm bringing this complaint before you.

JUPITER: My dear daughter, what do you hope to gain by moving me to tears with these laments? Don't you know how much I have always loved you? Are you worried that I won't want to help you, or that I won't be able to?

VENUS: Since I am the most aggrieved mother in the world, I can only speak as those who grieve. Despite all the kindness and love you've shown me, I can't be so bold as to ask you for anything other than what you would willingly grant to a perfect stranger. I ask you for justice, and for vengeance on the most terrible woman who ever existed, who has left my son Cupid in the state you see him in now. She is Folly, the most despicable Fury that hell has ever known.

JUPITER: Folly! Was she so bold as to attack the one dearest to your heart? Believe me, if she has wronged you, whatever punishment she receives, she will be held up as an example. I thought there were no fights and quarrels anymore except among men, but if this impertinent woman has stirred up trouble so close to me, she will pay for it dearly. Nevertheless, we must still listen to her side of the story, so that she can't complain afterward. For even though I can determine the truth of the matter on my own, I don't want to set a precedent that could have serious consequences, namely, that of condemning a person without hearing the case. Let Folly therefore be summoned.

FOLLY: Noble and supreme Jupiter, I stand ready here to respond to whatever Love wishes to ask me. However, I have one request to make of you. Because I know that from the very beginning most of the young gods will be on Love's side, and that they could prejudice my case by interrupting me, while aiding Love's case by cheering on his words, I beg you to allow one of the gods to speak for me and another for Love, so that the rank of the parties involved won't receive more consideration than the merits of the case. And because I'm afraid I won't be able to find anyone who will want to speak for me, for fear of being labeled a friend of Folly or mad himself, I beg you to charge someone to protect me and to handle my defense.

JUPITER: Name whomever you would like, and I will order him to speak for you.

FOLIE: Je te suplie donq que Mercure en ait la charge. Car combien qu'il soit des grans amis de Venus, si suis je seure, que s'il entreprent parler pour moy, il n'oublira rien qui serve à ma cause.

JUPITER: Mercure, il ne faut jamais refuser de porter parole pour un miserable et afligé: Car ou tu le mettras hors de peine, et sera ta louenge plus grande, d'autant qu'auras moins ù de regard aus faveurs et richesses, qu'à la justice et droit d'un povre homme: ou ta priere ne lui servira de rien, et neanmoins ta pitié, bonté et diligence, seront recommandees. A cette cause tu ne dois diferer ce que cette povre afligee te demande: Et ainsi je veus et commande que tu le faces.

MERCURE: C'est chose bien dure à Mercure moyenner desplaisir à Venus. Toutefois, puis que tu me contreins, je feray mon devoir tant que Folie aura raison de se contenter.

JUPITER: Et toy, Venus, quel des Dieus choisiras tu? l'affeccion maternelle, que tu portes à ton fils, et l'envie de voir venger l'injure, qui lui ha esté faite, te pourroit transporter. Ton fils estant irrité, et navré recentement, n'y pourroit pareillement satisfaire. A cette cause, choisi quel autre tu voudras pour parler pour vous: et croy qu'il ne lui sera besoin lui commander: et que celui, à qui tu t'adresseras, sera plus aise de te faire plaisir en cet endroit, que toy de le requerir. Neanmoins s'il en est besoin, je le lui commanderay.

VENUS: Encor que lon ai semé par le monde, que la maison d'Apolon et la mienne ne s'accordoient gueres bien: si le crois je de si bonne sorte qu'il ne me voudra esconduire en cette necessité, lui requerant son ayde à cestui mien extreme besoin: et montrera par l'issue de cette afaire, combien il y ha plus d'amitié entre nous, que les hommes ne cuident.

APOLON: Ne me prie point, Deesse de beauté: et ne fais dificulté que ne te vueille autant de bien, comme merite la plus belle des Deesses. En outre le témoignage, qu'en pourroient rendre tes jardins, qui sont en Cypre et Ida, si bien par moy entretenus, qu'il n'y ha rien plus plaisant au monde: encore connoitras tu par l'issue de cette querelle combien je te porte d'affeccion et me sens fort aise que, te retirant vers moy en cet afaire, tu declaires aus hommes comme faussement ils ont controuvé, que tu avois conjuré contre toute ma maison.

JUPITER: Retirez vous donq un chacun, et revenez demain à semblable heure, et nous mettrons peine d'entendre et vuider vos querelles.

FOLLY: Then I ask you to assign Mercury this task. For although he is one of Venus's best friends, I'm certain that if he undertakes my defense, he won't overlook anything that might help my cause.

JUPITER: Mercury, no one should ever decline to speak on behalf of the unfortunate and the downtrodden. For either you will get such a person out of trouble, to your own greater glory for having shown less concern for favors and riches than for justice and the rights of a poor man; or else your arguments will do him no good at all, but your sympathy, kindness, and hard work will nonetheless be admired. For these reasons you mustn't put off doing what this poor woman asks of you. Such is not only my wish, but my command.

MERCURY: It's a difficult thing indeed for Mercury to displease Venus. However, since you require me to do this, I will fulfill my duty so well that Folly cannot help but be satisfied.

JUPITER: And you, Venus, which one of the gods will you choose to represent you? The motherly affection you have for your son, and the desire to see his injury avenged, could make your emotions get the better of you. Your son, so angry from his recent injury, would hardly be up to the task either. In light of this, go ahead and choose whomever else you would like to speak for you, and trust me, he won't need to be forced into it. Whomever you turn to will be happier to oblige you in this matter than you will be to ask him. But still, should it be necessary, I will order him to do so.

VENUS: Even though rumor has it that Apollo's house and my own haven't gotten along very well at times, I still believe him to be so good-natured that if I asked his help in this difficult situation he wouldn't let me down in my hour of need. Indeed the outcome of this case will show that there's much more goodwill between us than people think.

APOLLO: You don't need to beg me, goddess of beauty. You have no cause for worry, since I wish you all the good that the most beautiful of goddesses deserves. You see for yourself the evidence of this in your gardens on Cyprus and on Mount Ida, which I take such good care of that there are no lovelier places on earth.[61] And when you see how this dispute turns out, you'll know even better how much I love you, and how happy I am that by turning to me in these circumstances, you've made it clear to everyone how wrong they were to imagine you'd conspired against my entire family.

JUPITER: You are all free to go now. Come back here tomorrow at the same time, and we will do our best to hear you out and resolve your dispute.

DISCOURS 4

Cupidon vient donner le bon jour à Jupiter.

JUPITER: Que dis tu petit mignon? Tant que ton diferent soit terminé, nous n'aurons plaisir de toy. Mais ou est ta mere?

AMOUR: Elle est allee vers Apolon, pour l'amener au consistoire des Dieus. Ce pendant elle m'a comandé venir vers toy te donner le bon jour.

JUPITER: Je la plein bien pour l'ennui qu'elle porte de ta fortune. Mais je m'esbahi comme, ayant tant ofensé de hauts Dieus et grans Seigneurs, tu n'as jamais ù mal que par Folie!

AMOUR: C'est pource que les Dieus et hommes, bien avisez, creingnent que ne leur face pis. Mais Folie n'a pas la consideracion et jugement si bon.

JUPITER: Pour le moins te devroient ils haïr, encore qu'ils ne t'osassent ofenser. Toutefois tous tant qu'ils sont t'ayment.

AMOUR: Je seroye bien ridicule, si ayant le pouvoir de faire les hommes estre aymez, ne me faisois aussi estre aymé.

JUPITER: Si est il bien contre nature, que ceus qui ont reçu tout mauvais traitement de toy, t'ayment autant comme ceus qui ont ù plusieurs faveurs.

AMOUR: En ce se montre la grandeur d'Amour, quand on ayme celui dont on est mal traité.

JUPITER: Je say fort bien par experience, qu'il n'est point en nous d'estre aymez: car, quelque grand degré ou je sois, si ay je esté bien peu aymé: et tout le bien qu'ay reçu, l'ay plus tot ù par force et finesse, que par amour.

AMOUR: J'ay bien dit que je fay aymer encore ceus, qui ne sont point aymez: mais si est il en la puissance d'un chacun le plus souvent de se faire aymer. Mais peu se treuvent, qui facent en amour tel devoir qu'il est requis.

JUPITER: Quel devoir?

AMOUR: La premiere chose dont il faut s'enquerir, c'est, s'il y ha quelque Amour imprimee: et s'il n'y en ha, ou qu'elle ne soit encor enracinee, ou qu'elle soit desja toute usee, faut songneusement chercher quel est le naturel de la personne aymee; et, connoissant le notre, avec les commoditez, façons, et qualitez estre semblables, en user: si non, le changer.

DISCOURSE 4

Cupid stops by to greet Jupiter.

JUPITER: What do you have to say, dear child? Until this dispute of yours is settled, we won't be able to enjoy your company. But where is your mother?

LOVE: She went to find Apollo, to bring him to the assembly of the gods. In the meantime she advised me to come pay you a visit.

JUPITER: I feel very badly for the pain she's suffering over your misfortune. But I must say I'm amazed, considering how many noble gods and great lords you've hurt, that only Folly has ever done you harm!

LOVE: That's because gods and men, wise as they are, are afraid I might do something even worse to them. But Folly doesn't have such good sense and judgment.

JUPITER: You'd think at the very least they would hate you, even though they don't dare do you any harm. Yet every single one of them still loves you.

LOVE: I would really look foolish if despite my power to make people love each other, I couldn't make them love me as well.

JUPITER: Yet it goes against nature that those whom you've treated so badly still love you as much as those for whom you've done so many favors.

LOVE: The true greatness of Love lies in this: when we love someone who treats us badly.[62]

JUPITER: I know all too well from experience that we have no control over whether we're loved — for even with my high rank, I've almost never been loved. All the good things that have happened to me, I've gotten by force and trickery rather than by love.

LOVE: I did say that I can spark love even in those who remain unloved in return; yet, most of the time it lies within the power of every person to make himself loved. But very few of them carry out the obligations that love demands.

JUPITER: What obligations?

LOVE: First we must ask if in some way love has left its mark. And if it has not — whether because it hasn't yet taken root, or because it has already worn off — then we must look carefully at the inner nature of the person we love. If we know that our own nature, with its traits, ways, and qualities, is compatible with theirs, we need to use it to our advantage; if not, we need to change.

[¶] Les Dames que tu as aymees, vouloient estre louees, entretenues par un long tems, priees, adorees: quell'Amour penses tu qu'elles t'ayent porté, te voyant en foudre, en Satire, en diverses sortes d'Animaus, et converti en choses insensibles? La richesse te fera jouir des Dames qui sont avares: mais aymer non. Car cette affeccion de gaigner ce qui est au cœur d'une personne, chasse la vraye et entiere Amour: qui ne cherche son proufit, mais celui de la persone, qu'il ayme. Les autres especes d'Animaus ne pouvoient te faire amiable. Il n'y ha animant courtois et gracieus que l'homme, lequel puisse se rendre suget aus complexions d'autrui, augmenter sa beauté et bonne grace par mile nouveaus artifices: plorer, rire, chanter, et passionner la personne qui le voit. La lubricité et ardeur de reins n'a rien de commun, ou bien peu, avec Amour. Et pource les femmes ou jamais n'aymeront, ou jamais ne feront semblant d'aymer pour ce respect. [¶] Ta magesté Royale encores ha elle moins de pouvoir en ceci; car Amour se plait de choses egales. Ce n'est qu'un joug, lequel faut qu'il soit porté par deus Taureaus semblables: autrement le harnois n'ira pas droit. Donq, quand tu voudras estre aymé, descens en bas, laisse ici ta couronne et ton sceptre, et ne dis qui tu es. Lors tu verras, en bien servant et aymant quelque Dame, que sans qu'elle ait egard à richesse ne puissance, de bon gré t'aymera. Lors tu sentiras bien un autre contentement, que ceus que tu as uz par le passé: et au lieu d'un simple plaisir, en recevras un double. Car autant y ha il de plaisir à estre baisé et aymé, que de baiser et aymer.

JUPITER: Tu dis beaucoup de raisons: mais il y faut un long tems, une sugeccion grande, et beaucoup de passions.

AMOUR: Je say bien qu'un grand Signeur se fache de faire longuement la court, que ses afaires d'importance ne permettent pas qu'il s'y assugettisse, et que les honneurs qu'il reçoit tous les jours, et autres passetems sans nombre, ne lui permettent croitre ses passions, de sorte qu'elles puissent mouvoir leurs amies à pitié. Aussi ne doivent ils atendre les grans et faciles contentemens qui sont en Amour. Mais souventefois j'abaisse si bien les grans, que je les fay à tous, exemple de mon pouvoir.

JUPITER: Il est tems d'aller au consistoire: nous deviserons une autrefois plus à loisir.

The women you've loved wanted to be praised, wooed at great length, implored, adored. What love do you imagine they could have felt for you, seeing you as a thunderbolt, a satyr, an array of animals, and even transformed into inanimate objects? Riches will allow you to enjoy the company of greedy women, but will not earn you their love — for the desire for gain within someone's heart drives away true and complete Love, which seeks no benefit for itself, but only for the one who is loved.[63] Changing yourself into other kinds of animals couldn't make you lovable. There is no other living creature as engaging and gracious as man, since only he can adjust to the moods of others and play up his attractiveness and charm with a thousand different techniques: crying, laughing, singing, and otherwise delighting the person who sees him. Lust and fire in the loins have nothing, or very little, to do with love. Therefore, women either will never fall in love, or at least will never appear to fall in love, on this account.

Then, too, your Royal Majesty is in a difficult position, in that love thrives best when things are equal. It's no more than a yoke that needs to be carried by two well-paired oxen; otherwise the harness will not stay on straight. And so, whenever you want to be loved, go on down to earth, leave your crown and scepter here, and don't tell anyone who you are. Then you will see, when you love and serve some lady well, that she will love you of her own free will, without thinking twice about your wealth or power. And then you will feel a kind of satisfaction unlike anything you have known in the past, and you will experience twice the pleasure. For there's every bit as much pleasure to be had in being kissed and loved, as in kissing and loving.

JUPITER: What you say certainly makes sense, but all this takes a very long time, a great deal of restraint, and a lot of emotion.

LOVE: I realize that a great lord finds it difficult to court a woman for a long period of time, since his important responsibilities keep him from devoting himself to it. Furthermore, the honors he receives every day, in addition to countless other distractions, don't allow his emotions to develop in ways that can move his beloved to pity. Therefore such lords mustn't expect the great and simple joys that can be found in love. Indeed, many times I bring the mighty down so low to show everyone how powerful I am.

JUPITER: It's time to go to the assembly now. We'll talk more about this later when we have the chance.

DISCOURS 5

APOLON: Si onques te falut songneusement pourvoir à tes afaires, souverein Jupiter, ou quand avec l'ayde de Briare tes plus proches te vouloient mettre en leur puissance, ou quand les Geans, fils de la Terre, mettans montaigne sur montaigne, deliberoient nous venir combattre jusques ici, ou quand le Ciel et la Terre cuiderent bruler: à cette heure, que la licence des fols est venue si grande, que d'outrager devant tes yeus l'un des principaus de ton Empire, tu n'a moins d'occasion d'avoir creinte, et ne dois diferer à donner pront remede au mal ja commencé. [¶] S'il est permis à chacun atenter sur le lien qui entretient et lie tout ensemble: je voy en peu d'heure le Ciel en desordre, je voy les uns changer leurs cours, les autres entreprendre sur leurs voisins une consommacion universelle: ton sceptre, ton trone, ta magesté en danger. Le sommaire de mon oraison sera conserver ta grandeur en son integrité, en demandant vengeance de ceus qui outragent Amour, la vraye ame de tout l'univers, duquel tu tiens ton sceptre. D'autant donq que ma cause est tant favorable, conjointe avec la conservacion de ton estat, et que neanmoins je ne demande que justice: d'autant plus me devras tu atentivement escouter. [¶] L'injure que je meintien avoir esté faite à Cupidon, est telle: Il venoit au festin dernier: et voulant entrer par une porte, Folie acourt apres lui, et lui mettant la main sus l'espaule le tire en arriere, et s'avance, et passe la premiere. Amour voulant savoir qui c'estoit, s'adresse à elle. Elle lui dit plus d'injures, qu'il n'apartient à une femme de bien à dire. De là elle commence se hausser en paroles, se magnifier, fait Amour petit. Lequel se voyant ainsi peu estimé, recourt à la puissance, dont tu l'as tousjours vù, et permets user contre toute personne. Il la veut faire aymer: elle evite au coup. Et feignant ne prendre en mal, ce que Cupidon lui avoit dit, recommence à deviser avec lui: et en parlant tout d'un coup lui leve les yeus de la teste. Ce fait, elle se vient à faire si grande sur lui, qu'elle lui fait entendre de ne lui estre possible le guerir, s'il ne reconnoissoit qu'il ne lui avoit porté l'honneur qu'elle meritoit. [¶] Que ne feroit on pour recouvrer la joyeuse vuë du Soleil? Il dit, il fait tout ce qu'elle veut. Elle

DISCOURSE 5

APOLLO: If ever there was a time when you needed to be mindful of your own interests, supreme Jupiter — either when your closest allies tried, with the help of Briareus, to make you submit to their power, or else when the Giants, the sons of Earth, piling mountain upon mountain, resolved to come all the way up here to fight us, or else even when heaven and earth were thought to be burning up — the time is now.[64] The license of fools has gone so far as to offend, before your very eyes, one of the leading figures of your kingdom. You have every reason to be alarmed, and you mustn't put off finding a way to repair promptly the damage that's already been done.

If anyone is permitted to violate the bond that sustains and ties everything together, then I predict that very soon the heavens will fall into chaos. I foresee that some will change their course of action and that others will set out to wreak destruction on their neighbors — all placing your scepter, your throne, and your royal authority in danger. The essential goal of my speech will be to preserve your greatness fully intact, by demanding vengeance on those who have wronged Love, the true soul of the whole universe over which you rule. Therefore, because my cause is so worthy, and so inextricably tied to the preservation of your kingdom, and since, after all, I am only asking for justice, it's all the more crucial that you listen to me carefully.

The offense that I submit was done to Cupid is the following: He was about to arrive at your last banquet, and as he was trying to go through the door, Folly comes running up behind him, and laying a hand on his shoulder, pulls him back, moves in front of him, and goes in first.[65] Wanting to know who she was, Love speaks to her directly. She responds with further insults not befitting a respectable lady. Then she starts to boast, glorifying herself, and demeaning Love. Seeing himself held in such little regard, he resorts to the power that you've witnessed time and time again, and that you allow him to use against everyone. He wants to make her fall victim to love, but she avoids his arrow. And pretending not to take offense at what Cupid said to her, she starts up a conversation with him again; and as she's talking all of a sudden she yanks his eyes right out of his head. Having done this, she goes on to lord it over him — so much so that she has him understand that he can't be healed unless he concedes that he didn't show her the esteem she deserved.

What wouldn't anyone do to regain the joyous sight of the sun?

le bande, et pense ses plaies en attendant que meilleure ocasion vinst de lui rendre la vuë. Mais la traytresse lui mit un tel bandeau, que jamais ne sera possible lui oter: par ce moyen voulant se moquer de toute l'ayde que tu lui pourrois donner: et encor que tu lui rendisse les yeus, qu'ils fussent neanmoins inutiles. Et pour le mieus acoutrer lui ha baillé de ses esles, a fin d'estre aussi bien guidé comme elle. [¶] Voila deus injures grandes et atroces faites à Cupidon. On l'a blessé, et lui ha lon oté le pouvoir et moyen de guerir. La plaie se voit, le delit est manifeste: de l'auteur ne s'en faut enquerir. Celle qui ha fait le coup, le dit, le presche, en fait ses contes par tout. Interrogue la: plus tot l'aura confessé que ne l'auras demandé. Que reste il? Quand il est dit: qui aura tiré une dent, lui en sera tiré une autre: qui aura arraché un œil, lui en sera semblablement crevé un, celà s'entent entre personnes égales. Mais quand on ha ofensé ceus, desquels depend la conservacion de plusieurs, les peines s'aigrissent, les loix s'arment de severité, et vengent le tort fait au publiq. [¶] Si tout l'Univers ne tient que par certeines amoureuses composicions, si elles cessoient, l'ancien Abime reviendroit. Otant l'amour, tout est ruïné. C'est donq celui, qu'il faut conserver en son estre: c'est celui, qui fait multiplier les hommes, vivre ensemble, et perpetuer le monde, par l'amour et solicitude qu'ils portent à leurs successeurs. Injurier cet Amour, l'outrager, qu'est ce, sinon vouloir troubler et ruïner toutes choses? Trop mieus vaudroit que la temeraire se fust adressee à toy: car tu t'en fusses bien donné garde. Mais s'estant adressee à Cupidon, elle t'a fait dommage irreparable, et auquel n'as ù puissance de donner ordre. Cette injure touche aussi en particulier tous les autres Dieus, Demidieus, Faunes, Satires, Silvains, Deesses, Nynfes, Hommes, et Femmes: et croy qu'il n'y ha Animant, qui ne sente mal, voyant Cupidon blessé. [¶] Tu as donq osé, ô detestable, nous faire à tous despit, en outrageant ce que tu savois estre de tous aymé. Tu as ù le cœur si malin, de navrer celui qui apaise toutes noises et querelles. Tu as osé atenter au fils de Venus: et ce en la court de Jupiter: et as fait qu'il y ha ù ça haut moins de franchise, qu'il n'y ha la bas entre les hommes, es lieus qui nous sont consacrez. [¶] Par tes foudres, ô Jupiter, tu abas les arbres, ou quelque povre femmelette gar-

And so he says and does everything she wants. She bandages him and wraps his wounds until a more favorable moment comes along to restore his sight. But the traitress put a bandage on him that will never be able to be removed. By doing this, she is trying to thwart all the help you might be able to give him — for now, even if you were to give him back his eyes, they'd be of no use to him. And to deck him out still better, she gave him some of her wings, so that he could make his way around as easily as she does.

Here, then, are two grave and heinous offenses committed against Cupid. He has been wounded, and the power and means to be healed have been taken away from him. The wound is in plain sight; the crime is clear; there's no doubt about who did it. She who did the deed says so, proclaims it publicly, and tells her story far and wide. Go ahead and question her: she'll admit it before you can even finish asking her about it. What then remains to be done? When they say "an eye for an eye, a tooth for a tooth," the saying is understood as applying to equals. But when someone has hurt those on whom the preservation of others depends, the penalties become harsher and the laws more severely enforced in order to avenge the wrong done to the entire social order.

If the entire universe holds together only because of certain bonds forged by Love, should these bonds cease to exist, the abyss of long ago would return again. If you take away Love, everything else is ruined. He must therefore be preserved in his previous state, for he is the one who makes people multiply, live together, and perpetuate the human race by the love and care they have for their offspring. To injure Love, to humiliate him, what is this if not an attempt to disturb and wreck everything? It would have been far better if this foolhardy woman had attacked you, for you would have been ready to protect yourself. But by attacking Cupid, she did you irreparable harm, over which you had no say. This crime also affects every single one of the other gods, demigods, fauns, satyrs, sylvans, goddesses, nymphs, men, and women. I believe there's no creature alive who isn't saddened at seeing Cupid hurt.

You have therefore dared, oh hateful woman, to offend us all by abusing the thing you knew we all loved. You bore such a grudge in your heart that you wounded the one who puts all our disputes and quarrels to rest. You went so far as to attack the son of Venus in Jupiter's own court, and because of your deed, the very places set aside for our refuge here on high now offer less safe haven than there is down below among men.[66]

With your thunderbolts, Jupiter, you strike down trees, or some

dant les brebis, ou quelque meschant garsonneau, qui aura moins dine-
ment parlé de ton nom: Et cette cy, qui, mesprisant ta magesté, ha
violé ton palais, vit encores! et ou? au ciel: et est estimee immortelle,
et retient nom de Deesse! Les roues des Enfers soutiennent elles une
ame plus detestable que cette cy? Les montaignes de Sicile couvrent
elles de plus execrables personnes? Et encores n'a elle honte de se pre-
senter devant vos divinitez: et lui semble (si je l'ose dire) que serez tous
si fols, que de l'absoudre. [¶] Je n'ay neanmoins charge par Amour de
requerir vengeance et punicion de Folie. Les gibets, potences, roues,
couteaus, et foudres ne lui plaisent, encor que fust contre ses malveuil-
lans, contre lesquels mesmes il ha si peu usé de son ire, que, oté quel-
que subit courrous de la jeunesse qui le suit, il ne se trouva jamais un
seul d'eus qui ait voulu l'outrager, fors cette furieuse. Mais il laisse le
tout à votre discrecion, ô Dieus: et ne demande autre chose, sinon que
ses yeus lui soient rendus, et qu'il soit dit, que Folie ha ù tort de l'in-
jurier et outrager. Et à ce que par ci apres n'avienne tel desordre, en cas
que ne veuillez ensevelir Folie sous quelque montaigne, ou la mettre à
l'abandon de quelque aigle, ce qu'il ne requiert, vous vueillez ordon-
ner, que Folie ne se trouvera pres du lieu ou Amour sera, de cent pas à
la ronde. Ce que trouverez devoir estre fait, apres qu'aurez entendu de
quel grand bien sera cause Amour, quand il aura gaigné ce point: et de
combien de maus il sera cause, estant si mal acompagné, mesmes à
present qu'il n'a perdu les yeus. Vous ne trouverez point mauvais que je
touche en brief en quel honneur et reputacion est Amour entre les
hommes, et qu'au demeurant de mon oraison je ne parle guere plus
que d'eus. [¶] Donques les hommes sont faits à l'image et semblance
de nous, quant aus esprits: leurs corps sont composez de plusieurs et
diverses complexions: et entre eus si diferent tant en figure, couleur et
forme, que jamais en tant de siecles, qui ont passé, ne s'en trouva, que
deus ou trois pers, qui se ressemblassent: encore leurs serviteurs et do-
mestiques les connoissoient particulierement l'un d'avec l'autre. Estans
ainsi en meurs, complexions, et forme dissemblables, sont neanmoins
ensemble liez et assemblez par une benivolence, qui les fait vouloir
bien l'un à l'autre: et ceus qui en ce sont les plus excellens, sont les plus
reverez entre eus. Delà est venue la premiere gloire entre les hommes.
Car ceus qui avoient inventé quelque chose à leur proufit estoient es-
timez plus que les autres. Mais faut penser que cette envie de proufiter
en publiq, n'est procedee de gloire, comme estant la gloire posterieure
en tems.

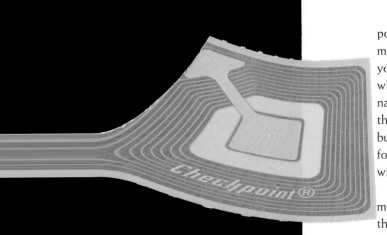

poor, frail woman looking after her sheep, or some bad little boy who may have disrespected your name. Yet this woman, despite scorning your glory and violating the very seat of your throne, still lives! And where? In heaven, where she's considered immortal and still keeps the name of goddess! Do the wheels of hell hold a soul more loathsome than hers?[67] Do the mountains of Sicily have anyone more atrocious buried beneath them?[68] And still she's not ashamed to show herself before your gods, and she seems to believe (if I may dare say it) that you will all be foolish enough to forgive her.

However, Love hasn't asked me to demand revenge and punishment against Folly. He dislikes gallows, scaffolds, wheels, knives, and thunderbolts, even against those who wish him ill. Even on them, he has taken out so little of his anger, that outside of some brief fits of temper among his youthful followers, not a single one has ever tried to do him any harm, except this madwoman. But he leaves everything to your discretion, oh gods, and asks nothing except that his eyes be given back to him, and that it be declared that Folly was wrong to injure and humiliate him. And so that no such disturbance ever occurs again, in case you decide not to bury Folly under some mountain, or to leave her as a victim to some eagle — which he's not asking of you — may you see fit to order Folly not to come within a hundred steps of wherever Love may be.[69] You'll reach the conclusion that this must be done once you come to understand what great good Love will accomplish when he wins his case, and just how much trouble he'll cause with such a dreadful companion, especially now that he's lost his eyes. I trust you won't object if I touch briefly upon the honor and reputation Love holds among men, and if in the rest of my speech, I hardly talk of anything else.

When it comes to their spirits, men are made in our image and likeness; their bodies are composed of many varied features and are so different in shape, color, and form that never in all the past centuries have there been more than two or three pairs who looked exactly alike — and even then their servants and valets could tell them apart. But although they differ in appearance, character, and custom, they are nevertheless bound and united together by a kindness that makes them bear good will toward one another; and those who excel at this are the most revered. From this came the first notion of fame among men, since those who had invented something for the benefit of all were more highly esteemed than others.[70] But we must consider that this desire to benefit society isn't a result of fame, because fame follows later in time.

[¶] Quelle peine croyez vous qu'a ù Orphee pour destourner les hommes barbares de leur acoutumee cruauté? pour les faire assembler en compagnies politiques? pour leur mettre en horreur le piller et robber l'autrui? Estimez vous que ce fust pour gain? duquel ne se parloit encores entre les hommes, qui n'avoient fouillé es entrailles de la terre? La gloire, comme j'ay dit, ne le pouvoit mouvoir. Car n'estans point encore de gens politiquement vertueus, il n'y pouvoit estre gloire, ny envie de gloire. L'amour qu'il portoit en general aus hommes, le faisoit travailler à les conduire à meilleure vie. C'estoit la douceur de sa Musique, que lon dit avoir adouci les Loups, Tigres, Lions: attiré les arbres, et amolli les pierres. Et quelle pierre ne s'amolliroit entendant le dous preschement de celui qui amiablement la veut atendrir pour recevoir l'impression de bien et honneur? [¶] Combien estimez vous que Promethee soit loué là bas pour l'usage du feu, qu'il inventa? Il le vous desroba, et encourut votre indignacion. Estoit ce qu'il vous voulust ofenser? je croy que non: mais l'amour, qu'il portoit à l'homme, que tu lui baillas, ô Jupiter, commission de faire de terre, et l'assembler de toutes pieces ramassees des autres animaus. Cet amour que lon porte en general à son semblable, est en telle recommandacion entre les hommes, que le plus souvent se trouvent entre eus qui pour sauver un païs, leur parent, et garder l'honneur de leur Prince, s'enfermeront dedens lieus peu defensables, bourgades, colombiers: et quelque asseurance qu'ils ayent de la mort, n'en veulent sortir à quelque composicion que ce soit, pour prolonger la vie à ceus que lon ne peut assaillir que apres leur ruïne. [¶] Outre cette afeccion generale, les hommes en ont quelque particuliere l'un envers l'autre, et laquelle, moyennant qu'elle n'ait point le but de gain, ou de plaisir de soymesme, n'ayant respect à celui, que lon se dit aymer, est en tel estime au monde, que lon ha remarqué songneusement par tous les siecles ceus, qui se sont trouvez excellens en icelle, les ornant de tous les plus honorables titres que les hommes peuvent inventer. Mesmes ont estimé cette seule vertu estre sufisante pour d'un homme faire un Dieu. Ainsi les Scythes deïfierent Pylade et Oreste, et leur dresserent temples et autels, les apelans les Dieus d'amitié. Mais avant iceus estoit Amour, qui les avoit liez et uniz ensemble.

How difficult do you suppose it was for Orpheus to make savage men turn away from their accustomed cruelty?[71] To get them to come together in civic assemblies? To make them come to loathe stealing and pillaging? Do you think he did this for personal profit? At that time such profit wasn't even a subject of conversation among men, who hadn't as yet started to dig up the bowels of the earth. Fame, as I've said, couldn't move him. Because people didn't yet have ambitions in the public sphere, there couldn't be a question of fame, or a desire for fame. Rather, the all-encompassing love he had for his fellow men made him strive to guide them toward a better life. It was the sweetness of his music, they say, that tamed wolves, tigers, and lions, enticed trees, and softened stones. Indeed, what stone wouldn't grow soft when hearing the sweet exhortation of someone who lovingly wishes to soften it so that it can be imprinted with goodness and honor?

How much praise do you imagine Prometheus is given down below for discovering how to use fire? He stole it from you, and was subjected to your wrath. But was it really that he wanted to offend you? I don't think so. Rather it was because of his love for man, whom you yourself, oh Jupiter, charged him to fashion out of earth and to put together with different parts gathered from other animals. This universal love of one's fellow man is so highly prized among men that quite often some of them, in order to save their country or their family, or to protect the honor of their prince, will barricade themselves in some almost indefensible places, such as small villages or cottages — and however sure they may be of their own death, they will refuse to come out no matter what concession might be offered to them. In so doing these men try to prolong the lives of those who can only be vulnerable to attack after their own demise.

Beyond this more overarching sense of love, men may have a special love toward another person. As long as its goals are not personal gain or selfish pleasure, which show no true regard for the person one claims to love, this type of love is held in such high esteem in the world that throughout history, those seen as towering above others in the greatness of their love have been carefully singled out and graced with the most honorable titles ever invented by men. This virtue alone has even been considered worthy enough to turn a man into a god. Accordingly, the Scythians deified Pylades and Orestes, and put up temples and altars in their names, calling them the gods of friendship.[72] But before these two, there was Love, who bound and united them together.

[¶] Raconter l'opinion, qu'ont les hommes des parens d'Amour, ne seroit hors de propos, pour montrer qu'ils l'estiment autant ou plus, que nul autre des Dieus. Mais en ce ne sont d'un acord, les uns le faisant sortir de Chaos et de la Terre: les autres du Ciel et de la Nuit: aucuns de Discorde et de Zephire: autres de Venus la vraye mere, l'honorant par ces anciens peres et meres, et par les effets merveilleus que de tout tems il ha acoutumé montrer. Mais il me semble que les Grecs d'un seul surnom qu'ils t'ont donné, Jupiter, t'apelant amiable, témoignent assez que plus ne pouvoient exaucer Amour, qu'en te faisant participant de sa nature. Tel est l'honneur que les plus savans et plus renommez des hommes donnent à Amour. Le commun populaire le prise aussi et estime pour les grandes experiences qu'il voit des commoditez, qui proviennent de lui. [¶] Celui qui voit que l'homme (quelque vertueus qu'il soit) languit en sa maison, sans l'amiable compagnie d'une femme, qui fidelement lui dispense son bien, lui augmente son plaisir, ou le tient en bride doucement, de peur qu'il n'en prenne trop, pour sa santé, lui ote les facheries, et quelquefois les empesche de venir, l'appaise, l'adoucit, le traite sain et malade, le fait avoir deus corps, quatre bras, deus ames, et plus parfait que les premiers hommes du banquet de Platon, ne confessera il que l'amour conjugale est dine de recommandacion? et n'atribuera cette felicité au mariage, mais à l'amour qui l'entretient. Lequel, s'il defaut en cet endroit, vous verrez l'homme forcené, fuir et abandonner sa maison. La femme au contraire ne rit jamais, quand elle n'est en amour avec son mari. Ilz ne sont jamais en repos. Quand l'un veut reposer, l'autre crie. Le bien se dissipe, et vont toutes choses au rebours. Et est preuve certeine, que la seule amitié fait avoir en mariage le contentement, que lon dit s'y trouver. [¶] Qui ne dira bien de l'amour fraternelle, ayant veu Castor et Pollux, l'un mortel estre fait immortel à moitié du don de son frere? Ce n'est pas estre frere, qui cause cet heur (car peu de freres sont de telle sorte) mais l'amour grande qui estoit entre eus. Il seroit long à discourir, comme Jonathas sauva la vie à David: dire l'histoire de Pythias et Damon: de celui qui quitta son espouse à son ami la premiere nuit, et s'en fuit vagabond par le monde. Mais pour montrer quel bien vient d'amitié, j'allegueray le dire d'un grand Roy, lequel,

It wouldn't be out of place here to state the opinions men have concerning Love's parents in order to show that they esteem him just as much as or more than any of the other gods. But on this issue they don't all agree: some believe he was born of Chaos and Earth, others of Heaven and Night; some of Discord and Zephyrus, and still others of Venus, his true mother.[73] They all revere him for his ancient ancestors, as well as for the marvelous feats he has always accomplished throughout the ages. But it seems to me, Jupiter, that by virtue of one name they've given you, calling you the loving one, the Greeks have shown convincingly enough that they could bestow no higher praise upon Love than making you share in his very nature.[74] Such is the honor that the most learned and celebrated of men confer upon Love. Ordinary people prize and respect him, too, thanks to their vast experience of the benefits that come from him.

Anyone who sees a man (however virtuous he may be) pining away in his home, without the loving company of a woman who devotedly showers him with her kindness; who increases his pleasure or gently keeps him in check for fear that he delights in it too much for his own health; who takes away his troubles and sometimes even keeps them from happening; who calms him, soothes him, and takes care of him in sickness and in health; and who allows him to have two bodies, four arms, and two souls, making him more perfect than the first men in Plato's *Symposium* — won't such an observer admit that married love is to be highly recommended?[75] And he'll attribute this great happiness not to marriage itself, but to the love that sustains it. For if love is missing here, you'll see that man, at his wit's end, flee and abandon his home. The woman, for her part, never laughs when she doesn't love her husband. They never have any peace. When one of them wants to rest, the other one yells. All the pleasure disappears, and everything goes wrong. This is undeniable proof that love alone brings about the happiness they say can be found in marriage.

Who won't speak well of fraternal love after considering the case of Castor and Pollux, where the mortal one came to share the gift of immortality offered to him by his brother?[76] It's not the mere fact of being brothers that gives rise to such good fortune (for there are few brothers like them), but rather the great love existing between them. It would take a long time to explain how Jonathan saved the life of David, to tell the story of Damon and Pythias, and of the man who on their very first night together entrusted his wife to his friend and ran off to wander the world.[77] But so as to show what good comes from friendship,

ouvrant une grenade, interrogué de quelles choses il voudroit avoir autant, comme il y avoit de grains en la pomme, respondit: de Zopires. C'estoit ce Zopire, par le moyen duquel il avoit recouvré Babilone. Un Scyte demandant en mariage une fille, et sommé de bailler son bien par declaracion, dit: qu'il n'avoit autre bien que deus amis, s'estimant assez riche avec telle possession pour oser demander la fille d'un grand Seigneur en mariage. [¶] Et pour venir aus femmes, ne sauva Ariadne la vie à Thesee? Hypermnestre à Lyncee? Ne se sont trouvees des armees en danger en païs estranges, et sauvees par l'amitié que quelques Dames portoient aus Capiteines? des Rois remiz en leurs principales citez par les intelligences, que leurs amies leur avoient pratiquees secretement? Tant y ha de povres soudars, qui ont esté eslevez par leurs amies es Contez, Duchez, Royaumes qu'elles possedoient. Certeinement tant de commoditez provenans aus hommes par Amour ont bien aydé à l'estimer grand. Mais plus que toute chose, l'afeccion naturelle, que tous avons à aymer, nous le fait eslever et exalter. Car nous voulons faire paroitre, et estre estimé ce à quoy nous nous sentons enclins. [¶] Et qui est celui des hommes, qui ne prenne plaisir, ou d'aymer, ou d'estre aymé? Je laisse ces Mysanthropes, et Taupes cachees sous terre, et enseveliz de leurs bizarries, lesquels auront par moy tout loisir de n'estre point aymez, puis qu'il ne leur chaut d'aymer. S'il m'estoit licite, je les vous depeindrois, comme je les voy decrire aus hommes de bon esprit. Et neanmoins il vaut mieus en dire un mot, à fin de connoitre combien est mal plaisante et miserable la vie de ceus, qui se sont exemptez d'Amour. [¶] Ils dient que ce sont gens mornes, sans esprit, qui n'ont grace aucune à parler, une voix rude, un aller pensif, un visage de mauvaise rencontre, un œil baissé, creintifs, avares, impitoyables, ignorans, et n'estimans personne: Loups garous. Quand ils entrent en leur maison, ils creingnent que quelcun les regarde. Incontinent qu'ils sont entrez, barrent leur porte, serrent les fenestres, mengent sallement sans compagnie, la maison mal en ordre: se couchent en chapon le morceau au bec. Et lors à beaus gros bonnets gras de deus doits d'espais, la camisole atachee avec esplingues enrouillees jusques au dessous du nombril, grandes chausses de laine venans à mycuisse, un oreiller bien chaufé et sentant sa gresse

I'll cite the words of a great king, who when opening a pomegranate was asked what things he would wish to have in as great a number as the seeds in the fruit and replied: "Zopyruses." It was this same Zopyrus thanks to whom he had won back Babylon.[78] A Scythian, who when asking the hand of a girl in marriage was required to present a declaration of his worldly goods, said that he had no goods other than his two friends, but that with such assets he considered himself wealthy enough to presume to ask for the daughter of a great lord in marriage.[79]

And now, if we turn to women, didn't Ariadne save the life of Theseus, and Hypermnestra the life of Lynceus?[80] Haven't armies who found themselves in danger in foreign lands been saved by the affection certain ladies felt for the captains? Haven't kings been brought back to their chief cities thanks to dealings their mistresses secretly carried out for them? Many a poor mercenary has been promoted to the earldoms, dukedoms, and kingdoms that his mistress possessed. Clearly the great many benefits made available to men through Love have helped him achieve his high standing. But more than anything else, the natural tendency of us all to Love makes us revere and glorify him.[81] For we want that to which we feel naturally drawn to shine forth and be prized.

And what sort of man takes no pleasure either in loving or in being loved? I'll leave these misanthropes and moles hidden underground and buried in their own bizarre behavior. Since to them it matters so little to love, I could care less if they aren't loved in return.[82] With your permission, I'd portray them to you as I see them described by intelligent men. Indeed, it's perhaps worth saying a word about them, so you'll come to know just how unpleasant and miserable the lives of those who have refused love truly are.

They say these are gloomy, humorless people, completely lacking in refinement when they speak. They have gruff voices, distracted gaits, scowling faces, and downcast eyes. They are suspicious, stingy, ruthless, ignorant, and disdainful of everyone — in short, like werewolves. When they enter their homes, they're afraid someone might be watching them. As soon as they're inside, they bar the doors and lock the windows. They eat messily all by themselves, the house in total squalor, and go up to bed early with pieces of food still in their mouths. And then, there they are, in their nice big nightcaps covered with grease two inches thick, their nightshirts, held up with rusty pins, hanging down below their belly buttons, and their thick wool stockings pulled up to the middle of their thighs. Their steamy pillows smell

fondue: le dormir acompagné de toux, et autres tels excremens dont ils remplissent les courtines. Un lever pesant s'il n'y a quelque argent à recevoir: vieilles chausses repetassees, soulier de païsant: pourpoint de drap fourré: long saye mal ataché devant: la robbe qui pend par derriere jusques aus espaules: plus de fourrures et pelisses: calottes et larges bonnets couvrans les cheveus mal pignez: gens plus fades à voir, qu'un potage sans sel à humer. [¶] Que vous en semble il? Si tous les hommes estoient de cette sorte, y auroit il pas peu de plaisir de vivre avec eus? Combien plus tot choisiriez vous un homme propre, bien en point, et bien parlant, tel qu'il ne s'est pù faire sans avoir envie de plaire à quelcun! Qui ha inventé un dous et gracieus langage entre les hommes? et ou premierement ha il esté employé? ha ce esté à persuader de faire guerre au païs? eslire un Capiteine? acuser ou defendre quelcun? Avant que les guerres se fissent, paix, alliances et confederacions en publiq: avant qu'il fust besoin de Capiteines, avant les premiers jugemens que fites faire en Athenes, il y avoit quelque maniere plus douce et gracieuse, que le commun: de laquelle userent Orphee, Amphion, et autres. Et ou en firent preuve les hommes, sinon en Amour? Par pitié on baille à manger à une creature, encore qu'elle n'en demande. On pense à un malade, encore qu'il ne veuille guerir. Mais qu'une femme ou homme d'esprit, prenne plaisir à l'afeccion d'une personne, qui ne la peut descouvrir, lui donne ce qu'il ne peut demander, escoute un rustique et barbare langage: et tout tel qu'il est, sentant plus son commandement, qu'amoureuse priere, celà ne se peut imaginer. [¶] Celle, qui se sent aymee, ha quelque autorité sur celui qui l'ayme: car elle voit en son pouvoir, ce que l'Amant poursuit, comme estant quelque grand bien et fort desirable. Cette autorité veut estre reveree en gestes, faits, contenances, et paroles. Et de ce vient, que les Amans choisissent les façons de faire, par lesquelles les personnes aymees auront plus d'ocasion de croire l'estime et reputacion que lon ha d'elles. On se compose les yeus à douceur et pitié, on adoucit le front, on amollit le langage, encore que de son naturel l'Amant ust le regard horrible, le front despité, et langage sot et rude: car il ha incessamment au cœur l'object de l'amour, qui lui cause un desir d'estre dine d'en recevoir faveur, laquelle il scet bien ne pouvoir avoir sans changer son naturel. Ainsi entre les hommes Amour cause une connoissance

of melted grease, and their sleep is interrupted by coughing and other such secretions that get all over the bed curtains. They get out of bed sluggish — unless they are expecting to collect some money. They put on patched old breeches and peasants' shoes, doublets lined with fur, long coats sloppily fastened in front with capes hanging down to the shoulders in the back, still more furs and fur skins, and skullcaps and big hats covering their disheveled hair. It's more distasteful to look at these people than it is to drink a soup without salt.

What do you think of them? If all men were like this, it wouldn't be much fun living with them, would it? Wouldn't you much rather see a man who is well groomed, well dressed, and well spoken — such that he couldn't exist without having the desire to please someone? Who invented kind and gracious speech among men, and how was it first used? Was it to convince a country to go to war? To elect a captain? To accuse or defend someone? Before wars, peace treaties, alliances, and confederations came to be declared publicly, before there was any need for captains, before the first judgments that you had handed down in Athens, there was a kinder, more gracious way of speaking than what is in common use — one that was practiced by Orpheus, Amphion, and others.[83] And where did men demonstrate this if not in love? Out of pity we give food to an unfortunate creature, even if he doesn't ask for it. We care for a sick person, even if he has no desire to get well. But that an intelligent woman or man could take pleasure in the affection of someone who can't express it, or give what that person is incapable of asking for, or pay attention to a crude and unrefined speech — which, such as it is, seems more like a command than a loving appeal — this is beyond all imagining.

A woman who feels she is loved holds a certain authority over the man who loves her, for she sees that some special and highly desirable thing her lover is seeking lies in her own power. Proper respect needs to be paid to this authority through bearing, actions, demeanor, and words. And that's why lovers choose to behave in ways designed best to convince the women they love of the esteem and admiration they have for them. They make their eyes look kind and sympathetic, they assume a gentle expression, they soften their speech — even if normally the lover in question has a frightening gaze, a vexed expression, and a crude and stupid way of speaking. For ever present in his heart is the object of his love, which makes him want to be worthy of gaining her favor, which he knows he won't be able to do without changing his natural disposition. And so it is that among men Love leads to self-knowledge.[84]

de soymesme. Celui qui ne tache à complaire à personne, quelque perfeccion qu'il ait, n'en ha non plus de plaisir, que celui qui porte une fleur dedens sa manche. Mais celui qui desire plaire, incessamment pense à son fait: mire et remire la chose aymee: suit les vertus, qu'il voit lui estre agreables, et s'adonne aus complexions contraires à soymesme, comme celui qui porte le bouquet en main, donne certein jugement de quelle fleur vient l'odeur et senteur qui plus lui est agreable. [¶] Apres que l'Amant ha composé son corps et complexion à contenter l'esprit de l'aymee, il donne ordre que tout ce qu'elle verra sur lui, ou lui donnera plaisir, ou pour le moins elle n'y trouvera à se facher. De là ha ù source la plaisante invencion des habits nouveaus. Car on ne veut jamais venir à ennui et lasseté, qui provient de voir tousjours une mesme chose. L'homme a tousjours mesme corps, mesme teste, mesme bras, jambes, et piez: mais il les diversifie de tant de sortes, qu'il semble tous les jours estre renouvelé. Chemises parfumees de mile et mile sortes d'ouvrages: bonnet à la saison, pourpoint, chausses jointes et serrees, montrans les mouvemens du corps bien disposé, mille façons de bottines, brodequins, escarpins, souliers, sayons, casaquins, robbes, robbons, cappes, manteaus: le tout en si bon ordre, que rien ne passe. [¶] Et que dirons nous des femmes, l'habit desquelles, et l'ornement de corps, dont elles usent, est fait pour plaire, si jamais rien fut fait. Est il possible de mieus parer une teste, que les Dames font et feront à jamais? avoir cheveus mieus dorez, crespes, frizez? acoutrement de teste mieus seant, quand elles s'acoutreront à l'Espagnole, à la Françoise, à l'Alemande, à l'Italienne, à la Grecque? Quelle diligence mettent elles au demeurant de la face? Laquelle, si elle est belle, elles contregardent tant bien contre les pluies, vents, chaleurs, tems et vieillesse, qu'elles demeurent presque tousjours jeunes. Et si elle ne leur est du tout telle, qu'elles la pourroient desirer, par honneste soin la se procurent; et l'ayant moyennement agreable, sans plus grande curiosité, seulement avec vertueuse industrie la continuent, selon la mode de chacune nacion, contree, et coutume. [¶] Et avec tout celà, l'habit propre comme la feuille autour du fruit. Et s'il y ha perfeccion du corps, ou lineament qui puisse, ou doive estre vù et montré, bien peu le cache l'agencement du vétement: ou, s'il est caché, il l'est en sorte, que lon le cuide plus beau et delicat. Le sein aparoit de tant plus beau, qu'il semble qu'elles ne le veuillent estre vù: les ma-

A man who makes no effort to please anyone, no matter how perfect he might be, gets no more satisfaction out of his virtues than someone who carries a flower inside his sleeve. But the man who desires to please thinks of nothing else but his goal: he observes the one he loves over and over again; he aspires to the qualities that he sees make her happy, and strives to develop ways that go counter to his own nature — just as the man who carries a bouquet in his hand learns to judge what flower has the fragrance and perfume that she will like the most.

After the lover has adjusted his physical appearance and his behavior to suit his beloved, he vows that everything she sees on him either will delight her, or at the very least will not displease her. This is how the appealing notion of new clothes first originated, since no one ever wants to end up getting bored and tired at seeing the same thing over and over again. A man always has the same body, the same head, the same arms, legs, and feet, but he can change his appearance in so many ways that every day he looks like a new person: perfumed shirts in a thousand different styles; hats for every season; doublets and tight, close-fitting stockings to reveal the movements of a well-proportioned body; a thousand varieties of buttoned and laced boots, flat and low-heeled shoes; jackets and overblouses, robes, coats, capes, cloaks — the whole wardrobe so well organized that nothing is left out.

And what will we say of women, whose clothing and other fashion accessories are designed to please, if ever anything was! Is it possible to beautify someone's appearance any better than ladies do now and will always do? To have hair more golden, crimped, and curled? Or hats more attractive than when they deck themselves out, whether in the Spanish, French, German, Italian, or Greek styles? To what great pains do they go to look after their face? If it's beautiful, they protect it so carefully against rain, wind, heat, time, and old age that they stay young almost forever. Even if it's not at all what they might like it to be, through diligent attention they manage to acquire the face they want; and when it's reasonably pleasing, they keep it that way — without extreme measures, but simply with devoted effort, following the fashion of their particular country, region, and customs.

In addition to all this, their clothing compliments them as nicely as the leaf around a fruit. If their body or any of its features is so perfect that it could or should be seen and revealed, the fit of their garments does little to conceal it, or if it does, it's in a way that makes it appear even more lovely and pleasing. Women's breasts look all the more beautiful if it seems as if they don't want them to be seen; and

melles en leur rondeur relevees font donner un peu d'air au large esto-mac. Au reste, la robbe bien jointe, le corps estreci ou il le faut: les manches serrees, si le bras est massif: si non, larges et bien enrichies: la chausse tiree: l'escarpin façonnant le petit pié (car le plus souvent l'amoureuse curiosité des hommes fait rechercher la beauté jusques au bout des piez:) tant de pommes d'or, chaines, bagues, ceintures, pen-dans, gans parfumez, manchons: et en somme tout ce qui est de beau, soit à l'acoutrement des hommes ou des femmes, Amour en est l'auteur. [¶] Et s'il ha si bien travaillé pour contenter les yeus, il n'a moins fait aus autres sentimens: mais les ha tous emmiellez de nouvelle et propre douceur. Les fleurs que tu fiz, ô Jupiter, naitre es mois de l'an les plus chaus, sont entre les hommes faites hybernalles: les arbres, plantes, herbages, qu'avois distribuez en divers païs, sont par l'estude de ceus qui veulent plaire à leurs amies, rassemblez en un verger: et quelque-fois suis contreint, pour ayder à leur afeccion, leur departir plus de chaleur que le païs ne le requerroit. Et tout le proufit de ce, n'est que se ramentevoir par ces petis presens en la bonne grace de ces amis et amies. [¶] Diray je que la Musique n'a esté inventee que par Amour? et est le chant et harmonie l'effect et signe de l'Amour parfait. Les hommes en usent ou pour adoucir leurs desirs enflammez, ou pour donner plaisir: pour lequel diversifier tous les jours ils inventent nou-veaus et divers instrumens de Luts, Lyres, Citres, Doucines, Violons, Espinettes, Flutes, Cornets: chantent tous le jours diverses chansons: et viendront à inventer madrigalles, sonnets, pavanes, passemeses, gaillardes, et tout en commemoracion d'Amour: comme celui, pour lequel les hommes font plus que pour nul autre. C'est pour lui que lon fait des serenades, aubades, tournois, combats tant à pié qu'à che-val. En toutes lesquelles entreprises ne se treuvent que jeunes gens amoureus: ou s'ils s'en treuvent autres meslez parmi, ceus qui ayment emportent tousjours le pris, et en remercient les Dames, desquelles ils ont porté les faveurs. Là aussi se raporteront les Comedies, Tragedies, Jeux, Montres, Masques, Moresques. [¶] Dequoy allege un voyageur son travail, que lui cause le long chemin, qu'en chantant quelque chanson d'Amour, ou escoutant de son compagnon quelque conte et fortune amoureuse? L'un loue le bon traitement de s'amie: l'autre se pleint de la cruauté de la sienne. Et mile accidens, qui interviennent en amours: lettres descouvertes, mauvais raports, quelque voisine jalouse,

when they are lifted up so that their roundness shows, they make a large belly less noticeable. As for the rest, a well-knit gown, drawn in tightly to the body where necessary; narrow sleeves if the arms are full and if not, wide, richly trimmed ones; close-fitting stockings; slippers shaping a dainty foot (for men's romantic curiosity frequently makes them look for beauty all the way down to the tips of the toes); and then all kinds of round golden pendants, chains, rings, belts, earrings, perfumed gloves, and muffs — in sum, everything beautiful in the apparel of either men or women owes its fashioning to Love.

And if he's worked so hard to please the eyes, he's done no less for the other senses, for he's delighted them all with new pleasures designed just for them. Flowers that you, Jupiter, made to grow during the hottest months of the year, men have made bloom in winter as well; trees, plants, and pastures that you had divided up among different regions are now placed together in a single orchard by the efforts of men who want to please the women they love. Sometimes, in order to help along their affections, I myself am forced to provide them with more heat than the land would require. And the benefit of all this is simply — by means of these little gestures — to be remembered and kept in the good graces of their loved ones.

Need I say that music was invented by none other than Love, and that song and harmony are the sign and mark of perfect love? Men turn to music to soothe their burning desires, or to provide enjoyment, which they vary from day to day by inventing new and different instruments such as lutes, lyres, zithers, oboes, violins, virginals, flutes, and cornets.[85] They sing different songs every day, and so have come to invent madrigals, sonnets, pavanes, passamezzos, and lively waltzes, and all of them to celebrate Love, for whom men will go to greater lengths than for anyone else.[86] It's for him that they sing serenades and aubades, and organize tournaments and jousts both on foot and on horseback.[87] In all these activities only young people in love take part, or if by chance others mix in among them, those who are in love always carry away the prize, and for this they thank the ladies whose colors they wore. Comedies, tragedies, games, performances, masquerades, and morris dances likewise come from the same source.[88]

What better eases the fatigue of a traveler after his long journey than singing some love song, or listening to his companion recount some story or adventure about love? One man praises the kindness of his beloved; another laments the cruelty of his. And then there are the thousand chance misfortunes that turn up in love: intercepted letters,

quelque mari qui revient plus tot que lon ne voudroit: quelquefois
s'apercevant de ce qui se fait: quelquefois n'en croyant rien, se fiant sur
la preudhommie de sa femme: et à fois eschaper un souspir avec un
changement de parler: puis force excuses. [¶] Brief, le plus grand
plaisir qui soit apres amour, c'est d'en parler. Ainsi passoit son chemin
Apulee, quelque Filozofe qu'il fust. Ainsi prennent les plus severes
hommes plaisir d'ouir parler de ces propos, encores qu'ils ne le veuil-
lent confesser. Mais qui fait tant de Poëtes au monde en toutes
langues? n'est ce pas Amour? lequel semble estre le suget, duquel tous
Poëtes veulent parler. Et qui me fait attribuer la poësie à Amour: ou
dire, pour le moins, qu'elle est bien aydee et entretenue par son
moyen? c'est qu'incontinent que les hommes commencent d'aymer, ils
escrivent vers. Et ceus qui ont esté excellens Poëtes, ou en ont tout
rempli leurs livres, ou, quelque autre suget qu'ils ayent pris, n'ont osé
toutefois achever leur euvre sans en faire honorable mencion. Orphee,
Musee, Homere, Line, Alcee, Saphon, et autres Poëtes et Filozofes:
comme Platon, et celui qui ha ù le nom de Sage, ha descrit ses plus
hautes concepcions en forme d'amourettes. Et plusieurs autres escri-
veins voulans descrire autres invencions, les ont cachées sous sem-
blables propos. [¶] C'est Cupidon qui ha gaigné ce point, qu'il faut que
chacun chante ou ses passions, ou celles d'autrui, ou couvre ses dis-
cours d'Amour, sachant qu'il n'y ha rien, qui le puisse faire mieus este
reçu. Ovide ha tousjours dit qu'il aymoit. Petrarque en son langage ha
fait sa seule afeccion aprocher à la gloire de celui, qui ha representé
toutes les passions, coutumes, façons, et natures de tous les hommes,
qui est Homere. Qu'a jamais mieus chanté Virgile, que les amours
de la Dame de Carthage? ce lieu seroit long, qui voudroit le traiter
comme il meriteroit. Mais il me semble qu'il ne se peut nier, que
l'Amour ne soit cause aus hommes de gloire, honneur, proufit, plaisir:
et tel, que sans lui ne se peut commodément vivre. Pource est il estimé
entre les humains, l'honorans et aymans, comme celui qui leur ha
procuré tout bien et plaisir. [¶] Ce qui lui ha esté bien aisé, tant qu'il
ha ù ses yeus. Mais aujourdhui, qu'il en est privé, si Folie se mesle de
ses afaires, il est à creindre, et quasi inevitable, qu'il ne soit cause d'au-
tant de vilenie, incommodité, et desplaisir, comme il ha esté par le
passé d'honneur, proufit, et volupté. Les grans qu'Amour contreingnoit

false reports, some jealous neighbor, some husband who returns earlier than expected, sometimes figuring out what's going on, sometimes not believing any of it, trusting in the loyalty of his wife, who in trying to change the subject sometimes lets out a sigh — and then, a litany of excuses.[89]

In short, the greatest pleasure there is, after love, is talking about it. That's how Apuleius kept himself amused on his travels, philosopher though he was.[90] And thus even the sternest men enjoy hearing people talk about such things, even if they don't care to admit it. Who is the one responsible for creating so many poets, in so many languages, throughout the world? Isn't it Love? This seems to be the subject on which all poets wish to speak. And what makes me attribute poetry to Love, or to say, at least, that poetry is promoted and nourished through his skill? It's that from the very minute men fall in love, they start writing verses. And those poets who are most admired either have totally filled their books with love, or else, even if they've treated other subjects, nevertheless haven't dared complete their works without making worthy mention of it: among them are Orpheus, Musaeus, Homer, Linus, Alcaeus, Sappho, as well as other poets and philosophers, such as Plato and the one known as the Sage, who depicted his loftiest ideas in the form of amusing love stories.[91] A number of other writers, when trying to express other ideas, disguised them in similar language.

Cupid has surely won this point: that everyone must sing either of his own passions or those of others, or else embellish his speeches with love, knowing there's nothing else that can make him more popular. Ovid always said that he loved.[92] In his own language, Petrarch raised his one great love close to the height of glory given to the poet who portrayed all the passions, customs, behaviors, and natures of all men — that is, Homer himself. When did Virgil ever sing better than when he told of Dido's love?[93] This account would be long indeed for anyone who really wanted to do it the justice it deserves. But it seems to me impossible to deny that Love is responsible for the reputation, honor, profit, and pleasure of mankind, so much so that without him, it would be impossible to get the proper joy out of life. This is why he is valued so highly by human beings, who honor and love him as the one who has provided them with every pleasure and every good thing.

He could do all of this very easily as long as he had his eyes. But now that he's without them, if Folly meddles in his affairs, I fear he will almost inevitably become the cause of as much nastiness, trouble, and distress as he was in the past of honor, good fortune, and pleasure.

aymer les petis et les sugetz qui estoient sous eus, changeront en sorte qu'ils n'aymeront plus que ceus dont ils en penseront tirer service. Les petits, qui aymoient leurs Princes et Signeurs, les aymeront seulement pour faire leurs besongnes, en esperance de se retirer quand ils seront pleins. Car ou Amour voudra faire cette harmonie entre les hautes et basses personnes, Folie se trouvera pres, qui l'empeschera: et encore es lieus ou il se sera ataché. Quelque bon et innocent qu'il soit, Folie lui meslera de son naturel: tellement que ceus qui aymeront, feront tousjours quelque tour de fol. Et plus les amitiez seront estroites, plus s'y trouvera il de desordre quand Folie s'y mettra. Il retournera plus d'une Semiramis, plus d'une Biblis, d'une Mirrha, d'une Canace, d'une Phedra. [¶] Il n'y aura lieu saint au monde. Les hauts murs et treilliz garderont mal les Vestales. La vieillesse tournera son venerable et paternel amour, en fols et juvenils desirs. Honte se perdra du tout. Il n'y aura discrecion entre noble, païsant, infidele, ou More, Dame, maitresse, servante. Les parties seront si inegales, que les belles ne rencontreront les beaus, ains seront conjointes le plus souvent avec leurs dissemblables. Grands Dames aymeront quelquefois ceus dont ne daigneroient estre servies. Les gens d'esprit s'abuseront autour des plus laides. Et quand les povres et loyaus amans auront langui de l'amour de quelque belle: lors Folie fera jouir quelque avolé en moins d'une heure du bien ou l'autre n'aura pù ateindre. [¶] Je laisse les noises et querelles, qu'elle dressera par tout, dont s'en ensuivra blessures, outrages, et meurtres. Et ay belle peur, qu'au lieu, ou Amour ha inventé tant de sciences, et produit tant de bien, qu'elle n'ameine avec soy quelque grande oisiveté acompagnee d'ignorance: qu'elle n'empesche les jeunes gens de suivre les armes et de faire service à leur Prince: ou de vaquer à estudes honorables: qu'elle ne leur mesle leur amour de paroles detestables, chansons trop vileines, ivrongnerie et gourmandise: qu'elle ne leur suscite mile maladies, et mette en infiniz dangers de leurs personnes. Car il n'y ha point de plus dangereuse compagnie que de Folie. Voila les maus qui sont à creindre, si Folie se trouve autour d'Amour. Et s'il avenoit que cette meschante le voulust empescher ça haut, que Venus ne voulust plus rendre un dous aspect avec nous autres, que

Those in high places, whom Cupid required to love the lowly folk and the subjects beneath them, will change in such a way that from now on they'll love only those who they believe will be of service to them. The lowly folk, who used to love their princes and lords, will love them only to get what they need from them, hoping to leave once they have the means. For wherever Love wants to create harmony between noble and lowly people, Folly will be right there to keep him from doing it, even in places where he's already made his mark. However good and innocent he may be, Folly will intrude and impart some of her own qualities, to the point where those who fall in love will always act foolishly. And the closer the relationships, the more chaotic it will be once Folly gets involved. More than one Semiramis, more than one Byblis, Mirrha, Canace, and Phaedra will be among us once again.[94]

No sacred places will be left in the world. High walls and fences will be unable to protect the vestal virgins. Even old age will turn its revered paternal love into foolish youthful desires. All sense of shame will be lost. There will be no distinction between nobleman or peasant, infidel or Moor, lady, mistress, or maidservant. The parties will be so unequal that beautiful women won't meet up with handsome men, but will be united most of the time with those most unlike them. Great ladies will sometimes fall in love with men they wouldn't even deign to have as their servants. Intelligent men will waste their time in the company of unattractive women. And then, when poor, devoted suitors have been pining away for the love of some beautiful woman, Folly will see to it that some thoughtless interloper enjoys in no time the favor that the others couldn't attain.

I won't even go into the quarrels and disputes she'll stir up everywhere, and the insults, injuries, and murders that will follow. And I'm terribly afraid that where Love has forged so much knowledge and brought about so much good, Folly will bring with her only widespread idleness accompanied by ignorance. I fear that she might prevent young men from taking up arms and serving their prince, or from pursuing worthy studies; that she might degrade their love with foul words, vulgar songs, drunkenness, and greed; and that she might make them vulnerable to a thousand sicknesses and place their lives in constant danger. For there is no more dangerous company in the world than Folly's. Here, then, are the evils to be feared should Folly be anywhere close to Love. And if it should happen that this malicious woman wanted — up here on high — to keep Venus from looking

Mercure ne voulust plus entretenir nos alliances, quelle confusion y auroit il? [¶] Mais j'ay promis ne parler que de ce qui se fait en terre. Or donq, Jupiter, qui t'apeles pere des hommes, qui leur es auteur de tout bien, leur donnes la pluie quand elle est requise, seiches l'humidité superabondante: considere ces maus qui sont preparez aus hommes, si Folie n'est separee d'Amour. Laisse Amour se resjouir en paix entre les hommes: qu'il soit loisible à un chacun de converser privément et domestiquement les personnes qu'il aymera, sans que personne en ait creinte ou soupson: que les nuits ne chassent, sous pretexte des mauvaises langues, l'ami de la maison de s'amie: que lon puisse mener la femme de son ami, voisin, parent, ou bon semblera, en telle seurté que l'honneur de l'un ou l'autre n'en soit en rien ofensé. Et à ce que personne n'ait plus mal en teste, quand il verra telles privautez, fais publier par toute la Terre, non à son de trompe ou par ataches mises aus portes des temples, mais en mettant au cœur de tous ceus qui regarderont les Amans, qu'il n'est possible qu'ils vousissent faire ou penser quelque Folie. Ainsi auras tu mis tel ordre au fait avenu, que les hommes auront ocasion de te louer et magnifier plus que jamais, et feras beaucoup pour toy et pour nous. Car tu nous auras delivrez d'une infinité de pleintes, qui autrement nous seront faites par les hommes, des esclandres que Folie amoureuse fera au monde. [¶] Ou bien si tu aymes mieus remettre les choses en l'estat qu'elles estoient, contreins les Parques et Destinees (si tu y as quelque pouvoir) de retourner leurs fuseaus, et faire en sorte qu'à ton commandement, et à ma priere, et pour l'amour de Venus, que tu as jusques ici tant cherie et aymee, et pour les plaisirs et contentemens que tous tant que nous sommes, avons reçuz et recevons d'Amour, elles ordonnent, que les yeus seront rendus à Cupidon, et la bande otee: à ce que le puissions voir encore un coup en son bel et naïf estre, piteus de tous les cotez dont on le sauroit regarder, et riant d'un seulement. [¶] O Parques, ne soyez à ce coup inexorables que lon ne die que vos fuseaus ont esté ministres de la cruelle vengeance de Folie. Ceci n'empeschera point la suite des choses à venir. Jupiter composera tous ces trois jours en un, comme il fit les trois nuits, qu'il fut avec Alcmene. Je vous apelle, vous autres Dieus, et vous Deesses, qui tant avez porté et portez d'honneur à Venus. Voici l'endroit ou lui pouvez rendre les faveurs que d'elle avez reçues.

kindly on the rest of us, or to keep Mercury from maintaining our alliances, what chaos would come out of this?

But I promised to speak only of what takes place on earth. So now then, Jupiter, you who call yourself the father of men and who are the source of all their good, you who bring them rain when it's needed and who dry out any excess moisture, consider these ills that lie in store for men, if Folly isn't separated from Love. Permit Love to enjoy living in peace among men, and allow each and every person to get together privately, and behind closed doors, with those they love, without fear or suspicion. Let no lover be forced to flee his beloved's house at nightfall out of worry about nasty gossip. Rather, let anyone take the wife of his friend, neighbor, or relative wherever he wants, with full assurance that the reputation of neither one of them will in any way be compromised. And so that no one harbors ill thoughts anymore when he witnesses such intimate scenes, let it be known all over the earth — not by the blare of trumpets or notices posted on temple doors but by instilling it in the hearts of all of them — that the lovers they see couldn't possibly want to commit or even to consider any act of folly. By taking these measures, you'll resolve this entire matter in a way that will give men reason to praise and honor you more than ever, and you'll be doing yourself and us a great favor. For you'll spare us from the neverending complaints that otherwise men will make to us about the scandals that Folly, if partnered with Love, will cause in the world.[95]

Or else, if you prefer to go back to the way things were before, insist that the Fates and Destinies (if you have any power over them) rewind their spindles.[96] Make it clear upon your command and my request, and for the love of Venus who up to this very day you've always loved and cherished, and for the pleasure and satisfaction that all of us — no matter who we are — have received and still receive from Love, that they order Cupid's eyes to be returned to him and his bandage removed. Then we will be able to see him once again in his beautiful and natural state, moving us to pity from every angle we look at him, but happy, at least, to have his eyes back.[97]

Oh Fates, this time don't be so merciless that your spindles will be said to have been the agents of Folly's cruel vengeance. This will have no impact on the course of things yet to come. Jupiter will contract these three days into a single one, just as he prolonged into three nights the time he spent with Alcmene.[98] I call upon you other gods and goddesses, who have paid and still pay such great homage to Venus, for here is your chance to return the favors she's done for you.

[¶] Mais de qui plus dois je esperer, que de toy, Jupiter? laisseras tu plorer en vain la plus belle des Deesses? n'auras tu pitié de l'angoisse qu'endure ce povre enfant dine de meilleure fortune? Aurons nous perdu nos veuz et prieres? Si celles des hommes te peuvent forcer et t'ont fait plusieurs fois tomber des mains, sans mal faire, la foudre que tu avois contre eus preparee: quel pouvoir auront les notres, ausquels as communiqué ta puissance et autorité? Et te prians pour personnes, pour lesquelles toymesme (si tu ne tenois le lieu de commander) prierois volontiers: et en la faveur desquelles (si je puis savoir quelque secret des choses futures) feras, possible, apres certeines revolucions, plus que ne demandons, assugetissant à perpetuité Folie à Amour, et le faisant plus cler voyant que nul autre des Dieus. J'ay dit.

Incontinent qu'Apolon ut fini son acusacion, toute la compagnie des Dieus par un fremissement, se montra avoir compassion de la belle Deesse là presente, et de Cupidon son fils. Et ussent volontiers tout sur lheure condamné la Deesse Folie: Quand l'equitable Jupiter par une magesté Imperiale leur commanda silence, pour ouir la defense de Folie enchargée à Mercure, lequel commença à parler ainsi:

MERCURE: N'atendez point, Jupiter, et vous autres Dieus immortels, que je commence mon oraison par excuses (comme quelquefois font les Orateurs, qui creingnent estre blamez, quand ils soutiennent des causes apertement mauvaises) de ce qu'ay pris en main la defense de Folie, et mesmes contre Cupidon, auquel ay en plusieurs endrois porté tant d'obeïssance, qu'il auroit raison de m'estimer tout sien: et ay tant aymé la mere, que n'ay jamais espargné mes allees et venues, tant qu'ay pensé lui faire quelque chose agreable. La cause, que je defens, est si juste, que ceus mesmes qui ont parlé au contraire, apres m'avoir ouy, changeront d'opinion. L'issue du diferent, comme j'espere, sera telle, que mesme Amour quelque jour me remercira de ce service, que contre lui je fay à Folie. [¶] Cette question est entre deus amis, qui ne sont pas si outrez l'un envers l'autre, que quelque matin ne se puissent reconcilier, et prendre plaisir l'un de l'autre, comme au paravant. Si à l'apetit de l'un, vous chassez l'autre, quand ce desir de vengeance sera passé (laquelle incontinent qu'elle est achevee commence à desplaire:) si vous ordonnez quelque cas contre Folie, Amour en aura le premier regret. Et n'estoit cette ancienne amitié et aliance de ces deus, meintenant aversaires, qui les faisoit si uniz et conjoins, que ja-

But from whom must I hope more than from you, Jupiter? Will you leave the most beautiful of all goddesses to weep in vain? Will you take no pity on the distress being endured by this poor child who deserves a better fate? Will our wishes and prayers all be for nothing? If the prayers of men can move you, and have made you many times drop harmlessly from your hands the thunderbolts you'd prepared to use against them, then what power will our prayers have — we with whom you've shared a measure of your strength and authority? And so I beseech you on behalf of those for whom you yourself would willingly plead (if it weren't in your place to rule), and in whose favor (since I can foresee some of the secrets of things to come) you'll perhaps do even more, in time, than what we are asking now.[99] You may, one day, bring Folly under Love's authority forever, and make him more clear-sighted than any of the other gods. I rest my case.

Immediately after Apollo had finished presenting his case, the entire assembly of the gods murmured, thereby showing their compassion for the beautiful goddess present among them and for her son Cupid. Indeed, they would willingly have condemned the goddess Folly at that very moment. But the upright Jupiter, in his imperial majesty, demanded their silence in order to hear the defense of Folly entrusted to Mercury, who began to speak thus:

MERCURY: You should not expect me, Jupiter and you other immortal gods, to begin my speech with apologies (as orators sometimes do for fear of being blamed when they defend clearly wrongful causes) for having assumed Folly's defense — even against Cupid, whom I have dutifully obeyed in so many circumstances that he would have every reason to count me as one of his own. Moreover, I've loved his mother so much that I've never failed to go to any lengths, so long as I thought I could do something to please her. The cause that I'm defending is so just that even those who have spoken out against it will change their minds once they've heard what I have to say. The outcome of this dispute, I hope, will be such that even Love will one day thank me for my efforts to uphold Folly against him.

This is really an issue between two friends, who aren't so angry at each other that they might not someday make up and enjoy each other's company as they did before. If at the demand of one of them you get rid of the other, or if you rule against Folly, then, when the desire for vengeance has passed (for once satisfied it always becomes distasteful), Love himself will be the first to regret it. Were it not for the longstanding friendship and alliance between these two newly declared adver-

mais n'avez fait faveur à l'un, que l'autre ne s'en soit senti: je me defierois bien que puissiez donner bon ordre sur ce diferent, ayans tous suivi Amour fors Pallas: laquelle estant ennemie capitale de Folie, ne seroit raison qu'elle voulust juger sa cause. [¶] Et toutefois n'est Folie si inconnue ceans, qu'elle ne se ressente d'avoir souventefois esté la bien venue, vous aportant tousjours avec sa troupe quelques cas de nouveau pour rendre vos banquets et festins plus plaisans. Et pense que tous ceus de vous, qui ont aymé, ont aussi bonne souvenance d'elle, que de Cupidon mesme. Davantage elle vous croit tous si equitables et raisonnables, qu'encore que ce fait fust le votre propre, si n'en feriez vous que la raison. [¶] J'ay trois choses à faire. Defendre la teste de Folie, contre laquelle Amour ha juré; respondre aus acusacions que j'entens estre faites à Folie: et à la demande qu'il fait de ses yeus. Apolon, qui ha si long tems ouy les causeurs à Romme, ha bien retenu d'eus à conter tousjours à son avantage. Mais Folie, comme elle est tousjours ouverte, ne veut point que j'en dissimule rien: et ne vous en veut dire qu'un mot, sans art, sans fard et ornement quelconque. Et, à la pure verité, Folie se jouant avec Amour, ha passé devant lui pour gaigner le devant, et pour venir plus tot vous donner plaisir. Amour est entré en colere. Lui et elle se sont pris de paroles. Amour l'a taché navrer de ses armes qu'il portoit. Folie s'est defendue des siennes, dont elle ne s'estoit chargee pour blesser personne, mais pource que ordinairement elle les porte. Car, comme vous savez, ainsi qu'Amour tire au cœur, Folie aussi se gette aus yeus et à la teste, et n'a autres armes que ses doits. Amour ha voulu montrer qu'il avoit puissance sur le cœur d'elle. Elle lui ha fait connoitre qu'elle avoit puissance de lui oter les yeus. Il ne se pleingnoit que de la deformité de son visage. Elle esmue de pitié la lui ha couvert d'une bande à ce que lon n'aperçust deus trous vuides d'iceus, enlaidissans sa face. [¶] On dit que Folie ha fait double injure à Amour: premierement, de lui avoir crevé les yeus: secondement, de lui avoir mis ce bandeau. On exaggere le crime fait à une personne aymee d'une personne, dont plusieurs ont afaire. Il faut respondre à ces deus injures. Quant à la premiere, Je dy: que les loix et raisons humaines ont permis à tous se defendre contre ceus qui les voudroient ofenser, tellement que ce, que chacun fait en se defendant, est estimé bien et justement fait. Amour ha esté l'agresseur. Car combien que

saries, one that joined and united them so closely that you've never granted a favor to one without its benefiting the other too, I would have little confidence that you could resolve this dispute fairly. After all, everyone has been known to follow Love except Pallas, Folly's mortal enemy, who'd have no reason to wish even to consider her cause.[100]

Still, Folly is hardly so unknown in this place that she doesn't recall the many times she was welcomed here. She and her troupe always brought you some new entertainment to make your banquets and parties more enjoyable. And I think that all of you who have been in love remember her as clearly as you remember Cupid himself. Furthermore, she believes you are all so fair-minded and reasonable that even if this were your own dispute, you could only handle it sensibly.

There are three things I must do: defend Folly's very person whom Love has denounced; answer the accusations that I understand are being made against Folly; and respond to Love's request that his eyes be given back to him. Apollo, who for so long has heard lawyers plead their cases in Rome, has surely learned from them how to argue to his own advantage.[101] But Folly, since she is always so open, doesn't want me to hide a thing. Rather, she wants me to speak to you using only simple, uncontrived words and no flowery rhetoric. And so, the simple truth of the matter is that Folly, trying to have a little fun with Love, passed in front of him to get ahead, and to arrive earlier in order to please you. Love got very angry. The two of them began to argue. Love tried to wound her with the weapons he was carrying. Folly defended herself with her own, which she'd brought along not to hurt anyone, but simply because she normally has them with her. For, as you know, whereas Love takes aim at the heart, Folly attacks the eyes and head, with no weapons other than her fingers. Love wanted to prove that he had power over her heart. She let him know that she had the power to put out his eyes. He complained only about his face being disfigured. Moved to pity, she covered it with a bandage so no one could see the two empty holes that made his face so unsightly.

They say that Folly inflicted a double injury on Love: first, to have put out his eyes, and second, to have put on the bandage. There is a tendency to exaggerate crimes when the victim is loved by a person who is implicated in the lives of so many others.[102] These two injuries must therefore be addressed. As for the first, I say that human laws and judgment have always allowed everyone to defend themselves against those who would wish to harm them, to the point that anything done in self-defense is considered proper and acceptable. Love was the aggressor.

Folie ait premierement parlé à Amour, ce n'estoit toutefois pour quereler, mais pour s'esbatre, et se jouer à lui. Folie s'est defendue. Duquel coté est le tort? Quand elle lui ust pis fait, je ne voy point comment on lui en ust pù rien demander. [¶] Et si ne voulez croire qu'Amour ait esté l'agresseur, interroguez le. Vous verrez qu'il reconnoitra verité. Et n'est chose incroyable en son endroit de commencer tels brouilliz. Ce n'est d'aujourdhui, qu'il ha esté si insuportable, quand bon lui ha semblé. Ne s'ataqua il pas à Mars, qui regardoit Vulcan forgeant des armes, et tout soudein le blessa? et n'y ha celui de cette compagnie, qui n'ait esté quelquefois las d'ouir ces bravades. Folie rit tousjours, ne pense si avant aus choses, ne marche si avant pour estre la premiere, mais pource qu'elle est plus pronte et hative. Je ne say que sert d'alleguer la coutume toleree à Cupidon de tirer de son arc ou bon lui semble. Car quelle loy ha il plus de tirer à Folie, que Folie n'a de s'adresser à Amour? Il ne lui ha fait mal: neanmoins il s'en est mis en son plein devoir. [¶] Quel mal ha fait Folie, rengeant Amour, en sorte qu'il ne peut plus nuire, si ce n'est d'aventure? Que se treuve il en eus de capital? y ha il quelque guet à pens, ports darmes, congregacions illicites, ou autres choses qui puissent tourner au desordre de la Republique? C'estoit Folie et un enfant, auquel ne falloit avoir egard. Je ne say comment te prendre en cet endroit, Apolon. S'il est si ancien, il doit avoir apris à estre plus modeste, qu'il n'est: et s'il est jeune, aussi est Folie jeune, et fille de Jeunesse. A cette cause, celui qui est blessé, en doit demeurer là. Et dorenavant que personne ne se prenne à Folie. Car elle ha, quand bon lui semblera, dequoy venger ses injures: et, n'est de si petit lieu, qu'elle doive soufrir les jeunesses de Cupidon. [¶] Quant à la seconde injure, que Folie lui ha mis un bandeau, ceci est une pure calomnie. Car en lui bandant le dessous du front, Folie jamais ne pensa lui agrandir son mal, ou lui oter le remede de guerir. Et quel meilleur témoignage faut il, que de Cupidon mesme? Il a trouvé bon d'estre bandé: il ha connu qu'il avoit esté agresseur, et que l'injure provenoit de lui: il ha reçu cette faveur de Folie. Mais il ne savoit pas qu'il fust de tel pouvoir. Et quand il ust sù, que lui ust nuy de le prendre? Il ne lui devoit jamais estre oté: par consequent donq ne lui de-

For although Folly spoke first to Love, it wasn't to get into an argument but to joke with him and have a good time. Folly defended herself. Who, then, was in the wrong? Even if she'd done something worse to him, I don't see how any case could possibly be brought against her.

And if you're unwilling to believe that Love was the aggressor, just ask him. You'll see that he'll admit the truth. After all, it's hardly unheard of for him to start such disagreements. Today isn't the first time he's been so troublesome simply because he felt like it. Didn't he attack Mars, who was watching Vulcan forge weapons, and wound him out of the blue? [103] There's not a single member of this assembly who hasn't at some point grown tired of hearing him brag about himself. Folly, on the other hand, is always laughing. She doesn't think about things so far in advance, or walk so far ahead for the sake of being first, but because she's quicker and swifter. I don't know what good it does to bring up the custom that's always allowed Cupid to shoot his arrows wherever he pleases. For what more right does he have to take aim at Folly than Folly has to attack Love? He didn't wind up hurting her, but he certainly gave it his very best effort.

What wrong has Folly committed by subduing Love so that he can no longer cause any harm, except by chance? Of what grave consequence is this dispute? Have there been ambushes, armed forces, illicit meetings, or other things that could throw the Republic into disarray? What we have here is simply Folly and a child, to whom it was not necessary to pay great respect. I don't quite know how to understand your position on this point, Apollo. If he's been around for so long, he should have learned to be more modest by now; and if he's young, so is Folly, the daughter of the goddess Youth. Because of this, the one who's been hurt should leave well enough alone. And from now on, no one should get in Folly's way, for she has what it takes to pay back any wrongs against her whenever she wants. Surely her status isn't so low that she should have to tolerate Cupid's childish behavior.

As for the second injury, that Folly put a bandage on him, this is pure slander. When she applied the bandage below his forehead, Folly never intended to aggravate his injury or to eliminate any chance for his recovery. And what better evidence is needed than what Cupid said himself? He willingly agreed to be bandaged. He knew he'd been the aggressor and that his injury was his own fault. He welcomed this favor from Folly, but he didn't know just how powerful the bandage was. But even if he'd known, what harm would it have done him to accept it? Since it was never to be removed, his eyes were never meant

voient estre ses yeus rendus. Si ses yeus ne lui devoient estre rendus, que lui nuit le bandeau? Que bien tu te montres ingrat à ce coup, fils de Venus, quand tu calomnies le bon vouloir que t'ay porté, et interpretes à mal ce que je t'ay fait pour bien. [¶] Pour agraver le fait, on dit que c'estoit en lieu de franchise. Aussi estoit ce en lieu de franchise, qu'Amour avoit assailli. Les autels et temples ne sont inventez à ce qu'il soit loisible aus meschans d'y tuer les bons, mais pour sauver les infortunez de la fureur du peuple, ou du courrous d'un Prince. Mais celui qui pollue la franchise, n'en doit il perdre le fruit? S'il ust bien succedé à Amour, comme il vouloit, et ust blessé cette Dame, je croy qu'il n'ust pas voulu que lon lui eust imputé ceci. Le semblable faut qu'il treuve bon en autrui. [¶] Folie m'a defendu que ne la fisse miserable, que ne vous suppliasse pour lui pardonner, si faute y avoit: m'a defendu le plorer, n'embrasser vos genous, vous adjurer par les gracieus yeus, que quelquefois avez trouvez agreables venans d'elle, ny amener ses parens, enfans, amis, pour vous esmouvoir à pitié. Elle vous demande ce que ne lui pouvez refuser, qu'il soit dit: qu'Amour par sa faute mesme est devenu aveugle. [¶] Le second point qu'Apolon ha touché, c'est qu'il veut estre faites defenses à Folie de n'aprocher dorenavant Amour de cent pas à la ronde. Et ha fondé sa raison sur ce, qu'estant en honneur et reputacion entre les hommes, leur causant beaucoup de bien et plaisirs, si Folie y estoit meslee, tout tourneroit au contraire. Mon intencion sera de montrer qu'en tout cela Folie n'est rien inferieure à Amour, et qu'Amour ne seroit rien sans elle: et ne peut estre, et regner sans son ayde. Et pource qu'Amour ha commencé à montrer sa grandeur par son ancienneté, je feray le semblable: et vous prieray reduire en memoire comme incontinent que l'homme fut mis sur terre, il commença sa vie par Folie: et depuis ses successeurs ont si bien continué, que jamais Dame n'ut tant bon credit au monde. [¶] Vray est qu'au commencement les hommes ne faisoient point de hautes folies, aussi n'avoient ils encores aucuns exemples devant eus. Mais leur folie estoit à courir l'un apres l'autre: à monter sus un arbre pour voir de plus loin: rouler en la vallee: à menger tout leur fruit en un coup: tellement que l'hiver n'avoient que menger. Petit à petit ha cru Folie avec le tems. Les plus esventez d'entre eus, ou pour avoir rescous des loups et autres

to be given back to him. And if his eyes weren't meant to be given back to him, what harm is there in the bandage? How thankless you seem, son of Venus, when you belittle my goodwill toward you, and when you misinterpret what I did for your own good.[104]

To make matters worse, they say that this happened in a sacred place.[105] But if so, then it was also in this sacred place that Love launched his attack. Altars and temples aren't created to provide a lawful haven for evildoers to kill honorable people, but to protect the unfortunate from the rage of the masses or from the anger of a prince. But shouldn't someone who violates a sacred place also forfeit its safety? If Love had really managed to wound this lady, as he was trying to do, I don't think he would have wanted to have a charge like this brought against him. He must give the same benefit of the doubt to others.

Folly has forbidden me to make her appear pathetic, or to beg you to forgive her if there was fault on her part. She's likewise forbidden me to weep, or to throw myself at your feet, or to implore you with endearing glances such as have pleased you at times when coming from her, or to bring in her family, children, or friends to move you to pity. She asks of you something you can't refuse: to have it be declared that Love is to blame for his own blindness.

The second point Apollo has touched upon is that from now on, he wants Folly to be prohibited from coming within a hundred paces of Love. He's based his reasoning on the idea that since Love enjoys such honor and esteem among men and provides them with so many pleasures and good things, if Folly were to intrude, everything would go wrong. But my purpose will be to show in all this that Folly is in no way inferior to Love — and moreover, that Love would be nothing without her, and that he can neither exist nor rule without her help. And in as much as to prove his greatness Love began by asserting his seniority, I'll do the same. I beg you to recall that from the very moment man was put on earth he began his life with Folly, and that ever since, his descendants have followed so closely in his footsteps that no other lady in the world has ever earned such a great reputation.

It's true that in the beginning men didn't rise to the heights of folly, since they didn't yet have any examples to follow.[106] Their folly consisted of running after one another, climbing trees to see farther ahead, rolling down into valleys, and consuming their entire harvest all at once, so that by the time winter came along, they had nothing left to eat. Little by little, folly grew with time. The most brazen among them — either because they saved their friends' and neighbors'

bestes sauvages, les brebis de leurs voisins et compagnons, ou pour avoir defendu quelcun d'estre outragé, ou pource qu'ils se sentoient ou plus forts, ou plus beaus, se sont fait couronner Rois de quelque feuillage de Chesne. Et croissant l'ambicion, non des Rois, qui gardoient fort bien en ce tems les Moutons, Beufs, Truies et Asnesses, mais de quelques mauvais garnimens qui les suivoient, leur vivre a esté separé du commun. Il ha fallu que les viandes fussent plus delicates, l'habillement plus magnifique. Si les autres usoient de laiton, ils ont cherché un metal plus precieus, qui est l'or. Ou l'or estoit commun, ils l'ont enrichi de Perles, Rubis, Diamans, et de toutes sortes de pierreries. Et, ou est la plus grand'Folie, si le commun ha ù une loy, les grans en ont pris d'autres pour eus. Ce qu'ils ont estimé n'estre licite aus autres, se sont pensé estre permis. [¶] Folie ha premierement mis en teste à quelcun de se faire creindre: Folie ha fait les autres obéïr. Folie ha inventé toute l'excellence, magnificence, et grandeur, qui depuis à cette cause s'en est ensuivie. Et neanmoins, qui ha il plus venerable entre les hommes, que ceus qui commandent aus autres? Toymesme, Jupiter, les apelles pasteurs de Peuples: veus qu'il leur soit obeï sous peine de la vie: et neanmoins l'origine est venue par cette Dame. Mais ainsi que tousjours as acoutumé faire, tu as converti à bien ce que les hommes avoient inventé à mal. [¶] Mais, pour retourner à mon propos, quels hommes sont plus honorez que les fols? Qui fut plus fol qu'Alexandre, qui se sentant soufrir faim, soif, et quelquefois ne pouvant cacher son vin, suget à estre malade et blessé, neanmoins se faisoit adorer comme Dieu? Et quel nom est plus celebre entre les Rois: quelles gens ont esté pour un tems en plus grande reputacion, que les Filosofes? Si en trouverez vous peu, qui n'ayent esté abruvez de Folie. Combien pensez vous qu'elle ait de fois remué le cerveau de Chrysippe? Aristote ne mourut il de dueil, comme un fol, ne pouvant entendre la cause du flus et reflus de l'Euripe? Crate, getant son tresor en la mer, ne fit il un sage tour? Empedocle qui se fust fait immortel sans ses sabots d'erain, en avoit il ce qui lui en failloit? Diogene avec son tonneau: et Aristippe qui se pensoit grand Filosofe, se sachant bien ouy d'un grand Signeur, estoient ils sages? Je croy qui regarderoit bien avant leurs opinions, que lon les trouveroit aussi crues, comme leurs cerveaus estoient mal faits. Combien y ha il d'autres sciences au monde, les-

lambs from wolves or other wild animals, or defended someone against abuse, or just because they considered themselves stronger or more handsome — had themselves crowned kings with oak leaves. And as ambition grew — not among the kings themselves, who at that time were doing a perfectly good job of guarding the sheep, cattle, pigs, and donkeys — but among some ne'er-do-wells in the company of the royal followers, their way of life became cut off from that of ordinary people. Their meats had to be more tender, their clothing more magnificent. If others were using brass, they sought out a more precious metal, gold. Where gold was common, they embellished it with pearls, rubies, diamonds, and all sorts of jewels. And here's where the greatest folly lies: when common people obey one law, and powerful people adopt others of their own. Whatever they consider unacceptable for others, they believe permissible for themselves.

Folly first gave someone the idea of making himself feared, and then she made others obey him. Folly created all the excellence, grandeur, and might that have gone along with this ever since. And still, who is more revered among men than those who have authority over others? You yourself, Jupiter, call them the peoples' shepherds, and want them to be obeyed at the cost of life itself — and yet it all began with this lady. As has always been your custom, you have changed into good what men created for evil.

But, to get back to my argument, what men are more honored than those touched by madness? Who was more mad than Alexander? [107] Although he was aware of suffering from hunger and thirst, although he was unable at times to hold his wine, and despite his vulnerability to sickness and injury, he nonetheless made men worship him like a god. What name among kings is more famous than his? What individuals, for a time, had greater reputations than the philosophers? Yet you'll find few of them who haven't grown intoxicated by Folly. How many times do you think she stirred up Chrysippus's brain? [108] Didn't Aristotle die, grieving like a madman, because he couldn't understand the cause of the ebbs and flows of Euripus? [109] Did Crates do a wise thing when he threw his treasure into the ocean? [110] And Empedocles, who would have been thought immortal if it hadn't been for his bronze sandals, was he as wise as he should have been? [111] Diogenes with his barrel, and Aristippus, who considered himself a great philosopher simply because he knew he had the ear of a great lord — were they wise? [112] I believe that anyone who studied their opinions carefully would find them as primitively developed as their minds. How many other fields of knowledge

quelles ne sont que pure resverie? encore que ceus qui en font professions, soient estimez grans personnages entre les hommes? Ceus qui font des maisons au Ciel, ces geteurs de points, faiseurs de caracteres, et autres semblables, ne doivent ils estre mis en ce reng? N'est à estimer cette fole curiosité de mesurer le Ciel, les Estoiles, les Mers, la Terre, consumer son tems à conter, getter, aprendre mile petites questions, qui de soy sont foles: mais neanmoins resjouissent l'esprit: le font aparoir grand et subtil autant que si c'estoit en quelque cas d'importance. [¶] Je n'auroy jamais fait, si je voulois raconter combien d'honneur et de reputacion tous les jours se donne à cette Dame, de laquelle vous dites tant de mal. Mais pour le dire en un mot: Mettez moy au monde un homme totalement sage d'un coté, et un fol de l'autre: et prenez garde lequel sera plus estimé. Monsieur le sage atendra que lon le prie, et demeurera avec sa sagesse tout seul, sans que lon l'apelle à gouverner les Viles, sans que lon l'apelle en conseil: il voudra escouter, aller posément ou il sera mandé: et on ha afaire de gens qui soient pronts et diligens, qui faillent plus tot que demeurer en chemin. Il aura tout loisir d'aller planter des chous. [¶] Le fol ira tant et viendra, en donnera tant à tort et à travers, qu'il rencontrera en fin quelque cerveau pareil au sien qui le poussera: et se fera estimer grand homme. Le fol se mettra entre dix mile harquebuzades, et possible en eschapera: il sera estimé, loué, prisé, suivi d'un chacun. Il dressera quelque entreprise escervelee, de laquelle s'il retourne, il sera mis jusques au ciel. Et trouverez vray, en somme, que pour un homme sage, dont on parlera au monde, y en aura dix mile fols qui seront à la vogue du peuple. [¶] Ne vous sufit il de ceci? assembleráy je les maus qui seroient au monde sans Folie, et les commoditez qui proviennent d'elle? Que dureroit mesme le monde, si elle n'empeschoit que lon ne previt les facheries et hazars qui sont en mariage? Elle empesche que lon ne les voye et les cache: à fin que le monde se peuple tousjours à la maniere acoutumee. Combien dureroient peu aucuns mariages, si la sottise des hommes ou des femmes laissoit voir les vices qui y sont? Qui ust traversé les mers, sans avoir Folie pour guide? se commettre à

are there in the world that are nothing more than sheer dreaming, even though people consider those who profess them to be celebrities? Those astrologers who divine the heavenly bodies, those magicians casting their dice, those sorcerers forging their charms, and others like them — mustn't we include them in the same category? It's impossible to fathom this mad curiosity to measure the sky, the stars, the oceans, the earth, to use up one's time calculating, advancing, and studying a thousand little questions that in themselves are frivolous, but that nevertheless delight the mind — and make it appear as remarkable and subtle as if it were engaged in a matter of true importance.[113]

I would never be able to finish if I wanted to recount how much honor and fame is granted every day to this lady, about whom you have such bad things to say. But to sum it up in a few words: show me a totally wise man on the one hand, and one guided by Folly on the other, and then observe carefully which one will be regarded more highly. The wise gentleman will wait for someone to seek him out, but will be left all alone with his wisdom. No one will call on him to govern cities, or even to ask for advice. He'll be more than happy to listen, to go at a deliberate pace wherever he's summoned. Yet the world needs individuals who are swift and ready to act, who would sooner make a mistake than dawdle along on their path. That wise man will have all the time in the world to retire to the country and plant cabbages.[114]

The fool, for his part, will come and go so often, making so much happen without any particular rhyme or reason, that he'll eventually meet up with a mind like his own who will goad him on, and he'll come to be considered a great man. That fool will put himself in the line of fire of ten thousand gunshots and will still possibly escape unscathed — and for this he'll be admired, acclaimed, prized, and followed by everyone. He'll devise some outrageous scheme, for which, if he pulls it off, he'll be praised to high heaven. You will thus find it true, in sum, that for every wise man who is talked about in the world, there will be ten thousand fools who are popular with the people.

Isn't this enough to satisfy you? Should I make a list of all the ills that would exist in the world without Folly, and all the good things that come about thanks to her? How would the world go on if she didn't prevent people from knowing ahead of time all the problems and pitfalls of marriage? She stops us from seeing them, and she hides them so that the world continues to repopulate itself in the usual way. How long would any marriage last, if the foolishness of men or women permitted its flaws to be seen? Who would have crossed the

la misericorde des vents, des vagues, des bancs, et rochers, perdre la terre de vuë, aller par voyes inconnues, trafiquer avec gens barbares et inhumains, dont est il premierement venu, que de Folie? Et toutefois par là, sont communiquees les richesses d'un païs à autre, les sciences, les façons de faire, et ha esté connue la terre, les proprietez, et natures des herbes, pierres et animaus. Quelle folie fust ce d'aller sous terre chercher le fer et l'or? combien de mestiers faudroit il chasser du monde, si Folie en estoit bannie? la plus part des hommes mourroient de faim: Dequoy vivroient tant d'Avocats, Procureurs, Greffiers, Sergens, Juges, Menestriers, Farseurs, Parfumeurs, Brodeurs, et dix mile autres mestiers? [¶] Et pource qu'Amour s'est voulu munir, tant qu'il ha pù, de la faveur d'un chacun, pour faire trouver mauvais que par moy seule il ait reçu quelque infortune, c'est bien raison qu'apres avoir ouy toutes ses vanteries, je lui conte à la verité de mon fait. Le plaisir, qui provient d'Amour, consiste quelquefois ou en une seule personne, ou bien, pour le plus, en deus, qui sont, l'amant et l'amie. Mais le plaisir que Folie donne, n'a si petites bornes. D'un mesme passetems elle fera rire une grande compagnie. Autrefois elle fera rire un homme seul de quelque pensee, qui sera venue donner à la traverse. Le plaisir que donne Amour, est caché et secret: celui de Folie se communique à tout le monde. Il est si recreatif, que le seul nom esgaie une personne. Qui verra un homme enfariné avec une bosse derriere entrer en salle, ayant une contenance de fol, ne rira il incontinent? Que lon nomme quelque fol insigne, vous verrez qu'à ce nom quelcun se resjouira, et ne pourra tenir le rire. Tous autres actes de Folie sont tels, que lon ne peut en parler sans sentir au cœur quelque allegresse, qui desfache un homme et le provoque à rire. [¶] Au contraire, les choses sages et bien composees, nous tiennent premierement en admiracion: puis nous soulent et ennuient. Et ne nous feront tant de bien, quelques grandes que soient et cerimonieuses, les assemblees des grans Seigneurs et sages, que fera quelque folatre compagnie de jeunes gens deliberez, et qui n'auront ensemble nul respet et consideracion. Seulement icelle voir, resveille les esprits de l'ame, et les rend plus dispos à faire leurs naturelles operacions: Ou, quand on sort de ces sages assemblees, la teste fait mal: on est las tant d'esprit que de corps, encore que lon ne soit bougé de sus une sellette. [¶] Toutefois, ne faut estimer que les actes de Folie soient tousjours ainsi legers comme le saut des Bergers, qu'ils

seas, without Folly as his guide — surrendering himself to the mercy of the winds, waves, reefs, and rocks; losing sight of land, exploring uncharted waters; trading for the first time with barbaric, uncivilized people? How did these things come to happen, if not because of Folly? And yet, in this very way, riches, knowledge, and ways of living are passed from one country to another, and the earth has become known, along with the nature and properties of its herbs, stones, and animals. What sort of madness made men go underground in search of iron and gold? And how many livelihoods would have to be sacrificed if Folly were banished from the world? The majority of people would die of hunger. What would all the lawyers, prosecutors, clerks, bailiffs, judges, musicians, actors, perfumers, embroiderers — and those in ten thousand other occupations — live on?

Since Love has tried as hard as possible to win everyone's favor and to paint me in a bad light as the only one who ever did him any harm, it's only right, after listening to all his boasting, that I should tell them the truth about what I'm really like.[115] The pleasure that comes from Love at times involves just one person, or else at most two people, the lover and the beloved. But the pleasure that Folly brings has no such limits. She'll make a whole group of people laugh at the same joke; at another time she'll make a man laugh all by himself at some thought that strikes him in a funny way. The pleasure provided by Love is hidden and secret, whereas that given by Folly can be shared with everyone. It's so enjoyable that the very mention of her name brightens up a person's day. Wouldn't anyone break out laughing to see a hunchback enter the room, his face all covered with flour and behaving like a fool? Just bring up the name of any notorious fool, and you'll see that someone will find it so funny that he won't be able to keep from laughing. No one can talk about all the things that Folly does without feeling a joy in his heart that cheers him up and makes him laugh.

On the contrary, wise and carefully considered things attract our admiration at first, but then lose their novelty and become boring. And so gatherings of great lords and wise men, however grand and full of ceremony they might be, won't do us as much good as some frolicsome group of merry young men who, together, have no respect or esteem for anything. Just seeing such camaraderie lifts our spirits and makes them more inclined to follow their natural impulses — whereas we leave those learned gatherings with a headache and as tired in mind as in body, even though we haven't gotten up from our chairs.

However, you mustn't assume that Folly's acts are always as frivo-

font pour l'amour de leurs amies: ny aussi deliberez comme les petites gayetez des Satires: ou comme les petites ruses que font les Pastourelles, quand elles font tomber ceus qui passent devant elles, leur donnant par derriere la jambette, ou leur chatouillant leur sommeil avec quelque branche de chesne. Elle en ha, qui sont plus severes, faits avec grande premeditacion, avec grand artifice, et par les esprits plus ingenieus. Telles sont les Tragedies que les garçons des vilages premierement inventerent: puis furent avec plus heureus soin aportees es viles. Les Comedies ont de là pris leur source. La saltacion n'a ù autre origine: qui est une representacion faite si au vif de plusieurs et diverses histoires, que celui, qui n'oit la voix des chantres, qui acompaignent les mines du joueur, entent toutefois non seulement l'histoire, mais les passions et mouvemens: et pense entendre les paroles qui sont convenables et propres en tels actes: et, comme disoit quelcun, leurs piez et mains parlans. Les Bouffons qui courent le monde, en tiennent quelque chose. Qui me pourra dire, s'il y a chose plus fole, que les anciennes fables contenues es Tragedies, Comedies, et Saltacions? Et comment se peuvent exempter d'estre nommez fols, ceus qui les representent, ayans pris, et prenans tant de peines à se faire sembler autres qu'ils ne sont? [¶] Est il besoin reciter les autres passetems, qu'a inventez Folie pour garder les hommes de languir en oisiveté? N'a elle fait faire les somptueus Palais, Theatres, et Amphitheatres de magnificence incroyable, pour laisser témoignage de quelle sorte de folie chacun en son tems s'esbatoit? N'a elle esté inventrice des Gladiateurs, Luiteurs, et Athletes? N'a elle donné la hardiesse et dexterité telle à l'homme, que d'oser, et pouvoir combatre sans armes un Lion, sans autre necessité ou atente, que pour estre en la grace et faveur du peuple? Tant y en ha qui assaillent les Taureaus, Sangliers, et autres bestes, pour avoir l'honneur de passer les autres en folie: qui est un combat, qui dure non seulement entre ceus qui vivent de mesme tems, mais des successeurs avec leurs predecesseurs. [¶] N'estoit ce un plaisant combat d'Antoine avec Cleopatra, à qui dépendroit le plus en un festin? Et tout celà seroit peu, si les hommes ne trouvans en ce monde plus fols qu'eus, ne dressoient querelle contre les morts. Cesar se fachoit qu'il n'avoit encore commencé à troubler le monde en l'aage, qu'Alexandre le grand en avoit vaincu une grande partie. Combien Luculle et autres, ont ils laissé d'imitateurs, qui ont taché à les passer, soit à traiter les hommes en grand apareil, à amonceler les plaines, aplanir les mon-

lous as the leaps that shepherds make to please their beloveds, or as playful as the satyrs' merry little mischief, or the little tricks that shepherd girls play when they trip people who pass them from behind, or when they tickle them in their sleep with an oak branch. Folly has other, more serious, acts in her repertoire that are accomplished through great forethought and skill by the most ingenious minds. Among these are tragedies, which were first invented by village boys and later, fortunately, thanks to great effort, were brought to the cities. Comedies came out of the same origins. The same can be said for dance, a representation of many different tales so true to life that even someone who doesn't hear the voices of the singers accompanying the dancers' gestures still understands not only the story, but their emotions and moods. He believes he can hear the words that suit the dancers' movements, or, as someone once put it, their "talking" hands and feet. Clowns all over the world have learned something from this. Who can tell me if there is anything inspired more by Folly than the ancient tales found in tragedies, comedies, and dance? And how can those performers not be called fools, when they have taken and still take such pains to portray themselves as someone other than who they are?

Need I recount the other diversions that Folly has created to keep men from languishing in idleness? Didn't she have lavish palaces and theaters and unbelievably magnificent amphitheaters built, so as to reveal what brand of folly people from different eras indulged in the most? Didn't she come up with the idea of gladiators, fighters, and athletes? Didn't she give man such bravery and skill that he could dare to fight a lion unarmed — and win — for no other need or hope than to gain the favor and approval of the people? A great many men have fought bulls, boars, and other beasts just to have the honor of surpassing others in folly, and this competition goes on not only among those who are alive at the same time, but also in respect to those who come before and after them.

Wasn't there an amusing contest between Antony and Cleopatra to see who could spend the most on a banquet? Yet all this would amount to very little if some men, unable to find anyone else in the world more driven by folly than themselves, didn't try to compete against the dead. Caesar was upset that he'd hardly begun to disrupt the world by the same age at which Alexander the Great had already conquered a large part of it. How many imitators did Lucullus and others leave behind — men who tried to outshine them either by entertaining lavishly, or else by raising up plains, flattening down moun-

taignes, seicher les lacs, mettre ponts sur les mers (comme Claude Empereur), faire Colosses de bronze et pierre, arcs trionfans, Pyramides? Et de cette magnifique folie en demeure un long tems grand plaisir entre les hommes, qui se destournent de leur chemin, font voyages expres, pour avoir le contentement de ces vieilles folies. [¶] En somme, sans cette bonne Dame l'homme seicheroit et seroit lourd, malplaisant et songeart. Mais Folie lui esveille l'esprit, fait chanter, danser, sauter, habiller en mile façons nouvelles, lesquelles changent de demi an en demi an, avec tousjours quelque aparence de raison, et pour quelque commodité. Si lon invente un habit joint et rond, on dit qu'il est plus seant et propre: quand il est ample et large, plus honneste. Et pour ces petites folies, et invencions, qui sont tant en habillemens qu'en contenances et façons de faire, l'homme en est mieus venu, et plus agreable aus Dames. [¶] Et comme j'ay dit des hommes, il y aura grand' diference entre le recueil que trouvera un fol, et un sage. Le sage sera laissé sur les livres, ou avec quelques anciennes matrones à deviser de la dissolucion des habits, des maladies qui courent, ou à demesler quelque longue genealogie. Les jeunes Dames ne cesseront qu'elles n'ayent en leur compagnie ce gay et joly cerveau. Et combien qu'il en pousse l'une, pinse l'autre, descoiffe, leve la cotte, et leur face mile maus: si le chercheront elles tousjours. Et quand ce viendra à faire comparaison des deus, le sage sera loué d'elles, mais le fol jouira du fruit de leurs privautez. Vous verrez les Sages mesmes, encore qu'il soit dit que lon cherche son semblable, tomber de ce coté. Quand ils feront quelque assemblee, tousjours donneront charge que les plus fols y soient, n'estimant pouvoir estre bonne compagnie, s'il n'y ha quelque fol pour resveiller les autres. Et combien qu'ils s'excusent sur les femmes et jeunes gens, si ne peuvent ils dissimuler le plaisir qu'ils y prennent, s'adressant tousjours à eus, et leur faisant visage plus riant, qu'aus autres. [¶] Que te semble de Folie, Jupiter? Est elle telle, qu'il la faille ensevelir sous le mont Gibel, ou exposer au lieu de Promethee, sur le mont de Caucase? Est il raisonnable la priver de toutes bonnes compagnies, ou Amour sachant qu'elle sera, pour la facher y viendra, et conviendra que Folie, qui n'est rien moins qu'Amour, lui quitte la place? S'il ne veut estre avec Folie, qu'il se garde de s'y trouver. Mais

tains, emptying out lakes, or constructing bridges over the seas (like the Emperor Claudius), or else by erecting huge bronze and stone statues, victory arches, and pyramids?[116] And all this magnificent folly has brought great and enduring pleasure to people, who go out of their way and take special trips to enjoy these ancient vestiges of folly.

In sum, without this good lady men would shrivel up and turn into dull, disagreeable characters with their heads in the clouds. But Folly wakes ups their spirits and makes them sing, dance, leap about, and dress in a thousand new ways that change every six months, always with some semblance of logic and suitability. If someone designs a snug, close-fitting garment, they declare it more appropriate and proper; if it's big and roomy, they say it's more decent. Thanks to these little follies and inventions, which show up as much in dress as in manners and customs, men have better succeeded in making themselves more appealing to ladies.

Furthermore, as I've already said on the subject of men, there will be a great difference between the welcome received by a fool and by a wise man. The wise man will be left alone with his books, or with some stodgy old matrons to converse about the decline in morals or the sicknesses going around, or to unravel some complicated family tree.[117] The young ladies won't be satisfied until they're in the company of the witty and amusing fellow. And no matter how much he pushes one, pinches another, messes up their hair, pulls up their skirts, and does a thousand other annoying things, they will still always seek him out. And when the time comes to compare the two, they will praise the wise man, but it is the fool who will reap the fruits of their intimacy. You'll even see wise men themselves — although it's said that people seek out their own — behave the very same way. Whenever they organize some get-together, they'll always see to it that the most extravagant characters are present, because they feel that no gathering can be much fun unless some fool is there to liven up the others. And no matter how many excuses they make to the women and young people, they still can't hide how much they enjoy the company of these fools, talking to them at every opportunity and looking much happier to be with them than with others.

So what do you think about Folly now, Jupiter? Is she the sort of person who should be buried under Mount Gibil, or left out on Mount Caucasus like Prometheus?[118] Is it fair to deprive her of all good company, where "Love," knowing she's there, will show up just to upset her, and make Folly, who ranks no lower than Love, leave the place to

que cette peine, de ne s'assembler point, tombe sur elle, ce n'est raison.
Quel propos y auroit il, qu'elle ust rendu une compagnie gaie et de-
liberee, et que sur ce bon point la fallust desloger? Encore s'il deman-
doit que le premier qui auroit pris la place, ne fust empesché par
l'autre, et que ce fust au premier venu, il y auroit quelque raison. Mais
je lui montreray que jamais Amour ne fut sans la fille de Jeunesse, et ne
peut estre autrement: et le grand dommage d'Amour, s'il avoit ce qu'il
demande. Mais c'est une petite colere, qui lui ronge le cerveau, qui lui
fait avoir ces estranges afeccions: lesquelles cesseront quand il sera un
peu refroidi. [¶] Et pour commencer à la belle premiere naissance
d'Amour, qui ha il plus despourvu de sens, que la personne à la moin-
dre ocasion du monde vienne en Amour, en recevant une pomme
comme Cydipee? en lisant un livre, comme la Dame Francisque de
Rimini? en voyant, en passant, se rende si tot serve et esclave, et
conçoive esperance de quelque grand bien sans savoir s'il en y ha? Dire
que c'est la force de l'œil de la chose aymee, et que de là sort une su-
tile evaporacion, ou sang, que nos yeus reçoivent, et entre jusques au
cœur: ou, comme pour loger un nouvel hoste, faut pour lui trouver sa
place, mettre tout en desordre. Je say que chacun le dit: mais, s'il est
vray, j'en doute. Car plusieurs ont aymé sans avoir ù cette occasion,
comme le jeune Gnidien, qui ayma l'euvre fait par Praxitelle. Quelle
influxion pouvoit il recevoir d'un œil marbrin? Quelle sympathie y
avoit il de son naturel chaud et ardent par trop, avec une froide et
morte pierre? Qu'est ce donq qui l'enflammoit? Folie, qui estoit logee
en son esprit. Tel feu estoit celui de Narcisse. Son œil ne recevoit pas
le pur sang et sutil de son cœur mesme: mais la fole imaginacion du
beau pourtrait, qu'il voyoit en la fonteine, le tourmentoit. [¶] Exprimez
tant que voudrez la force d'un œil: faites le tirer mile traits par
jour: n'oubliez qu'une ligne qui passe par le milieu, jointe avec le sour-
cil, est un vray arc: que ce petit humide, que lon voit luire au milieu,
est le trait prest à partir: si est ce que toutes ces flesches n'iront en
autres cœurs, que ceus que Folie aura preparez. Que tant de grans per-
sonnages, qui ont esté et sont de present, ne s'estiment estre injuriez,
si pour avoir aymé je les nomme fols. Qu'ils se prennent à leurs Filo-
zofes, qui ont estimé Folie estre privacion de sagesse, et sagesse estre
sans passions: desquelles Amour ne sera non plus tot destitué, que la

him? If he doesn't want to be with Folly, let him stay away from her. To have the burden of their not meeting up with each other fall on her is not right. What sense would it make, at the very point when she's livened up a party, to have to send her away? If he were asking only that whoever arrives first not be bothered by the other one, and that the first one to arrive get to stay, then that would be reasonable. But I'll show Love that he has never been without Youth's daughter at his side, and it can never be otherwise — and the worst thing that could happen to Love would be if he got what he asked for.[119] It's just a momentary fit of anger preying on his mind and bringing on these strange moods; they'll go away once he calms down a little.

Let's start with the very beginnings of Love. What is more utterly absurd than the idea that a person should fall in love at the slightest provocation — after receiving an apple, like Cydippe, when reading a book, like Lady Francesca da Rimini, while just looking or walking along — and at once become a servant and slave, and to start hoping for something wonderful without knowing if there's anything to it?[120] As the story goes, the power lies in the beloved's eyes, and from them emanates a subtle vapor or humor that enters through our eyes and travels all the way into our heart — where, just as to house a new guest, everything else must be disrupted in order to make room for it.[121] I know everyone says this is so, but I doubt that it's true. Many have actually fallen in love without having experienced this phenomenon, such as the young Cnidian who became enamored with Praxiteles' statue.[122] What force could have entered into him from a marble eye? What affinity could there be between his far too hot and passionate nature and a cold, dead piece of stone? What, then, ignited his passion? It was Folly, who was firmly lodged in his heart. So it was with Narcissus's flame. His eye didn't come into contact with a pure and subtle vapor from his own heart, but still the mad image of the beautiful likeness he saw in the water tormented him.

Talk all you want about the power of the eye: have it shoot off a thousand arrows a day — and don't forget that a line that passes through the center of it, when joined to the eyebrow, is a true bow, and that the moist little dot you can see shining in the middle is an arrow set to fly. However, none of these arrows will penetrate any hearts other than those Folly has prepared. No important people, either past or present, should feel offended if I call them fools for having loved. Let them blame their own philosophers, who considered folly to be the absence of wisdom, and wisdom to be without passion. But love can no

Mer d'ondes et vagues: vray est, qu'aucuns dissimulent mieus leur pas-
sion: et s'ils s'en trouvent mal, c'est une autre espece de Folie. Mais ceus
qui montrent leurs afeccions estans plus grandes que les secrets de
leurs poitrines, vous rendront et exprimeront une si vive image de
Folie, qu'Apelles ne la sauroit mieus tirer au vif. [¶] Je vous prie imag-
iner un jeune homme, n'ayant grand afaire, qu'à se faire aymer: pigné,
miré, tiré, parfumé: se pensant valoir quelque chose, sortir de sa mai-
son le cerveau embrouillé de mile consideracions amoureuses: ayant
discouru mile bons heurs, qui passeront bien loin des cotes: suivi de
pages et laquais habillez de quelque livree representant quelque tra-
vail, fermeté, et esperance: et en cette sorte viendra trouver sa Dame
à l'Eglise: autre plaisir n'aura qu'à getter force œillades, et faire quel-
que reverence en passant. Et que sert ce seul regard? Que ne va il en
masque pour plus librement parler? Là se fait quelque habitude, mais
avec si peu de demontrance du coté de la Dame, que rien moins. [¶] A
la longue il vient quelque privauté: mais il ne faut encore rien entre-
prendre, qu'il n'y ait plus de familiarité. Car lors on n'ose refuser d'ouir
tous les propos des hommes, soient bons ou mauvais. On ne creint
ce que lon ha acoutumé voir. On prent plaisir à disputer les demandes
des poursuivans. Il leur semble que la place qui parlemente est demi
gaignee. Mais s'il avient, que, comme les femmes prennent volontiers
plaisir à voir debatre les hommes, elles leur ferment quelquefois rude-
ment la porte, et ne les apellent à leurs petites privautez, comme elles
souloient, voilà mon homme aussi loin de son but comme n'a gueres
s'en pensoit pres. Ce sera à recommencer. Il faudra trouver le moyen
de se faire prier d'acompagner sa Dame en quelque Eglise, aus jeus, et
autres assemblees publiques. Et ce pendant expliquer ses passions par
soupirs et paroles tremblantes: redire cent fois une mesme chose: pro-
tester, jurer, promettre à celle qui possible ne s'en soucie, et est tour-
nee ailleurs et promise. [¶] Il me semble que seroit folie de parler des
sottes et plaisantes Amours vilageoises: marcher sur le bout du pié, ser-
rer le petit doit; apres que lon ha bien bu, escrire sur le bout de la table
avec du vin, et entrelasser son nom et celui de s'amie: la mener pre-
miere à la danse, et la tourmenter tout un jour au Soleil. Et encore ceus,

sooner exist without passion than the sea can exist without waves and swells. It's true that some people hide their passion better than others, and that causes them suffering, which is in itself another kind of folly.[123] But those who reveal their feelings to be stronger than the secrets of their hearts will provide you with such a vivid image of folly that even Apelles himself couldn't paint a portrait more true to life.[124]

Let me ask you, if I may, to imagine a young man who hasn't much else to do other than to make himself loved. Once he has coiffed, dressed, perfumed, and admired himself, he leaves the house feeling quite self-confident, and with his head caught up in a thousand notions about love — having rehearsed in his mind a thousand happy scenarios that will never come about. He is followed by pages and servants decked out in uniforms with colors representing his long-suffering devotion, perseverance, and hope.[125] This is the way he'll go to meet his lady in church, but he'll get no pleasure out of it other than sending her pregnant glances and bowing to her in passing. What good are glances alone? Why doesn't he go wearing a mask so he can speak more freely? This is becoming something of a custom, but it gets so little response from the lady that it's hardly worth it.

Eventually he manages to see her in private, but he mustn't yet make any moves until they've gotten better acquainted. For then the lady won't dare refuse to hear everything he has to say, whether good or bad. Women aren't afraid of what they are used to seeing. They take pleasure in arguing with whatever their suitors ask. It seems to the men that a fortress willing to talk is already half won. But since women, however, really enjoy seeing men struggle, they sometimes slam the door in their faces, and don't invite them to get together in private as they used to do. If this is what happens, we find my man as far from his goal now as he thought he was close before. He'll have to start all over again. He'll have to find some way to get himself invited to accompany his lady to church, to games, and to other public events. And then, all the while, he'll have to explain his feelings with sighs and trembling words; to say the same thing a hundred times over; to repeat assurances, vows, and promises to someone who may not care in the slightest, and who may have set her sights or even committed herself to someone else.[126]

It might seem foolish of me to talk about the silly and amusing love affairs of country folk: how they walk around on tiptoe squeezing each other's little finger; how the man, after he's had a bit to drink, writes his beloved's name, intertwined with his own, with wine on the tabletop; how he leads her out first to dance, and teases her all day

qui par longues alliances, ou par entrees ont pratiqué le moyen de voir leur amie en leur maison, ou de leur voisin, ne viennent en si estrange folie, que ceus qui n'ont faveur d'elles qu'aus lieus publiques et festins: qui de cent soupirs n'en peuvent faire connoitre plus d'un ou deus le mois: et neanmoins pensent que leurs amies les doivent tous conter. [¶] Il faut avoir tousjours pages aus escoutes, savoir qui va, qui vient, corrompre des chambrieres à beaus deniers, perdre tout un jour pour voir passer Madame par la rue, et pour toute remuneracion, avoir un petit adieu avec quelque souzris, qui le fera retourner chez soy plus content, que quand Ulysse vid la fumee de son Itaque. Il vole de joye: il embrasse l'un, puis l'autre: chante vers: compose, fait s'amie la plus belle qui soit au monde, combien que possible soit laide. Et si de fortune survient quelque jalousie, comme il avient le plus souvent, on ne rit, on ne chante plus: on devient pensif et morne: on connoit ses vices et fautes: on admire celui que lon pense estre aymé: on parangonne sa beauté, grace, richesse, avec celui duquel on est jalous: puis soudein on le vient à despriser: qu'il n'est possible, estant de si mauvaise grace, qu'il soit aymé: qu'il est impossible qu'il face tant son devoir que nous, qui languissons, mourons, brulons d'Amour. On se pleint, on apelle s'amie cruelle, variable: lon se lamente de son malheur et destinee. Elle n'en fait que rire, ou lui fait acroire qu'à tort il se pleint: on trouve mauvaises ses querelles, qui ne viennent que d'un cœur soupsonneus et jalous: et qu'il est bien loin de son conte: et qu'autant lui est de l'un que de l'autre. Et lors je vous laisse penser qui ha du meilleur. [¶] Lors il faut connoitre que lon ha failli par bien servir, par masques magnifiques, par devises bien inventes, festins, banquets. Si la commodité se trouve, faut se faire paroitre par dessus celui dont on est jalous. Il faut se montrer liberal: faire present quelquefois de plus que lon n'a: incontinent qu'on s'aperçoit que lon souhaite quelque chose, l'envoyer tout soudein, encores qu'on n'en soit requis: et jamais ne confesser que lon soit povre. Car c'est une tresmauvaise compagne d'Amour, que Povreté: laquelle estant survenue, on connoit sa folie, et lon s'en retire à tard. Je croy que ne voudriez point ressembler encore à cet Amoureus, qui n'en ha que le nom.

long in the sunshine. And yet, those who thanks to longstanding agreements or other means have found a way to see their beloved in their own home, or at a neighbor's, don't give in to such foolish behavior as those who receive favors from her only in public places or at banquets — for these suitors, who out of the hundred sighs they breathe each month cannot make more than one or two of them be heard, still think their lady must be counting them all.

Such a man always needs to have pages on the lookout, to keep track of who's coming and going, to corrupt chambermaids with generous bribes, and to waste whole days at a time just waiting to see Madame go down the street. The only reward he gets for all this is a brief goodbye with a few smiles, which nevertheless make him return home happier than Ulysses was when he saw the smoke of his beloved Ithaca. He leaps for joy and hugs one person after another; he sings and writes poetry, and makes his beloved out to be the most beautiful woman in the world, no matter how unattractive she might be. If by chance he has cause to be jealous, as so often happens, he stops laughing and singing. He becomes thoughtful and sad, and recognizes his vices and faults. He admires the man he suspects is loved, and compares his own looks, charm, and wealth with the qualities of the rival he's jealous of. But then, all of a sudden he starts to lash out at him in contempt: that someone so lacking in charm couldn't possibly be loved, and that he couldn't possibly be doing his duty as well as those of us who are pining away, burning, and dying of love. He pities himself; he calls his beloved cruel and fickle; he bemoans his bad luck and his fate. She merely laughs about it, or makes him think that he's wrong to feel sorry for himself — that people look down on his complaints, which can only come from a suspicious and jealous heart, and that quite contrary to what he says, she doesn't fancy either one of them more than the other. I'll leave it to you to consider who has the upper hand.

He must then face the fact that despite all his devoted service, all the splendid masked balls, all the witty conversation, and all the parties and banquets — he has failed. If the opportunity comes up, he must make himself appear superior to the man he is jealous of. He must show he is generous by sometimes giving beyond his means. The moment he learns that she wants something, he must send it to her right away without being asked — and he must never admit to being poor. For poverty and love make most undesirable companions, because once that happens, the folly is obvious, and by the time he gets out of it, it's too late. I doubt you'd want to be like such a man, who is a lover in name only.

[¶] Mais prenons le cas que lon lui rie, qu'il y ait quelque reciproque amitié, qu'il soit prié se trouver en quelque lieu: il pense incontinent qu'il soit fait, qu'il recevra quelque bien, dont il est bien loin: une heure en dure cent: on demande plus de fois quelle heure il est: on fait semblant d'estre demandé: et quelque mine que lon face, on lit au visage qu'il y ha quelque passion vehemente. Et quand on aura bien couru, on trouvera que ce n'est rien, et que c'estoit pour aller en compagnie se promener sur l'eau, ou en quelque jardin: ou aussi tot un autre aura faveur de parler à elle que lui, qui ha esté convié. Encore ha il ocasion de se contenter, à son avis. Car si elle n'ust plaisir de le voir, elle ne l'ust demandé en sa compagnie. [¶] Les plus grandes et hazardeuses folies suivent tousjours l'acroissement d'Amour. Celle qui ne pensoit qu'à se jouer au commencement, se trouve prise. Elle se laisse visiter à heure suspecte. En quels dangers? D'y aller accompagné, seroit declarer tout. Y aller seul, est hazardeus. Je laisse les ordures et infeccions, dont quelquefois on est parfumé. Quelquefois se faut desguiser en portefaix, en cordelier, en femme: se faire porter dens un coffre à la merci d'un gros vilain, que s'il savoit ce qu'il porte, le lairroit tomber pour avoir sondé son fol faix. [¶] Quelquefois on est surpris, batuz, outragez et ne s'en ose lon vanter. Il se faut guinder par fenestres, par sus murailles, et tousjours en danger, si Folie n'y tenoit la main. Encore ceus cy ne sont que des mieus payez. Il y en ha qui rencontrent Dames cruelles, desquelles jamais on n'obtient merci. Autres sont si rusees, qu'apres les avoir menez jusques aupres du but, les laissent là. Que font ils? apres avoir longuement soupiré, ploré et crié, les uns se rendent Moynes: les autres abandonnent le païs: les autres se laissent mourir. [¶] Et penseriez vous, que les amours des femmes soient de beaucoup plus sages? les plus froides se laissent bruler dedens le corps avant que de rien avouer. Et combien qu'elles vousissent prier, si elles osoient, elles se laissent adorer: et tousjours refusent ce qu'elles voudroient bien que lon leur otast par force. Les autres n'atendent que l'ocasion: et heureus qui la peut rencontrer: Il ne faut avoir creinte d'estre esconduit.

But let's consider the case where there is some mutual good feeling, where a woman is friendly to him and asks him to meet her at a particular place. He immediately thinks he has it made, that he's about to receive some favor, which is far from the case. Each hour seems like a hundred. He asks again and again what time it is and pretends to have another engagement. But whatever outward appearance he tries to put on, his eager passion is still written all over his face. And after running as fast as he can to get there, he will find that it's nothing special — just to go with a group of people on a boat ride or on a garden stroll, where someone else will just as soon have the benefit of talking to her as will he — the one who was invited.[127] Still, in his opinion, he has reason to be happy, for if she didn't enjoy seeing him, she wouldn't have invited him to join her.

As love grows stronger, the greatest and most dangerous follies always follow. The woman who only thought about playing games in the beginning, finds herself smitten. She allows visitors at suspicious hours. What are the dangers involved? For a man to go there with a companion at his side would be to admit everything. But to go there alone is risky. I'll leave out the dirt and stench that are sometimes showered on him. Sometimes he has to dress up as a porter, a monk, or a woman; or to be carried around in a trunk at the mercy of some fat lout, who if he knew what he was carrying, would drop him upon realizing the absurdity of his load.

Sometimes these men are ambushed, beaten, and abused — and they dare not brag about it. They have to climb through windows and over walls, and would forever be in danger if Folly weren't there to give them a hand. Yet these lovers are only the most handsomely rewarded. There are some men who come across cruel ladies who never show them any mercy. Other women are so tricky that after leading them on to the brink of their goal, they leave them high and dry. What do these men do? After they've sighed, cried, and complained endlessly over a long period of time, some become monks, others flee the country, and still others just give up and die.

Might you think that women are more sensible when they fall in love? Even the coldest of them would sooner let their insides burn up than admit anything. And no matter how much they might like to beg, if they dared, they simply allow themselves to be adored, and always refuse what they'd be more than willing to have taken from them by force. Others are just waiting for the right opportunity, and lucky is the man who can take advantage of it. He mustn't be afraid of being

Les mieus nees ne se laissent veincre, que par le tems. Et se connoissans estre aymees, et endurant en fin le semblable mal qu'elles ont fait endurer à autrui, ayant fiance de celui auquel elles se descouvrent, avouent leur foiblesse, confessent le feu qui les brule: toutefois encore un peu de honte les retient, et ne se laissent aller, que vaincues, et consumees à demi. Et aussi quand elles sont entrees une fois avant, elles font de beaus tours. Plus elles ont resisté à Amour, et plus s'en treuvent prises. Elles ferment la porte à raison. Tout ce qu'elles creingnoient, ne le doutent plus. Elles laissent leurs ocupacions muliebres. Au lieu de filer, coudre, besongner au point, leur estude est se bien parer, promener es Eglises, festes, et banquets pour avoir tousjours quelque rencontre de ce qu'elles ayment. Elles prennent la plume et le lut en main: escrivent et chantent leurs passions: et en fin croit tant cette rage, qu'elles abandonnent quelquefois pere, mere, maris, enfans, et se retirent ou est leur cœur. [¶] Il n'y ha rien qui plus se fache d'estre contreint, qu'une femme: et qui plus se contreingne, ou elle ha envie montrer son afeccion. Je voy souventefois une femme, laquelle n'a trouvé la solitude et prison d'environ sept ans longue, estant avec la personne qu'elle aymoit. Et combien que nature ne lui ust nié plusieurs graces, qui ne la faisoient indine de toute bonne compagnie, si est ce qu'elle ne vouloit plaire à autre qu'à celui qui la tenoit prisonniere. J'en ay connu une autre, laquelle absente de son ami, n'alloit jamais dehors qu'acompagnee de quelcun des amis et domestiques de son bien aymé: voulant tousjours rendre témoignage de la foy qu'elle lui portoit. En somme, quand cette afeccion est imprimee en un cœur genereus d'une Dame, elle y est si forte, qu'à peine se peut elle efacer. [¶] Mais le mal est, que le plus souvent elles rencontrent si mal: que plus ayment, et moins sont aymees. Il y aura quelcun, qui sera bien aise leur donner martel en teste, et fera semblant d'aymer ailleurs, et n'en tiendra conte. Alors les povrettes entrent en estranges fantasies: ne peuvent si aisément se defaire des hommes, comme les hommes des femmes, n'ayans la commodité de s'eslongner et commencer autre parti, chassans Amour avec autre Amour. Elles blament tous les hommes pour un. Elles apellent foles celles qui ayment. Maudissent le jour que premierement elles aymerent. Protestent de jamais n'aymer: mais celà ne leur dure gueres. Elles remettent incontinent devant les yeus ce qu'elles

rejected. Only with time do the most noble hearts consent to being conquered. Therefore when they finally know they are loved, when at long last they suffer the same pain they've caused to others, and when they come to trust the man to whom they've bared their souls, they admit their weakness and confess the flame burning within them. And yet, a bit of shame still holds them back, and they don't let themselves go completely until they're overcome and half consumed by their passion. But once they've gone this far, they get into some clever mischief. The more they've resisted love, the more they're caught up in it. They close the door to reason. They're no longer afraid of everything they used to have misgivings about. They neglect their womanly tasks. Instead of spinning, sewing, and working at needlepoint, they put all their effort into getting dressed up and going around to churches, parties, and banquets, so that they keep running into the ones they love. They take pen and lute in hand, and they write and sing about their passions. Finally this madness reaches a point where they sometimes abandon father, mother, husbands, and children, and take refuge where their heart is.

No one hates to be controlled more than a woman, yet no one is more capable of controlling herself than a woman who really wants to show her love. Many times I've see a woman who didn't find seven years of solitude and prison long, since she was with the person she loved. Although nature hadn't denied her many charms that made her fit for all good company, still she wanted to please no one else but the man who held her captive. I met another woman who, when her lover was away, never left the house unless one of his friends or servants went with her, because she wanted constantly to show her devotion to him. In short, once such feelings are sealed in a lady's generous heart, they are so strong that they can scarcely ever be erased.

But the sad thing is, more often than not, women have such bad luck that the more they love, the less they are loved in return. There will always be someone quite happy to fill their heads with jealous thoughts by acting as if he's in love with someone else, and showing no regard at all for their feelings. Then these poor souls start imagining all kinds of strange things. They can't break up with men as easily as men do with women, since it's much harder for them to go off and start a new relationship, discarding one love for another one. They blame all men on account of one. They call women in love fools. They curse the day when they first fell in love. They insist they will never fall in love again, but that doesn't last very long. All at once they picture again the

ont tant aymé. Si elles ont quelque enseigne de lui, elles la baisent, re-
baisent, sement de larmes, s'en font un chevet et oreiller, et s'escoutent
elles mesmes pleingnantes leurs miserables destresses. Combien en
voy je, qui se retirent jusques aus Enfers, pour essaier si elles pourront,
comme jadis Orphee, revoquer leurs amours perdues? [¶] Et en tous
ces actes, quels traits trouvez vous que de Folie? Avoir le cœur separé
de soymesme, estre maintenant en paix, ores en guerre, ores en treves:
couvrir et cacher sa douleur: changer visage mile fois le jour: sentir le
sang qui lui rougit la face, y montant: puis soudein s'enfuit, la laissant
palle, ainsi que honte, esperance, ou peur, nous gouvernent: chercher
ce qui nous tourmente, feingnant le fuir, et neanmoins avoir creinte de
le trouver: n'avoir qu'un petit ris entre mile soupirs: se tromper soy-
mesme: bruler de loin, geler de pres: un parler interrompu: un silence
venant tout à coup: ne sont ce tous signes d'un homme aliené de son
bon entendement? [¶] Qui excusera Hercule devidant les pelotons
d'Omphale? Le sage Roy Hebrieu avec cette grande multitude de
femmes? Annibal s'abatardissant autour d'une Dame: et mains autres,
que journellement voyons s'abuser tellement qu'ils ne se connoissent
eus mesmes. Qui en est cause, sinon Folie? Car c'est celle en somme,
qui fait Amour grand et redouté: et le fait excuser, s'il fait quelque
chose autre que de raison. [¶] Reconnois donq, ingrat Amour, quel tu
es, et de combien de biens je te suis cause? Je te fay grand: je te fay
eslever ton nom: voire et ne t'ussent les hommes reputé Dieu sans moy.
Et apres que t'ay tousjours acompagné, tu ne me veus seulement aban-
donner, mais me veus ranger à cette sugeccion de fuir tous les lieus ou
tu seras. [¶] Je croy avoir satisfait à ce qu'avois promis montrer: que
jusque ici Amour n'avoit esté sans Folie. Il faut passer outre, et montrer
qu'impossible est d'estre autrement. Et pour y entrer: Apolon, tu me
confesseras, qu'Amour n'est autre chose qu'un desir de jouir, avec une
conjonccion, et assemblement de la chose aymee. Estant Amour desir,
ou, quoy que ce soit, ne pouvant estre sans desir: il faut confesser
qu'incontinent que cette passion vient saisir l'homme, elle l'altere et
immue. Car le desir incessamment se demeine dedens l'ame, la poin-
gnant tousjours et resveillant. Cette agitacion d'esprit, si elle estoit na-
turelle, elle ne l'afligeroit de la sorte qu'elle fait: mais, estant contre son

very man they loved so much. If they have something belonging to him, they kiss it over and over again, cover it with tears, and use it as a cushion and pillow — and they pay attention to nothing but their own complaints about their miserable lot. How many have I seen, who would trail all the way down to the underworld, to try and find out, like Orpheus in times past, whether they can recover their lost loves? [128]

In all of these actions, do you observe the marks of anyone else but Folly? To have a heart divided against itself; to be at peace one minute, at war the next, and then at truce the next; to cover up and hide one's pain; to change expressions a thousand times a day; to feel the blood rush up and redden one's face, then suddenly drain away, leaving it pale, according to whether shame, hope, or fear besieges us; to go in search of what torments us, while pretending to run away from it, and yet to dread finding it; for every laugh, to breathe a thousand sighs; to deceive oneself, to burn from afar, but to freeze up close; to stumble on our words and fall abruptly silent — aren't these all signs of someone no longer in control of his senses?

Who will make excuses for Hercules when he unwound Omphale's yarn; or for the wise Hebrew king with his host of wives; or for Hannibal when he corrupted himself at the hands of a lady; or for so many others who we see delude themselves every day to the point that they don't even recognize themselves? [129] Who is responsible for all this, if not Folly? For in sum it's thanks to her that Love is great and feared, and she is his excuse if he acts irrationally.

And so, ungrateful Love, can you acknowledge who you are, and how many good things I bring about for you? [130] I make you great; I bring fame to your name — indeed, men might not even have held you up as a god without me. And after I've been your constant companion, you want not only to abandon me, but to make me consent to the idea of staying away from any place you might be.

I believe I've succeeding in showing what I promised I would: that up until this moment Love has never existed without Folly. [131] We must now go beyond this, and show that it can never be otherwise. To begin with, Apollo, you'll admit that love is nothing other than a desire for the pleasure of meeting and uniting with the object of our love. Since Love is desire, or since whatever it might be, it can't exist without desire, we must acknowledge that once this passion takes hold of a man, it alters and changes him. For desire ceaselessly struggles within the soul, always stabbing and arousing it. If this disturbance of spirit were natural, it wouldn't torment him the way it does; but since it goes against his na-

naturel, elle le malmeine, en sorte qu'il se fait tout autre qu'il n'estoit. Et ainsi en soy n'estant l'esprit à son aise, mais troublé et agité, ne peut estre dit sage et posé. Mais encore fait il pis: car il est contreint se descouvrir: ce qu'il ne fait que par le ministere et organe du corps et membres d'icelui. [¶] Estant une fois acheminé, il faut que le poursuivant en amours face deus choses: qu'il donne à connoitre qu'il ayme: et qu'il se face aymer. Pour le premier, le bien parler y est bien requis: mais seul ne suffira il. Car le grand artifice, et douceur inusitee, fait soupsonner pour le premier coup, celle qui l'oit: et la fait tenir sur ses gardes. Quel autre témoignage faut il? Tousjours l'ocasion ne se presente à combatre pour sa Dame, et defendre sa querelle. Du premier abord vous ne vous ofrirez à lui ayder en ses afaires domestiques. Si faut il faire à croire que lon est passionné. Il faut long tems, et long service, ardentes prieres, et conformité de complexions. [¶] L'autre point, que l'Amant doit gaigner, c'est se faire aymer: lequel provient en partie de l'autre. Car le plus grand enchantement, qui soit pour estre aymé, c'est aymer. Ayez tant de sufumigacions, tant de characteres, adjuracions, poudres, et pierres, que voudrez: mais si savez bien vous ayder, montrant et declarant votre amour: il n'y aura besoin de ces estranges receptes. Donq pour se faire aymer, il faut estre aymable. Et non simplement aymable, mais au gré de celui qui est aymé, auquel se faut renger, et mesurer tout ce que voudrez faire ou dire. Soyez paisible et discret. Si votre Amie ne vous veut estre telle, il faut changer voile, et naviguer d'un autre vent: ou ne se mesler point d'aymer. Zethe et Amphion ne se pouvoient acorder, pource que la vacacion de l'un ne plaisoit à l'autre . Amphion ayma mieus changer, et retourner en grace avec son frere. [¶] Si la femme que vous aymez est avare, il faut se transmuer en or, et tomber ainsi en son sein. Tous les serviteurs et amis d'Atalanta estoient chasseurs, pource qu'elle y prenoit plaisir. Plusieurs femmes, pour plaire à leurs Poëtes amis, ont changé leurs paniers et coutures, en plumes et livres. Et certes il est impossible plaire, sans suivre les afeccions de celui que nous cherchons. Les tristes se fachent d'ouir chanter. Ceus, qui ne veulent aller que le pas, ne vont volontiers avec ceus qui tousjours voudroient courir. [¶] Or me dites, si ces mutacions contre notre naturel ne sont vrayes folies, ou non exemptes

ture, it unsettles him to the point that he turns into a totally different person from who he was. Because his mind itself is not at peace, but troubled and upset, in no way can he be said to be wise or level-headed. But still worse, he is compelled to reveal what's on his mind, which he can only do by putting every part of his body to good use.

Once he's gotten started, the lover must do two things: he must let it be known he's in love, and he must make himself loved in return. For the first, he must have the ability to speak well, but that alone won't suffice. For contrived conversation and uncustomary compliments make the woman who hears them suspicious, and set her on her guard. What other expressions of esteem must he give? An opportunity to fight for the lady and defend her cause doesn't always present itself. At first, you shouldn't offer to help her with domestic matters. Yet you must convince her of how deeply in love you are — and this requires a long time, continuous service, fervent prayers, and compatible dispositions.

The second thing the lover must accomplish is to make the lady love him in return, and this comes naturally, in part, out of the first. For the most potent charm there is to make yourself loved, is simply to love. Conjure up as many sweet-smelling potions, magical spells, prayers, powders, and stones as you want: but if you know how to help your own cause by how you reveal and declare your love, there'll be no need for these extraordinary remedies. Thus in order to be loved, you must make yourself lovable — and not merely lovable, but lovable in ways that appeal to your beloved. You have to weigh and adapt everything you want to say or do to her liking. Try being gentle and discreet. But if your beloved doesn't want you to be like that, you have to change sails and steer by another wind, or else don't bother getting involved with love at all. Zethus and Amphion couldn't get along at first, because one of them hated the other's art.[132] Amphion chose to do something different, and to return to his brother's good graces.

If the woman you love is greedy, you must turn yourself into gold, and fall like this into her lap.[133] All of Atalanta's servants and suitors were hunters, simply because she enjoyed hunting.[134] A few women, in order to please their poet friends, have even exchanged their sewing and workbaskets for pens and books. Surely it's impossible to make a good impression without embracing whatever the one we're pursuing likes most. Gloomy people get upset when they hear someone singing. Those who only want to walk aren't happy to go along with those who would always prefer to run.

Now, tell me if these changes going against our nature are not

d'icelle? On dira qu'il se peut trouver des complexions si semblables, que l'Amant n'aura point de peine de se transformer es meurs de l'Aymee. Mais si cette amitié est tant douce et aisee, la folie sera de s'y plaire trop: en quoy est bien dificile de mettre ordre. Car si c'est vray amour, il est grand et vehement, et plus fort que toute raison. Et, comme le cheval ayant la bride sur le col, se plonge si avant dedens cette douce amertume, qu'il ne pense aus autres parties de l'ame, qui demeurent oisives: et par une repentance tardive, apres un long tems témoigne à ceus qui l'oyent, qu'il ha esté fol comme les autres. [¶] Or si vous ne trouvez folie en Amour de ce coté là, dites moy entre vous autres Signeurs, qui faites tant profession d'Amour, ne confessez vous, que Amour cherche union de soy avec la chose aymee? qui est bien le plus fol desir du monde: tant par ce, que le cas avenant, Amour faudroit par soymesme, estant l'Amant et l'Aymé confonduz ensemble, que aussi il est impossible qu'il puisse avenir, estant les especes et choses individues tellement separees l'une de l'autre, qu'elles ne se peuvent plus conjoindre, si elles ne changent de forme. Alleguez moy des branches d'arbres qui s'unissent ensemble. Contez moy toutes sortes d'Antes, que jamais le Dieu des jardins inventa. Si ne trouverez vous point que deus hommes soient jamais devenuz en un: et y soit le Gerion à trois corps tant que voudrez. [¶] Amour donq ne fut jamais sans la compagnie de Folie: et ne le sauroit jamais estre. Et quand il pourroit ce faire, si ne le devroit il pas souhaiter: pource que lon ne tiendroit conte de lui à la fin. Car quel pouvoir auroit il, ou quel lustre, s'il estoit pres de sagesse? Elle lui diroit, qu'il ne faudroit aymer l'un plus que l'autre: ou pour le moins n'en faire semblant de peur de scandaliser quelcun. Il ne faudroit rien faire plus pour l'un que pour l'autre: et seroit à la fin Amour ou aneanti, ou devisé en tant de pars, qu'il seroit bien foible. [¶] Tant s'en faut que tu doives estre sans Folie, Amour, que si tu es bien conseillé, tu ne redemanderas plus tes yeus. Car il en est besoin, et te peuvent nuire beaucoup: desquels si tu t'estois bien regardé quelquefois, toymesme te voudrois mal. [¶] Pensez vous qu'un soudart, qui va à l'assaut, pense au fossé, aus ennemis, et mile harquebuzardes qui l'atendent? non. Il n'a autre but, que parvenir au haut de

true folly, or at least not totally free of her influence? They say it's pos-
sible to find two natures so similar that the lover will have no trouble
adjusting himself to his beloved's ways. But if this relationship is so
pleasant and easy, the folly will be in getting carried away with it —
an impulse that's very hard to control. For if this is true love, it is in-
tense and powerful, and stronger than all reason. Like a horse with a
bridle around his neck, the lover will plunge so headlong into this
bittersweet adventure that he no longer thinks about the other parts
of his soul that remain idle. Finally, after a very long time, he proves
to everyone who will listen, through his belated show of regret, that
he's been as much of a fool as all the others.

Now if this doesn't make you find folly in love, then tell me, all you
lords, who've made love your very vocation, won't you admit that love
seeks out a union between the self and the beloved object? Surely there's
no madder desire in the world, for were it to happen, love itself would
vanish, since the lover and the beloved would be fused into one; and
moreover, this couldn't possibly happen, since individual species and
things are so separate from one another that they can't come together
unless they change form. Go ahead and give me the names of trees
whose branches have grown together. Or tell me about all the varieties
of plants grafted together that the god of gardens never created.[135] But
no matter how hard you try, you'll find no case whatsoever where two
men have ever become one, not even Geryon with his three bodies.[136]

And so Love has never been without Folly at his side, and never
could be. Even if somehow he were able to do this, he shouldn't wish
for it, because in the end no one would pay any attention to him. For
what power would he have, or what fame, if his companion were wis-
dom? She would tell him that no one should love one person more
than another — or at least they shouldn't make it appear they do —
for fear of offending someone. She would advise him that no one
should do more for one person than for another. Finally, then, Love
would either be reduced to nothing or spread so thin that he would be
extremely weak.

Love, it's so far from the truth that you should be without Folly,
you'd be well-advised not to ask for your eyes back. They won't do you
any good, and they could do you a great deal of harm. If you'd looked
hard at yourself when you still had them, you might even have wished
this fate on yourself.

Do you believe that a soldier going into battle stops to think about
the ditch, the enemies, and all the gunfire that await him? No, he has
no other goal than to reach the front of the line, and he doesn't give a

la bresche: et n'imagine point le reste. Le premier qui se mit en mer, n'imaginoit pas les dangers qui y sont. Pensez vous que le joueur pense jamais perdre? Si sont ils tous trois au hazard d'estre tuez, noyez, et destruiz. Mais quoy, ils ne voyent, et ne veulent voir ce qui leur est dommageable. Le semblable estimez des Amans: que si jamais ils voyent, et entendent clerement le peril ou ils sont, combien ils sont trompez et abusez, et quelle est l'esperance qui les fait tousjours aller avant, jamais n'y demeureront une seule heure. Ainsi se perdroit ton regne, Amour: lequel dure par ignorance, nonchaillance, esperance, et cecité, qui sont toutes damoiselles de Folie, lui faisans ordinaire compagnie. [¶] Demeure donq en paix, Amour: et ne vien rompre l'ancienne ligue qui est entre toy et moy: combien que tu n'en susses rien jusqu'à present. Et n'estime que je t'aye crevé les yeus, mais que je t'ay montré, que tu n'en avois aucun usage auparavant, encore qu'ils te fussent à la teste que tu as de present. [¶] Reste de te prier, Jupiter, et vous autres Dieus, de n'avoir point respect aus noms (comme je say que n'aurez) mais regarder à la verité et dinité des choses. Et pourtant, s'il est plus honorable entre les hommes dire un tel ayme, que, il est fol: que celà leur soit imputé à ignorance. Et pour n'avoir en commun la vraye intelligence des choses, ny pù donner noms selon leur vray naturel, mais au contraire avoir baillé beaus noms à laides choses, et laids aus belles, ne delaissez, pour ce, à me conserver Folie en sa dinité et grandeur. [¶] Ne laissez perdre cette belle Dame, qui vous ha donné tant de contentement avec Genie, Jeunesse, Bacchus, Silene, et ce gentil Gardien des jardins. Ne permetez facher celle, que vous avez conservee jusques ici sans rides, et sans pas un poil blanc. Et n'otez, à l'apetit de quelque colere, le plaisir d'entre les hommes. Vous les avez otez du Royaume de Saturne: ne les y faites plus entrer: et, soit en Amour, soit en autres afaires, ne les enviez, si pour apaiser leurs facheries, Folie les fait esbatre et s'esjouir. J'ay dit.

Quand Mercure ut fini la defense de Folie, Jupiter voyant les Dieus estre diversement afeccionnez et en contrarietez d'opinions, les uns se tenans du coté de Cupidon les autres se tournans à aprouver la cause de Folie: pour apointer le diferent và prononcer un arrest interlocutoire en cette maniere:

Pour la dificulté et importance de vos diferens, et diversité d'opinions, nous avons remis votre afaire d'ici à trois fois, sept fois, neuf

thought to the rest. The first man to brave the seas didn't imagine all the dangers to be found there. Do you believe that a gambler ever thinks about losing? And yet all three are at risk of being killed, drowned, or ruined. But they don't see, nor do they want to see, whatever puts them in harm's way. Think of it as being the same for lovers. If ever they came to see and understand clearly the peril they are in, how much they are deceived and misled, and the nature of the hope that makes them continually carry on, they would never last a single hour longer. And then, Love, your reign would be over, because it survives only by virtue of ignorance, distraction, hope, and blindness, which are all handmaidens of Folly and keep her company every day.

So be at peace, Love, and don't try to break up the longstanding alliance that you and I share, even though you were totally unaware of it until now.[137] And don't think of me as the one who put out your eyes, but rather as the one who's shown you that they were no more good to you before, when they were still in your head, than they are now.

In closing, I must beg you, Jupiter, and you other gods, not to focus on the names of those involved (as I know you won't), but to weigh the truth and the merit of the facts. And if people still see it as more noble to say someone's in love than to say he's a fool, let that be chalked up to their ignorance. Because they share no common understanding of the true sense of things, they have been unable to give them names reflecting their true nature, and have instead given beautiful names to ugly things and ugly names to beautiful ones.

For this very reason, you mustn't fail to see to it that Folly maintains her stature and dignity. Don't rule against this beautiful Lady, who has given you so much enjoyment along with Genius, Youth, Bacchus, Silenus, and that lovable keeper of gardens.[138] Don't risk wronging the one you've preserved up until now without wrinkles or a single white hair. And don't take away the source of pleasure among men just to appease some fit of anger. You removed them from Saturn's kingdom; don't make them go back there again.[139] Whether in love or other matters, don't begrudge them if to soothe their troubles Folly lets them play and enjoy themselves. I rest my case.

> *When Mercury had finished his defense of Folly, Jupiter saw that the gods were divided in their feelings and had conflicting opinions — some of them remaining on Cupid's side, and others shifting their support to Folly's cause. To settle the disagreement, he delivers a provisional verdict in the following manner:*[140]

In light of the complicated nature and importance of your disagreements, and the difference in opinion about them, we have post-

siecles. Et ce pendant vous commandons vivre amiablement ensemble, sans vous outrager l'un l'autre. Et guidera Folie l'aveugle Amour, et le conduira par tout ou bon lui semblera. Et sur la restitucion de ses yeus, apres en avoir parlé, aus Parques, en sera ordonné.

Fin du debat d'Amour et de Folie.

poned your case for three times seven times nine centuries.[141] Meanwhile we order you to live together in peace, without hurting one another. Since Love is blind, Folly will be his guide, and will lead him wherever he wishes.[142] And as to whether he will get his eyes back, I will hand down a decision after I've consulted with the Fates.

End of the Debate of Love and Folly.

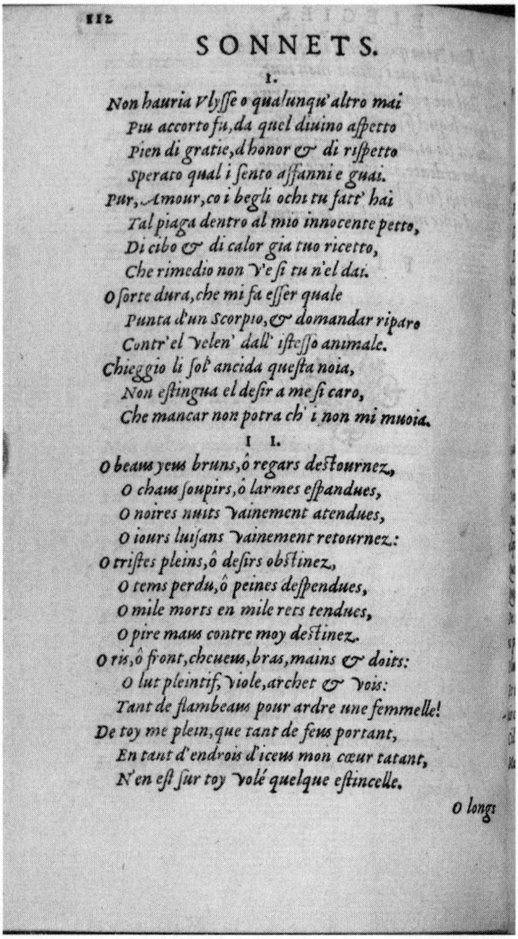

112

SONNETS.

I.

Non hauria Vlyſſe o qualunqu'altro mai
Piu accorto fu, da quel diuino aſpetto
Pien di gratie, d'honor & di riſpetto
Sperato qual i ſento affanni e guai.
Pur, Amour, co i begli ochi tu fatt' hai
Tal piaga dentro al mio innocente petto,
Di cibo & di calor gia tuo ricetto,
Che rimedio non V'e ſi tu n'el dai.
O ſorte dura, che mi fa eſſer quale
Punta d'un Scorpio, & domandar riparo
Contr'el Velen' dall' iſteſſo animale.
Chieggio li ſol' ancida queſta noia,
Non eſtingua el deſir a me ſi caro,
Che mancar non potra ch' i non mi muoia.

I I.

O beaus yeus bruns, ô regars deſtournez,
O chaus ſoupirs, ô larmes eſpandues,
O noires nuits Vainement atendues,
O iours luiſans Vainement retournez:
O triſtes pleins, ô deſirs obſtinez,
O tems perdu, ô peines deſpendues,
O mile morts en mile rets tendues,
O pire maus contre moy deſtinez.
O ris, ô front, cheueus, bras, mains & doits:
O lut pleintif, Viole, archet & Vois:
Tant de flambeaus pour ardre une femmelle!
De toy me plein, que tant de feus portant,
En tant d'endrois d'iceus mon cœur tatant,
N'en eſt ſur toy Volé quelque eſtincelle.

O longs

Figure 3. First two sonnets from the second edition of Labé's works, "Evvres de Louïze Labé Lionnoize. Reuues & corrigees par ladite Dame" (Gordon 1556.L25). Gordon Collections, Special Collections, University of Virginia Library.

II

POETRY

INTRODUCTION

Armed with the call for female selfhood and gender equality advanced polemically in her prose, yet ever mindful of the fundamental vulnerability shared by every human being, Louise Labé reframes these issues in her poetry via a stunning exposition of a woman's journey through love undertaken within and against the Petrarchan universe dominating the literary climate of her time. The elegies and sonnets represent two formally different but complementary articulations of her struggle to interrogate and revise the subjectivity of the conventional Petrarchan male speaker by exploiting the very obsessions and language of his discourse. Battling the pull of narcissistic self-absorption even when in the grips of the most intense emotion and the most wounding loss, Labé's lyric speaker reaches outward to seek genuine connection with the male beloved and with her male and female counterparts both in the real world and in the mythological world that serves as its metaphor. For Labé, the female subject is ultimately formed and validated through the joint labor of self-expression and interactive communication.

I shall develop the analysis of these lyric works in two ways. Given the challenge presented by the length and density of the three elegies, I shall first guide the reader through an interpretive overview of each text with the goal of highlighting those Petrarchan subversions that appear in more concise form in the sonnets. With respect to the sonnets themselves, after a brief overall contextualization and critical discussion of the inaugural poem written in Italian, my textual analysis will turn specifically to Annie Finch's innovative new translations and how they communicate and celebrate Labé's compelling lyric ethos.[1]

THE ELEGIES

Although the elegiac genre is strictly speaking a non-Petrarchan form —
since the *Canzoniere* contains no elegies — the Petrarchan presence remains
central to Labé's three elegies for several reasons. First of all, the French text
that furnished Labé's basic and most immediate model, Clément Marot's
group of love elegies entitled *Suite de l'adolescence Clémentine* (1534), already at-
tested to that author's liberal appropriation of Petrarchan diction and con-
ventions. Moreover, the complex physical and spiritual symptoms not only
of unattainable love, but of abandoned or lost love, as famously depicted by
the classical love elegists, had been broadly incorporated into Petrarch's own
lyric verse, as well as their bent toward narrative recounting or novelization — a feature that assumes new force in Labé's elegies through the intri-
cate yarn the speaker spins of her own personal history.

Annie Finch's translations of the speaker's saga (to my knowledge only
the second translation of these three texts in their entirety) maintain the
form and flavor of the original through their faithful and often ingenious ad-
aptation of Labé's decasyllabic rhyming couplets.[2] Finch also has created
titles for each elegy — as she has for each sonnet — an original move aimed
at increasing their immediacy and appeal to the reader.

Elegy 1 ("All-Conquering Love") begins with a dramatic presentation of
how Labé's speaker comes to assume her creative gift not only through the
intercession of Phoebus Apollo, god of poetry, but through the acknowl-
edgment of her female predecessor and counterpart in unreciprocated love,
Sappho, invoked indirectly through the geographical epithet of her origins
on the island of Lesbos:[3]

> The lyre he gave me once chanted the verse
> of love on Lesbos, in the olden times;
> now, in the same way, it will sing of mine.
> [Il m'a donné la lyre, qui les vers
> Souloit chanter de l'*Amour Lesbienne*:
> Et à ce coup pleurera de la mienne.][4]
>
> (ll. 14–16; emphasis added)

Labé's assertion of the Sapphic model restages the fundamental Pe-
trarchan dynamic in its iteration of unattainable passion; yet it simultane-
ously proposes an alternative response to the languishing despondency of
the Petrarchan male speaker. This response lies in the female speaker's as-
sumption of expressive power through the agency of her female predeces-
sor, an act realizing the narrator's call for self-empowerment through writing

in the dedicatory letter.[5] Indeed, the development of elegy 1 as a whole can be seen as a troubled and complex struggle between conventional Petrarchan passion in all its vanquishing force and the voice of the ambivalent female subject seeking support and validation.

Specifically, in the first half of the elegy Labé's speaker juxtaposes a rehearsal of her own fatal *innamoramento* and a subsequent plea addressed to her female audience. After dramatically evoking her amorous entrapment with the standard Petrarchan diction of fire, warfare, victimization, and Cupid's visual attack, she plaintively calls out for the understanding and empathy of her women readers:

> Oh, Women who read these words,
> Come sigh with me for the sorrows you have heard!
> And maybe one day I'll do the same for you,
> helping your pitiful voices to sound more true
> as you tell about your pain and your sad trial,
> lamenting in vain for times gone this long while.
> Whatever hardness lodges in your heart,
> Love will always conquer it through his special art, . . .
> So never think that anyone should blame
> the women whom hot Cupid has enflamed.
> [Dames, qui les lirez,
> De mes regrets avec moy soupirez.
> Possible, un jour, je feray le semblable,
> Et ayderay votre voix pitoyable
> A vos travaus et peines raconter,
> Au tems perdu vainement lamenter.
> Quelque rigueur qui loge en votre coeur,
> Amour s'en peut un jour rendre vainqueur. . . .
> N'estimez point que lon doive blamer
> Celles qu'a fait Cupidon inflamer.]
>
> (ll. 43–50, 53–54)

Here the striking dichotomy between an encouraging cry for solidarity from her equally vulnerable women peers on the one hand, and an unmistakable fear of their negative critical judgment on the other hand, involves more than the speaker's anxiety in respect to her deliberate breach of conventional female decorum. This duality figures more subtly and more deeply her quest to seek parallel access to the experience of grief heretofore privileged specifically as a male phenomenon in the Petrarchan tradition, and her effort to valorize the integrity and expression of female grief not through

the male lover's downward-spiraling self-absorption, but through the shared participation of women in a process of communal mourning.[6]

And yet the difficulty of this quest for validation against the backdrop of the reigning male ethos haunts the speaker in the second part of the elegy. In presenting two detailed examples of women caught in the erotic vulnerability and nonreciprocity characterizing the Petrarchan universe, she brutally shows that neither one accedes to the ennobled status of her male lyric counterpart in her crisis of grief. First, the Babylonian queen Semiramis, lauded for her manlike persona in military battle, is progressively and derogatorily feminized as the narrator relates and questions her fall into an incestuous infatuation with her own son — an infatuation so consuming that she loses her very sense of self: "Your love has, finally, estranged you from you,/yourself" (Ainsi Amour de toy t'a estrangee [l. 89]). Finally, a woman overwhelmed in old age by the type of unreciprocated passion she long ago instilled in others is pathetically depicted in foolish cosmetic attempts to forestall her own physical decay and reattract the object of her desire: "she tried to . . . camouflage / the wrinkles and the furrows, and to chase / the marks age had engraved deep in her face" (Voulant chasser le ridé labourage,/Que l'aage avoit gravé sur son visage [ll. 101–2]). What most strikes the reader is that although in both cases the women in question take on the *structural* position of the conventional male lover, either in the self-alienation caused by an invincible but sinful desire, or in the languishing after an uninterested lover, they do not take on the Sapphic lyre to "speak" and validate their plight — as Labé's speaker courageously tried to do in the first segment of the poem. Semiramis and the old woman therefore stand finally as the narrator's poignant exempla of the conventional devaluation of female grief as seen outside the privileged circle of male affective expression.

If elegy 1 moves beyond the speaker's personal *innamoramento* to evoke the overarching problematics of inscribing female loss in lyric verse, elegy 2 ("Such Endless Waiting") reengages the Sapphic and Petrarchan models in a striking return to the confessional mode inspired by Ovid's *Heroides*, one in which Labé's speaker reassumes her own position as desiring subject through an impassioned epistolary address to a departed male beloved. But her inscription of loss in the context of a feared abandonment allows the speaker to distance herself throughout the poem from the Petrarchan paradigm of radical unattainability by grounding and validating her grief not in a solitary psychic drama but in a prior *lived* love experience. Even as she employs a broad array of classic Petrarchan images and conceits early on to convey her plight in the face of her lover's absence (comparisons of herself to a ship longing for port and a slave longing for freedom, vacillations between jealousy toward an

imagined rival and disbelief that any such rival could supplant her), the speaker consistently uses diction that insists on the reality of their shared relationship: she addresses him directly as "Ami"; she invokes his written promise of a quick return, his vow of fidelity to her, and their mutual past love, with the unifying first-person-plural pronoun: *"our* former love" (*Notre* amour passee [l. 27; emphasis added]).[7]

The second half of elegy 2 presents two other key subversions of Petrarchan rhetoric that strengthen and valorize the position of the female subject. After first having the speaker playfully authorize her own beauty, talent, and fame uniquely via the praise won from learned men ("gens savans" and "gens d'esprit"), thereby elevating her own position in respect to any female rival, Labé strikingly deflates the idea that her narrator shares any real affinity with the idealized Petrarchan lady with whom the male lover can seek only a spiritual union:

> So come, taste well what others now desire;
> rest at the goal to which so many aspire.
> You know that elsewhere there's no one like me!
> I don't say others might not have more beauty —
> but no woman will ever love you more
> than I do now, or bring you higher honor.
> [Goute le bien que tant d'hommes desirent:
> Demeure au but ou tant d'autres aspirent:
> Et croy qu'ailleurs n'en auras une telle.
> Je ne dy pas qu'elle ne soit plus belle:
> Mais que jamais femme ne t'aymera,
> Ne plus que moy d'honneur te portera.]
>
> (ll. 69–74)

Indeed, rather than entreating her lover to aspire to a higher plane in the Neoplatonic mode frequently adopted by the Petrarchan male poet, Labé's speaker seductively invites him to return and "taste" the prize of the real-life woman who openly speaks ("I don't *say*" ["Je ne *dy* pas"]) to the possibility that she may not be the most beautiful, but that her own capacity to love him and to bring him honor — through the very identity she has forged by self-expression in the public and private worlds — goes unexcelled. In thus portraying her speaker as a vibrant and responsive subject, Labé asserts the legitimacy of a woman's claim to take on the first-person role of the suffering male lover and validates the voice of her loss.

An additional legitimation of that voice occurs at the very end of the poem, when Labé has the speaker first envision her own death should her

lover not return, and then record the actual inscription to be engraved on her tomb:

> MY LOVE, I BURNED FOR YOU UNTIL DESIRE
> CONSUMED MY BODY. THEN THE FLAMES GREW
>   HIGHER.
> I'M STILL BURNING UNDER THE ASHES OF THIS
>   PYRE.
> ONLY YOUR TEARS CAN EVER QUENCH THE FIRE.
> [PAR TOY, AMI, TANT VESQUI ENFLAMMEE,
> QU'EN LANGUISSANT PAR FEU SUIS CONSUMEE,
> QUI COUVE ENCOR SOUS MA CENDRE EMBRAZEE
> SI NE LE RENS DE TES PLEURS APAIZEE.]

(ll. 101–4)

What is particularly telling here is that although Labé exploits the Petrarchan convention of the speaker's death (real or metaphorical) at the hands of love, she does so in a way that is fundamentally un-Petrarchan. Whereas the traditional male lover attempts to find solace in the hope that his own death will allow him to reunite with the beloved in heaven, Labé's speaker rejects the imperative to look to any such spiritual union or transcending afterlife. Rather, her one request to her lover is that at her grave he himself shed the tears that alone could help relieve her suffering — that is, that he take part in an active *mutual* mourning that would constitute an authentic validation of her loss.

The appeal for empathetic solidarity carries over to the start of the third and final elegy ("Oh, Women of Lyon"), where Labé's speaker reengages her plea to her female co-citizens:

> Oh, women of Lyon, whenever you read
> these writings of mine, so full of love and need —
> all the worries, grudges, tears, sobs, and regret
> that the piteous music of these songs has set —
> please don't condemn me for simplicity
> because of my youthful weakness. If it be
> that I'm in error . . .
> [Quand vous lirez, ô Dames Lionnoises,
> Ces miens escrits pleins d'amoureuses noises,
> Quand mes regrets, ennuis, despits, et larmes
> M'orrez chanter en pitoyables carmes,

Ne veuillez pas condamner ma simplesse,
Et jeune erreur de ma fole jeunesse,
Si c'est erreur . . .]

(ll. 1–7)

Perhaps the best-known excerpt of any of Labé's three long narrative poems, these lines seem to figure a cyclical return to the concerns and vicissitudes of elegy 1. Yet the reprisal of Labé's appeal to her female audience introduces important transitions in her speaker's perspective toward the three dominant concerns of the earlier poem: the conflictive interplay between external validation and external judgment; the autobiographical narration and aftermath of Love's brutal attack; and the role of exempla as didactic elaborations. First, in unmistakably reinvoking the renowned "youthful error" (giovenile errore) confessed by Petrarch in the opening sonnet of the *Canzoniere*, she puts into question with the simple three-word conditional clause "Si c'est erreur" (If it be that I'm in error) whether her own experience in love even constitutes any wrongdoing.[8] She then further dilutes the traditional Petrarchan link between erotic passion and transgression by reviewing a litany of other vices and sins to which women and men are mutually susceptible, thereby seeking to forestall condemnation by her readers of either sex and to assert her speaking voice without the stigma of shame.

As Labé's speaker moves to displace any blame for her personal imperfections onto Amour, god of love, she invokes female exempla not to focus on their narratives of amorous woe, but rather to expand and to dramatize the story of her own *innamoramento* introduced more apologetically in elegy 1. Interestingly, with a self-comparison to the female warriors of Ariosto's *Orlando furioso* ("You might / have compared me to great Bradamante with ease, / or to Roger's sister, the renowned Marphise" [Pour Bradamante, ou la haute Marphise, / Suer de Roger, il m'ust, possible, prise (ll. 41–42)]), she aligns herself in part with her earlier example, Semiramis, whose manly military talents could not fight off Amour's assault — but with an essential difference: whereas Semiramis remained silent and paralyzed in the opening elegy, Labé's speaker here implicitly assumes and valorizes the voice of the warrior queen and empowers it as her own.[9]

In the extended presentation of the narrator's perilous encounter with love in the second half of the elegy, Labé inscribes the female subject's unapologetic appropriation of the full range of the Petrarchan male speaker's "privileged" suffering: psychic disruption, physiological torment, and self-alienation experienced relentlessly over time. But even within the space of

that suffering, the poet seeks to challenge its unremitting isolation in two crucial ways. The final exempla employed in the service of this challenge are no longer those of victimized women alone, but those of the mythological couples Jason-Medea and Paris-Oenone, whose stories feature in part the abandonment of the female figures by their male partners — an abandonment recalling the desertion feared by the speaker in elegy 2. Here, as there, the speaker is not content to accept anguished solitude as the sole stance available to the female lover:

> Those women deserved the love that they had earned,
> and loving, to have been loved in return.
> If those who are loved can leave love in the past,
> shouldn't we who aren't loved let it go, at last? [10]
> [Si meritoient elles estre estimees,
> Et pour aymer leurs Amis, estre aymees.
> S'estant aymé on peut Amour laisser
> N'est il raison, ne l'estant, se lasser?]

(ll. 89–92)

The first two lines above assert unmistakably the right of the female exempla to be loved in return — to claim a mutual sharing of love that defies the dynamics of Petrarchan subjectivity. Moreover, in using the nonspecific pronoun "on" (those) in the rhetorical question that follows, Labé asks her readers to appraise why *anyone*— whether male or female — would not grow weary of unrequited love, thereby suggesting her resistance to its privileged status in the reigning lyric discourse.

In a final rhetorical gesture of challenge, Labé ends her last elegy by addressing directly the god of love himself in a series of imperatives designed to incite change in the very tradition in which he plays such an important metaphoric role:

> If you really want me to love to the very end,
> make him whom I love most, my all, my friend,
> . . .
> let him feel, in his blood, his bones, and in his soul,
> an equal — or a hotter — desire boil.
> Then your burdens won't weigh as heavily on me,
> since someone who shares them will keep me company.
> [Mais si tu veus que j'ayme jusqu'au bout,
> Fay que celui que j'estime mon tout,
> . . .

Sente en ses os, en son sang, en son ame,
Ou plus ardente, ou bien egale flame.
Alors ton faix plus aisé me sera,
Quand avec moy quelcun le portera.]

(ll. 97–98, 101–4)

Here the poetess dismantles and transforms the posture of the female speaker in the concluding lines of both previous elegies. She can no longer be resigned, as at the end of elegy 1, to the vision of love as ongoing nonreciprocity; nor can she find satisfaction in elegy 2's image of the lover grieving with and for her at her own tomb. Rather, by daring to envision her relationship with her partner as an all-encompassing and "equal" (if not "hotter") flame, and by figuring their love as a shared burden, Labé's speaker challenges Amour to make good on his own glorification of mutual love posited in his conversation with Jupiter in discourse 4 of the *Debate*, and in so doing introduces the model for amatory experience she will explore further in the sonnets.

THE SONNETS AND THEIR NEW TRANSLATION

In contrast to the sustained narration of the elegies, Louise Labé's celebrated twenty-four-sonnet cycle offers a series of fascinating short vignettes that expand the overarching dialogue between the female poetic speaker and her male lyric heritage. Relinquishing the attempt to impose any strict linear progression or evolution on her verse, Labé rehearses throughout her collection the full array of motifs and settings through which she simultaneously appropriates and subverts Petrarchan poetics, from the violence of Love's attack, to the anguish of loss and separation, to the appeal for female empathy and noncensuring judgment, to the creation of scenarios of achieved and consummated *mutual* love.[11] Indeed, even as she is nurtured by her filiation with the ancient Sapphic lyre, the poetess explicitly acknowledges her own lyric origins in the world of Petrarch's *Canzoniere* not only by adapting the sonnet form privileged in his volume, but by composing her own inaugural sonnet in Italian (aptly entitled by Finch "The Sting"). A brief look at portions of this incipit in juxtaposition with the famed opening of the *Canzoniere* illuminates the struggle for independence and innovation enacted throughout Labé's sonnets.[12]

"The Sting" begins:

Not even Ulysses, or someone as wise as he,
would guess that a face like yours — so full of grace
and honor and respect — such a divine face —

> could bring suffering like the pain you're causing me.
> [Non havria Ulysse o qualunqu'atro mai
> Più accorto fu, da quel divino aspetto
> Pien di gratie, d'honor et di respetto
> Sperato qual i'sento affanni e guai.]

(ll. 1–4)

Whereas the Petrarchan speaker begins with a renowned plea for the compassion of his audience ("Voi ch'ascoltate in rime sparse" [You who hear in scattered rhymes]) in face of an at first unspecified youthful error ("mio primo giovenile errore"), Labé's speaker invokes immediately the living agent of her pain against the backdrop of a mythological allusion to Ulysses.[13] Presented grammatically in a kind of negation, the opening invocation of this powerful male figure known for his mental acumen subverts the notion that *male* intellect (and attendant *male* expression) have any innate superiority in understanding, assimilating, and communicating the trials of love — thus arming the female speaker with yet another validation of her right to take up the Petrarchan "lyre." Labé's rich reference to the *Odyssey's* wise and heroic wanderer, which reinscribes Petrarch's own frequent use of the journey metaphor, works on several other levels to suggest the values and direction she will embrace in her love experience. First, despite her admission here and further on of the acute anguish that Amour's attack on her has produced — dramatized by the conventional and paradoxical image of the scorpion, whose sting can be assuaged only by its own venom (ll. 10–11) — Labé's speaker at no point links this pain to the repentant stance and pervasive sense of spiritual divagation that overwhelm the Petrarchan narrator throughout his opening poem, displacing even the indirect mention of his fateful amorous fall. Implicitly set against this errant and futile wandering provoked by the yet unvoiced image of the inaccessible Laura, the prolonged and tumultuous voyage of Ulysses ends in reunion with his long-waiting, long-suffering mate, Penelope. This intertext activates the implicit hope that even in her suffering, Labé's speaker might reenact such a reunion at the conclusion of her own journey.[14]

Finally, whether or not such a hope comes to fruition, in the final lines of her inaugural sonnet Labé affirms an affective posture and itinerary for her speaker that diverge sharply from the stance of the male speaker not only at the end of Petrarch's opening poem but throughout the *Canzoniere*:

> I am wounded. I ask you only to kill the pain,
> but *not to extinguish* the burning I crave to feel,
> this desire whose broken life would break my own.

[Chieggo li sol' ancida questa noia,
Non estingua el desir a me si caro,
Che mancar no potrà ch'i' non mi muoia.]

(ll. 12–14; emphasis added)

In stark contrast to the disillusioned Petrarchan lover, who recognizes that "whatever pleases in the world is a brief dream" (Che quanto piace al mondo è breve sogno [l. 14]), and in the inaugural sonnet elides the very *desire* that fuels his shame and that in numerous subsequent poems he openly struggles to conquer, Labé's speaker here embraces the notion of a desire that might transcend or exist independently from emotional suffering, an outward-flowing force providing her with the very impetus to go on with her life. Perhaps more than anything else, it is this valorization of erotic desire as such a life-perpetuating force that constitutes Louise Labé's central innovation, one that permits her — despite and through the deprivation at the heart of her lyric tradition — to preserve intact a sense of both selfhood and otherness, and a vision of their unification in a rich and mutually fulfilling relationship.

The new conceptualization of male-female love experience proposed by Labé in the twenty-three French sonnets following her inaugural poem finds a vibrant vehicle of communication in Annie Finch's exciting new translations. In addition to her invention of titles for each poem, what distinguishes Finch's translations of the sonnets from those of her predecessors — in both collected volumes and anthology selections — is that they follow the actual Petrarchan sonnet rhyme schemes and their variations used by Labé. Previously, translators working with rhyming verse have opted to use the English sonnet rhyme scheme, or else a looser variation of the Petrarchan scheme, because it requires fewer rhymings on a single sound. And yet one of the main characteristics of Labé's own language is the insistent repetition of sounds — rhymes, assonances, and alliteration — a repetition that underscores the accelerating intensity of emotion in her poetry. Finch's expressive diction — and her ability to avoid the artificiality inherent in imitating such a repetitive rhyming pattern — creates a set of translations conveying the integration of affective immediacy and technical virtuosity that is both the hallmark of the original poems and the center of their appeal to the contemporary reader.

I would now like to introduce Annie Finch's rich dialogue with Labé's sonnet sequence by examining several examples that highlight at once the poetess's articulation of female suffering and her creation of a new poetics of reciprocity challenging the traditional Petrarchan paradigm. In sonnet 3

("Long-Felt Desires"}, the translator movingly adapts the presentation of the speaker's anguished passion in the two opening quatrains:

> Long-felt desires, hopes as long as vain —
> sad sighs — slow tears accustomed to run sad
> into as many rivers as two eyes can add,
> pouring like fountains, endless as the rain —
> cruelty beyond humanity, a pain
> so hard it makes compassionate stars go mad
> with pity: these are the first passions I've had.
> Do you think Love could root in my soul again?
> [O longs desirs, ô esperances vaines,
> Tristes soupirs et larmes coutumieres
> A engendrer de moy maintes rivieres,
> Dont mes deus yeus sont sources et fontaines:
>
> Ô cruautéz, ô durtez inhumaines,
> Piteus regars des celestes lumieres:
> Du coeur transi ô passions premieres
> Estimez vous croitre encore mes peines?]

(ll. 1–8)

Here Finch elects to tone down the enumerated apostrophes and exclamations so frequent in Labé's work without sacrificing the almost desperate sense of the speaker's pain. The intense character of this suffering is communicated by a refocusing of more rhymes not on the poet's water and light images, but on the quality of the speaker's emotional experience ("run sad," "go mad," "the first passions I've had"). Furthermore, the visceral pull of "first passions" (recalling the Petrarchan *innamoramento*) emerges in the replacement of the apostrophe in Labé's line 7 by the speaker's poignant affirmation of vulnerability and by her image of passion's "rooting" in the soul — a harsher rendering of Labé's original verb of organic growth ("croitre," l. 8).

In her recasting of the tercets, where this "rooting" of passion is graphically described, Finch's choice of diction to fulfill the rhyme scheme is particularly apt in defining the qualities of the *innamoramento*'s wound:

> If it arched the great bow back again at me,
> licked me again with fire, and stabbed me *deep*
> with the violent worst, as awful as *before,*
> the wounds that cut me everywhere would *keep*
> me shielded, so there would be no place free
> for love. It covers me. It will pierce no *more.*

[Qu'encor Amour su moy son arc essaie,
Que nouveaus feus me gette et nouveaus dars:
Qu'il se despite, et pis qu'il pourra face:

Car je suis tant navree en toutes pars,
Que plus en moy une nouvelle plaie,
Pour m'empirer ne pourroit trouver place.]

(ll. 9–14; emphasis added)

Although the rhyming of "deep" and "keep" juxtaposes two words that function as different parts of speech and are apparently unrelated in meaning, it stresses both the profound internal rupture and sustained action of Love's attack. Likewise, although Finch modifies the syntax of Labé's final line in order to incorporate two more blunt affirmations of the speaker's state, she maintains the corresponding rhythmic fragmentation of the original line. Furthermore, in rhyming the concluding word "more" with line 11's "before," she shows the speaker's acceptance that both past and future have been engulfed by the power of her passion in the present moment.

Two poems later, in sonnet 5 ("Bright Venus"}, the perspective of the speaker's suffering changes in that she reaches out directly for the potential comfort and partnership of Venus, goddess of love, as an antidote to her nocturnal isolation from the rest of sleeping humanity: "Listen, bright Venus —*errant* in the *air*!/ Listen to my clear voice move, as I sing . . ." (*Clere Venus, qui erres par les Cieus,/ Entens ma voix qui en pleins chantera* [ll. 1–2; emphasis added]).[15] The translator begins with the plaintive imperative that does not occur until line 2 of the original, at the same time maintaining Labé's hypnotic internal rhyme in the first line. By thus insisting on the centrality of the imperative, Finch stresses the desire of the speaker to connect with her female celestial counterpart — a desire nevertheless conflicted, as Tom Conley has suggested, because it is infused with anxiety as to whether the "errant" goddess possesses the focused empathy to fulfill this bond.[16] Moreover, Finch continues to emphasize this subtle interplay between the speaker's appeal for a complex emotional connection and Venus's uncertain capacity to provide it in lines 6–8, by rhyming the speaker's accelerating expression of tears with her longed-for projection of the goddess as compassionate witness — but a witness anticipated even now as "troubled" by the expression of the speaker's voice: "and as you look you'll see much, much more *weeping*./ More tears will dampen my bed, with your eyes *watching*,/ though they *trouble* the sight of witnesses so rare" (Mon œil veillant s'atendrira bien mieus,/ Et plus de *pleurs* te *voyant* gettera [emphasis added]).

Sonnet 7 ("Soul and Body") provides a particularly beautiful translation of the Neoplatonic theme of the transmigration of souls evoked frequently in Labé's poetry. Although the experiential point of departure of the poem involves separation from the male beloved, here the poetic speaker uses this motif as a vehicle to address him directly, to invite her absent partner into conversation, and to include the implicit support of the rest of humankind in her reflection. The translation once again captures Labé's validation of otherness in its own diction and dialogic strategies. Whereas the original sonnet opens with the impersonal pronoun "on," Finch uses the more informal, collective first-person-plural pronoun:

> *We* know this: everything that feels life *move*
> dies, if the soul and body separate.
> Now, I'm the body, and you are my own soul mate.
> So where have you gone to now, my life, my *love?*
> [*On* voit mourir toute chose animee,
> Lors que du corps l'ame sutile part:
> Je suis le corps, toy la meilleure part:
> Ou es tu donq, o ame bien aymee?]
>
> (ll. 1–4; emphasis added)

This opening takes away the slightly austere abstractness that the reader may sense in the original poem. Furthermore, the slant rhyme between "move" and "love" suggests the speaker's passion as an intense movement toward the other. Finch develops this dynamic push toward unification by repeating the verb "move" twice more in lines 8 and 11, as well as by ingeniously varying and reformulating the original French imperatives and assertions of need dominating the rest of the poem: "Don't make me stay here soulless while you rove" (l. 6); "Don't wait!/ This body of yours has reached a terrible state!" (ll. 6–7); "I need you now; I need how you move above /me" (ll. 8–9); "Come easily, so it's not dangerous / for us to meet again" (ll. 9–10); "don't be too hard on me" (l. 11).[17]

The final imperative "Restore," newly added to Finch's translation of the final tercet, is an especially effective verb, rhymed as it is with the sonnet's closing word "before"— for it speaks not to a crisis of inaccessibility but to the reconstruction of a togetherness once possessed.

> *Restore*
> your beauty to me gently — so it will prove
> gentle, although it was so cruel before.
> [Non de rigueur: mais de grace amiable,

Qui doucement me *rende* ta beauté,
Jadis cruelle, à present favorable.]

(ll. 12–14; emphasis added)

Given that the imperative form used in the translation has more insistency than the subjunctive form ("rende"} in the French text, this anticipated restoration paradoxically involves not simply the relationship as it was "before," but the creation of a more stable, mutually satisfying union, no longer threatened by the "cruelty" of rupture.

Even in its thematization of a separation much more definitive in kind, the moving and well-known sonnet 14 ("The Point of Death") still records — against the Petrarchan grain — the lyric speaker's attempt to assess and preserve a precious past *lived* experience. In affirming her desire to continue living as long as she can actively express the beauty and mourn the loss of that experience, the female subject celebrates the power of memory and its preservation in the act of writing, thus enacting the very imperative of Labé's dedicatory letter. Finch's translation seizes poignantly the prioritization of lived (rather than unattainable) experience driving the poem, rephrasing the speaker's regret in line 2 over "l'heur passé avec toy" (literally, "happy time spent with you"— the word "heur" incorporating connotations of both time and happiness) into sorrow over the more sharply defined loss of a fully reciprocal and unconflicted union: "mourning our *shared hours*, gone now, so long gone" (emphasis added). The translator likewise reiterates the speaker's simultaneous embrace of the empathy of others, clarifying Labé's elliptical reflexive structure in line 4 ("Pourra ma voix, et un peu faire entendre") by speaking of "a voice *someone* might hear" (emphasis added).

In the two final stanzas of the poem, which detail the projected loss of expressive power that alone would cause the speaker to renounce life, Finch's rhyming of "death" and "breath" and her enjambment immediately following "breath" ("I'll never want to reach the point of *death*!/ Though when my eyes grow dry and this voicing *breath*/is broken" ["Je ne souhaitte encor point mourir. / Mais quand mes yeus je sentiray tarir,/Ma voix cassee . . ."; ll. 9–11; emphasis added]). create an effect of physical breathlessness, as if the speaker were indeed about to exhale her final sigh. At the same time, the unlikely revisionary rhyme of "powerless" and "press" in her lines 11 and 13 ("and my hand is *powerless*/ . . . then, I'll *press*/death to come cover my clearest day with night" ["Et ma main impuissante /. . . Prirey la Mort noircir mon plus cler jour"; ll. 11, 14; emphasis added]). suggests paradoxically that the loss of expressive power unleashes one more act of strength: it sets into motion the human drive toward death.

Finally, beyond the various presentations of suffering and separation in which the female speaker nevertheless seeks alternatives to narcissistic languishing, Labé's most frequently anthologized poem, sonnet 18 ("Kiss Me Again"), places the celebration of lived experience squarely in the present and projects its continuation into an earthly future. In this famous "kisses" sonnet, inspired by the Roman poet Catullus's famous song to his Lesbia, Labé invites the reader to delight in a scene of lovemaking upon which her speaker will then articulate her own set of values in respect to erotic love:

> Kiss me again, rekiss me, and then kiss
> me again, with your richest, most succulent
> *kiss;* then adore me with another *kiss,* meant
> to steam out fourfold the very hottest *hiss*
> from my love-hot coals. Do I hear you *moaning?* This
> is my plan to soothe you: ten more *kisses,* sent
> just for your pleasure. Then, both sweetly bent
> on love, we'll enter joy through doubleness.
> [Baise m'encor, rebaise moy et baise:
> Donne m'en un de tes plus savoureus,
> Donne m'en un de tes plus amoureus:
> Je t'en rendray quatre plus chaus que braise.
>
> Las, te pleins tu? ça que ce mal j'apaise,
> En te'n donnant dix autres doucereus.
> Ainsi meslans nos baisers tant heureus
> Jouissons nous l'un de l'autre à notre aise.]
>   (ll. 1–8; emphasis added)

These lines have been widely discussed for their use of the erotic stage to illustrate the author's emphasis on mutuality and reciprocity — from the repeated imperative "Kiss me" to the quickening rate of exchange in these embraces.[18] The translation embodies this hyperbolic repetition and acceleration. After imitating literally the first line in which the word "kiss" is used three times as a verb, Finch eschews Labé's taste for mere numbers ("one," "four," "ten") and repeats the noun "kiss" three more times in various positions in the upcoming lines. Her rhyming of this mantra with the "hiss" exuding from the metaphoric "hot coals" of the lover's passion creates an onomatopoetic effect of intensely smoldering fire. As if to push the sensual overtones to the limit, she also does not translate the speaker's flirtatious question in line 5 in its primary sense of complaint but rather gives it an erotically charged resonance —"Are you moaning?" Labé's culminating imperative for

mutual pleasure conveyed in multiple reflexive structures at the end of the second quatrain emerges in the translation in slightly different fashion: a call for joy in "doubleness" that anticipates the *"double* vie" advocated in Labé's own line 9 ("Lors double vie à chacun en suivra") and in its alliterative glossing by Finch as "two loving lives to tend" (emphasis added).

Given that the final four enigmatic lines of the sonnet are meant to reveal what kind of "double life" Louise Labé has in mind, they form one of the more important challenges to any translator of this otherwise deceptively straightforward poem:

> I'll tell you *something honest* now, my love:
> it's very bad for me to live apart.
> There's no way I can have a happy heart
> without some place outside myself to *move.*
>
> [Permets m'Amour penser *quelque folie:*
>
> Tousjours suis mal, vivant discrettement,
> Et ne me puis donner contentement,
> Si hors de moy ne fay quelque saillie.]

(ll. 10–14; emphasis added)

Rather than translating the key words "quelque folie" directly as "madness," Finch intriguingly communicates them through the unexpected expression "something honest." But if "folie" fundamentally represents desires that do not conform to the tenets of logical reason and conventional social propriety, such desires — although perhaps viewed from the outside as "mad" when voiced by a sixteenth-century woman — indeed constitute the basis of what for Louise Labé is true honesty and authenticity in being. To express herself honestly, Labé's speaker decries the artificial nobility of living "apart" from her lover and rejects traditional Petrarchan solipsism by voicing her need in the final line for "some place outside myself to move." Just as she does in sonnet 7, Finch uses the slant rhyme between "love" (l. 11) and "move" (a verb derived from Labé's culminating noun "saillie" [a "sally forth"]) to provocative effect. For the poetess, love is once again a *move* outside the self toward the other, and this dictum here becomes both the speaker's most fervent desire and her ultimate and most compelling expression of "honesty."

The parallel "honesty" in all of Annie Finch's new translations conveys not only Louise Labé's distinctive contribution to Petrarchan poetics but also that courageous spirit of directness and vulnerability that enhances her modernity and appeal in our twenty-first-century world. The productive paradox of the translator's work is that in patiently and artfully going back to

recuperate the original rhyme schemes of Labé's verse, she herself restores the immediacy of perhaps the first fully defined early modern female subject and the gift of her hard-earned wisdom. In so doing, Annie Finch has left for us her own authentic gift.

Deborah Lesko Baker

POETRY TRANSLATOR'S NOTE

As I have grown to know Louise Labé's poems from the inside out, and grown with them myself through the process of translation, I feel I have found a paradoxical reason that Labé has won so many admirers and disciples over the centuries. Labé is strengthened as an individual, made more complex, by her focus on her feelings toward another. Her elaborate metaphors and frank self-reflection in the face of intricate feelings are as heroic, in their own context, as Emily Dickinson's. Labé's passion, her courage, her playfulness, and her pain reflect struggles not only of the emotions but of the spirit.

Labé wrote just after the height of the Petrarchan influence on Renaissance love poetry, when disillusion with the Petrarchan tradition of the idealized woman and her frustrated lover had begun to set in. She used a female poetic voice both to explore the validity of the Petrarchan tradition for expressing female passion and to critique that tradition. Whether she is entreating kisses in her famous sonnet 18, voicing classic paradoxes in sonnet 8, lamenting male impotence in sonnet 16, or casting herself in a forest encounter with Diana in sonnet 19, she plays with and off the traditional Petrarchan love sonnet, teasing and adding fresh twists to the old imagery. But always, whether in the role of nymph, martyr, philosopher, mocker, or seductress, she is unflinching in claiming her own passion.

Labé's play with the Petrarchan tradition is rendered more piercing by her skill in its conventional forms. She found a material obdurate and resistant enough to exercise her skill and shape her emotions in the Petrarchan or Italian sonnet form, with its complex and repeated rhyme schemes (the basic form, rhymed *abba,abba,cdcdcd,* and its variations). However, Labé's previous translators have avoided translating Labé's sonnets into the Italian sonnet form, choosing instead the English sonnet. Perhaps this is because the English language has fewer rhyming words than Italian, and the English sonnet form, used most famously by Shakespeare, requires only two words to rhyme on any one sound (the basic form is *abab,cdcd,efef,gg*).

When I started this project I decided to render Labé's poems in accordance with their original designs. I felt it important to translate each of

Labé's poems not only into the Italian sonnet form but also into the particular version of the Italian sonnet rhyme scheme she had originally found for it, because the poems' ceaseless, anguished struggle with love has its appropriate incarnation in the repetitive intensity of Labé's rhymes. Often these involve four, six, or even eight words rhymed on a single sound. My use of the original rhyming patterns intends at once to echo Labé's original music, to emphasize the insistent emotion of the poems, and to force the syntax and the logical connections between parts into patterns whose complexity enacts the organization of the original.

There were many times when I was sure I had finally found the sonnet that I would be forced to translate into an English rather than an Italian rhyme scheme, the one that would get the better of me. Each time, however, a solution emerged eventually that would allow me to maintain the original rhyme scheme. After a while I began to feel I was being guided by Labé's spirit; I found myself in the habit of murmuring, "Thank you, Louise," as I worked. I have translated the work of a number of different poets, but I have never felt such an intimate connection with the presiding spirit of the poems as I felt in translating Labé's poetry.

I am indebted to Deborah Lesko Baker and Albert Rabil for their support of the idea of adding my own titles to the poems; writing the titles gave me the opportunity to acknowledge the essential core of each of the sonnets I had grown to know so well. I would also like to express my appreciation for the work of Labé's previous translators Edith Farrell and Graham Dunstan Martin, and my grateful indebtedness to the detailed notes on each of Labé's sonnets by Peter Sharratt in the Edinburgh Bilingual Library edition of the sonnets. Finally I would like to recognize, as a touchstone of excellence, the marvelous, little-known translation of sonnet 22 in A. D. Hope's *Collected Poems*.

Annie Finch

ELEGIES

Elégie 1

Au tems qu'Amour, d'hommes et Dieus vainqueur,
Faisoit bruler de sa flamme mon cœur,
En embrasant de sa cruelle rage
Mon sang, mes os, mon esprit et courage:
Encore lors je n'avois la puissance
De lamenter ma peine et ma souffrance.
Encor Phebus, ami des Lauriers vers,
N'avait permis que je fisse des vers:
Mais maintenant que sa fureur divine,
Remplit d'ardeur ma hardie poitrine,
Chanter me fait, non le bruians tonnerres
De Jupiter, ou les cruelles guerres
Dont trouble Mars, quand il veut, l'Univers.
Il m'a donné la lyre, qui les vers
Souloit chanter de l'amour Lesbienne:
Et à ce coup pleurera de la mienne.
O dous archet, adouci moy la voix,
Qui pourroit fendre et aigrir quelquefois,
En recitant tant d'ennuis et douleurs,
Tant de despits fortunes et malheurs.
Trempe l'ardeur, jadis mon cœur tendre
Fut en brulant demi reduit en cendre.
Je sen desja un piteus souvenir,
Qui me contreint la larme à l'œil venir.
Il m'est avis que je sen les alarmes,
Que premiers j'ù d'Amour, je voy les armes,

152

ELEGIES

ELEGY 1 [All-Conquering Love]

At first when Love — whose power can make gods grow tame [19]—
brought down inside my heart a burning flame,
embracing with his cruel and furious rage
my blood, my bones, my spirit, and my courage,
I was tender and did not yet have the strength
to sing out my pain and suffering at length;
Phoebus, the friend of laureled poetry,[20]
had not yet allowed my verse to come to me.
But now that his divine furor has filled
my valiant breast, I feel my ardor build
and it makes me sing — though not of the bruising thunder
of Zeus, nor of the wars we suffer under[21]
at the will of Mars, when he moves the universe.[22]
The lyre he gave me once chanted the verse
of love on Lesbos, in the olden times;[23]
now, in the same way, it will sing of mine.
So sweeten my voice for me, sweet arching bow.
I know it cracks or sours sometimes with woe,
reciting so many troubles, so little gladness,
so many hard turns of fortune, such deep sadness.
Soften my passion. Once it made my tender heart
burn half to cinders; and now whenever I start
to relive the piteous memories of those years,
they force my sobs and constrain my eyes to tears.
Already it seems I hear the same alarms
that I heard first from Love; now I see the arms

Dont il s'arma en venant m'assaillir.
C'estoit mes yeus, dont tant faisois saillir
De traits, à ceus qui trop me regardoient
Et de mon arc assez ne se gardoient.
Mais ces miens traits ces miens yeus me defirent,
Et de vengeance estre exemple me firent.
Et me moquant, et voyant l'un aymer,
L'autre bruler et d'Amour consommer:
En voyant tant de larmes espandues,
Tant de soupirs et prieres perdues,
Je n'aperçu que soudein me vint prendre
Le mesme mal que je soulois reprendre:
Qui me persa d'une telle furie,
Qu'encor n'en suis apres long tems guerie:
Et meintenant me suis encor contreinte
De rafreschir d'une nouvelle pleinte
Mes maus passez. Dames, qui les lirez,
De mes regrets avec moy soupirez.
Possible, un jour, je feray le semblable,
Et ayderay votre voix pitoyable
A vos travaus et peines raconter,
Au tems perdu vainement lamenter.
Quelque rigueur qui loge en votre cœur,
Amour s'en peut un jour rendre vainqueur.
Et plus aurez lui esté ennemies,
Pis vous fera, vous sentant asservies.
N'estimez point que lon doive blamer
Celles qu'a fait Cupidon inflamer.
Autres que nous, nonobstant leur hautesse,
Ont enduré l'amoureuse rudesse:
Leur cœur hautein, leur beauté, leur lignage,
Ne les ont su preserver du servage
De dur Amour: les plus nobles esprits
En sont plus fort et plus soudain espris.
Semiramis, Royne tant renommee,
Qui mit en route avecques son armee
Les noirs squadrons des Ethiopiens,
Et en montrant louable exemple aus siens
Faisoit couler de son furieus branc
Des ennemies les plus braves le sang,

with which he girded himself to take me on.
My eyes were the ones that shot the arrows, then;
others would stop and gaze at me too long,
not able to guard themselves against my strong
bow. But my arrows wound my own eyes now,
in a model of revenge. While mocking how
one loved, another was consumed and burned —
how so many tears were poured, so many turned
to prayers and sighs in vain — I didn't see
how the same fate was overtaking me.
And it got such a furious grip into my soul
that after so long a time, I'm *still* not whole.
Once more I feel it, now: the old constraint
opening freshly again, with a fresh complaint,
wounds from the past. Oh, Women who read these words,
Come sigh with me, for the sorrows you have heard!
And maybe one day I'll do the same for you,
helping your pitiful voices to sound more true
as you tell about your pain and your sad trial,
lamenting in vain for times gone this long while.
Whatever hardness lodges in your heart,
Love will always conquer it through his special art,
and the more you have made him your enemy,
the worse he'll act when you are at his mercy.
So never think that anyone should blame
the women whom hot Cupid has enflamed!
Even those whose power and rank have seemed most great
still had to bear the rudeness of Love's weight.
Their haughty hearts, their beauty, their high breed
could not protect them from the awful need
to serve hard Love. He traps the noblest souls
most suddenly, and in the strongest coils!
Even mighty Semiramis, a queen so proud[24]
she led her powerful army to put to rout
the dark squadrons of the Ethiopians
(and as an example to her troops, made run
along her furious sword's clean shining blade
her bravest enemies' congealing blood),
and then desired to go conquer still more,
bringing all of her neighbors out to war —

Ayant encor envie de conquerre
Tous ses voisins, ou leur mener la guerre,
Trouva Amour, qui si fort la pressa,
Qu'armes et loix veincue elle laissa.
Ne meritoit sa Royalle grandeur
Au moins avoir un moins facheus malheur
Qu'aymer son fils? Royne de Babylonne,
Ou est ton cœur qui es combaz resonne?
Qu'est devenu ce fer et cet escu,
Dont tu rendois le plus brave veincu?
Ou as tu mis la Marciale creste,
Qui obombroit le blond or de ta teste?
Ou est l'espee, ou est cette cuirasse,
Dont tu rompois des ennemis l'audace?
Ou sont fuiz tes coursiers furieus,
Lesquels trainoient ton char victorieus?
T'a pù si tot un foible ennemi rompre?
Ha pù si tot ton cœur viril corrompre,
Que le plaisir d'armes plus ne te touche:
Mais seulement languis en une couche?
Tu as laissé les aigreurs Marciales,
Pour recouvrer les douceurs geniales.
Ainsi Amour de toy t'a estrangee,
Qu'on te diroit en une autre changee.
Donques celui lequel d'amour esprise
Pleindre me voit, que point il ne mesprise
Mon triste deuil: Amour, peut estre, en brief
En son endroit n'aparoitra moins grief.
Telle j'ay vù qui avoit en jeunesse
Blamé Amour: apres en sa vieillesse
Bruler d'ardeur, et pleindre tendrement
L'ápre rigueur de son tardif tourment.
Alors de fard et eau continuelle
Elle essayoit se faire venir belle,
Voulant chasser le ridé labourage,
Que l'aage avoit gravé sur son visage.
Sur son chef gris elle avoit empruntee
Quelque perruque, et assez mal antee:
Et plus estoit à son gré bien fardee,
De son Ami moins estoit regardee:
Lequel ailleurs fuiant n'en tenoit conte,

even her Love pressed too hard, until she saw
that she was vanquished, and gave up war and law.
Didn't her royal grandeur at least deserve
a love less maddened than to make her serve
her son in love? Oh Babylon's Queen, in state,
where is *your* heart, which war made resonate?
What has become of the great spear and shield
with which you made even the bravest yield?
Where have you laid your helmet, with its bold
and martial crest shadowing your head's blonde gold?
Where is your cuirass; where is the slim blade
that struck your boldest enemies afraid?
Where are the furious coursers who drew you on
in your chariot of victory? So soon
have you been broken, and by so feeble a foe!
Is your high, virile heart so soon laid low
that now the pleasures of arms no longer touch
you? Do you simply languish on your couch?
Far behind you've left Mars's hard and bitter ways,
learning again how sweet Love's nature stays.
Your own love has, finally, estranged you from you,
yourself; and now it seems you're someone new.
And so, when someone sees that I'm in love
and lamenting, I hope my sadness will not move
their mind to scorn. In such a very brief
time, Love could cause them not one bit less grief!
I saw a woman once, who blamed and scorned
Love in her youth; but in old age, she turned
to burning passion, and tenderly lamented
the late, bitter hardship with which she was tormented.
Then, with continual washing and with rouge,
she tried to bring back beauty, camouflage
the wrinkles and the furrows, and to chase
the marks age had engraved deep in her face.
On her gray head she wore a wig, a puff
of borrowed hair, and badly curled enough.
The more she was, to her eyes, nicely painted,
the less her love looked at her; he nearly fainted,
then paid no attention, ran far away so fast—
he thought her ugly, and was quite embarrassed
to be loved by her. And so the poor old dear

Tant lui sembloit laide, et avoit grand'honte
D'estre aymé d'elle. Ainsi la povre vieille
Recevoit bien pareille pour pareille.
De maints en vain un tems fut reclamee,
Ores qu'elle ayme, elle n'est point aymee.
Ainsi Amour prend son plaisir, à faire
Que le veuil d'un soit à l'autre contraire.
Tel n'ayme point, qu'une Dame aymera:
Tel ayme aussi, qui aymé ne sera:
Et entretient, neanmoins, sa puissance
Et sa rigueur d'une vaine esperance.

got just exactly what seemed to be fair;
in times long past, men had clamored for her in vain;
now *she* loved, and it only earned her pain.
And so Love takes his pleasure, always setting
the will of one against another, letting
this one not love, though a woman loves him well,
and that one love, who's not loved, truth to tell —
but yet who encourages Love's awful strength
by holding hard to a vain hope — and at such length!

Elégie 2

D'un tel pouvoir le serf point ne desire
La liberté, ou son port le navire,
Comme j'atens, helas, de jour en jour,
De toy, Ami, le gracieus retour.
Là j'avais mis le but de ma douleur,
Qui fineroit, quand j'aurois ce bon heur
De te revoir: mais de la longue atente,
Helas, en vain mon desir se lamente.
Cruel, Cruel, qui te faisoit promettre
Ton brief retour en ta premiere lettre?
As tu si peu de memoire de moy,
Que de m'avoir si tot rompu la foy?
Comme oses tu ainsi abuser celle
Qui de tout tems t'a esté si fidelle?
Or' que tu es aupres de ce rivage
Du Pau cornu, peut estre ton courage
S'est embrasé d'une nouvelle flame,
En me changeant pour prendre une autre Dame:
Jà en oubli inconstamment est mise
La loyauté que tu m'avois promise.
S'il est ainsi, et que desja la foy
Et la bonté se retirent de toy:
Il ne me faut esmerveiller si ores
Toute pitié tu as perdu encores.
O combien ha de pensee et de creinte,
Tout aparsoy, l'ame d'Amour ateinte!
Ores je croy, vu notre amour passee,
Qu'impossible est, que tu m'aies laissee:
Et de nouvel ta foy je me fiance,
Et plus qu'humeine estime ta constance.
Tu es, peut estre, en chemin inconnu
Outre ton gré malade retenu.
Je croy que non: car tant suis coutumiere
De faire aus Dieus pour ta santé priere,
Que plus cruels que tigres ils seroient,
Quand maladie ils te prochasseroient:
Bien que ta fole et volage inconstance
Meriteroit avoir quelque soufrance.

ELEGY 2 [Such Endless Waiting]

With a yearning such as slaves could hardly know
for liberty — or ships aching to go
to harbor — alas! I wait from day to day
for you, dear gracious love, to bring my way,
at last, the long-awaited end of sorrow,
the long-postponed eternal glad tomorrow
of seeing you! But ah, such endless waiting,
that's the cause of this vain, passionate berating.
So cruel, so cruel . . . didn't you pledge a solemn vow,
when you first wrote, that you'd be back by now?
Do you have so little memory of me
that your promises are broken so easily?
How do you dare abuse me? How could you wrong
one who has stayed so loyal, for so long?
If you're still lingering near the crescent shore
of the river Po,²⁵ it could just be that your
sweet heart has been consumed by other fire,
changing my own for some other's desire,
and forgetting, in that hard inconstancy,
your solemn vow of faithfulness to me.
If this is really so — if it *is* true
that faith and goodness have abandoned you —
I shouldn't be the slightest bit surprised
that you don't feel compassion for my cries!
Yes, so many hard thoughts, and so many hard fears, come
on the poor souls where Love has made a home,
But I *will* keep faith, because of our former love,
that you'll find it impossible to rove.
I'll vow, again, my faith in your own faith,
I'll esteem your constancy more than my breath!
But what if you're lost alone on an unknown road —
or a terrible illness is dwelling in your blood —
though I doubt that, because I have such skill
at praying to the Gods to keep you well,
they would be crueler than tigers in a spat
to send you any sickness after that
(though silly, faithless, cruel inconstancy
does deserve some suffering!). Well, as for me,

Telle est ma foy, qu'elle pourra sufire
A te garder d'avoir mal et martire.
Celui qui tient au haut Ciel son Empire
Ne me sauroit, ce me semble, desdire:
Mais quand mes pleurs et larmes entendroit
Pour toy prians, son ire il retiendroit.
J'ay de tout tems vescu en son service,
Sans me sentir coulpable d'autre vice
Que te d'avoir bien souvent en son lieu,
Damour forcé, adoré comme Dieu.
Desja deus fois, depuis le promis terme,
De ton retour, Phebe ses cornes ferme,
Sans que de bonne ou mauvaise fortune
De toy, Ami, j'aye nouvelle aucune.
Si toutefois pour estre enamouré
En autre lieu, tu as tant demeuré,
Si say je bien que t'amie nouvelle
A peine aura le renom d'estre telle,
Soit en beauté, vertu, grace et faconde,
Comme plusieurs gens savans par le monde
M'ont fait à tort, ce croy je, estre estimee.
Mais qui pourra garder la renommee?
Non seulement en France suis flatee,
Et beaucoup plus, que ne veus, exaltee.
La terre aussi que Calpe et Pyrenee
Avec la mer tiennent environnee,
Du large Rhin les roulantes areines,
Le beau païs auquel or' te promeines,
Ont entendu (tu me l'as fait à croire)
Que gens d'esprit me donnent quelque gloire.
Goute le bien que tant d'hommes desirent:
Demeure au but ou tant d'autres aspirent:
Et croy qu'ailleurs n'en auras une telle.
Je ne dy pas qu'elle ne soit plus belle:
Mais que jamais femme ne t'aymera,
Ne plus que moy d'honneur te portera.
Maints grans Signeurs à mon amour pretendent,
Et à me plaire et servir prets se rendent,
Joutes et jeus, maintes belles devises
En ma faveur sont par eus entreprises:

my faith is strong. And it will guard you well
from all the evils that might do you ill.
Even He whose empire is the highest sky
cannot think worse of me because I pray
for you. As my tears and cries come pouring down
for your sake, He'll undo His angry frown;
I've lived to serve Him my entire life long,
and I don't think I've done anything wrong
(except to make you a god: Love forces me
to place you where only a god should be!).
Now, the silver moon has closed her silver horns[26]
twice, since the day you promised to return,
and no news of you at all. I haven't heard
anything good or bad — not a single word.
If you've made up your mind to stay away
because you've fallen in love, well, I'll just say
that if you ever did find another love,
she couldn't earn the fame of the one you have —
whether in virtue, beauty, skill, or graces.
Quite well-known people, and in many places,
have (wrongly, I think!) chosen to praise my name
(though who can count on everlasting fame?).
I'm lucky to be flattered here in France
(far more than I'm happy with) — by fame enhanced,
and not only here. Where the Carps and Pyrenees[27]
cup that rich land between surrounding seas,
and by the Rhine, between the shores that roll,
and the lovely green country where you stroll,
they've heard of me. You've told me it is so —
that I hold some glory, in the eyes of those who know.
So come, taste well what others now desire;
rest at the goal to which so many aspire.
You know that elsewhere there's no one like me!
I don't say others might not have more beauty —
but no woman will ever love you more
than I do now, or bring you higher honor.
Many great lords have tried to win my love,
offering themselves to please me, and to prove
their worth. They've jousted, gamed, worn fine devices[28]
to try to win my favor by their enterprises —

Et neanmoins, tant peu je m'en soucie,
Que seulement ne les en remercie:
Tu es tout seul, tout mon mal et mon bien:
Avec toy tout, et sans toy je n'ay rien:
Et n'ayant rien qui plaise à ma pensee,
De tout plaisir me treuve delaissee,
Et pour plaisir ennui saisir me vient.
Le regretter et plorer me convient,
Et sur ce point entre en tel desconfort,
Que mile fois je souhaite la mort.
Ainsi, Ami, ton absence lointeine
Depuis deus mois me tient en cette peine,
Ne vivant pas, mais mourant d'une Amour
Lequel m'occit dix mile fois le jour.
Revien donq tot, si tu as quelque envie
De me revoir encor' un coup en vie.
Et si la mort avant ton arrivee
Ha de mon corps l'aymante ame privee,
Au moins un jour vien, habillé de dueil,
Environner le tour de mon cercueil.
Que plust à Dieu que lors fussent trouvez
Ces quatre vers en blanc marbre engravez.

PAR TOY, AMI, TANT VESQUI ENFLAMMEE,
QU'EN LANGUISSANT PAR FEU SUIS CONSUMEE,
QUI COUVE ENCOR SOUS MA CENDRE EMBRAZEE
SI NE LE RENS DE TES PLEURS APAIZEE.

but in spite of all that, I care so very little,
I've hardly even thanked them for their trouble.
Only you are all my bad and all my good;
you are my all. Except you, it's understood
that nothing satisfies me. There's nothing left;
I'm abandoned by any pleasure, lost, bereft —
no more delight. Grief and care alone seize me —
only regret and complaint will keep me company.
And in this state, among such miseries,
I have wished a thousand times for Death to ease
my mood. My love, your absence is terribly wrong;
it has kept me in this state two whole months long,
not living, but dying of desire; and it makes me pay
every time it kills me — ten thousand times a day! [29]
Come back right now, if you ever want to see
me alive again. But if it has to be
that death finds its way to me before you do,
and takes away this soul, which so loves you —
find me once, at least. Dress yourself all in black.
Come circle around my tomb: forward, then back.
And if it pleases God, your eyes will find
on the white carved marble headstone these four lines:

MY LOVE, I BURNED FOR YOU UNTIL DESIRE
CONSUMED MY BODY. THEN THE FLAMES GREW HIGHER.
I'M STILL BURNING UNDER THE ASHES OF THIS PYRE.
ONLY YOUR TEARS CAN EVER QUENCH THE FIRE.

Elégie 3

Quand vous lirez, ô Dames Lionnoises,
Ces miens escrits pleins d'amoureuses noises,
Quand mes regrets, ennuis, despits et larmes
M'orrez chanter en pitoyables carmes,
Ne veuillez pas condamner ma simplesse,
Et jeune erreur de ma fole jeunesse,
Si c'est erreur: mais qui dessous les Cieus
Se peut vanter de n'estre vicieus?
L'un n'est content de sa sorte de vie,
Et tousjours porte à ses voisins envie:
L'un forcenant de voir la paix en terre,
Par tous moyens tache y mettre la guerre:
L'autre croyant povreté estre vice,
A autre Dieu qu'or, ne fait sacrifice:
L'autre sa foy parjure il emploira
A decevoir quelcun qui le croira:
L'un en mentant de sa langue lezarde,
Mile brocars sur l'un et l'autre darde:
Je ne suis point sous ces planettes nee,
Qui m'ussent pù tant faire infortunee.
Onques ne fut mon œil marri, de voir
Chez mon voisin mieus que chez moy pleuvoir.
Onq ne mis noise ou discord entre amis:
A faire gain jamais ne me soumis.
Mentir, tromper, et abuser autrui,
Tant m'a desplu, que mesdire de lui.
Mais si en moy rien y ha d'imparfait,
Qu'on blame Amour: c'est lui seul qui l'a fait.
Sur mon verd aage en ses laqs il me prit,
Lors qu'exerçoi mon corps et mon esprit
En mile et mile euvres ingenieuses,
Qu'en peu de tems me rendit ennuieuses.
Pour bien savoir avec l'esguille peindre
J'eusse entrepris la renommee estreindre
De celle là, qui plus docte que sage,
Avec Pallas comparoit son ouvrage.
Qui m'ust vù lors en armes fiere aller,
Porter la lance et bois faire voler,

ELEGY 3 [Oh, Women of Lyon]

Oh, women of Lyon, whenever you read
these writings of mine, so full of love and need —
all the worries, grudges, tears, sobs, and regret
that the piteous music of these songs has set —
please don't condemn me for simplicity
because of my youthful weakness. If it be
that I'm in error, who, under the skies,
can praise herself for having not one vice?
One is unhappy with her lot in life,
and watches her neighbors with envy like a knife;
another, striving to see peace come on earth,
tries so hard that he starts wars for all he's worth;
another, making a sin of poverty,
sacrifices only to the god of money;
another, perjuring her own Faith, will deceive
whoever trusts her enough to want to believe;
another, with a lizard-like poisoned tongue,
throws a thousand lying darts, and many are stung.
I wasn't born under those planets at all —
the ones that could have forced my luck to fall.
It never pained my eyes to have to see
better rain fall on my neighbor than on me.
I have not set discord among my friends,
or debased myself to further my own ends.
To lie, to trick, or to abuse another —
or to speak badly of anyone — makes me shudder.
So, if there's anything imperfect in my life,
blame Love. He is the cause of all my strife.
In my green youth he got a hold of me,
while I was exercising both my soul and body
in a hundred thousand ingenious feats of skill
which, in no time at all, he rendered dull.
Wanting to paint fine scenes in my sewing frame,
I had challenged myself to extinguish the great fame
of her who — surely more studious than wise — [30]
set her work against what Pallas had devised. [31]
And you should have seen me in armor, riding high,
gripping my lance, letting my arrows fly!

Le devoir faire en l'estour furieus,
Piquer, volter le cheval glorieus,
Pour Bradamante, ou la haute Marphise,
Seur de Roger, il m'ust, possible, prise.
Mais quoy? Amour ne peut longuement voir,
Mon cœur n'aymant que Mars et le savoir:
Et me voulant donner autre souci,
En souriant, il me disoit ansi:
"Tu penses donq, ô Lionnoise Dame,
Pouvoir fuir par ce moyen ma flame:
Mais non feras, j'ai subjugué les Dieus
Es bas Enfers, en le Mer et es Cieus.
Et penses tu que n'aye tel pouvoir
Sur les humeins, de leur faire savoir
Qu'il n'y ha rien qui de ma main eschape?
Plus fort se pense et plus tot je frape.
De me blamer quelquefois tu n'as honte,
En te fiant en Mars, dont tu fais conte:
Mais maintenant, voy si pour persister
En le suivant me pourras resister."
Ainsi parloit, et tout eschaufé d'ire
Hors de sa trousse une sagette il tire,
Et decochant de son extreme force,
Droit il tira contre ma tendre escorce,
Foible harnois, pour bien couvrir le cœur,
Contre l'Archer qui tousjours est vainqueur.
La bresche faite, entre Amour en la place,
Dont le repos premierement il chasse:
Et de travail qui me donne sans cesse,
Boire, manger, et dormir ne me laisse.
Il ne me chaut de soleil ne d'ombrage:
Je n'ay qu'Amour et feu en mon courage,
Qui me desguise, et fait autre paroitre,
Tant que ne peu moymesme me connoitre.
Je n'avois vù encore seize Hivers,
Lors que j'entray en ces ennuis divers:
Et jà voici le treiziéme Esté
Que mon cœur fut par Amour arresté.
Le tems met fin aus hautes Pyramides,
Le temps met fin aus fonteines humides:

I kept my head in the fury of the fight,
spurring my glorious wheeling horse. You might
have compared me to great Bradamante with ease,
or to Roger's sister, the renowned Marphise.[32]
But what of it? Love couldn't lend my heart
to Mars and study for long; soon he would start[33]
to lead me to other concerns. At first, for a while,
he only watched me. But then he called, with his smile,
"Oh woman of Lyon, do you believe
that my quick flames will grant you a reprieve?
No, they will not! I have subdued the gods
in hell below, in the sea, and in the clouds!
Now, don't you think I also can command
you humans, making sure you understand
my hand is so strong that no one can escape?
Those who think they're strongest are the first I take!
And you have dared to defy me without shame,
putting your faith in Mars, spreading his name!
Now, see if you are strong enough to persist
in following him — see if you can resist!"
So saying, now all red and hot with anger,
he pulled out an arrow with a fearsome clangor.
He loosed it with a strength that will never yield,
aiming it straight against my tender shield —
too feeble a harness to defend my heart
against that all-vanquishing Archer's solemn dart.
Now the wound is cut. When Love entered in my breast,
the first thing that he drove away was rest.
He brings me cares that will never be complete;
He will not let me drink, or sleep, or eat.
I can't feel sun, and I can't feel the shade.
Only fire and love fill me. And they don't fade;
they hide me. Now I have become so strange
I hardly remember, myself, how I have changed.
I was not even sixteen winters old
when all these cares took me into their hold,
and now it has been thirteen summers more
since Love first froze my heart to its young core.
The Pyramids were defeated, at last, by Time;
moist fountains will be dried, at last, by Time.

Il ne pardonne aus braves Colisees,
Il met à fin les viles plus prisees:
Finir aussi il ha acoutumé
Le feu d'Amour tant soit il allumé:
Mais, las! en moy il semble qu'il augmente
Avec le tems, et que plus me tourmente.
Paris ayma OEnone ardamment,
Mais son amour ne dura longuement:
Medee fut aymee de Jason,
Qui tot apres la mit hors sa maison.
Si meritoient elles estre estimees,
Et pour aymer leurs Amis, estre aymees.
S'estant aymé on peut Amour laisser
N'est il raison, ne l'estant, se lasser?
N'est il raison te prier de permettre,
Amour, que puisse à mes tourmens fin mettre?
Ne permets point que de Mort face espreuve,
Et plus que toy pitoyable la treuve:
Mais si tu veux que j'ayme jusqu'au bout,
Fay que celui que j'estime mon tout,
Qui seul me peut faire plorer et rire,
Et pour lequel si souvent je soupire,
Sente en ses os, en son sang, en son ame,
Ou plus ardente, ou bien egale flame.
Alors ton faix plus aisé me sera,
Quand avec moy quelcun le portera.

FIN

Time will not pardon the brave Coliseum;
it will topple each city that holds our esteem;
and Time is accustomed even to quenching the fire
of Love, no matter how hot the desire.
But, alas, in me the flame grows still more fervent
with Time, and brings on worse and worse torment!
Paris's desire for Oenone was strong,[34]
but his love didn't last for very long;
Medea was loved by Jason, so we hear[35] —
but soon enough he threw her out the door.
Those women deserved the love that they had earned,
and, loving, to have been loved in return.
If those who are loved can leave love in the past,
shouldn't we who aren't loved let it go, at last?
So shouldn't I pray to you now, Love, to cease
this torture, and to let me rest in peace?
Don't make me look Death in the face to prove
that Death is more compassionate than Love!
If you really want me to love to the very end,
make him whom I love most, my all, my friend,
the only one who can bring me tears or laughter,
for whom I have sighed so often, follow after:
let him feel, in his blood, his bones, and in his soul,
an equal — or a hotter — desire boil.
Then your burdens won't weigh as heavily on me,
since someone who shares them will keep me company.[36]

END

SONNETS

1

Non havria Ulysse o qualunqu'atro mai
Più accorto fu, da quel divino aspetto
Pien di gratie, d'honor et di rispetto
Sperato qual i' sento affanni e guai.

Pur, *Amour*, co i begli occhi tu fatt'hai
Tal piaga dentro al mio innocente petto,
Di cibo et di calor già tuo ricetto,
Che rimedio non v'è si tu n'el dai.

O sorte dura, che mi fa esser quale
Punta d'un Scorpio, et domandar riparo
Contr'el velen' dall'istesso animale.

Chieggo li sol' ancida questa noia,
Non estingua el desir a me si caro,
Che mancar non potrà ch'i' non mi muoia.

[handwritten marginal notes:]
tu meurs et tu vis
paradox et cyclique.
verbatim M Italien.
pungere = punto — a
la punta
elle poète
l'enjambement
La forme est circulaire d'un scorpion.

SONNETS

1 [The Sting]

Not even Ulysses, or someone as wise as he,[37]
would guess that a face like yours — so full of grace
and honor and respect — such a divine face —
could bring suffering like the pain you're causing me.
Yes, Love, your eyes in all their piercing beauty[38]
have stabbed my innocent breast in the same place
once nourished and kept warm in your embrace;
and still, you are my only remedy.
Hard destiny makes me act like one who's been
stung by a scorpion but still hopes to heal,[39]
taking an antidote of the same poison.
I am wounded. I ask you only to kill the pain,
but not to extinguish the burning I crave to feel,
this desire whose broken life would break my own.[40]

2

O beaus yeus bruns, ô regars destournez,
O chaus soupirs, ô larmes espandues,
O noires nuits vainement atendues,
O jours luisans vainement vainement retournez:

O tristes pleins, ô desirs obstinez,
O tems perdu, ô peines despendues,
O mile morts mile rets tendues,
O pires maus contre moy destinez.

O ris, ô front, cheveus, bras, mains et doits:
O lut pleintif, viole, archet et vois:
Tant de flambeaus pour ardre une femmelle!

myself full of you.
De toy me plein, que tant de feus portant,
En tant d'endrois d'iceus mon cœur tatant,
N'en est sur toy volé quelque estincelle.

*le lut est sur
le cœur.*

*lyrical cause
from lyre.*

2 [Handsome Brown Eyes]

Ah handsome brown eyes — ah eyes that turn away —
ah burning sighs; ah tears that stretch so far;
ah night I wait in vain for, without a star;
ah luminous and vainly returning day —
oh sad complaints; oh love's stubborn play;
oh lost hours; oh wasted pain and war;
oh thousand deaths, each in a tightened snare;
oh sullen evils that design against my way.
Ah laugh, ah forehead, hair, arm, hand, and finger,[41]
ah plaintive lute, viola, bow, and singer —[42]
so many flames to engulf one single woman!
I despair of you; you carry so many fires
to touch my secret places and desires,
but not one spark flies back, to make you human.

3

O longs desirs, ô esperances vaines,
Tristes soupirs et larmes coutumieres
A engendrer de moy maintes rivieres,
Dont mes deus yeus sont sources et fontaines:

O cruautez, ô durtez inhumaines,
Piteus regars des celestes lumieres:
Du coeur transi ô passions premieres,
Estimez vous croitre encore mes peines?

Qu'encor Amour su moy son arc essaie,
Que nouveaus feus me gette et nouveaus dars:
Qu'il se despite, et pis qu'il pourra face:

Car je suis tant navree en toutes pars,
Que plus en moy une nouvelle plaie,
Pour m'empirer, ne pourrait trouver place.

3 [Long-Felt Desires]

Long-felt desires, hopes as long as vain —
sad sighs — slow tears accustomed to run sad
into as many rivers as two eyes can add,
pouring like fountains, endless as the rain —
cruelty beyond humanity, a pain
so hard it makes compassionate stars go mad
with pity: these are the first passions I've had.
Do you think Love could root in my soul again?
If he arched the great bow back again at me,[43]
licked me again with fire, and stabbed me deep
with the violent worst, as awful as before,
the wounds that cut me everywhere would keep
me shielded, so there would be no place free
for love. It covers me. It will pierce no more.[44]

4

Depuis qu'Amour cruel empoisonna
Premierement de son feu ma poitrine,
Tousjours brulay de sa fureur divine,
Qui un seul jour mon cœur n'abandonna.

Quelque travail, dont assez me donna,
Quelque menasse et procheine ruïne:
Quelque penser de mort qui tout termine,
De rien mon cœur ardent et n'estonna.

Tant plus qu'Amour nous vient fort assaillir,
Plus il nous fait nos forces recueillir,
Et toujours frais en ses combats fait estre:

Mais ce n'est pas qu'en rien nous favorise,
Cil qui les Dieus et les hommes mesprise:
Mais pour plus fort contre les fors paroitre.

4 [Stronger among the Strong]

Ever since I felt cruel Love first poison me [45]
with the first of many fires in my chest,
with a sacred flame that never lets me rest,
for one single day He has not let me be.
Whatever troubles He's brought me to see,
whatever approaching ruin or distress,
whatever thoughts of death's final conquest —
none of it could shake my heart's desire free.
The more that Love assails us with His powers,
the more He makes us recollect what is ours
and reenter the fight, refreshed, before too long.
It's not because He favors us in any way,
He who scorns gods and men and makes them pay —
it's just so He'll look stronger, among the strong.

5

Clere Venus, qui erres par les Cieus,
Entens ma voix qui en pleins chantera,
Tant que ta face au haut du Ciel luira,
Son long travail et souci ennuieus.

Mon œil veillant s'atendrira bien mieus,
Et plus de pleurs te voyant gettera.
Mieus mon lit mol de larmes baignera,
De ses travaus voyant témoins tes yeus.

Donq des humains sont les lassez esprits
De dous repos et de sommeil espris.
J'endure mal tant que le Soleil luit:

Et quand je suis quasi toute cassee,
Et que me suis mise en mon lit lassee,
Crier me faut mon mal toute la nuit.

5 [Bright Venus]

Listen, bright Venus — errant in the air! [46]
Listen to my clear voice move, as I sing
for your face, shining so high above everything,
about my long labor and my exhausting care.
My eyes grow softer with the night's long stare,
and as you look you'll see much, much more weeping.
More tears will dampen this bed, with your eyes watching,
though they trouble the sight of witnesses so rare.
Humans are weary now. Their spirits sleep
in a gentle hold of rest that pulls them deep.
But my pain will last as long as the sky is bright,
and when, almost completely broken, I
am pulled to my tear-wet bed, I'll plead and cry
with hurt that will hold me through the whole long night.

6

Deus ou trois fois bienheureus le retour
De ce cler Astre, et plus heureus encore
Ce que son œil de regarder honore.
Que celle là recevroit un beau jour,

Qu'elle pourroit se vanter d'un bon tour
Qui baiseroit le plus beau don de Flore,
Le mieus sentant que jamais vid Aurore,
Et y feroit sur mes levres sejour!

C'est à moy seule à qui ce bien est dù,
Pour tant de pleurs et tant de tems perdu:
Mais le voyant, tant lui feray de feste,

Tant emploiray de mes yeux le pouvoir,
Pour dessus lui plus de credit avoir,
Qu'en peu de temps feray grande conqueste.

6 [Aurora's Lessons]

It's twice happy, three times happy, the return
of his clear Star. And happier in turn[47]
is she his gaze will honor: I discern
how she will spend a happy day's sojourn,
so very proud of the rare luck she will earn
when Flora's gifts, of handsomest kisses, burn —
the most fragrant lessons Aurora could ever learn,
she on whose lips that sweet bliss will adjourn![48]
And *I* am the one to whom this gift should go,
for all my tears, and my time lost in woe.
So, when I see him, I will show my best,
using my eyes so well in all their power
that I'll have the advantage; in that short hour,
I'll make myself a very grand conquest.

Symbiose — 2 things coming together.
musc./fem.

neo platonisme
l'homme symbolise
la femme qui parle
à l'homme.
au seul qui parle

7

On voit mourir toute chose animee,
Lors que du corps l'ame sutile part:
Je suis le corps, toy la meilleure part:
Ou es tu donq, o ame bien aymee?

l'ame represente
homme.

Ne me laissez par long temps pámee,
Pour me sauver apres viendrois trop tard.
Las, ne mets point ton corps en ce hazart:
Rens lui sa part et moitié estimee.

le corps une est
ame.

Mais fais, Ami, que ne soit dangereuse
Cette rencontre et revüe amoureuse,
L'accompagnant, non de severité,

Non de rigueur: mais de grace amiable,
Qui doucement me rende ta beauté,
Jadis cruelle, à present favorable.

mélange femme
et ame

l'homme de la
beauté de l'homme.
une rime feminine avec
les mots (f)
la femme embrace l'homme
âme.

7 [Soul and Body]

We know this: everything that feels life move
dies, if the soul and body separate.
Now, I'm the body, and you are my own soul mate.
So where have you gone to now, my life, my love?
Don't make me stay here soulless while you rove!
You'd come back too late to save my life! Don't wait!
This body of yours has reached a terrible state!
I need you now; I need how you move above
me. Come easily, so it's not dangerous
for us to meet again, all amorous;
don't be too hard on me, and I know you'll move
me to appreciate your grace. Restore
your beauty to me gently — so it will prove
gentle, although it was so cruel before.[49]

8

oxymorons

Je vis, je meurs: je me brule et me noye.
J'ay chaut estreme en endurant froidure:
La vie m'est et trop molle et trop dure.
J'ay grans ennuis entremeslez de joye:

Tout à coup je ris et je larmoye,
Et en plaisir maint grief tourment j'endure:
Mon bien s'en va, et à jamais il dure:
Tout en un coup je seiche et je verdoye.

Ainsi Amour inconstamment me meine:
Et quand je pense avoir plus de douleur,
Sans y penser je me treuve hors de peine.

Puis, quand je croy ma joye estre certeine,
Et estre au haut de mon desiré heur,
Il me remet en mon premier malheur.

→ phonetique verse. not technically the mid pt but she plays with it.

La ryme est aussi avec les accents.
des verbes sont très actif.

Quel est le style, c'est comme Ronsard.
le style Petrarchiste.
très universel.

8 [I Live, I Die]

I live, I die: I burn and I also drown.[50]
I'm utterly hot and all I feel is cold.
Life is too soft and too hard for me to hold;
my joy and my heavy burden are mixed in one.
I laugh at the same time that I weep and frown;
the tarnish of grief has marred my pleasure's gold;
my good flies away, but stays until it's old;
I wither just as I find out that I've grown.
This is how love guides me, so changeably
that when I think the pain has me controlled,
with my very next thought I find that I am free.
Then, just as I trust in joy so certainly
that the peak of a yearned-for hour makes me bold,
he shows me my familiar grief unfold.

de platonism.
Neo l'influence la
Symposium.
Banquet

9

Tout aussi tot que je commence à prendre
Dens le mol lit le repos desiré,
Mon triste esprit, hors de moy retiré,
S'en va vers toy incontinent se rendre.

Lors m'est avis que dedens mon sein tendre
Je tiens le bien, où j'ay tant aspiré,
Et pour lequel j'ay si haut souspiré,
Que de sanglots ay souvent cuidé fendre.

O dous sommeil, o nuit à moy heureuse!
Plaisant repos, plein de tranquilité,
Continuez toutes les nuiz mon songe: → melody & illusion.

Et si jamais ma povre ame amoureuse
Ne doit avoir de bien en verité,
Faites au moins qu'elle en ait en mensonge

mettez l'amour idéal
en hors / outside l'amour réel.

fiction
La republic banned poets . . . .

9 [A Dream]

As soon as I, at last, begin to take
the rest I have been needing in my soft bed,
my soul grows sad and, shivering, is led
to fly to you and surrender.[51] I mistake
myself, imagining my tender breast will make
a pillow for the longed-for, darling head
for which I've sighed so hard, for which I've shed
tears and sobbed sobs until I thought I'd break.
Sweet sleep! Night so full of happiness!
Tender rest, all tranquil and unvisited
by pain — keep sending this dream every night!
And if my poor soul ever can't possess
its actual good, then send to me, instead,
at least the lie — the wrong, deceptive sight.

10

Quand j'aperçoy ton blond chef couronné
D'un laurier verd, faire un Lut si bien pleindre,
Que tu pourrois à te suivre contreindre
Arbres et rocs: quand je te vois orné,

Et de vertus dix mile environné,
Au chef d'honneur plus haut que nul ateindre,
Et des plus hauts les louenges esteindre:
Lors dit mon cœur en soy passionné:

Tant de vertus qui te font estre aymé,
Qui de chacun te font estre estimé,
Ne te pourroient aussi bien faire aymer?

Et ajoutant à ta vertu louable
Ce nom encor de m'estre pitoyable,
De mon amour doucement t'enflamer?

10 [Ten Thousand Ornaments]

When I see your blond head in its laurel crown
and hear your melancholy lute strings sing[52]
with a sound that would seduce almost anything,
even rocks or trees;[53] when I hear of your renown,
all the ten thousand ornaments that surround
your virtue, endowing you more than a king
so the highest praise grows dim with your sparkling —
then my heart cries, in a secret passion of her own:
since all your graces are well-loved and known —
since everyone's esteem for you has grown
so strong — shouldn't these graces help you start
to love? To all the virtues that make you great
adding knowledge of my own pitiable state,
so that my love can softly inflame your heart?

11

O dous regars, o yeus pleins de beauté,
Petits jardins, pleins de fleurs amoureuses
Ou sont d'Amour les flesches dangereuses,
Tant à vous voir mon œil s'est arresté!

O cœur felon, o rude cruauté,
Tant tu me tiens de façons rigoureuses,
Tant j'ay coulé de larmes langoureuses,
Sentant l'ardeur de mon cœur tourmenté!

Donques, mes yeus, tant de plaisir avez,
Tant de bons tours par ses yeus recevrez:
Mais toy, mon cœur, plus les vois s'y complaire,

Plus tu languiz, plus en as de soucis,
Or devinez si je suis aise aussi,
Sentant mon œil estre à mon cœur contraire

11 [Opposition]

Ah! The soft looks of your so beautiful eyes
are tiny gardens growing amorous flowers;
Love's dangerous arrows nestle in their bowers,[54]
and my eye has been arrested by the prize.
Ah! Your violent heart is so rude and cruel: it lies,
and binds me with such unrelenting powers
that my tears pour down in oh, such languorous showers,
at the torture of my ripe heart's ardent cries!
My eyes, you have discovered such great pleasure,
so much good fortune in his two eyes' treasure —
but my heart, the more you see the eyes' condition,
the more you languish, the more you feel the pain.
Do you think that I feel easy, that I gain,
when I feel my eyes and my heart in opposition?

12

Lut, compagnon de ma calamité,
De mes soupirs témoin irreprochable,
De mes ennuis controlleur véritable,
Tu as souvent avec moy lamenté:

Et tant le pleur piteus t'a molesté,
Que commençant quelque son delectable,
Tu le rendois tout soudein lamentable,
Feignant le ton que plein avoit chanté.

Et si tu veus efforcer au contraire,
Tu te destens et si me contreins taire:
Mais me voyant tendrement soupirer,

Donnant faveur à ma tant triste pleinte:
En mes ennuis me plaire suis contreinte,
Et d'un dous mal douce fin esperer.

12 [To My Lute]

Lute, my companion in calamity,[55]
irreproachable witness of my sighs,[56]
faithful secretary of all my cries,
you have lamented so often with me
that my tears have driven you deep into pity.
Now, if a delicious sound starts to arise,
you turn it back to a sad lament, disguise
it with tones you've sung so much more frequently.
No matter how I try to force you the other way,
you struggle, and loosen your strings, and steal away
my song. Still, when you watch my tender sighing,
indulging me, listening again while I complain,
I know pleasure, I find an opposite in my pain,
and hope sweet suffering will lead me to sweet dying.

13

Oh si j'estois en ce beau sein ravie
De celui là pour lequel vois mourant:
Si avec lui vivre le demeurant
De mes cours jours ne m'empeschoit envie:

Si m'acollant me disoit, chere Amie,
Contentons nous l'un l'autre, s'asseurant
Que ja tempeste, Euripe, ne Courant
Ne nous pourra desjoindre en notre vie:

Si de mes bras le tenant acollé,
Comme du Lierre est l'arbre encercelé,
La mort venoit, de mon aise envieuse:

Lors que souef plus il me baiseroit,
Et mon esprit sur ses levres fuiroit,
Bien je mourrois, plus que vivante, heureuse.

13 [The Ivy and the Tree]

Oh, if I were taken to that handsome breast[57]
and ravished by him for whom I seem to die,
if I could live with him through all of my
short days, free of the envy of the rest;
if, clinging to me, he'd say, "We're so blessed,
dear love; let's be contented just to lie
together, proving to flood and stormy sky[58]
how life can never break our close caress"—
if I could tighten my arms around him, cling
as ivy surrounds a tree with its circling,
then death would be welcome to envy and destroy.
And if then he'd give me another thirsty kiss
till my spirit flew away through his sweet lips,
I would die instead of live, and with more joy.[59]

14

Tant que mes yeux pourront larmes espandre,
A l'heur passé avec toy regretter:
Et qu'aus sanglots et soupirs resister
Pourra ma voix, et un peu faire entendre:

Tant que ma main pourra les cordes tendre
Du mignard Lut, pour tes graces chanter:
Tant que l'esprit se voudra contenter
De ne vouloir rien fors que toy comprendre:

Je ne souhaitte encor point mourir.
Mais quand mes yeus je sentiray tarir,
Ma voix cassee, et ma main impuissante,

Et mon esprit en ce mortel sejour
Ne pouvant plus montrer signe d'amante:
Prirey la Mort noircir mon plus cler jour.

14 [The Point of Death]

While my eyes can still pour out fountains of tears,
mourning our shared hours, gone now, so long gone;
while my slow sighs and sobs can still bemoan
the loss of you in a voice someone might hear;
while my hands can still caress this lute to clear
praises for any grace you might have shown,
and while my spirit remembers to bend alone
on you, on nothing that's outside your sphere —
I'll never want to reach the point of death!
Though when my eyes grow dry and this voicing breath
is broken and my hand is powerless,
and when my spirit takes its mortal flight,
beating with no more signs of love — yes, then, I'll press
death to come and cover my clearest day with night.

15

Pour le retour du Soleil honorer,
Le Zephir, l'air serein lui apareille:
Et du sommeil l'eau et la terre esveille,
Qui les gardoit l'une de murmurer,

En dous coulant, l'autre de se parer
De mainte fleur de couleur nompareille.
Ja les oiseaus es arbres font merveille,
Et aus passans font l'ennui moderer:

Les Nynfes ja en mile jeus s'esbatent
Au cler de Lune, et dansans l'herbe abatent:
Veus tu Zephir de ton heur me donner,

Et que par toy toute me renouvelle?
Fay mon Soleil devers moy retourner,
Et tu verras s'il ne me rend plus belle.

[handwritten annotations:]

God of the west.
Soleil → homme
Terre → femme.

C'est un cycle
s'enrichir la rotation
porte fruit
Ils travaillent ensemble.

l'idée d'Androgyne.

L'idée de Soleil
homme qui retourne.

plus belle plus
Louise Labé

(c'est la force?)
Authon

15 [The Returning of the Sun]

In honor of the returning of the Sun,[60]
the Zephyr begins to move the peaceful air.[61]
Both water and earth have awakened out of their
deep sleep (which kept the first from its sweet run-
ning murmur, the second from dressing in the spun
rainbows that myriads of flowers wear).
The marvel of birds in trees has just begun,
cheering anyone who was passing in despair.
But nymphs still play at their thousand games and prance
in the clear Moon's light, beating the grass as they dance.
Oh Zephyr, will you give me some time with you,
so I can renew myself in your company?
Come help my Sun return into my view,
and see if he doesn't render me more lovely.

16

Apres qu'un tems la gresle et le tonnerre
Ont le haut mont de Caucase batu,
Le beau jour vient, de lueur revétu.
Quand Phebus ha son cerne fait en terre,

Et l'Ocean il regaigne à grand erre:
Sa sœur se montre avec son chef pointu.
Quand quelque tems le Parthe ha combatu,
Il prent la fuite et son arc il desserre.

Un tems t'ay vù et consolé pleintif,
Et defiant de mon feu peu hatif:
Mais maintenant que tu m'as embrasee,

Et suis au point auquel tu me voulois:
Tu as ta flame en quelque eau arrosee,
Et es plus froit qu'estre je ne soulois.

16 [Impotence]⁶²

After a time in which thunder and hail
have beaten the mountains — the Caucasian height — ⁶³
a fine day comes, and they're clothed again in light.
When Phoebus⁶⁴ has covered the land with his circling trail,
he dives to the ocean again, and his sister, pale
with her pointed crown, moves back into our sight.
When the Parthian warrior has spent some time in the fight,⁶⁵
he loosens his bow and turns from his travail.
When I saw you plaintive once, I consoled you, though
that provoked my fire, which was burning slow.
But now that you have given me your embrace
and I am just at the point where you wanted me,
you have quenched your own flame in some watery place;
now it's colder than my own could ever be.

17

Je fuis la vile, et temples, et tous lieus,
Esquels prenant plaisir à t'ouir pleindre,
Tu peus, et non sans force, me contreindre
De te donner ce qu'estimois le mieus.

Masques, tournois, jeus me sont ennuieus,
Et rien sans toy de beau ne me peindre:
Tant que tachant à ce désir esteindre,
Et un nouvel obget faire à mes yeus,

Et des pensers amoureus me distraire,
Des bois espais sui le plus solitaire:
Mais j'aperçoy, ayant erré maint tour,

Que si je veus de toy estre delivre,
Il me convient hors de moymesme vivre,
Ou fais encor que loin sois en sejour.

17 [I Run from Town and Temple]

I run from town and temple, everywhere[66]
that I felt pleased to hear of your desire
(you could, with just a little force, inspire
me to surrender — ah, surrender what they call rare . . .).
Masques, tournaments, and games are a dull affair;
without you, there is nothing to admire.
I'm struggling once again to quench my fire,
To find another object to hold my stare,
to distract me from these constant thoughts of love —
I'm the loneliest soul in this deserted grove!
Wandering further then, I realize:
if I really want to deliver myself from you,
I'll need to live outside myself. It's true.[67]
Or else you will have to move further from my eyes.

présent et imperatif.
↳ l'idée de contrôle — Baise-moi!
Baise de Louis Labé.

passionée

18

Baise m'encor, rebaise moy et baise:
Donne m'en un de tes plus savoureus,
Donne m'en un de tes plus amoureus:
Je t'en rendray quatre plus chaus que braise.

Las, te pleins tu? ça que ce mal j'apaise,
En t'en donnant dix autres doucereus.
Ainsi meslans nos baisers tant heureus
Jouissons nous l'un de l'autre à notre aise.

Lors double vie à chacun en suivra.
Chacun en soy et son ami vivra.
Permets m'Amour penser quelque folie:

Tousjours suis mal, vivant discrettement,
Et ne me puis donner contentement,
Si hors de moy ne fay quelque saillie.

Louis signs this love a., it is also her poetry..

seperation et reunion.

le fadur, parce que, c'est le but.

→ seperate from.
seperament.

n'est pas réelle dans le réalité.

une sorte de symbose. establ

l'idéal n'existe pas.

une sorte de folie

jump out

12 13 (14)

une sorte de folie She is obsessed to be kissed. She exaggerates.

très exaggeré

Catulle — un poète Latin

Folie à forcé la repetition.
La force de l'amour et le rôle est symbose et une cyclique.

18 [Kiss Me Again]

Kiss me again, rekiss me, and then kiss [68]
me again, with your richest, most succulent
kiss; then adore me with another kiss, meant
to steam out fourfold the very hottest hiss
from my love-hot coals. Do I hear you moaning? This
is my plan to soothe you: ten more kisses, sent
just for your pleasure. Then, both sweetly bent
on love, we'll enter joy through doubleness,
and we'll each have two loving lives to tend:
one in our single self, one in our friend.
I'll tell you something honest now, my love: [69]
it's very bad for me to live apart.
There's no way I can have a happy heart
without some place outside myself to move. [70]

19

Diane estant en l'espesseur d'un bois,
Apres avoir mainte beste assenee,
Prenoit le frais, de Nynfes couronnee.
J'allois resvant comme fay maintefois,

Sans y penser: quand j'ouy une vois,
Qui m'apela, disant, Nynfe estonnee,
Que ne t'es tu vers Diane tournee?
Et me voyant sans arc et sans carquois,

Qu'as-tu trouvé, o compagne, en ta voye,
Qui de ton arc et flesches ait fait proye?
Je m'animay, respons je, à un passant,

Et lui getay en vain toutes mes flesches
Et l'arc apres: mais lui les ramassant
Et les tirant me fit cent et cent bresches.

19 [A Meeting with Diana]

Diana, standing in the clearing of a wood[71]
after she had hunted her prey and shot it down,
breathed deep. Her nymphs had woven her a green crown.
I walked, as I often do, in a distracted mood,
not thinking — when I heard a voice, subdued
and quiet, call, "Astonished nymph, don't frown;
have you lost your way to Diana's sacred ground?"
Since I had no quiver, no arrows, it pursued,
"Dear friend, who were you meeting with today?
Who has taken your bow and arrows away?"
I said, "I found an enemy on the path,
and hurled my arrows at him, but in vain —
and then my bow — but he picked them up in wrath,
and with my arrows shot back hundreds of kinds of pain."

20

Predit me fut, que devoit fermement
Un jour aymer celui dont la figure
Me fut descrite: et sans autre peinture
Le reconnu quand vy premierement:

Puis le voyant aymer fatalement,
Pitié je pris de sa triste aventure:
Et tellement je forçay ma nature,
Qu'antant que lui aymay ardentement.

Qui n'ust pensé qu'en faveur devoit croitre
Ce que le Ciel et destins firent naitre?
Mais quand je voy si nubileus aprets,

Vents si cruels et tant horrible orage:
Je croy qu'estoient les infernaus arrets,
Qui de si loin m'ourdissoient ce naufrage.

20 [The Seer]

A seer told me of a man who stood
firm in his love, and described this steadfast lover.
I needed no other picture; I knew I would
know him—and I did, when I first looked him over.
And when I realized that his love was good,
I was shaken to pity by his sad endeavor,
forced myself to love him, and found I could
love him right back, with just as hot a fever.
Who wouldn't think that this love, birthed alive
by the union of Fate and Heaven, was bound to thrive?
Ah! When I see how thick the storm clouds form,
how cruel the winds blow, how angry the sea foam,
I think Hell is the place that birthed this storm,
bearing its long-foretold disaster home.[72]

21

Quelle grandeur rend l'homme venerable?
Quelle grosseur? quel poil? quelle couleur?
Qui est des yeus le plus emmieleur?
Qui fait plus tot une playe incurable?

Quel chant est plus à l'homme convenable?
Qui plus penetre en chantant sa douleur?
Qui un dous lut fait encore meilleur?
Quel naturel est le plus amiable?

Je ne voudrois le dire assurément,
Ayant Amour forcé mon jugement:
Mais je say bien et de tant je m'assure,

Que tout le beau que lon pourroit choisir,
Et que tout l'art qui ayde la Nature,
Ne me sauroient acroitre mon desir.

Les cheveux
La poitrine.
Le blason
Quel voix qui chante.

21 [Love Forces My Judgment]

Which height makes a man earn the most admiration?[73]
Which weight? Which hair? What color of skin and face?
Which eyes brim fullest with the honeyed grace
that spurs the most incurable sensation?
What song brings a man's voice the highest glorification,
its sadness penetrating the deepest place?
On whose voice does a lute leave the sweetest trace?
Which nature best feels love's warm palpitation?
I wouldn't want to claim that I know best,
since Love forces my judgment; nevertheless,[74]
I do know one thing well — yes, I'm quite sure
that all the beauty I could choose to explore,
and all the art that might improve on Nature,
would never increase my desire one bit more.

22

Luisant Soleil, que tu es bien heureus,
De voir toujours de t'Amie la face:
Et toy, sa seur, qu'Endimion embrasse,
Tant te repais de miel amoureus.

Mars voit Venus: Mercure aventureus
De Ciel en Ciel, de lieu en lieu se glasse:
Et Jupiter remarque en mainte place
Ses premiers ans plus gays et chaleureus.

Voilà du Ciel la puissante harmonie,
Qui les esprits divins ensemble lie:
Mais s'ils avoient ce qu'ils ayment lointein,

Leur harmonie et ordre irrevocable
Se tourneroit en erreur variable,
Et comme moy travailleroient en vain.

22 [Celestial Loves]

How you shine, oh Sun, with happiness, to see
your love's own silver, gazing, steady face.[75]
Your sister Moon, whom Endymion embraced,[76]
is filled now with the feast of Love's fine honey.
And Mars sees Venus, and Mercury still ventures[77]
from Sky to Sky, from place to glistening place,
and Jupiter notices everywhere the trace
of his many youthful hot and gay adventures.
See how, with the strength of the Sky's harmonies,
these heavenly bodies link their different ways.
If those celestial loves were to separate,
their harmony and irrevocable order
would change and vary in a turning error —
and they'd strive as I do, vainly, against fate.

23

Las! que me sert, que si parfaitement
Louas jadis ma tresse doree,
Et de mes yeus la beauté comparee
A deus Soleils, dont Amour finement

Tira les trets causez de ton tourment?
Ou estes vous, pleurs de peu de duree?
Et Mort par qui devoit estre honoree
Ta ferme amour et iteré serment?

Donques c'estoit le but de ta malice
De m'asservir sous ombre de service?
Pardonne moy, Ami, à cette fois,

Estant outree et de despit et d'ire:
Mais je m'assur', quelque part que tu sois,
Qu'autant que moy tu soufres de martire.

23 [This Tangle]

What good is it how well, alas, you sang
those long-ago praises to my rich gold hair,
or told me that my gorgeous eyes compared
to suns from which Love's brightest arrows sprang,[78]
tormenting you again with each sharp new pang?
Oh tears, that dry so quickly in the air;
oh Death, on which you promised you would swear
your love — and where your solemn vows still hang
(or was the aim of your deceitful malice
to enslave me, while seeming to be in my service?).
This time, oh love, I know you'll pardon me
this tangle of all my anger and grief entwined;
since I know for sure, wherever you may be,
you endure your martyrdom, as I do mine.

24

Ne reprenez, Dames, si j'ai aymé:
Si j'ay senti mile torches ardentes,
Mile travaus, mile douleurs mordentes:
Si en pleurant, j'ay mon tems consumé,

Las que mon nom n'en soit par vous blamé.
Si j'ay failli, les peines sont presentes,
N'aigrissez point leurs pointes violentes:
Mais estimez qu'Amour, à point nommé,

Sans votre ardeur d'un Vulcan excuser,
Sans la beauté d'Adonis acuser,
Pourra, s'il veut, plus vous rendre amoureuses:

En ayant moins que moy d'ocasion,
Et plus d'estrange et forte passion.
Et gardez vous d'estre plus malheureuses.

FIN DES EUVRES DE LOVÏSE
LABÉ LIONNOIZE.

24 [Sisters, Do Not Reproach Me]

Sisters, do not reproach me that I've felt
such love it makes a thousand torches burn,[79]
had a thousand cares, a thousand sorrows turn
my days to days that tears consume and melt.
Rough words like yours shouldn't burden my name with guilt;
if I've failed, you'll know I feel all the pain I earn.[80]
So stop sharpening those needles. Someday you'll learn
how high Love flames every time it burns heartfelt,
even if there's no Vulcan as an excuse,[81]
no beauty like Adonis's to accuse.[82]
On a whim, Love can force you to burn until —
even with less occasion than I have —
you'll suffer a stronger, and a stranger, love.
So watch out — you could be far more unhappy still.

END OF THE WORKS OF LOUISE
LABÉ, LYONNAISE

NOTES

CHAPTER ONE

1. The present edition reproduces the definitive text of François Rigolot in his 2004 edition of the *Complete Works*.

2. From its opening invocation of the "harsh laws of men," the *Letter* takes its place among what Colette Winn has called the "transgressive" female-authored texts challenging the social restrictions placed on early modern women ("La femme écrivain au XVIe siècle: Ecriture et transgression," *Poétique* 84 [1990]: 442–43).

3. The text of Labé's letter is preceded by an explicit dedication in abbreviated form: A.M.C.D.B.L. ("A Mademoiselle Clémence de Bourges, Lyonnaise"). Jones (*Currency of Eros*, 159) and Berriot (*La Belle Rebelle*, 183) have read in Labé's insertion of the epithet "Lyonnaise" the author's highlighting of the common urban citizenship she shared with Clémence, over and above their class differences.

4. Two male-authored French documents published in the years prior to Labé's works demonstrate important resonances with her dedicatory letter. Antoine de Moulin's preface to the 1545 edition of Pernette du Guillet's *Rymes*, addressed to the women of Lyon, urges the female collective to follow in Pernette's literary footsteps and strive toward her acclaim. As Madeleine Lazard underlines, Labé's own preface "responds" to Moulin's exhortations — not through a male intermediary, but in the poetess's own voice (*Louise Labé*, 121). In a different vein, Claude de Taillemont's *Discours des champs faits à l'honneur et l'exaltation de l'Amour et des Dames* (Discourses on the Spheres Related to the Honor and Praise of Love and of Women [Lyon, 1553]), deplore the past barriers to female learning and argue for equal access for women and men to educational opportunity. In his recent critical book on Labé, François Rigolot posits the polemic links and temporal proximity between Taillemont's defense and her letter as an important example of the solidarity and exchange in the Lyonnais intellectual community that nurtured Labé's literary and cultural formation (*Louise Labé Lyonnaise*, 22–27). Moving farther back in time, prose defenses of women founded on exempla had long been the typical mode, as shown in Boccaccio's *De claris mulieribus* (Of Famous Women, c. 1380) and Christine de Pizan's 1405 *Livre de la Cité des Dames* (Book of the City of Ladies). Other sixteenth-century male defenses of women still frequently adopted the model of exemplarity, sometimes alternating with conventional Petrarchan stereotypes that placed women on pedestals and thus elided the

issue of active social change. Examples of such works include Castiglione's 1537 courtly polemic *Il Cortegiano* (The Book of the Courtier), Cornelius Agrippa's *De nobilitate et praecellentia foeminei sexus* (Declamation on the Nobility and Preeminence of the Female Sexe, 1529), and François de Billon's *Le Fort inexpugnable de l'honneur du sexe feminin* (The Inextinguishable Strength of the Honor of the Female Sex), published the same year as Labé's own volume, 1555.

5.   Ann Rosalind Jones (*Currency of Eros*, chap. 1) and Constance Jordan (*Renaissance Feminism*, 175) explore the background and socioeconomic implications of the distaff and spindle emblem in early modern Europe, a period of mercantile expansion during which it lost much of its urgent domestic necessity, but maintained its power as an image of women's confinement to the home.

6.   Cotgrave's 1611 *Dictionarie of the French and English Tongues* offers the following range of definitions for the term *vertu:* Virtue, goodnesse, honestie, sinceritie, integritie; worth, perfection, desert, merit; also valour, prowesse, manhood; also energie, efficacie, force, power, might. Huguet's seven-volume 1950 dictionary of sixteenth-century French language presents similar threads of meaning: *force, courage, vaillance* (valor), *talent, propriété* (propriety); *pouvoir* (power), *qualité* (upstanding character).

7.   Cathy Yandell, *Carpe Corpus: Time and Gender in Early Modern France* (Newark: University of Delaware Press, 2000), beautifully analyzes against the backdrop of the male Lyonnais establishment what she calls the "temporality of virtue" in Labé's works, from the *Letter's* challenge to the distaff and spindle to the poetry's vigilant consciousness of both the gift and the burden of investing time in self-expression (111–27).

8.   François Rigolot's updated 2004 edition of Labé's works introduces the term *"secondes concepcions"* (*"second* impressions"), and I have followed this change in my translation. This replaces the 1986 edition's other plausible orthographic transcription of the term as *"fecondes* impressions" (*"fertile* impressions"), given that Labé is clearly drawing a distinction between earlier and later impressions, as Daniel Martin's exhaustive 1999 study of Labé's works has also argued (*Signe[s] d'Amante*, 43). The earlier transcription nevertheless retains a certain appeal, since more "fertile" or developed ideas are clearly the product of the later perspective of which Labé speaks. For an important discussion of Labé's notion of literary composition and recomposition, see Jordan, *Renaissance Feminism*, 176–77.

9.   In an earlier study I have observed that "the rapidly accumulating diction of pleasure in the second half of the *Epistre* divides into two different networks, such that the more abstract and global terms of enjoyment ('contentement,' 'resjouit,' and later, 'aise') are related to intellectual activity, as against the more narrowly suggestive vocabulary evoking purely sensual satisfaction ('voluptez,' 'delectables')" (*Subject of Desire*, 36).

10.   Rigolot, Préface to *Œuvres complètes*, 21–22 (my translation).

11.   For a discussion of the projection of responsibility onto others as a frequent rhetorical tactic in the prefaces of women writers, see Anne Larsen, "'Un honneste passetems': Strategies of Legitimation in French Renaissance Women's Prefaces," *L'Esprit Créateur* 30, no. 4 (1990): 17–19. One effect of adducing advance outside support for potentially controversial or even censurable writing, of course, is to attract

the interest and curiosity of other readers (see Jones, *Currency of Eros*, 173, and Lesko Baker, *Subject of Desire*, 19).

12.   One likely imperative for the author's strong attribution of both external support and responsibility for the publication of her works is the important fact, stressed by Lazard, that Labé stands alone among sixteenth-century French women writers in having received the so-called "privilege du Roy" (the king's authorization to publish) without the expressed intervention or facilitation of a specific male intermediary (*Louise Labé*, 122).

13.   For discussions of the hybrid generic sources of the *Debate*, see Edith Benkov, "The Re-making of Love: Louise Labé's *Débat de Folie et d'Amour*," *Symposium* 46, no. 2 (1992): 95–98; Berriot, *La Belle Rebelle*, 170–72; Christiane Lauvergnat-Gagnière, "La rhétorique dans le *Débat de Folie et d'Amour*," in Demerson, *Louise Labé*, 53–56; Lazard, *Louise Labé*, 131; and Rigolot, Préface to *Œuvres complètes*, 10–11.

14.   As Lazard notes (*Louise Labé*, 134), the idea of making Folly responsible for Cupid's blindness is original to Labé.

15.   Anne R. Larsen, "Louise Labé's *Débat de Folie et d'Amour*: Feminism and the Defense of Learning," *Tulsa Studies in Women's Literature* 2 (1983): 46.

16.   Given the centrality of the confrontation between the two sexes in this scene, I have chosen to specify the female gendering of the repeated nominal adjective "fole."

17.   For an extended analysis of the rest of discourse 1 in the context of the protagonists' opening exchange, see Lesko Baker, *Subject of Desire*, 47–58.

18.   Martin reveals other important "thematic echoes" between the letter and the *Debate*'s first discourse, namely, varying presentations of the motifs of *glory* (the misplaced, self-attributed glory of Cupid versus the authentic glory obtainable by women through writing); *guidance* (Folly's self-portrayal as the guide for Love's arrows and ultimately for the blinded god himself versus Labé's own request for a guide in the person of Clémence de Bourges); and *public enlightenment* (Folly's self-purported modesty in not announcing her role in the praise attributed to Love, versus Labé's imperative to her female counterparts to illuminate the world on the rightful status of women as "companions" alongside men, the common vocabulary in this theme's presentation being the expression "faire entendre au monde" [to make the world understand]). *Signe(s) d'Amante*, 117–20.

19.   As stated by François Rigolot and Julianne Jones Wright, Folly's culminating act (the blinding of Love) serves literally to obliterate the "objectifying look" with which the love god has viewed her. She can therefore no longer be simply a misunderstood reflection of his male suppositions. "Les irruptions de Folie: Fonction idéologique du porte-parole dans les *Œuvres* de Louise Labé," *L'Esprit Créateur* 30 no. 4 (1990): 74.

20.   See ibid., 76.

21.   Labé's critique here alludes to the Petrarchan speaker's tendency — hyperbolized in the genre of the Renaissance *blason*— to laud the female object fragmentally in terms of her specific body parts, a phenomenon discussed in depth by Nancy Vickers in "Diana Described: Scattered Woman and Scattered Rhyme," *Critical Inquiry* 8 (1981): 265–79. As Jones has argued, in the listing of male attributes in sonnet 2 and in the longer interrogation of male attributes in sonnet 21, Labé turns the

gender tables on this descriptive mode, amusingly deriding its objectifying conse-
quences (*Currency of Eros*, 168–70).

22.   On the medieval rooting of the tradition of highborn love, see Berriot, *La Belle Rebelle*, 163.

23.   Labé will in fact use a similar image of joint labor at the end of the final elegy, when she evokes Love's "burden" ("faix," l. 103) as easier to bear when shared with another person.

24.   It is these instances of otherwise inexplicable pronoun slippage that Rigolot and Wright refer to as the "irruptions" of Folly's own voice into Mercury's oral argument ("Les irruptions de Folie," 78–81). In addition to the attempt to claim her verbal autonomy on the social and judicial stage, Folly's intrusions subtly anticipate Labé's rejection of the lady's mute posture in Petrarchan male lyric and her own poetic restoration of that silenced voice (Lesko Baker, *Subject of Desire*, 73–74).

25.   See Robert D. Cottrell, "The Problematics of Opposition in Louise Labé's *Débat de Folie et d'Amour*," *French Forum* 12, no. 1 (1987): 39.

26.   Mercury's amusing enumeration of these contradictions is as follows:

> To have a heart divided against itself; to be at peace one minute, at war the next, and then at truce the next; to cover up and hide one's pain; to change expressions a thousand times a day; to feel the blood rush up and redden one's face, then suddenly drain away, leaving it pale, according to whether shame, hope, or fear besiege us; to go in search of what torments us, while pretending to run away from it, and yet to dread finding it; for every laugh, to breathe a thousand sighs; to deceive oneself, to burn from afar, but to freeze up close; to stumble on our words and fall abruptly silent — aren't these all signs of *someone no longer in control of his senses?*

> (Avoir le cœur separé de soymesme, estre maintenant en paix, ores en guerre, ores en treves: couvrir et cacher sa douleur: changer visage mile fois le jour: sentir le sang qui lui rougit la face, y montant: puis soudein s'enfuit, la laissant palle, ainsi que honte, esperance, ou peur, nous gouvernent: chercher ce qui nous tourmente, feingnant le fuir, et neanmoins avoir creinte de le trouver: n'avoir qu'un petit ris entre mile soupirs: se tromper soymesme: bruler de loin, geler de pres: un parler interrompu: un silence venant tout à coup: ne sont ce tous signes d'*un homme aliené de son bon entendement?* [Pp. 122–123 below; emphasis added.])

27.   Rigolot observes and analyzes this key pronoun ambiguity in "Gender vs. Sex Difference in Louise Labé's Grammar of Love," in *Rewriting the Renaissance: The Discourses of Sexual Difference in Early Modern Europe*, ed. Margaret W. Ferguson, Maureen Quilligan, and Nancy J. Vickers (Chicago: University of Chicago Press, 1986), 295, and in "Quel genre d'amour pour Louise Labé," *Poétique* 55 (1983), 313. I state my own reasons for attributing the final pronoun to Love in the final note for my translation of discourse 5.

28.   Labé uses initials only to identify her dedicatee: Mademoiselle Clémence de Bourges, Lionnoize (see, 00 and n. 9 above). As mentioned earlier, Labé's insistence on referring to this young noblewoman with a formal invocation of her Lyonnais heritage attests to her pride in a shared female citizenship that blurs and supersedes their class differences (see p. 6, n. 9, and n. 3 above).

29.   As confirmed by Cotgrave and Huguet, the sixteenth-century meanings of the French term *science* go back to its Latin etymologies (*scio, scire:* "to know"), and it is therefore best translated as "learning" (or, by extension, "education") or "knowledge," depending upon the context. The word *discipline(s)* pertains especially to the work of gaining knowledge, i.e. *study,* and, by extension in the plural, the materials to be mastered, i.e., *studies.*

30.   The French term "usage" can refer to the actual use or using of something, or else to social custom or convention. Although translators Anne-Marie Bourbon (*Debate of Folly and Love* [New York: Peter Lang, 2000], 15) and Edith Farrell (*Louise Labé's Complete Works* [Troy, NY: Whitson, 1986], 27) have both adopted the first sense, I have preferred the second, as has Jeanne Prine ("Louise Labé," 149), because I feel it suggests more clearly the sense that material goods come to women principally through their societal bonds and commitments to men.

31. For a discussion of the multiple resonances of the word "virtue" (*vertu*) in the sixteenth century and its exploitation along gendered lines in this paragraph, see p. 22 and nn. 6–7 above.

32.   Concerning the emblem of the distaff and spindle, see p. 22 and n. 5 above.

33.   Labé's French phrase "contentement de soy," describing the particular nature of intellectual pleasure, could have the sense of either the satisfaction or contentment experienced within the self (the sense followed by Bourbon and Farrell) or the satisfaction or contentment uniquely produced by study (the sense followed by Prine). Although I tend to favor the first option, I have tried to capture both resonances in my translation.

34.   Jupiter, Olympian king of gods and men.

35.   Love, god of love, popularly known as Cupid, and the son of Venus.

36.   Folly, daughter of Youth, first popularly allegorized as a goddess in the Renaissance by Erasmus, as pointed out by translators Anne-Marie Bourbon (*Debate of Folly and Love,* 24) and Edith Farrell (*Louise Labé's Complete Works,* 6).

37.   Bourbon raises the issue of Labé's frequent shifts in verb tense in the *Debate,* as illustrated in the very first two sentences of the preliminary Argument. Although there is indeed an element of stylistic dissonance here in the rapid change from the past to the present tense, I have maintained this transition, because it immediately draws the reader into the "presentness" and dramatic vibrancy of the protagonists' upcoming encounter in the opening discourse.

38.   Venus, goddess of love and beauty, and mother of Cupid.

39.   Apollo, god of poetry, music, and prophecy and Love's representative at Jupiter's hearing.

40.   Mercury, god of eloquence and cleverness, known as the messenger of the gods, and Folly's representative at Jupiter's hearing.

41.   Given the centrality of the confrontation between the two sexes in this scene, I have chosen to specify the female gendering of the repeated nominalized adjective "fole."

42.   The French phrase, "vendre tes coquilles," is certainly one of the most colorful expressions in the *Debate* and one of the most difficult to translate. A more literal

version of Labé's sentence ("Ce n'est pas a moy a qui tu dois vendre *tes coquilles*.") is fol-lowed in Farrell's translation: "Don't try to sell your *pilgrim's shells* to me" (32). As Bour-bon has noted in her own translation (38), these *"coquilles"* refer to the shells brought back by religious pilgrims from Santiago de Compostela and then sold for profit. Folly means here to equate Love's inflated rhetoric with worthless, misrepresented merchandise offered to the gullible buyer. However, Max Engammare, the editor of Droz Press, has recently pointed out that the *q* in "coquilles" was most likely inserted by Labé's printer to deflect attention away from the otherwise socially inappropriate term "couilles" (referring to the male testicles), this while leaving its resonance to the reader's imagination. In that context, I wish to thank François Rigolot for suggesting the translation "strut your stuff," which exploits the ambiguous connotation of "stuff" (boasting, nonsense, merchandise, virility).

43.   Saturn, former ruler of the universe, overthrown by his son Jupiter. Mars, god of war. Satyrs, fauns, and sylvans, minor rural and woodland deities.

44.   Pallas, another name for Athena, goddess of war and wisdom and a masterful weaver of tapestries. In elegy 3, Labé's speaker will reinvoke and measure herself against Pallas's artisanal talents.

45.   Neptune, god of the sea, accompanied by his attendants, the Tritons.

46.   Pluto, god of the underworld, stole Proserpina away as she screamed for her mother and whisked her off to Hades.

47.   Vulcan, god of fire and forger of arms for the gods.

48.   The Furies, three snaked-haired female spirits who avenged unpunished crimes. Harpies, monsters of prey with the head and upper body of a woman and the legs, tail, and claws of a bird.

49.   In this sentence, I have translated the polyvalent term "vertu" as "power," ap-plying to Love the typical male-gendered connotations of this word discussed in the introduction to this chapter (see p. 22).

50.   The serpent of Epidaurus, known for its keen sight, became a medical emblem symbolizing the watchful eye of doctors over the health of their patients.

51.   Circe, an enchantress who changed men to swine in Homer's *Odyssey*. Medea, the volatile sorceress who assisted Jason in his quest for the Golden Fleece.

52.   In the series of famous transformation myths included in Ovid's *Metamorphoses*, Jupiter turns himself into a bull to carry off the Phoenician princess Europa; into a golden rain to father Perseus by the nymph Danaë; and into an eagle to snatch up the nymph Asteria.

53.   Vulcan, Venus's husband, caught his wife and Mars in bed together by setting up chains in which they were entrapped.

54.   The smitten Paris's abduction of Helen from King Menelaus of Sparta was the famous catalyst of the Trojan War.

55.   As movingly recounted in book 4 of the *Aeneid*, Queen Dido of Carthage wel-comed Aeneas and his entourage to her shores after the fall of Troy, only to fall so deeply in love with him that when his fortune finally beckoned him to embark for Italy, she committed suicide on a funeral pyre.

56. After the death of her husband, King Mausolus of Caria, Queen Artemisia memorialized him with the construction of the fourth-century BCE Mausoleum, one of the seven wonders of the ancient world. But still wild with grief, she is said to have met her own death after drinking a mixture containing her husband's ashes.

57. In Greek and Roman mythology, the Fates were the three goddesses who controlled human life and destiny through their work at the spinning wheel. Accordingly, the first goddess, Clotho, was responsible for spinning the thread of life; the second, Lachesis, for deciding upon its length; and the third, Atropos, for cutting it off.

58. I have chosen to translate literally Venus's characterization of Folly as "the most wretched *thing* of all" ("la plus miserable *chose* du monde") in order to emphasize how Labé attributes to both Love and his mother the misogynist rhetorical tactic of dehumanizing the female protagonist as part of their attempt to claim power and superiority over her. This linguistic strategy is repeated later in the scene, when Venus likens Folly to a "mad beast" ("beste si furieuse").

59. Diomedes, a Greek warrior at the siege of Troy, injured Venus's wrist as she struggled to save Aeneas, the Trojan hero and her son with Anchises.

60. Adonis, a young man esteemed for his exceptional beauty and loved by Venus. According to some sources, Apollo grew so jealous of Adonis's affections for Venus that he sent a wild boar to kill the boy, thereby provoking Venus's wrath. It is this history that Venus alludes to further on when she requests Apollo to be Love's defender.

61. In his role as god of the sun, Apollo nurtured and cultivated lands, among them Venus's gardens on the island of Cyprus and on Mount Ida in Crete.

62. In this discourse, "love" as an abstract concept begins to be interwoven more frequently with "Love" as the name for the male protagonist, Cupid. (Prior to this discourse, the noun as concept is used only once (in the plural: "Amours"), designating the "love story" of Dido toward the end of discourse1.) Here in discourse 4, as well as in discourse 5, Labé most frequently (although not in every single instance), retains the capitalization of the term regardless of its referent. In my translation, beyond the references to the love god himself, I will choose the uppercase or lowercase spelling according to the context, capitalizing the word only when it refers simultaneously to the character and the concept (as in this sentence), or when the concept is used in an overarching proverbial or aphoristic formulation.

63. A reinvocation of Jupiter's metamorphoses first mentioned in the *Debate*'s opening scene, and glossed above, n. 52.

64. Jupiter sustained challenges to his rule by a race of ancient giant deities, also known as the Titans, who tried to reach the heavens from earth by piling mountains one on top of the other, but who were buried under the rubble of their own structures when the Olympian king hurled his thunderbolt. Briareus, a monstrous giant with a hundred hands, was supposedly allied with the Olympians against the Titans but himself joined a rebellion against Jupiter. So numerous were the attacks to Jupiter's power that his retaliatory thunderbolts at one point threatened to burn up the entire universe.

65. Anne-Marie Bourbon (*Debate of Folly and Love,* 134 n. 3) rightly points out the syntactical ambiguity opening this sentence, where the word "dernier" could be taken to modify "festin" ("the last banquet") or Love himself ("il," i.e., the last one to arrive at the

banquet). Although, as she indicates, the previous action in discourse 1 invites the second interpretation, I have followed Edith Farrell in selecting the other option, since it seems to me unlikely that Apollo — Love's defender — would wish to draw attention to the tardiness of his own client. Beginning here, when Apollo describes the opening encounter between Love and Folly, Labé shifts once again to the present tense, as she did in the Argument. I continue to uphold this tense shift for the same reasons of dramatic vibrancy that I adduced in my translation of the Argument.

66.   Bourbon's note (*Debate of Folly and Love*, 134 n. 6) describing Folly's attack as a violation of the protected sacred site of Jupiter's palace helps to clarify the accurate sense of this difficult sentence.

67.   Apollo refers to the story of Ixion, who was fastened eternally to a burning wheel in Hades as punishment for his attempt to seduce Jupiter's wife, Juno.

68.   Sicily's Aetna was one of the mountains under which Jupiter buried the Giants who rebelled against his reign.

69.   Apollo here invokes the famous punishment inflicted by Jupiter on Prometheus, who for having stolen fire from the gods was imprisoned on Mount Caucasus, where every day an eagle came and devoured his liver.

70.   This sentence and the following one pose problems, owing to the ambiguity of the referent in the phrase "A leur profit," as noted by Bourbon (*Debate of Folly and Love*, 135) and shown by the wide divergence between her translation and that of Farrell. I have basically followed Bourbon's interpretation, which makes more sense in context, although my reading of the difficult phrase "n'est procedee de gloire" in the second sentence differs from hers.

71.   Orpheus, the mythological Thracian musician and poet whose magical skill on the lyre could delight and appease even the most brutal men and animals, as well as trees, rocks, and other elements of the natural world.

72.   In Greek legend, Orestes, the son of Agamemnon and Clytemnestra, would likely have been murdered along with his father by his mother and her lover Aegisthus, had he not been sent in secret by his sister, Electra, to the home of his uncle, King Strophios. There Orestes was raised alongside his cousin Pylades, and the two became inseparable lifelong friends.

73.   As Rigolot notes in his edition (*Œuvres complètes*, 70 n.1), the reference to different theories concerning Love's origins suggests Labé's familiarity with Plato's *Symposium*. Among the ancient forces deified here, Zephyrus is the personification of the west wind, considered among the gentlest of the wood-land gods.

74.   Philios, the name sometimes attributed to Jupiter, comes from the Greek *philos* (friend) and *philein* (to love).

75.   Plato's androgyne combined both male and female characteristics in one unified being.

76.   Castor and Pollux were the twin sons of Leda. Castor was fathered by Leda's husband, Tyndarus, whereas Pollux was fathered by Jupiter, who had seduced the faithful Leda by assuming the form of a swan. Their fraternal love was so great that when Jupiter decided to grant immortality to the wounded Pollux following a battle that claimed Castor's life, Pollux asked that he be able to share this immortality with

his dead brother. According to legend, Jupiter granted this request and conferred immortality to each of them on alternate days.

77.   These three allusions span Old Testament, classical, and medieval contexts. As recounted in the first book of Samuel, when King Saul revealed to his son Jonathan his intention to kill David, Jonathan pleaded with his father to recall David's defense of the kingdom of Israel against the Philistines and finally convinced the king to spare David's life. In Roman legend, Damon and Pythias were such devoted friends that when Pythias had been condemned to death for challenging King Dionysius of Syracuse but wished a stay of his execution to finalize his affairs, Damon offered himself up as a pledge of Pythias's return — an act that moved the king to pardon them both. Alexis, the peripatetic saint of medieval lore, was said to have left his marriage bed and entrusted his bride to his friend in order to flee and answer God's calling. Bourbon's note (*Debate of Folly and Love*, 136) also relates this allusion to an episode in book 10 of the *Decameron*, where Gisippo gives his bride, Sofronia, to his lovesick friend Tito Quinzio Fulvo on his wedding night.

78.   King Darius tried for many months to conquer Babylon, succeeding finally when his devoted companion Zopyrus feigned betrayal and gained command of the Babylonian army, only to stage their defeat.

79.   As the story goes, the king of Bosphorus scorned the request by the young Scythian Arsacomas to marry his daughter, but Arsacomas, aided by his two cherished friends, eventually prevailed and won the princess's hand.

80.   In one of the most renowned stories in classical mythology, King Minos's daughter, Ariadne, out of love for the great slayer of monsters Theseus, provided the hero with the thread that allowed him to find his way out of the labyrinth after he destroyed the Minotaur. Hypermnestra was the only one of the Danaides, the fifty daughters of King Danaus forced into marriage to the fifty sons of the king's twin brother, who disobeyed her father's order to kill her husband, Lynceus.

81.   This sentence and the previous one are excellent examples of instances in which the word "Love" can be taken to refer simultaneously to Cupid and to the abstract concept (see n. 62 above). In my translation I have retained the capitalization prioritizing the male protagonist as the primary referent in both sentences, given the context of Apollo's defense.

82.   Rigolot remarks that the word "mysanthropes" was a recent addition to the French lexicon, and that it was used and defined by Rabelais in the *Brief Declaration* appearing with his *Fourth Book (Quart Livre)* (*Œuvres complètes*, 72 n. 1). Rabelais's inspiration seems likely both in the scatological humor and the hyperbolic enumerations in the following comic passage.

83.   Like his fellow poet and musician Orpheus (see n. 71 above), Amphion exercised magical power with his song. When he played his lyre, the stones being used to build the walls of Thebes fell into place all by themselves.

84.   I retain the uppercase spelling for the conceptual notion of "Love" in this aphoristic sentence (see n. 62 above). Rigolot notes Labé's allusion to Plato's notion of love in the *Symposium* (*Œuvres complètes*, 74 n. 1).

85.   Virginals or spinets (*espinettes*) were small varieties of single-keyboard harpsichords in use during the sixteenth century.

86.   Pavanes (*pavanes*) were slow, elegant early modern court dances of Spanish and Italian origin that gained popularity in France; passamezzos (*passemeses*) were faster Italian dances; and *gaillardes* (which I have translated as "lively waltzes") were very fast French dances set in three-quarter tempo.

87.   Aubades were musical pieces played or sung at dawn or during the morning, in contrast to serenades performed in the evening.

88.   Morris dances were old folk dances common especially in England during special celebrations such as May Day.

89.   As Bourbon notes, the referent in the final part of this sentence is grammatically obscure in the French text (*Debate of Folly and Love*, 137 n. 40); given the nature and context of the vignette being recounted, I translate this segment as applying to the wife.

90.   A Roman philosopher and satirist from the second century CE, Apuleius was the author of *The Golden Ass*, a romance widely read in early modern Europe recounting the experiences of a young man magically transformed into an ass.

91.   Musaeus and Linus were two mythological poets and musicians linked with Orpheus, the second of whom incurred Apollo's jealousy and was purportedly killed by him. Alcaeus and Sappho were seventh-century BCE Greek poets, male and female respectively, from the island of Lesbos. The original text of Sappho's most famous love poem had just been recovered and published in Venice in the mid-1550s, and this ancient woman writer famed for her passionate lyrics inspires the opening section of Labé's first elegy. The "Sage" refers to Socrates, so named and prized above all others for his wisdom.

92.   In addition to the *Metamorphoses*, Ovid (43 BCE–17 CE) was the author of the *Amores*, a volume of short love poems; the *Heroïdes*, a volume of verse letters written in the voices of women abandoned by their lovers; *Ars amatoria* (The Art of Love), a handbook on love; and *Remedia amoris* (The Remedies of Love), an advice book for the lovelorn.

93.   See n. 55 above.

94.   The women enumerated here were notorious for their deviant passions. As narrated in Labé's first elegy, Semiramis, the widowed queen and fierce leader of Babylon, abandoned her armies to indulge her incestuous passion for her own son. The unhappy loves of the nymph Byblis for her twin brother, Caunus, and of Myrrha for her father, King Cyniras, to whom she bore a child, Adonis, are recounted at length in books 9 and 10, respectively, of Ovid's *Metamorphoses*. Canace was ordered by her father to kill herself after giving birth to her brother Macareus's child. Finally, Phaedra, daughter of King Minos, whom Theseus married after killing the Minotaur, fell in love with her stepson, Hippolytus, and in a jealous rage ordered his death at the hands of Neptune before committing suicide herself.

95.   In the final two sentences of this paragraph I have changed the verb tenses in Labé's original text from the future perfect to the simple future, in order to make the passage more colloquial and less ponderous. The use of the conditional in these entreaties to Jupiter might sound more natural still, but it is clearly advantageous for Apollo to keep his discourse in the future in order convey his expectation that Jupiter will indeed take the course of action being recommended. Likewise, I have had to be

creative in my translation of "Folie amoureuse" (normally, "Folly in love") to give idiomatic sense to the expression.

96.   See n. 57 above.

97.   The last part of this sentence in the French text is very difficult to decipher, and has been glossed both by Rigolot (*Œuvres complètes*, 80 n. 1) and Bourbon (*Debate of Folly and Love*, 138 n. 54). I have taken the license to reformulate these enigmatic phrases in such a way that contextually they make sense.

98.   In one of his famous transformations, Jupiter disguised himself as Amphitryon, the husband of Alcmene, and impregnated her with the future Hercules. During this seduction Jupiter did not allow the sun to rise for three days in order to extend his "night" of love with Alcmene.

99.   By intimating his knowledge of the future, Apollo is referring to his role as god of prophecy. In this final pronouncement, the word "revolucions" in the French text, as defined in the sixteenth-century lexicon, suggests the passage of time, as calculated by the length of the orbits of planets and stars.

100.   One of Pallas Athena's notable features was her virginity, and thus her refusal to submit to Cupid's temptations. Likewise, her role as goddess of wisdom places her in antagonistic opposition to Folly.

101.   As Bourbon (*Debate of Folly and Love*, 138 n. 61) notes, Apollo's statue embodying truth was the site of trials held in the Roman Forum.

102.   I agree with Bourbon that this sentence is somewhat obscure in French and that the person who loves and champions the victim (Love) here is his mother Venus. However, the expression "avoir affaire à" (to be involved, entangled, or implicated in) does not to my knowledge include the specific sense of having sexual affairs, as is reflected in her translation and explanation (*Debate of Folly and Love*, 97 and 138 n. 63).

103.   The indirect references to Venus continue here, as Love's attack on Mars catalyzed his adulterous liaison with Vulcan's wife. See n. 53 above.

104.   This is the first of the four instances in discourse 5 where the slippage from third-person to first-person pronouns indicates Folly's own interruption of Mercury's argument. See p. 34 and n. 24 above.

105.   See n. 66 above.

106.   As in the case of the substantive "love" (*amour*), the noun "folly" (*folie*) begins to be used more frequently to evoke an abstract concept, in addition to the name of the female protagonist. Here again Labé is not completely consistent in her choice of uppercase or lowercase spelling. In my translation, therefore, beyond the unambiguous uppercase references to the protagonist, I will once again select the uppercase or lowercase spelling according to the context, capitalizing the word only when it refers simultaneously to the character and the concept (see n. 62 above).

107.   Alexander the Great (356 – 323 BCE), king of Macedon, was notorious not only for his military conquests but for his drunken excesses.

108.   A Greek philosopher from Zeno's third-century BCE school of stoicism and one of the founders of the Athenian Academy, Chrysippus was renowned for his voluminous writings.

109.   Euripus was the strait between the island of Euboea and Boetia in ancient Greece, well-known for its violent and unpredictable currents in both directions. As Bourbon (*Debate of Folly and Love*, 139 n. 71) notes, the great Aristotle is said to have drowned there, unable to overcome his grief at being unable to solve the puzzle of its currents. Euripus becomes a central image in Labé's sonnet 13, where it subverts the classic Petrarchan topos of the stormy seas as a metaphor of the lyric speaker's disorientation and serves rather as a purely external phenomenon against which the unified lovers protect themselves. (Lesko Baker, *Subject of Desire*, 141–42).

110.   Crates, a fourth-century BCE cynic philosopher and follower of Diogenes, got rid of his worldly possessions so that he could live and teach the ascetic life. One story recounts that Diogenes convinced him to throw his entire fortune into the sea.

111.   Empedocles was a fifth-century BCE Greek philosopher who attempted to show that he was a god by seeking a death in which he would leave no mortal trace and diving into the crater of Mount Etna. His misrepresentation of himself became apparent when one of his brass sandals was coughed back up by the volcano.

112.   Diogenes was the eminent cynic philosopher from the fourth century BCE who touted his austere lifestyle by living in a tub. Socrates' follower Aristippus believed he shared his mentor's greatness because he enjoyed the undivided attention of Denys the Tyrant.

113.   Both Farrell and Bourbon have chosen to translate this sentence in the form of a rhetorical question, following the model of the previous sentence. However, Labé's original text does not present this sentence as a question, and I have preferred to retain its declarative form, which entails a slightly different but, I believe, legitimate grammatical interpretation of the opening verbal structure.

114.   As Bourbon (*Debate of Folly and Love*, 139 n. 76) points out, the expression "to go plant one's cabbages" popularly carries the connotation of retiring to country life. I combine the literal and figural renderings in my translation.

115.   For the second time, the unexpected switch to the first-person pronoun signals Folly's brief appropriation of Mercury's voice (see n. 104 above). The translation of Folly's resolve to "dire mon fait" is not without ambiguity. Farrell and Bourbon have translated this phrase as referring to Folly's legal "case." However, I prefer to assume that "mon fait" refers to a person's character or way of being (as documented in the *Dictionnaire Robert*), especially since the following segment of Mercury's oration deals with Folly's role in the world rather than with her "legal" dispute with Cupid.

116.   Lucullus was a first-century BCE Roman consul and general who was renowned for his wealth and luxury, which he gained the reputation for displaying in magnificent feasts. Claudius was emperor of Rome from 41 to 54 CE. As Rigolot (*Œuvres complètes* 90 n. 3) notes, the inspiration for Labé's parenthetical reference may come from the fact that Claudius was born in her home city of Lyon.

117.   In respect to Labé's phrase "la dissolucion des habits," although in modern French the term *habits* refers exclusively to fashion or dress, in sixteenth-century French it may apply to customs or manners. In my translation I have taken the license to color this second connotation more strongly by proposing the word "morals," which I believe works well with the sense of "decline" communicated by the word

"dissolucion." I nevertheless see no lexical inaccuracy in Farrell's choice to translate the phrase as "excesses in customs" (74) (since *dissolucion* carries this sense as well), or in Bourbon's preference to translate it as "indecency of clothes" (113).

118.   Mercury here refers back to the opening section of Apollo's oration, which evoked the burying of the Titans under Mount Etna (Mount Gibil) as well as the chaining of Prometheus to Mount Caucasus. See nn. 64, 69 above.

119.   Folly's Olympian mother was Jeunesse, the goddess of youth. In my translation of the final clause of this sentence, I have adapted in English the paraphrase provided by Rigolot in modern French (*Œuvres complètes* 92 n. 1).

120.   In the first of these two allusions to the sudden onset of love, the Greek noblewoman Cydippe was said to have received an apple from her suitor of humble means, Acontius, on which he had cleverly inscribed a message in his beloved's own name, vowing on the goddess Artemis-Diana that she would marry and remain true to him. The second reference is to the renowned passage in Dante's *Inferno* recounting how Paolo and Francesca, a married woman, fell in love as they read the adulterous tale of Lancelot and Guinevere.

121.   Here Mercury begins a critique of the Neoplatonic theorist Marsilio Ficino's commentary on the visual origins of Petrarchan love, what is known as the Petrarchan *innamoramento*.

122.   The young man in question was from Cnidus, a city in ancient Asia Minor that housed a well-known statue of Venus-Aphrodite in the temple named in her honor.

123.   Bourbon and Farrell have both translated "et s'ils s'en trouvent mal" with the hypothetical "if," suggesting the uncertain nature of the lover's suffering. I prefer the emphatic sense of "si," since there seems little doubt that Mercury views concealed passion as heightening internal anguish and as a mark, as he states, of another brand of folly.

124.   Apelles was a Greek painter from the fourth century BCE famed in particular for his self-portrait and his portraits of Alexander the Great and others.

125.   As noted by Bourbon (*Debate of Folly and Love*, 141 n. 95) and Rigolot (*Oeuvres complètes*, 93 n. 3), the symbolism in the colors of the servants' uniforms demonstrates character traits popularized in the *Blason des couleurs*: red for long-suffering devotion, blue for determination, and green for hope.

126.   Both Bourbon and Farrell have introduced the suitor's lovesick gestures by the adverb "meanwhile." But Labé's term "ce pendant," in sixteenth-century usage, can have the sense of "during" or "in the midst of." It makes sense if the lady has slammed the door on the suitor and refused to see him privately that he would need to pledge his passion once he had succeeded in meeting her publicly, rather than while he is banished from her company.

127.   Bourbon (121) conveys in her translation the sense that another man will definitely supplant the suitor as the lady's talking companion, whereas Farrell (79) sees the "rival" as having as much chance as the suitor in engaging her in conversation. I believe that both translations can be justified grammatically (depending on differing adverbial interpretations of the expression "aussi tot . . . que"); however, I incline more to an adaptation of Farrell's, especially given that in the following

sentence the suitor, in my reading, is still said to consider himself "happy." (In that subsequent sentence, where there are ambiguous pronoun structures, Bourbon also attributes to the woman, rather than to the suitor himself, the opinion that he should still be happy (see *Debate of Folly and Love*, 141 n. 99), which fits well with her reading of the previous sentence).

128.   In one of the most famous myths recounted in Ovid's *Metamorphoses* (book 10), the magical musician Orpheus pleads for the return of his wife Eurydice after her premature death and moves the gods to secure her release from the underworld on the condition that as he leads her back he will not turn around and look at her until they have reached the upper world. But just before they arrive on earth, in his eagerness to see her Orpheus glances behind him, and Eurydice falls back into the depths and is lost to her husband forever.

129.   Greek legend tells that the gods had the great hero Hercules sold as a slave to Omphale, queen of Lydia, to make amends for his murder of one of Mercury's friends. Hercules fell passionately in love with the queen, submitting himself to her whims to the extent that he dressed as a woman and did her spinning while she wore his lion skin. The wise King Solomon of Israel (tenth century BCE) kept a large number of wives. Hannibal, the second-century BCE Carthaginian general famed for crossing the Alps to invade Italy in the Punic Wars, was said to have debauched himself in a sordid love affair.

130.   Folly's third interruption of Mercury's speech extends this time for three sentences, which feature multiple incursions of first-person subject and object pronouns (see nn. 104, 115 above).

131.   It is interesting that Mercury resumes his argument by reasserting his own "I," which he has used only in rare instances since the early part of his exposition. It suggests, perhaps, that he feels too much intervention on the part of his client will not work in their favor.

132.   Amphion and Zethus were twin sons born to Antiope, daughter of King Nycteus of Thebes, after Zeus disguised himself as a satyr and impregnated her in her sleep. After fleeing her father's wrath and marrying the king of Scyion, Antiope was captured and forced to return to Thebes by her uncle when he laid siege to her husband's city. Amphion and Zethus were born on her journey back to Thebes and were abandoned to be raised by shepherds. Zethus himself became a shepherd and came to hate his brother on account of Amphion's magical skill on the lyre. However, Amphion regained Zethus's regard when, through his music, he made the stones fall into place for the wall around Thebes, their mother's birthplace (see n. 83 above).

133.   Mercury indirectly refers to one of Jupiter's most famous erotic escapades (already evoked in the opening discourse by Folly herself): his seduction of Danaë in the disguise of a golden rain (see n. 52 above).

134.   Atalanta was a beautiful, swift-footed young maiden who had been abandoned at birth and raised in the woods by hunters under the protection of the goddess Artemis-Diana. Like her protectress, Atalanta excelled at hunting and spurned the advances of all those who fell in love with her. Since she could run faster than anyone else, she would challenge each of her suitors to a footrace, promising to marry whichever one could defeat her. Hippomenes finally accomplished that feat,

but only with the help of Venus, who gave him three golden apples to throw into Atalanta's path, thereby making her slow down enough to lose the race.

135.   The god of gardens refers to Priapus, the son of Venus and Bacchus, who was said to be endowed with a huge phallus in a constant state of erection, and who thereby became associated with procreative power. He enjoyed a great following among the Romans, who often placed his statue in gardens to promote the growth of flowers and fruits.

136.   A huge monster with three bodies and three heads, Geryon possessed a herd of red cattle coveted by King Eurysthius, who sent Hercules to slay the creature and seize the animals in what became the hero's tenth great labor.

137.   For the fourth and last time, Folly breaks into the argument and interrupts Mercury's defense in order to have her final, unapologetic say (see nn. 104, 115, and 130 above).

138.   In his closing argument, Mercury associates Folly with a group of pleasure-loving deities: Genius, god of nature; Youth, Folly's mother; Bacchus, god of wine and revelry; and Priapus, already evoked in his virile role as god of gardens (see n. 135 above).

139.   In Roman mythology, Saturn was assimilated to the Greek god Cronos, one of the Titans who challenged Jupiter's reign. Here Mercury recalls the adulatory recounting of Jupiter's retaliation by which Apollo began his speech.

140.   In a style similar to that of the opening Argument, the tense shifts rapidly from past to present in Labé's "stage direction." I have once again chosen to maintain this transition, since the switch to the present in the final sentence lends a certain immediacy to Jupiter's decree.

141.   Clearly the idea being presented here is that the final verdict will not be handed down for centuries to come, implying that the relationship between Love and Folly is an eternal issue. It seems appropriate to retain the curious numerical wording, however, according to the letter of the text.

142.   Rigolot (*Œuvres complètes*, 15 and 103 n. 2) has drawn prominent attention to the ambiguous nature of the French pronoun "lui" (him or her) in this sentence, for it leaves open the possibility that although Folly is leading the way, either protagonist could be giving directions. From the point of view of critical analysis, this grammatical slippage provides a rich focal point of Labé's clever assertion of the notion of interdependency she espouses so vehemently (see Lesko Baker, *Subject of Desire*, 80–81). Farrell's translation accentuates the ambiguity by avoiding attribution of the pronoun, in an impersonal phrase where she has Folly guiding Love "wherever it seems best" (*Louise Labé's Complete Works*, 87). Bourbon (*Debate of Folly and Love*, 133 and 142–43 n. 123), on the other hand, chooses to attribute the prerogative of selecting the path to Love, arguing that this is more consistent with Jupiter's deferential temporary verdict. Since for the purposes of translation (versus analysis), it seems to me undesirable to elide the reference of a pronoun that is clearly center stage in the sentence, I have adopted Bourbon's stance. Not only is her conceptual argument convincing but there is a grammatical argument to be made that normally a pronoun should refer to the immediate antecedent, which in this case is indeed Love.

CHAPTER TWO

Note— all notes below are by Deborah Lesko Baker.

1.   For helpful overviews concerning the thematic structuring of the elegies and sonnets and/or the various strands of dialogue between them, see especially Keith Cameron, *Louise Labé*, 42–25 and 61–85; and François Lecercle, "L'erreur d'Ulysse: Quelques hypothèses sur l'organisation du *Canzoniere* de Louise Labé," in Demerson, *Louise Labé*, 207–21, reprinted in Alonso and Viennot, *Louise Labé 2005*, 169–80. For a much more extensive discussion of these structural and intertextual issues, see Daniel Martin, *Signe(s) d'Amante*, 157–67, 185–96, and 197–375.

2.   In order to sustain and prioritize the rhyme scheme of the original, Finch occasionally makes small modifications to Labé's decasyllabic lines by adding or suppressing a syllable.

3.   In her book *Fictions of Sappho: 1546–1937* (Chicago: University of Chicago Press, 1989), Joan DeJean underlines Labé's central role in the French literary appropriation of Sappho as a figure representing the claim to female writing: "She is the first of a number of French women writers, notably Scudéry and Stael, elaborately to stage her accession to authorship through an identification with the original woman writer, as the process by which she becomes a Sappho in her own right" (38–39). For an overview of the rebirth of Sappho in the literary circles of early modern Europe, see Lazard, *Louise Labé* (111–16); for more extended discussion, see Rigolot, *Louise Labé Lyonnaise*, 31–67, and "Louise Labé et la redécouverte de Sappho," *Nouvelle Revue du seizième siècle* 1 (1983): 19–31.

4.   The present edition reproduces the definitive text of François Rigolot in his 2004 edition of the *Complete Works*.

5.   Mary B. Moore elaborates on this connection in her recent study, *Desiring Voices: Women Sonneteers and Petrarchism* (Carbondale: Southern Illinois University Press, 2000), observing that Labé extends her Sapphic filiation well beyond the dynamics of unrequited heterosexual desire, via a "move [that] fuses intellectual and erotic aspects of female subjectivity, simultaneously displaying learning and wit and a spectacular role as desirable woman" (94).

6.   For an excellent discussion of the cultural privileging of male grief and the typical devaluation of female grief, see Schiesari, *Gendering of Melancholia*, 160–66. For a fuller elaboration of this phenomenon in the context of Labé's first elegy, see Lesko Baker, *Subject of Desire*, 98–101.

7.   For a discussion of the intertextual debt to Ovid's *Heroides* in the second elegy, see Martin, *Signe(s) d'Amante*, 176–78, and Rigolot, *Louise Labé Lyonnaise*, 83–85.

8.   Cathy Yandell (*Carpe Corpus*, 123–25) shrewdly analyzes the subversion of Petrarchan "error" in the elegies, as well as in the final sonnet, through Labé's accumulated use of the ambiguous conjunction "si" (if), which highlights how the speaker questions her transgression, rather than admitting it.

9.   For a discussion of the speaker's multiple but problematic challenges to female gender stereotypes in this section of elegy 3, see Moore, *Desiring Voices*, 106–7.

10.   Although not addressed directly to the beloved in epistolary form, the bitter reminiscences of abandonment in these allusions once again recall the powerful intertext of Ovid's *Heroides* (see n. 7 above).

11.   This purposeful lack of linearity is perhaps most strikingly demonstrated by Labé's return in the final sonnet to the imperative to forestall blame on the part of her female co-citizens by yet another warning addressing their equal susceptibility to the snares of unhappy passion. Thus, the quest for legitimation and the anxiety of potential judgment against the backdrop of cultural and literary norms remain part of the poet's psychic struggle. Nonetheless, as Martin (*Signe[s] d'Amante*, 374–76) points out, if Labé frames the end of her sequence with an intertextual play on the obsessive theme of error in Petrarch's inaugural sonnet, her stance is nevertheless different: ostensibly humble, yet unashamed and unapologetic with respect to her own loves; didactic and admonitory, although sympathetic, toward those who have not yet traveled the path of her amatory experience.

12.   For key discussions devoted to Petrarch's opening poem and/or the new lyric speaking voice and subjectivity it inaugurated throughout early modern Europe, see especially DellaNeva, *Song and Counter-song*, 86–88; Freccero, "Fig Tree and the Laurel"; Mazzota, "*Canzoniere* and the Language of the Self"; and Sturm-Maddox, *Petrarch's Metamorphoses* (4–5). For a more extended analysis of the dialogue between the opening sonnets of Labé and Petrarch, see Lesko Baker, *Subject of Desire*, 125–36.

13.   The brief excerpts from the *Canzoniere*, along with their English translations, are from Robert Durling's bilingual edition, *Petrarch's Lyric Poems*.

14.   For additional commentary on the key role of the figure of Ulysses in Labé's opening sonnet, see Kennedy, *Authorizing Petrarch*, 165–66; Lecercle, "L'erreur d'Ulysse, 216–20; and Rigolot, *Louise Labé Lyonnaise*, 80–86. For an excellent analysis of the sonnet as a whole, with an emphasis on the epistemological issues suggested by the Ulysses figure and the complex implication of the scorpion's wound, see Moore, *Desiring Voices*, 107–11.

15.   For a discussion of the relationship of Labé's sonnet addressing Venus to Petrarch's sonnet 216, see Kennedy, *Authorizing Petrarch*, 171–73.

16.   In his sensitive analysis of this sonnet, Tom Conley evokes how the poetess's voice "labors to speak ambiguously and with affective complexity that the figure of Venus cannot represent." He goes on to posit that "the goddess is invoked only in order to be castigated through the counter image of a female who strives toward an intersubjective union that does not deny her a space of autonomy." Foreword to Lesko Baker, *Subject of Desire*, xi–xiii.

17.   "Ne me laissez par long temps pámee" (l. 5); "Las, ne mets point ton corps en ce hazart" (l. 7); "Rens lui sa part et moitié estimee" (l. 8); "Mais fais, Ami, que ne soit dangereuse / Cette rencontre . . ." (ll. 9–10); "L'accompagnant, non de severité" (l. 11). For an etymological analysis of the adjective "dangerous" ("dangereuse") used at the end of line 9 by both Labé and Finch and its relationship to the power dynamics between the speaker and her lover, see Kennedy, *Authorizing Petrarch*, 175.

18.   Recent in-depth discussions of this anthology favorite, as well as its Latin and neo-Latin backgrounds, have been undertaken by Jones, *Currency of Eros*, 171–72;

Peggy Kamuf, "A Double Life (Femmeninism II)," in *Men in Feminism*, ed. Alice Jardine and Paul Smith (New York: Methuen, 1987), 93–97; Kennedy, *Authorizing Petrarch*, 190–93; Lesko Baker, *Subject of Desire*, 153–61, and "Re-reading the 'folie': Louise Labé's Sonnet XVIII and the Renaissance Love Heritage," *Renaissance and Reformation / Renaissance et Réforme* 17.1 (1993), 5–14; Moore, *Desiring Voices*, 119–23; and Rigolot, *Louise Labé Lyonnaise*, 216–25, and "Signature et signification: Les Baisers de Louise Labé," *Romanic Review* 75.1 (1984), 10–24.

19.   Labé's lyric works open with an immediate invocation of the god of Love (Cupid), who remains a dramatic personified force throughout her poetry, particularly in the narratives of elegies 1 and 3.

20.   Phoebus, another name for Apollo, god of the sun, poetry, music, and prophecy. As recounted in book 1 of Ovid's *Metamorphoses*, he was in love with the nymph Daphne, who, in order to stave off his unwanted advances, entreated her father to transform her into a laurel tree. The heartbroken Apollo nevertheless cut off one of the laurel branches and used it ever thereafter to adorn his lyre.

21.   Zeus, the Greek name for the celestial king Jupiter, wielder of the thunderbolt.

22.   Mars, the brutal god of war. Jupiter's only legitimate son by his wife, Juno, Mars was notorious for his adulterous love affair with Venus. See chapter 1, n. 53.

23.   Lesbos, the ancient name of Mytilene, an island in the Aegean Sea sacred to the poet Sappho, Labé's female model of lyric inspiration. See nn. 3 and 5 above.

24.   Semiramis, the warlike Babylonian queen, following her husband's death deserted her nation's troops after surrendering to an incestuous love for her own son, Ninus. Already mentioned by Apollo in discourse 5 of the *Debate* (see ch. 1 n. 94) as an example of disordered passion, Semiramis returns in Labé's elegy as an example of the extremes to which victimization by Love may lead. See the introduction above.

25.   The Po River, located in northern Italy and flowing into the Adriatic Sea. This river was known for its serpentine meanderings and was therefore sometimes represented as a god with horns, which explains Labé's French expression "Pau cornu" (literally, "horned Po").

26.   Phoebe, one of the Greek names for Diana, goddess of the moon. That her "silver horns" (Diana was associated with silver moonlight, in contrast to the golden sunlight prized by her brother Apollo) have closed twice indicates that the full moon has come and gone two times since the lover's expected return.

27.   The Pyrenees are the mountain range between France and Spain. The name "Calpe" poses more of a problem. According to Rigolot, it refers to Gibraltar (*Oeuvres complètes*, 112), and Edith Farrell follows the same direction by translating it as the "Pillars named for Hercules" (*Louise Labé's Complete Works*, 92)— that is, the two points of land on either side of the Strait of Gibraltar. However, it may refer rather to the town of Calpe on the Spanish Mediterranean coast, which is dominated by an impressively high rock at the edge of the sea.

28.   As explained by Rigolot (*Oeuvres complètes*, 113), "devices" ("devises") were ornamental colors worn by knights in honor of their cherished ladies.

29.   Although the problem is elided in Finch's English translation, the original French lines 91–92 ("Ne vivant pas, mais mourant d'*une* Amour / *Lequel* m'occit dix mile fois le jour, emphasis added") present another grammatical slippage pertaining to gender, as we have seen in the provisional verdict issued at the end of the *Debate*. Rigolot addresses this instance in the same articles mentioned in chapter 1, nn. 27 and 142.

30.   The referent here is Arachne, in Greek mythology a young woman who excelled at weaving and who challenged the goddess Pallas Athena, celebrated for her own stitching skills, to a tapestry-weaving contest. Arachne's artistry was so extraordinary that the goddess destroyed the work and transformed her into a spider, destined forever to spin her web. The story is recounted in depth at the beginning of book 6 of Ovid's *Metamorphoses*.

31.   See chapter 1, n. 44.

32.   Bradamant and Marfisa, were two female warriors in Ariosto's epic *Orlando Furioso*, a recasting of a legend from the ancient Carolingian dynasty. As noted by Edith Farrell (*Complete Works of Louise Labé*, 136), Bradamant, known as the Virgin Knight and wielder of a magic spear that caused the downfall of any knight it touched, fell in love with Marfisa's brother, the Moor Ruggiero, and following his conversion became his wife.

33.   See n. 22 above.

34.   Paris, one of the sons of Priam, king of Troy, was married to the nymph Oenone, but abandoned her for Helen, the wife of the Greek king Menelaus. Helen's kidnaping by Paris was the celebrated catalyst of the Trojan War.

35.   Medea was the sorceress who enabled Jason and his Argonauts to obtain the Golden Fleece. When he later reneged on his promise to marry her and instead wed Creusa, daughter of King Creon of Thebes, the enraged Medea murdered her rival, as well as the two sons she had borne Jason.

36.   As she concludes her final elegy, Labé returns to the image of love as equal, shared burden, thereby recalling Cupid's advice to Jupiter in discourse 4: "love thrives best when things are equal. It's no more than a yoke that needs to be carried by two well-paired oxen; otherwise the harness will not stay on straight."

37.   Ulysses, one of the greatest of Greek heros, known especially for the intelligence, cunning, and trickery he displayed during the Trojan War. After the war, he embarked on his famous ten-year odyssey, filled with multiple adventures and fraught with numerous dangers, finally arriving home in Ithaca where he was reunited with his faithful wife, Penelope.

38.   Just as in elegy 1, personified Love appears almost immediately in Labé's opening sonnet and remains the speaker's formidable opponent but indispensable companion throughout the sonnet cycle, invoked explicitly in sonnets 3, 4, 8, 11, 18, 21, 23, and 24.

39.   Labé highlights the image of the scorpion, with its toxic stinging tail, to metaphorize her own *innamoramento* in the traditional mode of violent attack (see Paolo Budini, "Le sonnet italien de Louise Labé," in Alonso and Viennot, *Louise Labé 2005*, 152; reprinted from *Francophonia* 20 [1991], 48; and Berriot, *La Belle Rebelle*, 82–83). Images

of real or mythological poisonous creatures are common in Petrarchan poetry to dramatize the beginnings of love, as is attributing to them the paradoxical ability both to wound and cure their victim.

40.   For a discussion of this inaugural poem in dialogue with the opening of Petrarch's *Canzoniere*, see the introduction above, esp. n. 12.

41.   As mentioned in the introduction to chapter 1, Venus's need to validate herself exclusively through Cupid's visual appreciation of her own beauty inaugurates a critique of Petrarchan adaptations of the *blason*, verse involving the male praise of specific female body parts. This sonnet—and particularly this line cataloguing the beguiling physical attributes of the male lover—provides an example of Labé's "table-turning" satirization of this convention that Ann Rosalind Jones has highlighted (see ch. 1, n. 21). Sonnet 2's play with the rich *blason* tradition is also discussed by Kennedy, *Authorizing Petrarch*, 166–69, and Moore, *Desiring Voices*, 111–14.

42.   The power of music—and of verse—not only to reveal but to provoke passion is central in Labé's poetry, beginning with her invocation of the Apollonian and Sapphic lyre in elegy 1. The lute is a classic instrument representing this power, and recalls, of course, the author's revelation in the dedicatory letter that she had been substantially trained in music. Across the sonnets both the female speaker and the male lover take turns as its players (the lover here and in sonnet 10, the female speaker in sonnets 12 and 14), and this alternation provides a motor that enhances her capacity to both feel and voice love. For discussion of the importance of the lute as a representation of the link between music and poetry, and its role in Labé's work, see Yandell, *Carpe Corpus*, 117–19.

43.   See n. 38 above.

44.   For a commentary on sonnet 3 in the context of Finch's translation, see the introduction above.

45.   See n. 38 above.

46.   Sonnet 5 marks the first direct appearance of Venus in Labé's works since discourses 2 and 3 of the *Debate*, where she represented the voice of female censure and opposition to Folly, and the embodied glorification of the male gaze (see the introduction to chapter 1, pp. 30–31). Here the speaker seeks instead an empathetic bonding with her celestial counterpart in passion. For a commentary on the ambivalence of that bonding in the context of Finch's translation, see introduction above, p. 145 including n. 16; for the backgrounds grounding the divided depictions of Venus in the mid-sixteenth century, see Rigolot, *Louise Labé Lyonnaise*, 167–70.

47.   The "clear Star" evokes the sun (Apollo), which in its cyclic daily dawnings also figures the hoped-for return of the male beloved.

48.   The syntax and referents here are somewhat ambiguous. Rigolot identifies the "she" (lines 4, 5, and 9) as the moon (Luna, sister of Apollo), figuring the female lover who would attract the gaze of her solar partner (*Œuvres complètes*, 124 n. 2). Another plausible variation on this popular lyric coupling would be to identify the "she" with Aurora herself, goddess of the dawn (and a sister of both Apollo and Luna), who is specifically named in line 7 and is kissed by the daytime blooming of Flora's (the divinity of spring and flowers) most fragrant gift—most likely, as Rigolot notes, the rose.

49.   For a discussion of how Finch's translation of sonnet 7 brings a vibrant intensity to the frequent Neoplatonic theme involving the transmigration of lovers' souls, see the introduction above, pp. 146–147.

50.   Composed of endless antitheses in varied grammatical formulations, sonnet 8 is Labé's version of Petrarch's famous sonnet 134 "Pace non trovo et non ò da far guerra" (Peace I do not find, and I have no wish to make war). Although Petrarch's poem is far from one of his most subtle, moving, or ingenious, it became the hallmark of the tortured and conflicted male lyric speaker and was widely imitated across the stage of European Petrarchism. As is the case with Labé here, such imitations of *Canzoniere* 134 are not typically strong sites of revision or subversion, but rather artful rhetorical gestures to the tradition.

51.   This oneiric flight of the speaker's soul toward the male beloved is described in line 3 of the French as a flight "hors de moy" (literally, "outside myself"). This expression, repeated by Labé in sonnet 17 and most famously in sonnet 18, has physical, spiritual, and psychological dimensions, but in all cases subverts the sense of the phrase in male Petrarchan poetry, where it reflects the divided and alienated self of the anguished lover (see Lesko Baker, *Subject of Desire,* 160).

52.   See n. 42 above.

53.   Here the speaker implicitly compares the speaker to the great musician Orpheus in his ability to move even inanimate objects (see ch. 1, n. 71).

54.   See n. 38 above.

55.   See n. 42 above. In taking up the lute herself for the first time here in the sonnet sequence, she dramatically positions it as the first word of the poem, personifying and addressing it directly as her constant emotional partner. As Yandell puts it, "the lute serves here as the embodiment of the poet's contradictory sentiments and the pretext for a dialogic exchange" and holds the status of "companion, witness and implied interlocutor" (*Carpe Corpus,* 119).

56.   In the intimate communion the speaker has evoked, the lute has become an "*irreproachable* witness" ("témoin irreprochable"), thus implicitly more reliable than the revered but "errant" Venus to whom she appeals as her witness in sonnet 5 (see n. 46 above).

57.   This provocative scene of union and reciprocal passion imagined by the speaker constitutes one of Labé's most compelling and well-known sonnets, and also one where the Petrarchan paradigms of separation and inaccessibility are most pointedly challenged. For a discussion of this challenge through the poetess's rereading of Ovidian narratives, see Jones, *Currency of Eros,* 165–67; for the full range of the poem's erotic resonances, see Kennedy, *Authorizing Petrarch,* 191–92; for the multiple subversions of Petrarchan images and rhetorical structures, see Lesko Baker, *Subject of Desire,* 137–45, and "Louise Labé's Conditional Imperatives: Subversion and Transcendence of the Petrarchan Tradition" in Alonso and Viennot, *Louise Labé 2005,* 133–50, reprinted from *Sixteenth Century Journal* 21, no. 4 (1990): 523–41.

58.   Euripus, the violent strait between the ancient Greek islands of Euboea and Boetia, was alluded to in discourse 5 of the *Debate* as the dramatic site of Aristotle's drowning (see ch. 1, n. 109). As already mentioned in that note, Euripus ("Euripe")

recurs in line 7 of the French sonnet (translated by Finch as "flood"), where, along with the image of the "tempeste" ("stormy sky"), it strikingly overturns the Petrarchan use of the sea storm as a representation of the lyric speaker's disordered state— thus remaining a fierce manifestation of nature that further unites the lovers in an embrace of mutual protection.

59.   The escape of the speaker's spirit (i.e., her life breath, from the Latin *spiritus*) caused by the ecstasy of her lover's kisses figures an erotic love-death based on the conventional motif of the *mors osculi* (death from the kiss). For background on this motif and its use in both sonnets 13 and 18, see Rigolot, *Louise Labé Lyonnaise*, 220–21, 233–34.

60.   See n. 47 above for a similar solar configuring of the male beloved.

61.   Zephyr, the god of the west wind, known for its soft, gentle breezes, and therefore pointing, both literally and metaphorically, to favorable and auspicious conditions. As seen later in the poem, the speaker will playfully try to coax Zephyr to stay in her presence and to ease the return of her fair weather "sun."

62.   The welcome return of fair weather after the storm at the beginning of sonnet 16 belies the speaker's frustration to come, powerfully captured by Finch's title.

63.   Mount Caucasus, where Prometheus was chained by the gods for having stolen their fire. See ch. 1, n. 69.

64.   Phoebus, another name for the sun god, Apollo, is first used by Labé in her inaugural elegy (see n. 47 above).

65.   The Parthian soldiers, from the ancient kingdom of Parthia southeast of the Caspian Sea, were known for firing parting shots with their arrows as they retreated or pretended to retreat from the enemy.

66.   Labé takes as her intertext here Petrarch's famous sonnet 35, "Solo e pensoso i più deserti campi / vo mesurando a passi tardi et lenti"("Alone and filled with care, I go measuring the most deserted fields"). For an in-depth analysis of Labé's rewriting of this sonnet, see Kennedy, *Authorizing Petrarch*, 184–89, and also Moore, *Desiring Voices*, 116–19.

67.   See n. 51 above. Labé's recasting of the "hors de moymesme" ("outside myself") phenomenon in this second instance is suggested in the discussions of both Kennedy, *Authorizing Petrarch*, 188, and Moore, *Desiring Voices*, 118.

68.   Sonnet 18 is Labé's most famous and widely published single text, and also one in which the subversion of conventional Petrarchan and Neoplatonic motifs and diction is most acute— as well as more subtle than meets the eye. The poem is discussed in the context of the translation in the introduction to this chapter (p. 148–149, and important recent critical studies of the poem are also listed there in n. 18.

69.   See n. 38 above. This line is both richly intriguing and pivotal, particularly in terms of how to read the key terms "Amour" ("Love") and "quelque folie" (literally, "some kind of folly" and translated provocatively, as the introduction above explains, as "something honest"). Finch has conveyed "Love" as "my love," referring directly to her lover; for other interpretive possibilities of this apostrophe and/or of the "folly" that Labé proposes in the final tercet of the sonnet, see especially Jones,

Currency of Eros, 72; Kamuf, "Double Life," 93–94; Kennedy, *Authorizing Petrarch*, 192–93; Lesko Baker, *Subject of Desire*, 158–61, and "Re-reading the 'folie,'" 9–12; Moore (122–23); and Rigolot, *Louise Labé Lyonnaise*, 222–25, and "Signature et signification," 18–21.

70.   See nn. 51 and 67 above. This is Labé's final reiteration of the expression "hors de moy" ("outside myself") in her sonnets.

71.   Diana, sister of Apollo, Roman goddess of hunting, virginity, and the moon (hence, among her other names is Luna; see n. 48 above). As the virgin huntress, she is known to wreak vengeance with her arrows whenever she is offended. In this sonnet the goddess, having just slain her latest prey, stands in stark contrast to the unsuspecting female speaker, who has unsuccessfully attacked her own victim and remains weaponless and wounded after his counterattack.

72.   The Petrarchan images of "orage" (storm) and "naufrage" (literally "shipwreck," translated by Finch with apt dramatic effect as "disaster") here do not serve as backdrops to protective union of the lovers against the tempest as they did earlier (see n. 58 above). They prefigure instead a catastrophic aftermath to a mutual love that destiny seemed to fulfill.

73.   In contrast to the (purposefully) melodramatic enumerations of sonnet 2, this poem—with its opening list of mock-serious questions—is a more playful example of Labé's gently satirical gesture to the Renaissance *blason* tradition. See n. 41 above, and chapter 1, n. 21.

74.   See n. 38 above.

75.   Sonnet 22 begins with another reference to the loving reciprocity between Apollo (the sun) and his sister Diana (Luna, the moon). See n. 48 above.

76.   After Luna fell in love with the beautiful young shepherd Endymion, Jupiter put him into a deep, everlasting sleep so that the goddess could gaze upon and caress him forever.

77.   Another allusion to Mars's adulterous passion for Venus (see n. 4 above, and ch. 1, n. 53). Having served as Folly's defender in his role as god of eloquence (see ch. 1, n. 40), Mercury appears here in his role as messenger of the gods in the heavens and on earth.

78.   See n. 38 above.

79.   As observed in n. 19 above, in her twenty-fourth sonnet, the concluding text in her volume, the poetess puts forth one final time the emotional address to her sister citizens undertaken in her first and third elegies—an address complexly invested with pleas for compassion rather than blame, with touches of anxiety yet void of contrition, and above all with an urgent quest from the voice of experience to unite her peers by convincing them to understand their common and inevitable vulnerability to love. On this combination of impulses, see Jones, *Currency of Eros*, 176–77; Lesko Baker, *Subject of Desire*, 219–20; and Rigolot, *Louise Labé Lyonnaise*, 194–95.

80.   As in elegy 3, Labé employs the conditional "si" (if), refusing any definitive admission of error.

81.   Implicitly comparing her female audience to Venus, married to the repulsive-looking Vulcan (see ch. 1, n. 53), the speaker warns that unattractive physical appearance in a partner is no excuse for amorous wandering.

82.   Angered by the refusal of the princess Myrrha to marry, Venus forced her to fall in love and copulate with her own father. The fruit of this incestuous union was a son, Adonis, whose beauty was so remarkable that Venus fell in love with him and persuaded Jupiter to let her live with the boy for a portion of each year—an infidelity vis-à-vis not only her husband, Vulcan, but her own lover, Mars. Labé's admonition here is that since it is unlikely her peers will come across a partner as stunning as Adonis, they will likewise not be able to blame their passion on their lover's irresistible physical charms.

SERIES EDITORS'
BIBLIOGRAPHY

PRIMARY SOURCES

Alberti, Leon Battista. *The Family in Renaissance Florence.* Trans. Renée Neu Watkins. Columbia, SC: University of South Carolina Press, 1969.

Arenal, Electa and Stacey Schlau, eds. *Untold Sisters: Hispanic Nuns in Their Own Works.* Trans. Amanda Powell. Albuquerque, NM: University of New Mexico Press, 1989.

Astell, Mary (1666–1731). *The First English Feminist: Reflections on Marriage and Other Writings.* Ed. and Introd. Bridget Hill. New York: St. Martin's Press, 1986.

Atherton, Margaret, ed. *Women Philosophers of the Early Modern Period.* Indianapolis, IN: Hackett Publishing Co., 1994.

Aughterson, Kate, ed. *Renaissance Woman: Constructions of Femininity in England: A Source Book.* London & New York: Routledge, 1995.

Barbaro, Francesco (1390–1454). *On Wifely Duties.* Trans. Benjamin Kohl in Kohl and R. G. Witt, eds., *The Earthly Republic.* Philadelphia: University of Pennsylvania Press, 1978, 179–228. Translation of the Preface and Book 2.

Behn, Aphra. *The Works of Aphra Behn.* 7 vols. Ed. Janet Todd. Columbus, OH: Ohio State University Press, 1992–96.

Boccaccio, Giovanni (1313–75). *Famous Women.* Ed. and trans. Virginia Brown. The I Tatti Renaissance Library. Cambridge, MA: Harvard University Press, 2001.

———. *Corbaccio or the Labyrinth of Love.* Trans. Anthony K. Cassell. Second revised edition. Binghamton, NY: Medieval and Renaissance Texts and Studies, 1993.

Booy, David, ed. *Autobiographical Writings by Early Quaker Women.* Aldershot and Brookfield: Ashgate Publishing Co., 2004.

Brown, Sylvia. *Women's Writing in Stuart England: The Mother's Legacies of Dorothy Leigh, Elizabeth Joscelin and Elizabeth Richardson.* Thrupp, Stroud, Gloceter: Sutton, 1999.

Bruni, Leonardo (1370–1444). "On the Study of Literature (1405) to Lady Battista Malatesta of Moltefeltro." In *The Humanism of Leonardo Bruni: Selected Texts.* Trans. and Introd. Gordon Griffiths, James Hankins, and David Thompson. Binghamton, NY: Medieval and Renaissance Studies and Texts, 1987, 240–51.

Castiglione, Baldassare (1478–1529). *The Book of the Courtier.* Trans. George Bull. New York: Penguin, 1967; *The Book of the Courtier.* Ed. Daniel Javitch. New York: W. W. Norton & Co., 2002.

Christine de Pizan (1365–1431). *The Book of the City of Ladies.* Trans. Earl Jeffrey Richards. Foreword Marina Warner. New York: Persea Books, 1982.

————. *The Treasure of the City of Ladies.* Trans. Sarah Lawson. New York: Viking Penguin, 1985. Also trans. and introd. Charity Cannon Willard. Ed. and introd. Madeleine P. Cosman. New York: Persea Books, 1989.

Clarke, Danielle, ed. *Isabella Whitney, Mary Sidney and Aemilia Lanyer: Renaissance Women Poets.* New York: Penguin Books, 2000.

Crawford, Patricia and Laura Gowing, eds. *Women's Worlds in Seventeenth-Century England: A Source Book.* London & New York: Routledge, 2000.

"Custome Is an Idiot": Jcobean Pamphlet Literature on Women. Ed. Susan Gushee O'Malley. Afterword Ann Rosalind Jones. Chicago and Urbana: University of Illinois Press, 2004.

Daybell, James, ed. *Early Modern Women's Letter Writing, 1450–1700.* Houndmills, England & New York: Palgrave, 2001.

Elizabeth I: Collected Works. Ed. Leah S. Marcus, Janel Mueller, and Mary Beth Rose. Chicago: University of Chicago Press, 2000.

Elyot, Thomas (1490–1546). *Defence of Good Women: The Feminist Controversy of the Renaissance.* Facsimile Reproductions. Ed. Diane Bornstein. New York: Delmar, 1980.

Erasmus, Desiderius (1467–1536). *Erasmus on Women.* Ed. Erika Rummel. Toronto: University of Toronto Press, 1996.

Female and Male Voices in Early Modern England: An Anthology of Renaissance Writing. Ed. Betty S. Travitsky and Anne Lake Prescott. New York: Columbia University Press, 2000.

Ferguson, Moira, ed. *First Feminists: British Women Writers 1578–1799.* Bloomington, IN: Indiana University Press, 1985.

Galilei, Maria Celeste. *Sister Maria Celeste's Letters to her father, Galileo.* Ed. and trans. Rinaldina Russell. Lincoln, NE & New York: Writers Club Press of Universe.com, 2000; *To Father: The Letters of Sister Maria Celeste to Galileo, 1623–1633.* Trans. Dava Sobel. London: Fourth Estate, 2001.

Gethner, Perry, ed. *The Lunatic Lover and Other Plays by French Women of the 17th and 18th Centuries.* Portsmouth, NH: Heinemann, 1994.

Glückel of Hameln (1646–1724). *The Memoirs of Glückel of Hameln.* Trans. Marvin Lowenthal. New Introd. Robert Rosen. New York: Schocken Books, 1977.

Harline, Craig, ed. *The Burdens of Sister Margaret: Inside a Seventeenth-Century Convent.* New Haven: Yale University Press, abr. ed., 2000.

Henderson, Katherine Usher and Barbara F. McManus, eds. *Half Humankind: Contexts and Texts of the Controversy about Women in England, 1540–1640.* Urbana, IL: Indiana University Press, 1985.

Hoby, Margaret. *The Private Life of an Elizabethan Lady: The Diary of Lady Margaret Hoby 1599–1605.* Phoenix Mill, Great Britain: Sutton Publishing, 1998.

Humanist Educational Treatises. Ed. and trans. Craig W. Kallendorf. The I Tatti Renaissance Library. Cambridge, MA: Harvard University Press, 2002.

Hunter, Lynette, ed. *The Letters of Dorothy Moore, 1612–64.* Aldershot and Brookfield: Ashgate Publishing Co., 2004.

Joscelin, Elizabeth. *The Mothers Legacy to her Unborn Childe.* Ed. Jean leDrew Metcalfe. Toronto: University of Toronto Press, 2000.

Kaminsky, Amy Katz, ed. *Water Lilies, Flores del agua: An Anthology of Spanish Women Writers from the Fifteenth Through the Nineteenth Century.* Minneapolis, MN: University of Minnesota Press, 1996.

Kempe, Margery (1373–1439). *The Book of Margery Kempe.* Trans. and ed. Lynn Staley. A Norton Critical Edition. New York: W.W. Norton, 2001.

King, Margaret L., and Albert Rabil, Jr., eds. *Her Immaculate Hand: Selected Works by and about the Women Humanists of Quattrocento Italy.* Binghamton, NY: Medieval and Renaissance Texts and Studies, 1983; second revised paperback edition, 1991.

Klein, Joan Larsen, ed. *Daughters, Wives, and Widows: Writings by Men about Women and Marriage in England, 1500–1640.* Urbana, IL: University of Illinois Press, 1992.

Knox, John (1505–72). *The Political Writings of John Knox: The First Blast of the Trumpet against the Monstrous Regiment of Women and Other Selected Works.* Ed. Marvin A. Breslow. Washington: Folger Shakespeare Library, 1985.

Kors, Alan C., and Edward Peters, eds. *Witchcraft in Europe, 400–1700: A Documentary History.* Philadelphia: University of Pennsylvania Press, 2000.

Krämer, Heinrich, and Jacob Sprenger. *Malleus Maleficarum* (ca. 1487). Trans. Montague Summers. London: Pushkin Press, 1928; reprinted New York: Dover, 1971.

Larsen, Anne R. and Colette H. Winn, eds. *Writings by Pre-Revolutionary French Women: From Marie de France to Elizabeth Vigée-Le Brun.* New York & London: Garland Publishing Co., 2000.

de Lorris, William, and Jean de Meun. *The Romance of the Rose.* Trans. Charles Dahlbert. Princeton: Princeton University Press, 1971; reprinted University Press of New England, 1983.

Marguerite d'Angoulême, Queen of Navarre (1492–1549). *The Heptameron.* Trans. P. A. Chilton. New York: Viking Penguin, 1984.

Mary of Agreda. *The Divine Life of the Most Holy Virgin.* Abridgment of *The Mystical City of God.* Abr. by Fr. Bonaventure Amedeo de Caesarea, M.C. Trans. from French by Abbé Joseph A. Boullan. Rockford, IL: Tan Books, 1997.

Mullan, David George. *Women's Life Writing in Early Modern Scotland: Writing the Evangelical Self, c. 1670–c. 1730.* Aldershot and Brookfield: Ashgate Publishing Co., 2003.

Myers, Kathleen A. and Amanda Powell, eds. *A Wild Country Out in the Garden: The Spiritual Journals of a Colonial Mexican Nun.* Bloomington: Indiana University Press, 1999.

Russell, Rinaldina, ed. *Sister Maria Celeste's Letters to Her Father, Galileo.* San Jose & New York: Writers Club Press, 2000.

Teresa of Avila, Saint (1515–82). *The Life of Saint Teresa of Avila by Herself.* Trans. J. M. Cohen. New York: Viking Penguin, 1957.

Travitsky, Betty, ed. *The Paradise of Women: Writings by Entlishwomen of the Renaissance.* Westport, CT: Greenwood Press, 1981.

Weyer, Johann (1515–88). *Witches, Devils, and Doctors in the Renaissance: Johann Weyer, De praestigiis daemonum.* Ed. George Mora with Benjamin G. Kohl, Erik Midelfort, and Helen Bacon. Trans. John Shea. Binghamton, NY: Medieval and Renaissance Texts and Studies, 1991.

Wilson, Katharina M., ed. *Medieval Women Writers.* Athens, GA: University of Georgia Press, 1984.

———, ed. *Women Writers of the Renaissance and Reformation.* Athens, GA: University of Georgia Press, 1987.

———, and Frank J. Warnke, eds. *Women Writers of the Seventeenth Century.* Athens, GA: University of Georgia Press, 1989.

Wollstonecraft, Mary. *A Vindication of the Rights of Men and a Vindication of the Rights of Women.* Ed. Sylvana Tomaselli. Cambridge: Cambridge University Press, 1995. Also *The Vindications of the Rights of Men, The Rights of Women.* Ed. D. L. Macdonald & Kathleen Scherf. Peterborough, Ontario, Canada: Broadview Press, 1997.

Women Critics 1660–1820: An Anthology. Edited by the Folger Collective on Early Women Critics. Bloomington, IN: Indiana University Press, 1995.

Women Writers in English 1350–1850: 15 published through 1999 (projected 30-volume series suspended). Oxford University Press.

Wroth, Lady Mary. *The Countess of Montgomery's Urania.* 2 parts. Ed. Josephine A. Roberts. Tempe, AZ: MRTS, 1995, 1999.

———. *Lady Mary Wroth's "Love's Victory": The Penshurst Manuscript.* Ed. Michael G. Brennan. London: The Roxburghe Club, 1988.

———. *The Poems of Lady Mary Wroth.* Ed. Josephine A. Roberts. Baton Rouge, LA: Louisiana State University Press, 1983.

de Zayas Maria. *The Disenchantments of Love.* Trans. H. Patsy Boyer. Albany, NY: State University of New York Press, 1997.

———. *The Enchantments of Love: Amorous and Exemplary Novels.* Trans. H. Patsy Boyer. Berkeley, CA: University of California Press, 1990.

SECONDARY SOURCES

Abate, Corinne S., ed. *Privacy, Domesticity, and Women in Early Modern England.* Aldershot and Brookfield: Ashgate Publishing Co., 2003.

Ahlgren, Gillian. *Teresa of Avila and the Politics of Sanctity.* Ithaca: Cornell University Press, 1996.

Akkerman, Tjitske & Siep Sturman, eds. *Feminist Thought in European History, 1400–2000.* London & New York: Routledge, 1997.

Allen, Sister Prudence, R.S.M. *The Concept of Woman: The Aristotelian Revolution, 750 B.C. – A.D. 1250.* Grand Rapids, MI: William B. Eerdmans Publishing Company, 1997.

———. *The Concept of Woman: Volume II: The early Humanist Reformation, 1250–1500.* Grand Rapids, MI: William B. Eerdmans Publishing Company, 2002.

Amussen, Susan D. And Adele Seeff, eds. *Attending to Early Modern Women.* Newark: University of Delaware Press, 1998.

Andreadis, Harriette. *Sappho in Early Modern England: Female Same-Sex Literary Erotics 1550–1714.* Chicago: University of Chicago Press, 2001.

Armon, Shifra. *Picking Wedlock: Women and the Courtship Novel in Spain.* New York: Rowman & Littlefield Publishers, Inc., 2002.

Backer, Anne Liot Backer. *Precious Women.* New York: Basic Books, 1974.

Ballaster, Ros. *Seductive Forms.* New York: Oxford University Press, 1992.

Barash, Carol. *English Women's Poetry, 1649–1714: Politics, Community, and Linguistic Authority.* New York & Oxford: Oxford University Press, 1996.

Battigelli, Anna. *Margaret Cavendish and the Exiles of the Mind.* Lexington, KY: University of Kentucky Press, 1998.

Beasley, Faith. *Revising Memory: Women's Fiction and Memoirs in Seventeenth-Century France.* New Brunswick: Rutgers University Press, 1990.

Becker, Lucinda M. *Death and the Early Modern Englishwoman.* Aldershot and Brookfield: Ashgate Publishing Co., 2003.

Beilin, Elaine V. *Redeeming Eve: Women Writers of the English Renaissance.* Princeton: Princeton University Press, 1987.

Benson, Pamela Joseph. *The Invention of Renaissance Woman: The Challenge of Female Independence in the Literature and Thought of Italy and England.* University Park, PA: Pennsylvania State University Press, 1992.

———— and Victoria Kirkham, eds. *Strong Voices, Weak History? Medieval and Renaissance Women in their Literary Canons: England, France, Italy.* Ann Arbor: University of Michigan Press, 2003.

Berry, Helen. *Gender, Society and Print Culture in Late-Stuart England.* Aldershot and Brookfield: Ashgate Publishing Co., 2003.

Bicks, Caroline. *Midwiving Subjects in Shakespeare's England.* Aldershot and Brookfield: Ashgate Publishing Co., 2003.

Bilinkoff, Jodi. *The Avila of Saint Teresa: Religious Reform in a Sixteenth-Century City.* Ithaca: Cornell University Press, 1989.

Bissell, R. Ward. *Artemisia Gentileschi and the Authority of Art.* University Park, PA: Pennsylvania State University Press, 2000.

Blain, Virginia, Isobel Grundy, & Patricia Clements, eds. *The Feminist Companion to Literature in English: Women Writers from the Middle Ages to the Present.* New Haven: Yale University Press, 1990.

Bloch, R. Howard. *Medieval Misogyny and the Invention of Western Romantic Love.* Chicago: University of Chicago Press, 1991.

Bogucka, Maria. *Women in Early Modern Polish Society, Against the European Background.* Aldershot and Brookfield: Ashgate Publishing Co., 2004.

Bornstein, Daniel and Roberto Rusconi, eds. *Women and Religion in Medieval and Renaissance Italy.* Trans. Margery J. Schneider. Chicago: University of Chicago Press, 1996.

Brant, Clare & Diane Purkiss, eds. *Women, Texts and Histories, 1575–1760.* London & New York: Routledge, 1992.

Briggs, Robin. *Witches and Neighbours: The Social and Cultural Context of European Witchcraft.* New York: HarperCollins, 1995; Viking Penguin, 1996.

Brink, Jean R., ed. *Female Scholars: A Tradition of Learned Women before 1800.* Montréal: Eden Press Women's Publications, 1980.

————, Allison Coudert, and Maryanne Cline Horowitz. *The Politics of Gender in Early Modern Europe.* Sixteenth Century Essays & Studies, V.12. Kirksville, MO: Sixteenth Century Journal Publishers, 1989.

Broude, Norma and Mary D. Garrard, eds. *The Expanding Discourse: Feminism and Art History.* New York: HarperCollins, 1992.

Brown, Judith C. *Immodest Acts: The Life of a Lesbian Nun in Renaissance Italy.* New York: Oxford University Press, 1986.

———— and Robert C. Davis, eds. *Gender and Society in Renaissance Italy.* London: Addison Wesley Longman, 1998.

Burke, Victoria E. Burke, ed. *Early Modern Women's Manuscript Writing.* Aldershot and Brookfield: Ashgate Publishing Co., 2004.

Bynum, Carolyn Walker. *Fragmentation and Redemption: Essays on Gender and the Human Body in Medieval Religion.* New York: Zone Books, 1992.

————. *Holy Feast and Holy Fast: The Religious Significance of Food to Medieval Women.* Berkeley: University of California Press, 1987.

Cambridge Guide to Women's Writing in English. Edited by Lorna Sage. Cambridge: University Press, 1999.

Cavallo, Sandra, and Lyndan Warner. *Widowhood in Medieval and Early Modern Europe.* New York: Longman, 1999.

Cavanagh, Sheila T. *Cherished Torment: The Emotional Geography of Lady Mary Wroth's Urania.* Pittsburgh: Duquesne University Press, 2001.

Cerasano, S. P. and Marion Wynne-Davies, eds. *Readings in Renaissance Women's Drama: Criticism, History, and Performance 1594–1998.* London & New York: Routledge, 1998.

Cervigni, Dino S., ed. *Women Mystic Writers. Annali d'Italianistica* 13 (1995) (entire issue).

——— and Rebecca West, eds. *Women's Voices in Italian Literature. Annali d'Italianistica* 7 (1989) (entire issue).

Charlton, Kenneth. *Women, Religion and Education in Early Modern England.* London & New York: Routledge, 1999.

Chojnacka, Monica. *Working Women in Early Modern Venice.* Baltimore: Johns Hopkins University Press, 2001.

Chojnacki, Stanley. *Women and Men in Renaissance Venice: Twelve Essays on Patrician Society.* Baltimore: Johns Hopkins University Press, 2000.

Cholakian, Patricia Francis. *Rape and Writing in the* Heptameron *of Marguerite de Navarre.* Carbondale and Edwardsville, IL: Southern Illinois University Press, 1991.

———. *Women and the Politics of Self-Representation in Seventeenth-Century France.* Newark: University of Delaware Press, 2000.

Christine de Pizan: A Casebook. Edited by Barbara K. Altmann and Deborah L. McGrady. New York: Routledge, 2003.

Clogan, Paul Maruice, ed. *Medievali et Humanistica: Literacy and the Lay Reader.* Lanham, MD: Rowman & Littlefield, 2000.

Clubb, Louise George (1989). *Italian Drama in Shakespeare's Time.* New Haven: Yale University Press.

Clucas, Stephen, ed. *A Princely Brave Woman: Essays on Margaret Cavendish, Duchess of Newcastle.* Aldershot and Brookfield: Ashgate Publishing Co., 2003.

Conley, John J., S.J. *The Suspicion of Virtue: Women Philosophers in Neoclassical France.* Ithaca, NY: Cornell University Press, 2002.

Crabb, Ann. *The Strozzi of Florence: Widowhood and Family Solidarity in the Renaissance.* Ann Arbor: University of Michigan Press, 2000.

Crowston, Clare Haru. *Fabricating Women: The Seamstresses of Old Regime France, 1675–1791.* Durham, NC: Duke University Press, 2001.

Cruz, Anne J. and Mary Elizabeth Perry, eds. *Culture and Control in Counter-Reformation Spain.* Minneapolis: University of Minnesota Press, 1992.

Datta, Satya. *Women and Men in Early Modern Venice.* Aldershot and Brookfield: Ashgate Publishing Co., 2003.

Davis, Natalie Zemon. *Society and Culture in Early Modern France.* Stanford: Stanford University Press, 1975. Especially chapters 3 and 5.

———. *Women on the Margins: Three Seventeenth-Century Lives.* Cambridge, MA: Harvard University Press, 1995.

DeJean, Joan. *Ancients Against Moderns: Culture Wars and the Making of a Fin de Siècle.* Chicago: University of Chicago Press, 1997.

———. *Fictions of Sappho, 1546–1937.* Chicago: University of Chicago Press, 1989.

———. *The Reinvention of Obscenity: Sex, Lies, and Tabloids in Early Modern France.* Chicago: University of Chicago Press, 2002.

————. *Tender Geographies: Women and the Origins of the Novel in France.* New York: Columbia University Press, 1991.

————. *The Reinvention of Obscenity: Sex, Lies, and Tabloids in Early Modern France.* Chicago: University of Chicago Press, 2002.

Dictionary of Russian Women Writers. Edited by Marina Ledkovsky, Charlotte Rosenthal, and Mary Zirin. Westport, CT: Greenwood Press, 1994.

Dixon, Laurinda S. *Perilous Chastity: Women and Illness in Pre-Enlightenment Art and Medicine.* Ithaca: Cornell University Press, 1995.

Dolan, Frances, E. *Whores of Babylon: Catholicism, Gender and Seventeenth-Century Print Culture.* Ithaca: Cornell University Press, 1999.

Donovan, Josephine. *Women and the Rise of the Novel, 1405–1726.* New York: St. Martin's Press, 1999.

Encyclopedia of Continental Women Writers. 2 vols. Edited by Katharina Wilson. New York: Garland, 1991.

De Erauso, Catalina. *Lieutenant Nun: Memoir of a Basque Transvestite in the New World.* Trans. Michele Ttepto & Gabriel Stepto; foreword by Marjorie Garber. Boston: Beacon Press, 1995.

Erdmann, Axel. *My Gracious Silence: Women in the Mirror of Sixteenth-Century Printing in Western Europe.* Luzern: Gilhofer and Rauschberg, 1999.

Erickson, Amy Louise. *Women and Property in Early Modern England.* London & New York: Routledge, 1993.

Ezell, Margaret J. M. *The Patriarch's Wife: Literary Evidence and the History of the Family.* Chapel Hill: University of North Carolina Press, 1987.

————. *Social Authorship and the Advent of Print.* Baltimore: Johns Hopkins University Press, 1999.

————. *Writing Women's Literary History.* Baltimore: Johns Hopkins University Press, 1993.

Farrell, Michèle Longino. *Performing Motherhood: The Sévigné Correspondence.* Hanover, NH and London: University Press of New England, 1991.

The Feminist Companion to Literature in English: Women Writers from the Middle Ages to the Present. Edited by Virginia Blain, Isobel Grundy, and Patricia Clements. New Haven, CT: Yale University Press, 1990.

The Feminist Encyclopedia of German Literature. Edited by Friederike Eigler and Susanne Kord. Westport, CT: Greenwood Press, 1997.

Feminist Encyclopedia of Italian Literature. Edited by Rinaldina Russell. Westport, CT: Greenwood Press, 1997.

Ferguson, Margaret W. *Dido's Daughters: Literacy, Gender, and Empire in Early Modern England and France.* Chicago: University of Chicago Press, 2003.

————, Maureen Quilligan, and Nancy J. Vickers, eds. *Rewriting the Renaissance: The Discourses of Sexual Difference in Early Modern Europe.* Chicago: University of Chicago Press, 1987.

Ferraro, Joanne M. *Marriage Wars in Late Renaissance Venice.* Oxford: Oxford University Press, 2001.

Fletcher, Anthony. *Gender, Sex and Subordination in England 1500–1800.* New Haven: Yale University Press, 1995.

French Women Writers: A Bio-Bibliographical Source Book. Edited by Eva Martin Sartori and Dorothy Wynne Zimmerman. Westport, CT: Greenwood Press, 1991.

Frye, Susan and Karen Robertson, eds. *Maids and Mistresses, Cousins and Queens: Women's Alliances in Early Modern England.* Oxford: Oxford University Press, 1999.

Gallagher, Catherine. *Nobody's Story: The Vanishing Acts of Women Writers in the Marketplace, 1670–1820.* Berkeley: University of California Press, 1994.

Garrard, Mary D. *Artemisia Gentileschi: The Image of the Female Hero in Italian Baroque Art.* Princeton: Princeton University Press, 1989.

Gelbart, Nina Rattner. *The King's Midwife: A History and Mystery of Madame du Coudray.* Berkeley: University of California Press, 1998.

Glenn, Cheryl. *Rhetoric Retold: Regendering the Tradition from Antiquity Through the Renaissance.* Carbondale & Edwardsville, IL: Southern Illinois University Press, 1997.

Goffen, Rona. *Titian's Women.* New Haven: Yale University Press, 1997.

Goldberg, Jonathan. *Desiring Women Writing: English Renaissance Examples.* Stanford: Stanford University Press, 1997.

Goldsmith, Elizabeth C. *Exclusive Conversations: The Art of Interaction in Seventeenth-Century France.* Philadelphia: University of Pennsylvania Press, 1988.

———, ed. *Writing the Female Voice.* Boston: Northeastern University Press, 1989.

——— & Dena Goodman, eds. *Going Public: Women and Publishing in Early Modern France.* Ithaca: Cornell University Press, 1995.

Grafton, Anthony, and Lisa Jardine. *From Humanism to the Humanities: Education and the Liberal Arts in Fifteenth-and Sixteenth-Century Europe.* London: Duckworth, 1986.

Grassby, Richard. *Kinship and Capitalism: Marriage, Family, and Business in the English-Speaking World, 1580–1740.* Cambridge: Cambridge University Press, 2001.

Greer, Margaret Rich. *Maria de Zayas Tells Baroque Tales of Love and the Cruelty of Men.* University Park, PA: Pennsylvania State University Press, 2000.

Gutierrez, Nancy A. *"Shall She Famish Then?" Female Food Refusal in Early Modern England.* Aldershot and Brookfield: Ashgate Publishing Co., 2003.

Habermann, Ina. *Staging Slander and Gender in Early Modern England.* Aldershot and Brookfield: Ashgate Publishing Co., 2003.

Hackett, Helen. *Women and Romance Fiction in the English Renaissance.* Cambridge: Cambridge University Press, 2000.

Hall, Kim F. *Things of Darkness: Economies of Race and Gender in Early Modern England.* Ithaca, NY: Cornell University Press, 1995.

Hampton, Timothy. *Literature and the Nation in the Sixteenth Century: Inventing Renaissance France.* Ithaca, NY: Cornell University Press, 2001.

Hannay, Margaret, ed. *Silent But for the Word.* Kent, OH: Kent State University Press, 1985.

Hardwick, Julie. *The Practice of Patriarchy: Gender and the Politics of Household Authority in Early Modern France.* University Park, PA: Pennsylvania State University Press, 1998.

Harris, Barbara J. *English Aristocratic Women, 1450–1550: Marriage and Family, Property and Careers.* New York: Oxford University Press, 2002.

Harth, Erica. *Ideology and Culture in Seventeenth-Century France.* Ithaca: Cornell University Press, 1983.

——— *Cartesian Women. Versions and Subversions of Rational Discourse in the Old Regime.* Ithaca: Cornell University Press, 1992.

Harvey, Elizabeth D. *Ventriloquized Voices: Feminist Theory and English Renaissance Texts.* London & New York: Routledge, 1992.

Haselkorn, Anne M. & Betty Travitsky, eds. *The Renaissance Englishwoman in Print: Counterbalancing the Canon.* Amherst: University of Massachusetts Press, 1990.

Hendricks, Margo and Patricia Parker, eds. *Women, "Race," and Writing in the Early Modern Period.* London and New York: Routledge, 1994.

Herlihy, David. "Did Women Have a Renaissance? A Reconsideration." *Medievalia et Humanistica,* NS 13 (1985): 1–22.

Hill, Bridget. *The Republican Virago: The Life and Times of Catharine Macaulay, Historian.* New York: Oxford University Press, 1992.

Hills, Helen, ed. *Architecture and the Politics of Gender in Early Modern Europe.* Aldershot and Brookfield: Ashgate Publishing Co., 2003.

A History of Central European Women's Writing. Edited by Celia Hawkesworth. New York: Palgrave Press, 2001.

A History of Women in the West.
 Volume I: *From Ancient Goddesses to Christian Saints.* Ed. Pauline Schmitt Pantel. Cambridge, MA: Harvard University Press, 1992.
 Volume 2: *Silences of the Middle Ages.* Ed. Christiane Klapisch-Zuber. Cambridge, MA: Harvard University Press, 1992.
 Volume 3: *Renaissance and Enlightenment Paradoxes.* Ed. Natalie Zemon Davis and Arlette Farge. Cambridge, MA: Harvard University Press, 1993.

A History of Women Philosophers. Ed. Mary Ellen Waithe. 3 vols. Dordrecht: Martinus Nijhoff, 1987.

A History of Women's Writing in France. Ed. Sonya Stephens. Cambridge: Cambridge University Press, 2000.

A History of Women's Writing in Germany, Austria and Switzerland. Ed. Jo Catling. Cambridge: Cambridge University Press, 2000.

A History of Women's Writing in Italy. Ed. Letizia Panizza and Sharon Wood. Cambridge: University Press, 2000.

A History of Women's Writing in Russia. Edited by Alele Marie Barker and Jehanne M. Gheith. Cambridge: Cambridge University Press, 2002.

Hobby, Elaine. *Virtue of Necessity: English Women's Writing 1646–1688.* London: Virago Press, 1988.

Horowitz, Maryanne Cline. "Aristotle and Women." *Journal of the History of Biology* 9 (1976): 183–213.

Howell, Martha. *The Marriage Exchange: Property, Social Place, and Gender in Cities of the Low Countries, 1300–1550.* Chicago: University of Chicago Press, 1998.

Hufton, Olwen H. *The Prospect Before Her: A History of Women in Western Europe, 1: 1500–1800.* New York: HarperCollins, 1996.

Hull, Suzanne W. *Chaste, Silent, and Obedient: English Books for Women, 1475–1640.* San Marino, CA: The Huntington Library, 1982.

Hunt, Lynn, ed. *The Invention of Pornography: Obscenity and the Origins of Modernity, 1500–1800.* New York: Zone Books, 1996.

Hutner, Heidi, ed. *Rereading Aphra Behn: History, Theory, and Criticism.* Charlottesville, VA: University Press of Virginia, 1993.

Hutson, Lorna, ed. *Feminism and Renaissance Studies.* New York: Oxford University Press, 1999.

Italian Women Writers: A Bio-Bibliographical Sourcebook. Edited by Rinaldina Russell. Westport, CT: Greenwood Press, 1994.

Jaffe, Irma B. with Gernando Colombardo. *Shining Eyes, Cruel Fortune: The Lives and Loves of Italian Renaissance Women Poets.* New York: Fordham University Press, 2002.

James, Susan E. *Kateryn Parr: The Making of a Queen.* Aldershot and Brookfield: Ashgate Publishing Co., 1999.

Jankowski, Theodora A. *Women in Power in the Early Modern Drama.* Urbana, IL: University of Illinois Press, 1992.

Jansen, Katherine Ludwig. *The Making of the Magdalen: Preaching and Popular Devotion in the Later Middle Ages.* Princeton: Princeton University Press, 2000.

Jed, Stephanie H. *Chaste Thinking: The Rape of Lucretia and the Birth of Humanism.* Bloomington, IN: Indiana University Press, 1989.

Jordan, Constance. *Renaissance Feminism: Literary Texts and Political Models.* Ithaca: Cornell University Press, 1990.

Kagan, Richard L. *Lucrecia's Dreams: Politics and Prophecy in Sixteenth-Century Spain.* Berkeley: University of California Press, 1990.

Kehler, Dorothea and Laurel Amtower, eds. *The Single Woman in Medieval and Early Modern England: Her Life and Representation.* Tempe, AZ: MRTS, 2002.

Kelly, Joan. "Did Women Have a Renaissance?" In her *Women, History, and Theory.* Chicago: University of Chicago Press, 1984. Also in Renate Bridenthal, Claudia Koonz, and Susan M. Stuard, eds., *Becoming Visible: Women in European History.* Third edition. Boston: Houghton Mifflin, 1998.

———. "Early Feminist Theory and the *Querelle des Femmes.*" In *Women, History, and Theory.*

Kelso, Ruth. *Doctrine for the Lady of the Renaissance.* Foreword by Katharine M. Rogers. Urbana, IL: University of Illinois Press, 1956, 1978.

Kendrick, Robert L. *Celestical Sirens: Nuns and their Music in Early Modern Milan.* New York: Oxford University Press, 1996.

Kermode, Jenny and Garthine Walker, eds. *Women, Crime and the Courts in Early Modern England.* Chapel Hill: University of North Carolina Press, 1994.

King, Catherine E. *Renaissance Women Patrons: Wives and Widows in Italy, c. 1300–1550.* New York & Manchester: Manchester University Press (distributed in the U.S. by St. Martin's Press), 1998.

King, Margaret L. *Women of the Renaissance.* Foreword by Catharine R. Stimpson. Chicago: University of Chicago Press, 1991.

Krontiris, Tina. *Oppositional Voices: Women as Writers and Translators of Literature in the English Renaissance.* London & New York: Routledge, 1992.

Kuehn, Thomas. *Law, Family, and Women: Toward a Legal Anthropology of Renaissance Italy.* Chicago: University of Chicago Press, 1991.

Kunze, Bonnelyn Young. *Margaret Fell and the Rise of Quakerism.* Stanford: Stanford University Press, 1994.

Labalme, Patricia A., ed. *Beyond Their Sex: Learned Women of the European Past.* New York: New York University Press, 1980.

Lalande, Roxanne Decker, ed. *A Labor of Love: Critical Reflections on the Writings of Marie-Catherine Desjardina (Mme de Villedieu).* Madison, NJ: Fairleigh Dickinson University Press, 2000.

Lamb, Mary Ellen. *Gender and Authorship in the Sidney Circle.* Madison: University of Wisconsin Press, 1990.

Laqueur, Thomas. *Making Sex: Body and Gender from the Greeks to Freud.* Cambridge, MA: Harvard University Press, 1990.

Larsen, Anne R. and Colette H. Winn, eds. *Renaissance Women Writers: French Texts/ American Contexts*. Detroit, MI: Wayne State University Press, 1994.

Laven, Mary. *Virgins of Venus: Enclosed Lives and Broken Vows in the Renaissance Convent*. London: Viking, 2002.

Lerner, Gerda. *The Creation of Patriarchy* and *Creation of Feminist Consciousness, 1000–1870*. 2-vol. history of women. New York: Oxford University Press, 1986, 1994.

Levin, Carole and Jeanie Watson, eds. *Ambiguous Realities: Women in the Middle Ages and Renaissance*. Detroit: Wayne State University Press, 1987.

Levin, Carole, Jo Eldridge Carney, and Debra Barrett-Graves. *Elizabeth I: Always Her Own Free Woman*. Aldershot and Brookfield: Ashgate Publishing Co., 2003.

Levin, Carole, et al. *Extraordinary Women of the Medieval and Renaissance World: A Biographical Dictionary*. Westport, CT: Greenwood Press, 2000.

Levy, Allison, ed. *Widowhood and Visual Culture in Early Modern Europe*. Aldershot and Brookfield: Ashgate Publishing Co., 2003.

Lewalsky, Barbara Kiefer. *Writing Women in Jacobean England*. Cambridge, MA: Harvard University Press, 1993.

Lewis, Jayne Elizabeth. *Mary Queen of Scots: Romance and Nation*. London: Routledge, 1998.

Lindenauer, Leslie J. *Piety and Power: Gender and Religious Culture in the American Colonies, 1630–1700*. London and New York: Routledge, 2002.

Lindsey, Karen. *Divorced Beheaded Survived: A Feminist Reinterpretation of the Wives of Henry VIII*. Reading, MA: Addison-Wesley Publishing Co., 1995.

Lochrie, Karma. *Margery Kempe and Translations of the Flesh*. Philadelphia: University of Pennsylvania Press, 1992.

Longino Farrell, Michèle. *Performing Motherhood: The Sévigné Correspondence*. Hanover, NH: University Press of New England, 1991.

Lougee, Carolyn C. *Le Paradis des Femmes: Women, Salons, and Social Stratification in Seventeenth-Century France*. Princeton: Princeton University Press, 1976.

Love, Harold. *The Culture and Commerce of Texts: Scribal Publication in Seventeenth-Century England*. Amherst, MA: University of Massachusetts Press, 1993.

Lowe, K. J. P. *Nuns' Chronicles and Convent Culture in Renaissance and Counter-Reformation Italy*. New York: Cambridge University Press, 2003.

MacCarthy, Bridget G. *The Female Pen: Women Writers and Novelists 1621–1818*. Preface by Janet Todd. New York: New York University Press, 1994. (Originally published by Cork University Press, 1946–47).

Maclean, Ian. *Woman Triumphant: Feminism in French Literature, 1610–1652*. Oxford: Clarendon Press, 1977.

———. *The Renaissance Notion of Woman: A Study of the Fortunes of Scholasticism and Medical Science in European Intellectual Life*. Cambridge: Cambridge University Press, 1980.

MacNeil, Anne. *Music and Women of the Commedia dell'Arte in the Late Sixteenth Century*. New York: Oxford University Press, 2003.

Maggi, Armando. *Uttering the Word: The Mystical Performances of Maria Maddalena de' Pazzi, a Renaissance Visionary*. Albany: State University of New York Press, 1998.

Marshall, Sherrin. *Women in Reformation and Counter-Reformation Europe: Public and Private Worlds*. Bloomington, IN: Indiana University Press, 1989.

Masten, Jeffrey. *Textual Intercourse: Collaboration, Authorship, and Sexualities in Renaissance Drama*. Cambridge: Cambridge University Press, 1997.

Matter, E. Ann, and John Coakley, eds. *Creative Women in Medieval and Early Modern Italy.* Philadelphia: University of Pennsylvania Press, 1994. (sequel to the Monson collection, below)

McGrath, Lynette. *Subjectivity and Women's Poetry in Early Modern England.* Burlington, VT: Ashgate, 2002.

McLeod, Glenda. *Virtue and Venom: Catalogs of Women from Antiquity to the Renaissance.* Ann Arbor: University of Michigan Press, 1991.

Medwick, Cathleen. *Teresa of Avila: The Progress of a Soul.* New York: Alfred A. Knopf, 2000.

Meek, Christine, ed. *Women in Renaissance and Early Modern Europe.* Dublin-Portland: Four Courts Press, 2000.

Mendelson, Sara and Patricia Crawford. *Women in Early Modern England, 1550–1720.* Oxford: Clarendon Press, 1998.

Merchant, Carolyn. *The Death of Nature: Women, Ecology and the Scientific Revolution.* New York: HarperCollins, 1980.

Merrim, Stephanie. *Early Modern Women's Writing and Sor Juana Inés de la Cruz.* Nashville, TN: Vanderbilt University Press, 1999.

Messbarger, Rebecca. *The Century of Women: The Representations of Women in Eighteenth-Century Italian Public Discourse.* Toronto: University of Toronto Press, 2002.

Miller, Nancy K. *The Heroine's Text: Readings in the French and English Novel, 1722–1782.* New York: Columbia University Press, 1980.

Miller Naomi J. *Changing the Subject: Mary Wroth and Figurations of Gender in Early Modern England.* Lexington, KY: University Press of Kentucky, 1996.

———— and Gary Waller, eds. *Reading Mary Wroth: Representing Alternatives in Early Modern England.* Knoxville, TN: University of Tennessee Press, 1991.

Monson, Craig A., ed. *The Crannied Wall: Women, Religion, and the Arts in Early Modern Europe.* Ann Arbor: University of Michigan Press, 1992.

Moore, Cornelia Niekus. *The Maiden's Mirror: Reading Material for German Girls in the Sixteenth and Seventeenth Centuries.* Wiesbaden: Otto Harrassowitz, 1987.

Musacchio, Jacqueline Marie. *The Art and Ritual of Childbirth in Renaissance Italy.* New Haven: Yale University Press, 1999.

Newman, Barbara. *God and the Goddesses: Vision, Poetry, and Belief in the Middle Ages.* Philadelphia: University of Pennsylvania Press, 2003.

Newman, Karen. *Fashioning Femininity and English Renaissance Drama.* Chicago & London: University of Chicago Press, 1991.

O'Donnell, Mary Ann. *Aphra Behn: An Annotated Bibliography of Primary and Secondary Sources.* Aldershot and Brookfield: Ashgate Publishing Co., 2nd ed., 2004.

Okin, Susan Moller. *Women in Western Political Thought.* Princeton: Princeton University Press, 1979.

Ozment, Steven. *The Bürgermeister's Daughter: Scandal in a Sixteenth-Century German Town.* New York: St. Martin's Press, 1995.

————. *Flesh and Spirit: Private Life in Early Modern Germany.* New York: Penguin Putnam, 1999.

————. *When Fathers Ruled: Family Life in Reformation Europe.* Cambridge, MA: Harvard University Press, 1983.

Pacheco, Anita, ed. *Early [English] Women Writers: 1600–1720.* New York & London: Longman, 1998.

Pagels, Elaine. *Adam, Eve, and the Serpent.* New York: Harper Collins, 1988.

Panizza, Letizia, ed. *Women in Italian Renaissance Culture and Society.* Oxford: European Humanities Research Centre, 2000.

Parker, Patricia. *Literary Fat Ladies: Rhetoric, Gender and Property.* London and New York: Methuen, 1987.

Pernoud, Regine and Marie-Veronique Clin. *Joan of Arc: Her Story.* Rev. and trans. Jeremy DuQuesnay Adams. New York: St. Martin's Press, 1998 (French original, 1986).

Perry, Mary Elizabeth. *Crime and Society in Early Modern Seville.* Hanover, NH: University Press of New England, 1980.

———. *Gender and Disorder in Early Modern Seville.* Princeton: Princeton University Press, 1990.

Petroff, Elizabeth Alvilda, ed. *Medieval Women's Visionary Literature.* New York: Oxford University Press, 1986.

Perry, Ruth. *The Celebrated Mary Astell: An Early English Feminist.* Chicago: University of Chicago Press, 1986.

Rabil, Albert. *Laura Cereta: Quattrocento Humanist.* Binghamton, NY: MRTS, 1981.

Ranft, Patricia. *Women in Western Intellectual Culture, 600–1500.* New York: Palgrave, 2002.

Rapley, Elizabeth. *A Social History of the Cloister: Daily Life in the Teaching Monasteries of the Old Regime.* Montreal: McGill-Queen's University Press, 2001.

Raven, James, Helen Small and Naomi Tadmor, eds. *The Practice and Representation of Reading in England.* Cambridge: University Press, 1996.

Reardon, Colleen. *Holy Concord within Sacred Walls: Nuns and Music in Siena, 1575–1700.* Oxford: Oxford University Press, 2001.

Reiss, Sheryl E. and David G. Wilkins, ed. *Beyond Isabella: Secular Women Patrons of Art in Renaissance Italy.* Kirksville, MO: Turman State University Press, 2001.

Rheubottom, David. *Age, Marriage, and Politics in Fifteenth-Century Ragusa.* Oxford: Oxford University Press, 2000.

Richardson, Brian. *Printing, Writers and Readers in Renaissance Italy.* Cambridge: University Press, 1999.

Riddle, John M. *Contraception and Abortion from the Ancient World to the Renaissance.* Cambridge, MA: Harvard University Press, 1992.

———. *Eve's Herbs: A History of Contraception and Abortion in the West.* Cambridge, MA: Harvard University Press, 1997.

Roper, Lyndal. *The Holy Household: Women and Morals in Reformation Augsburg.* New York: Oxford University Press, 1989.

Rose, Mary Beth. *The Expense of Spirit: Love and Sexuality in English Renaissance Drama.* Ithaca, NY: Cornell University Press, 1988.

———. *Gender and Heroism in Early Modern English Literature.* Chicago: University of Chicago Press, 2002.

———, ed. *Women in the Middle Ages and the Renaissance: Literary and Historical Perspectives.* Syracuse: Syracuse University Press, 1986.

Rosenthal, Margaret F. *The Honest Courtesan: Veronica Franco, Citizen and Writer in Sixteenth-Century Venice.* Foreword by Catharine R. Stimpson. Chicago: University of Chicago Press, 1992.

Rublack, Ulinka, ed. *Gender in Early Modern German History.* Cambridge: Cambridge University Press, 2002.

Sackville-West, Vita. *Daughter of France: The Life of La Grande Mademoiselle.* Garden City, NY: Doubleday, 1959.

Sánchez, Magdalena S. *The Empress, the Queen, and the Nun: Women and Power at the Court of Philip III of Spain.* Baltimore: Johns Hopkins University Press, 1998.

Scaraffia, Lucetta and Gabriella Zarri. *Women and Faith: Catholic Religious Life in Italy from Late Antiquity to the Present.* Cambridge, MA: Harvard University Press, 1999.

Schiebinger, Londa. *The Mind has no Sex?: Women in the Origins of Modern Science.* Cambridge, MA: Harvard University Press, 1991.

————. *Nature's Body: Gender in the Making of Modern Science.* Boston: Beacon Press, 1993.

Schutte, Anne Jacobson, Thomas Kuehn, and Silvana Seidel Menchi, eds. *Time, Space, and Women's Lives in Early Modern Europe.* Kirksville, MO: Truman State University Press, 2001.

Schofield, Mary Anne and Cecilia Macheski, eds. *Fetter'd or Free? British Women Novelists, 1670–1815.* Athens, OH: Ohio University Press, 1986.

Schutte, Anne Jacobson. *Aspiring Saints: pretense of Holiness, Inquisition, and Gender in the Republic of Venice, 1618–1750.* Baltimore: Johns Hopkins University Press, 2001.

————, Thomas Kuehn, and Silvana Seidel Menchi, eds. *Time, Space, and Women's Lives in Early Modern Europe.* Kirksville, MO: Truman State University Press, 2001.

Seifert, Lewis C. *Fairy Tales, Sexuality and Gender in France 1690–1715: Nostalgic Utopias.* Cambridge, UK: Cambridge University Press, 1996.

Shannon, Laurie. *Sovereign Amity: Figures of Friendship in Shakespearean Contexts.* Chicago: University of Chicago Press, 2002.

Shemek, Deanna. *Ladies Errant: Wayward Women and Social Order in Early Modern Italy.* Durham, NC: Duke University Press, 1998.

Smith, Hilda L. *Reason's Disciples: Seventeenth-Century English Feminists.* Urbana, IL: University of Illinois Press, 1982.

————. *Women Writers and the Early Modern British Political Tradition.* Cambridge: Cambridge University Press, 1998.

Sobel, Dava. *Galileo's Daughter: A Historical Memoir of Science, Faith, and Love.* New York: Penguin Books, 2000.

Sommerville, Margaret R. *Sex and Subjection: Attitudes to Women in Early-Modern Society.* London: Arnold, 1995.

Soufas, Teresa Scott. *Dramas of Distinction: A Study of Plays by Golden Age Women.* Lexington, KY: The University Press of Kentucky, 1997.

Spencer, Jane. *The Rise of the Woman Novelist: From Aphra Behn to Jane Austen.* Oxford: Basil Blackwell, 1986.

Spender, Dale. *Mothers of the Novel: 100 Good Women Writers Before Jane Austen.* London & New York: Routledge, 1986.

Sperling, Jutta Gisela. *Convents and the Body Politic in Late Renaissance Venice.* Foreword by Catharine R. Stimpson. Chicago: University of Chicago Press, 1999.

Steinbrügge, Lieselotte. *The Moral Sex: Woman's Nature in the French Enlightenment.* Trans. Pamela E. Selwyn. New York: Oxford University Press, 1995.

Stephenson, Barbara. *The Power and Patronage of Marguerite de Navarre.* Aldershot and Brookfield: Ashgate Publishing Co., 2004.

Stocker, Margarita. *Judith, Sexual Warrior: Women and Power in Western Culture.* New Haven: Yale University Press, 1998.

Stretton, Timothy. *Women Waging Law in Elizabethan England*. Cambridge: Cambridge University Press, 1998.

Stuard, Susan M. "The Dominion of Gender: Women's Fortunes in the High Middle Ages." In Renate Bridenthal, Claudia Koonz, and Susan M. Stuard, eds. *Becoming Visible: Women in European History*. Third edition. Boston: Houghton Mifflin, 1998.

Summit, Jennifer. *Lost Property: The Woman Writer and English Literary History, 1380–1589*. Chicago: University of Chicago Press, 2000.

Surtz, Ronald E. *The Guitar of God: Gender, Power, and Authority in the Visionary World of Mother Juana de la Cruz (1481–1534)*. Philadelphia: University of Pennsylvania Press, 1991.

———. *Writing Women in Late Medieval and Early Modern Spain: The Mothers of Saint Teresa of Avila*. Philadelphia: University of Pennsylvania Press, 1995.

Suzuki, Mihoko. *Subordinate Subjects: Gender, the Political Nation, and Literary Form in England, 1588–1688*. Aldershot and Brookfield: Ashgate Publishing Co., 2003.

Teague, Frances. *Bathsua Makin, Woman of Learning*. Lewisburg, PA: Bucknell University Press, 1999.

Thomas, Anabel. *Art and Piety in the Female Religious Communities of Renaissance Italy: Iconography, Space, and the Religious Woman's Perspective*. New York: Cambridge University Press, 2003.

Tinagli, Paola. *Women in Italian Renaissance Art: Gender, Representation, Identity*. Manchester: Manchester University Press, 1997.

Todd, Janet. *The Secret Life of Aphra Behn*. London, New York, & Sydney: Pandora, 2000.

———. *The Sign of Angelica: Women, Writing and Fiction, 1660–1800*. New York: Columbia University Press, 1989.

Tomas, Natalie R. *The Medici Women: Gender and Power in Renaissance Florence*. Aldershot and Brookfield: Ashgate Publishing Co., 2004.

Traub, Valerie. *The Renaissance of Lesbianism in Early Modern England*. Cambridge: Cambridge University Press, 2002.

Valenze, Deborah. *The First Industrial Woman*. New York: Oxford University Press, 1995.

Van Dijk, Susan, Lia van Gemert & Sheila Ottway, eds. *Writing the History of Women's Writing: Toward an International Approach*. Proceedings of the Colloquium, Amsterdam, 9–11 September. Amsterdam: Royal Netherlands Academy of Arts and Sciences, 2001.

Vickery, Amanda. *The Gentleman's Daughter: Women's Lives in Georgian England*. New Haven: Yale University Press, 1998.

Vollendorf, Lisa, ed. *Recovering Spain's Feminist Tradition*. New York: MLA, 2001.

Walker, Claire. *Gender and Politics in Early Modern Europe: English Convents in France and the Low Countries*. New York: Palgrave, 2003.

Wall, Wendy. *The Imprint of Gender: Authorship and Publication in the English Renaissance*. Ithaca, NY: Cornell University Press, 1993.

Walsh, William T. *St. Teresa of Avila: A Biography*. Rockford, IL: TAN Books & Publications, 1987.

Warner, Marina. *Alone of All Her Sex: The Myth and Cult of the Virgin Mary*. New York: Knopf, 1976.

Warnicke, Retha M. *The Marrying of Anne of Cleves: Royal Protocol in Tudor England*. Cambridge: Cambridge University Press, 2000.

Watt, Diane. *Secretaries of God: Women Prophets in Late Medieval and Early Modern England.* Cambridge, England: D. S. Brewer, 1997.

Weaver, Elissa. *Convent Theatre in Early Modern Italy.* New York: Cambridge University Press, 2002.

Weber, Alison. *Teresa of Avila and the Rhetoric of Femininity.* Princeton: Princeton University Press, 1990.

Welles, Marcia L. *Persephone's Girdle: Narratives of Rape in Seventeenth-Century Spanish Literature.* Nashville: Vanderbilt University Press, 2000.

Whitehead, Barbara J., ed. *Women's Education in Early Modern Europe: A History, 1500–1800.* New York & London: Garland Publishing Co., 1999.

Wiesner, Merry E. *Working Women in Renaissance Germany.* New Brunswick, NJ: Rutgers University Press, 1986.

Wiesner-Hanks, Merry E. *Christianity and Sexuality in the Early Modern World: Regulating Desire, Reforming Practice.* New York: Routledge, 2000.

———. *Gender, Church, and State in Early Modern Germany: Essays.* New York: Longman, 1998.

———. *Gender in History.* Malden, MA: Blackwell, 2001.

———. *Women and Gender in Early Modern Europe.* Cambridge, UK: Cambridge University Press, 1993.

———. *Working Women in Renaissance Germany.* New Brunswick, NJ: Rutgers University Press, 1986.

Willard, Charity Cannon. *Christine de Pizan: Her Life and Works.* New York: Persea Books, 1984.

Winn, Colette and Donna Kuizenga, eds. *Women Writers in Pre-Revolutionary France.* New York: Garland Publishing, 1997.

Woodbridge, Linda. *Women and the English Renaissance: Literature and the Nature of Womankind, 1540–1620.* Urbana: University of Illinois Press, 1984.

Woodford, Charlotte. *Nuns as Historians in Early Modern Germany.* Oxford: Clarendon Press, 2002.

Woods, Susanne. *Lanyer: A Renaissance Woman Poet.* New York: Oxford University Press, 1999.

——— and Margaret P. Hannay, eds. *Teaching Tudor and Stuart Women Writers.* New York: MLA, 2000.

INDEX OF FIRST LINES AND TITLES

GENERAL INDEX

Page ranges for the dedicatory letter, the *Debate*, the elegies, and the sonnets include both the original and translated text.